W9-BZX-285

Music (top)

OS X®
Mavericks
onDemand

Que® Que Publishing, 800 East 96th Street, Indianapolis, IN 46240 USA

OS X® Mavericks on Demand

Copyright © 2014 by Perspection, Inc.
All rights reserved. No part of this book shall be reproduced, stored in a retrieval system, or transmitted by any means, electronic, mechanical, photocopying, recording, or otherwise, without written permission from the publisher. No patent liability is assumed with respect to the use of the information contained herein. Although every precaution has been taken in the preparation of this book, the publisher and author assume no responsibility for errors or omissions. Nor is any liability assumed for damages resulting from the use of the information contained herein.

Library of Congress Control Number: 2013951668

ISBN-13: 978-0-7897-5218-5
ISBN-10: 0-7897-5218-2

Printed and bound in the United States of America
First Printing: November 2013
16 15 14 13 4 3 2 1

Que Publishing offers excellent discounts on this book when ordered in quantity for bulk purchases or special sales.

For information, please contact: U.S. Corporate and Government Sales

 1-800-382-3419 or corpsales@pearsontechgroup.com

For sales outside the U.S., please contact: International Sales

 1-317-428-3341 or International@pearsontechgroup.com

Trademarks

All terms mentioned in this book that are known to be trademarks or service marks have been appropriately capitalized. Que cannot attest to the accuracy of this information. Use of a term in this book should not be regarded as affecting the validity of any trademark or service mark.

Warning and Disclaimer

Every effort has been made to make this book as complete and as accurate as possible, but no warranty or fitness is implied. The authors and the publishers shall have neither liability nor responsibility to any person or entity with respect to any loss or damage arising from the information contained in this book.

Publisher
Paul Boger

Associate Publisher
Greg Wiegand

Acquisitions Editor
Laura Norman

Managing Editor
Steve Johnson

Author
Steve Johnson

Page Layout
James Teyler

Interior Designers
Steve Johnson
Marian Hartsough

Photographs
Tracy Teyler

Indexer
Katherine Stimson

Proofreader
Beth Teyler

Team Coordinator
Cindy Teeters

Acknowledgments

Perspection, Inc.

OS X Mavericks on Demand has been created by the professional trainers and writers at Perspection, Inc. to the standards you've come to expect from Que publishing. Together, we are pleased to present this training book.

Perspection, Inc. is a software training company committed to providing information and training to help people use software more effectively in order to communicate, make decisions, and solve problems. Perspection writes and produces software training books, and develops multimedia and web-based training. Since 1991, we have written more than 100 computer books, with several bestsellers to our credit, and sold over 5 million books.

This book incorporates Perspection's training expertise to ensure that you'll receive the maximum return on your time. You'll focus on the tasks and skills that increase productivity while working at your own pace and convenience.

We invite you to visit the Perspection web site at:

www.perspection.com

Acknowledgments

The task of creating any book requires the talents of many hard-working people pulling together to meet impossible deadlines and untold stresses. We'd like to thank the outstanding team responsible for making this book possible: the writer, Steve Johnson; the production editor, James Teyler; proofer reader, Beth Teyler; and the indexer, Katherine Stimson.

At Que publishing, we'd like to thank Greg Wiegand and Laura Norman for the opportunity to undertake this project, Cindy Teeters for administrative support, and Sandra Schroeder for your production expertise and support.

Perspection

About the Author

Steve Johnson has written more than 80 books on a variety of computer software, including Adobe Photoshop CC, Adobe InDesign CC, Adobe Illustrator CC, Adobe Dreamweaver CS6, Adobe Edge Animate, Adobe Flash Professional CS5, Microsoft Windows 8, Microsoft SharePoint 2013, Microsoft Office 2013 and 2010, Microsoft Office 2008 for the Macintosh, and Apple OS X Mountain Lion. In 1991, after working for Apple Computer and Microsoft, Steve founded Perspection, Inc., which writes and produces software training. When he is not staying up late writing, he enjoys coaching baseball, playing golf, gardening, and spending time with his wife, Holly, and three children, JP, Brett, and Hannah. Steve and his family live in Northern California, but can also be found visiting family all over the western United States.

We Want to Hear from You!

As the reader of this book, *you* are our most important critic and commentator. We value your opinion and want to know what we're doing right, what we could do better, what areas you'd like to see us publish in, and any other words of wisdom you're willing to pass our way.

I welcome your comments. You can email or write me directly to let me know what you did or didn't like about this book—as well as what we can do to make our books better.

Please note that I cannot help you with technical problems related to the topic of this book.

When you write, please be sure to include this book's title and author as well as your name, email address, and phone number. I will carefully review your comments and share them with the author and editors who worked on the book.

Email: feedback@quepublishing.com

Mail: Que Publishing
 ATTN: Reader Feedback
 800 East 96th Street
 Indianapolis, IN 46240 USA

For more information about this book or another Que title, visit our web site at *www.quepublishing.com*. Type the ISBN (excluding hyphens) or the title of a book in the Search field to find the page you're looking for.

Contents

C

Introduction

Welcome to *OS X Mavericks on Demand*, a visual quick reference book that shows you how to work efficiently with Apple OS X Mavericks. This book provides complete coverage of basic to advanced OS X skills.

How This Book Works

You don't have to read this book in any particular order. We've designed the book so that you can jump in, get the information you need, and jump out. However, the book does follow a logical progression from simple tasks to more complex ones. Each task is presented on no more than two facing pages, which lets you focus on a single task without having to turn the page. To find the information that you need, just look up the task in the table of contents or index, and turn to the page listed. Read the task introduction, follow the step-by-step instructions in the left column along with screen illustrations in the right column, and you're done.

What's New

If you're searching for what's new in OS X Mavericks, just look for the icon: **New!**. The new icon appears in the table of contents and throughout this book so you can quickly and easily identify a new or improved feature in Mavericks. A complete description of each new feature appears in the New Features guide in the back of this book.

Keyboard Shortcuts

Most menu commands have a keyboard equivalent, such as ⌘+P, as a quicker alternative to using the mouse. A complete list of keyboard shortcuts is available on the web at *www.queondemand.com* or *www.perspection.com*.

How You'll Learn

How This Book Works

What's New

Keyboard Shortcuts

Step-by-Step Instructions

Real World Examples

Workshops

Get More on the Web

Step-by-Step Instructions

This book provides concise step-by-step instructions that show you "how" to accomplish a task. Each set of instructions includes illustrations that directly correspond to the easy-to-read steps. Also included in the text are time-savers, tables, and sidebars to help you work more efficiently or to teach you more in-depth information. A "Did You Know?" provides tips and techniques to help you work smarter, while a "See Also" leads you to other parts of the book containing related information about the task.

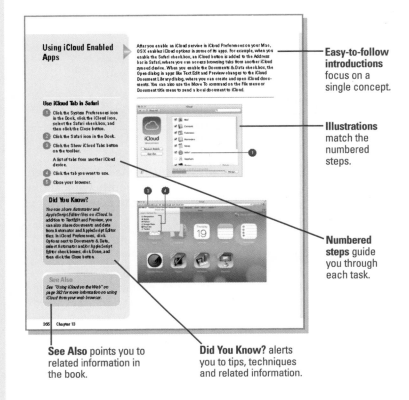

Easy-to-follow introductions focus on a single concept.

Illustrations match the numbered steps.

Numbered steps guide you through each task.

See Also points you to related information in the book.

Did You Know? alerts you to tips, techniques and related information.

Real World Examples

This book uses real world examples files to give you a context in which to use the task. By using the example files, you won't waste time looking for or creating sample files. You get a start file and a result file, so you can compare your work. Not every topic needs an example file, such as changing options, so we provide a complete list of the example files used through out the book. The example files that you need for project tasks along with a complete file list are available on the web at *www.queondemand.com* or *www.perspection.com*.

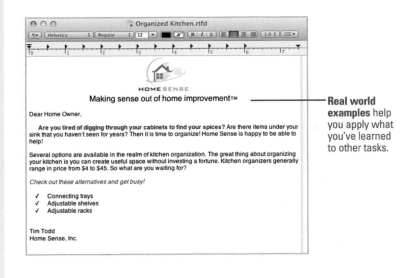

Real world examples help you apply what you've learned to other tasks.

Workshops

This book shows you how to put together the individual step-by-step tasks into in-depth projects with the Workshops. You start each project with a sample file, work through the steps, and then compare your results with project results file at the end. The Workshop projects and associated files are available on the web at www.queondemand.com or www.perspection.com.

Workshops

Introduction

The Workshops are all about being creative and thinking outside of the box. These workshops will help your right-brain soar, while making your left-brain happy; by explaining why things work the way they do. Exploring OS X Mavericks's possibilities is great fun; however, always stay grounded with knowledge of how things work. Knowledge is power.

Getting and Using the Project Files

Some projects in the Workshops may include a start file to help you get started with the project, and a final file to provide you with the results so you can see how well you accomplished the task. The first step in a project specifies whether you need a project file to complete it.

Before you can use the project files, you need to download them from the web. You can access the files at www.perspection.com. After you download the files from the web, uncompress the files into a folder on your hard drive to which you have easy access from OS X Mavericks.

Project 1: Viewing and Using Multiple Desktops

Skills and Tools: Desktop, Finder, Stacks, Mission Control, and Misc.

If your desktop gets cluttered, you can change view options or use stacks of folders with documents or applications to access material you're currently working on. If your dock starts to get cluttered, you can minimize windows to the associated application icon on the left side of the dock instead of minimizing windows to the right-side of the dock. With Mission Control, you can display and switch between windows in an easy to view grid with window tiles.

The Project

In this project, you'll display and customize the desktop and Finder to meet your workspace needs. You'll change view options for the desktop, create stacks, and use Mission Control to switch windows, minimize windows to the dock into an application icon. In addition, you'll show the date in the menu bar, show more commands in the menu bar, zoom desktop icons using the trackpad, and learn how to quickly get your Mac's serial number for support purposes.

The **Workshops** walks you through in-depth projects to help you put the OS X Mavericks to work.

Get More on the Web

In addition to the information in this book, you can also get more information on the web to help you get up to speed faster with OS X. Some of the information includes:

Transition Helpers

◆ **Only New Features.** Download and print the new feature tasks as a quick and easy guide.

Productivity Tools

◆ **Keyboard Shortcuts.** Download a list of keyboard shortcuts to learn faster ways to get the job done.

Keyboard Shortcuts

If a command on a menu includes a keyboard reference, known as a keyboard shortcut, to the right of the command name, you can perform the action by pressing and holding the first key, and then pressing the second key to perform the command quickly. In some cases, a keyboard shortcut uses one key or three keys. For three keys, simply press and hold the first two keys, and then press the third key. Keyboard shortcuts provide an alternative to using the mouse and make it easy to perform repetitive commands. If you don't like a global shortcut key combination, you can change it. See "Changing Keyboard Settings," on page 453 for details.

Finding a Keyboard Shortcut

The OS X Mavericks contains keyboard shortcuts for many commands and tasks in the different applications and utility programs. To find a keyboard shortcut for a menu command, click the menu with the command to display the keyboard shortcut keys. See the illustration below for key symbols on menus. To find a keyboard shortcut for a common task, use the list provided here. If you're searching for new keyboard shortcuts in Mavericks, just look for the letter: N. The N appears in the Keyboard Shortcuts table so you can quickly and easily identify new shortcuts.

Keyboard Shortcuts Index

Accessibility, 3
App Store, 8
Calendar, 8
Contacts, 9
Dialogs, 3
Dock, 3
Finder, 4
Folders, 6
Freezes, 2
iPhoto, 10
iTunes, 11
Mail, 12
Print Screen, 6
QuickTime, 14
Safari, 16
Shutting Down, 2
Spotlight, 6
Starting Up, 2
System, 7
Windows, 7

Additional content is available on the web.

More Content

◆ **Photographs.** Download photographs and other graphics to use in your documents.

◆ **More Content.** Download new content developed after publication.

You can access these additional resources on the web at *www.queondemand.com* or *www.perspection.com.*

Download and use **Photographs** to help you add impact to your documents.

Getting Started with OS X Mavericks

Introduction

OS X Mavericks is an **operating system (OS)**, a computer program that controls the basic operation of your Macintosh computer and the programs you run. A **program**, also known as an application, is task-oriented software you use to accomplish a specific task, such as word processing, managing files on your computer, or performing calculations.

The **Finder** is part of the Mac OS and starts when you turn on your computer. The Finder displays a menu bar and desktop on your screen that you can use to work with windows, icons, and files. A window can contain the contents of a file and the application in which it was created, icons (picture representations of an application or a file), or other usable data. This use of windows and icons is called a **graphical user interface** (GUI, pronounced "gooey"), meaning that you ("user") interact ("interface") with the computer through the use of graphics: icons and other meaningful words, symbols, and windows. A **file** is a collection of information (such as a letter or list of addresses) that has a unique name, distinguishing it from other files. You can use the Finder to open, copy, delete, list, and organize your computer files.

When you turn on your Macintosh computer, the Finder might ask you to log in. Your Macintosh is built to share with other people and work with other computers. If you are sharing your computer with others or accessing other computers over a network, you need to log in (type a user name and password) and log out to switch users or access information. When you're done working on your computer, you should put it to sleep for short periods or shut it down for longer stints.

Starting OS X

OS X automatically starts when you turn on your computer. When you first start OS X, you see the desktop screen, or a Login window depending on your installation. The OS X desktop screen indicates you are using a stand-alone computer (you're the only person using the computer), while the Login window identifies you're on a shared computer. After you click or type your user name in the Login window, and then possibly type a password, you'll see the OS X desktop.

Start OS X Using a Stand Alone Computer

1 Turn on your computer, and then wait while OS X loads.

The OS X Mavericks desktop screen appears.

Menu bar Desktop

Dock

Did You Know?

The Login window doesn't always appear. If OS X is set up to log in automatically, you don't normally see the Login window. However, if you select the Log Out command from the Apple menu, you do see the Login window. If you see the Login window, click Restart to log in again automatically.

You can start your Mac in Safe Mode. Safe Mode starts your Mac with the minimal OS X files for use with fixing problems. Restart your Mac and hold down the Right Shift key while booting up.

See Also

See "Adding a User Account" on page 398 for information on creating a user account.

See "Activating the Login Window" on page 397 for information on changing log in options.

For Your Information

Creating a Shared Computer

During the OS X installation process, you create a user account for the computer administrator and possibly other accounts for each person who uses your computer. An administrator account can create other user accounts, install software, and change computer settings. When you create accounts for more than one account, your computer changes from a stand-alone computer to a shared computer. Each user maintains separate files, a home folder, and preferences without affecting other users.

Start OS X Using a Shared Computer

1 Turn on your computer and wait while OS X loads.

The Login window opens.

2 Click or type your user name.

3 Type your password. Be sure to use the correct capitalization.

4 Press Return.

TROUBLE? *If you forget your password, your third attempt to type the password correctly displays your password hint, and a Reset button, where you can use the administrator's master password to create a new password.*

Did You Know?

The password is case-sensitive. Macintosh makes a distinction between uppercase and lowercase letters. Your password should be at least seven characters long, the optimal length for encryption, which is the process of logically scrambling data to keep a password secure.

You can set up your computer to automatically log in (by pass the Login window). Click the Apple menu, click System Preferences, click Users & Groups, and then select the administrator account. Next, click Login Options, select the Automatically Login pop-up, and then click an account. Type a password, and then click OK.

You can sleep, restart, and shut down from the Login window. In the Login window, click Sleep, Restart, or Shut Down, and then click the appropriate button or wait 60 seconds.

Login window

Exploring the Finder and Desktop

When you first start OS X, you see the Finder desktop with a transparent look and feel, or a log in screen (a way to identify yourself on the computer), depending on your installation. The desktop is an on-screen version of an actual desk, containing windows, icons, files, and applications. You can use the desktop to access, store, organize, modify, share, and explore information (such as a letter or a list of addresses), whether it resides on your computer, a network, or the Internet. The desktop contains icons that represent volumes (such as your Hard Disk to store data), applications, documents, folders, and the Trash. If you upgraded your Mac computer to OS X from a previous version, your desktop might contain many different icons. These icons can also appear a number of different ways depending on your view. When you open an icon, a window or application appears, displaying its contents or an application work environment. The bar at the bottom

Menu bar Menu status area

Finder window

Background picture on the desktop

Dock

of the desktop is called the **Dock** (if it's hidden, point to the bottom of the screen to display it); it allows you to start applications and switch among currently running ones. At the top of the screen is a **menu bar**, which contain commands you use to perform tasks and customize your environment. At the right end of the menu bar is the **menu status area**, which displays the time, date, current user, and application related icons—including Spotlight, Notifications, AirPort, Volume, Eject, and Bluetooth to name a few. Your list of icons may differ depending on the applications you have installed. The OS X dynamic user interface includes a transparent look and feel with design themes and a reflective floor for the Dock. A **design theme** is a professionally designed look and feel that coordinates all aspects of the user interface, including the desktop, menus, and windows.

Fast user switching

Desktop icons

Open application window

Recent documents

Open application windows

Application commands

Open Application icon in the Dock

Using the Mouse or Multi-Touch Gestures

Macintosh desktop computers typically come with a mouse that contains a single button, while Macintosh portable computers come with a Multi-Touch trackpad. A **mouse** is a handheld input device you roll across a flat surface (such as a desk or a mouse pad) while a **trackpad** is a small pad device you tap or slide your fingers across, which is known as a **gesture**. You use a mouse or trackpad to position the **mouse pointer**, the small symbol that indicates the pointer's relative position on the screen. When you move the mouse or drag the trackpad, the mouse pointer on the screen moves in the same direction. The shape of the mouse pointer changes to indicate different activities. However, the pointer usually looks like an arrow pointer. Once you move the mouse pointer (the arrow's tip) to a desired position on the screen (known as pointing), you use the mouse button or trackpad as a button to tell your computer what you want it to do by either clicking (press and release), double-clicking (press and release twice quickly), dragging (press and hold, then move and release), or pressing (press and hold).

With the Multi-Touch trackpad, you can use gestures to naturally interact with your computer. You can click anywhere on the trackpad as a button, pinch two fingers to zoom in and out, swipe a finger to flip through photos or rotate images, or brush two fingers to scroll. To see how to perform gestures, customize how gestures work, and set options from your trackpad or mouse, open Trackpad or Mouse preferences.

With OS X, you can perform even more gestures:

◆ **Rubber-band scrolling.** Swipe to the top or bottom of a list or a web page to scroll and it springs back.

◆ **Swipe forward and back.** Swipe left or right in apps, like Safari and Preview, to move between pages.

◆ **Tap to zoom.** Double-tap to zoom in on text or images in Safari and Preview.

◆ **Pinch to zoom.** Pinch using two fingers to precise zoom in or out of apps, like Safari, Preview, and iPhoto.

◆ **Swipe between full screen apps.** Swipe to move from one full screen apps to another.

◆ **Show Mission Control.** Swipe to open Mission Control.

◆ **Show Launchpad.** Pinch three fingers and your thumb to open Launchpad.

◆ **Show desktop.** Spread three fingers and your thumb to move all open windows off the screen, revealing the desktop.

In addition to the traditional mouse and trackpad, you can use other input devices, such as a mouse with two buttons (left and right), the Magic Mouse (a mouse device with a Multi-touch trackpad surface), the Magic Trackpad (a Multi-Touch trackpad device for a desktop computer), or writing tablet.

Dragging

Mouse pointer

Clicking

Pinching gesture

Multi-Touch trackpad

Working with Menus, Toolbars, and Panes

A **menu** is a list of commands that you use to accomplish certain tasks, such as when you use the View menu to open the Customize Toolbar dialog. A **command** is a directive that provides access to an application's features. Each application has its own set of menus, which are on the menu bar along the top of the application window. The menu bar organizes commands into groups of related operations. Each group is listed under the name of the menu, such as File or Help. To access the commands in a menu, you click the name of the menu, and then click the command name. If a menu command is gray, the option is not available at this time; availability depends on what is selected. If a command on a menu includes a keyboard reference, known as a **keyboard shortcut**, such as ⌘+1 for the As Icons command, you can perform the action by pressing and holding the first key, and then pressing the second key to perform the command quickly. When a menu command is followed by an ellipse (...), a dialog appears when you select it. On a menu, a **check mark** identifies a currently selected feature, meaning that the feature is enabled, or turned on. To disable, or turn off the feature, you click the command again to remove the check mark, or you can select another command (within the menu section, separated by gray lines) in its place. You can also carry out some of the most frequently used commands on a menu by clicking a button on a toolbar. A **toolbar** contains buttons that are convenient shortcuts for menu commands and navigation. A **pane** is a frame within a window, such as a Sidebar, where you can quickly access navigation controls. You can use menus, toolbar buttons, and commands in a pane to change how a window's contents appear.

Pane (Sidebar) Toolbar Check mark Keyboard shortcut Menu Submenu

Using Menus for Quick Results

The Finder uses several different types of menus to help you use the commands you need to get the results you want. The Finder uses four types of menus: pull-down, submenu, pop-up, and contextual. The **pull down** menu appears on the menu bar when you click a menu name or status icon in the menu status area. A **submenu** appears when you point to a menu with a triangle. A **pop-up** menu appears in a window or dialog when you click the double arrow. A **contextual** menu appears when you hold down the Control key while you click an item, such as an icon, text, or graphic or right-click an item. A contextual menu displays a list of commands related to the selected item. When you click a menu name, the menu stays open. If you don't want to select a menu command, you can click outside the menu or press the Esc key to close it.

Use a Pull Down Menu

1. Point to the name or menu status icon on the menu bar, and then click to open the menu.

2. Point to the menu option you want.

3. If a submenu opens, point to the menu option you want.

4. Click to select the command.

Did You Know?

You can rearrange menu status icons on the menu bar. Press and hold ⌘, and then drag the icon to reposition it.

Use a Contextual Menu

1. Point to the item on which you want to act upon.

2. Press and hold down the Control key, and then click to display a contextual menu.

 If you are using a mouse with two buttons, right-click the item.

3. Select the command you want.

Pull down menu Menu status icons

Submenu

Choosing Dialog Options

The Finder and OS X applications use dialogs to carry out options, provide alert messages, and gather information. A **dialog** is a window that opens when the Finder or an application wants to alert you of an event, or you select a menu command or button followed by an ellipsis. In a dialog, you acknowledge an alert message or select various options, and then provide information for completing the command.

Choose Dialog Options

All dialogs contain the same types of options, including the following:

- **Tabs.** Click a tab to display its options. Each tab groups a related set of options.

- **Option buttons.** Click an option button to select it. You can usually select only one in a group.

- **Check box.** Click the box to turn on or off the option. A checked box means the option is selected; a cleared box means it's not.

- **Pop-up menu.** Click the arrow to display a list of commands or options, and then click the one you want.

- **Entry field.** Click in the field, and then type the requested information.

- **Up and down arrows.** Click the up or down arrow to increase or decrease the number, or type a number in the field.

- **Scroll bar.** Drag a slider control to change screen position.

- **Preview area.** Many dialogs show an image that reflects the options you select.

- **Slider.** Drag a slider control to change a screen position.

- **Push button.** Click a button to perform an action or command. A button name followed by an ellipsis (...) opens another dialog.

Option button Pop-up menu

Help button Check box

Entry field

Push buttons

For Your Information

Navigating and Working in a Dialog

Rather than clicking to move around a dialog, you can press the Tab key to move from one field to the next. You can also use Shift+Tab to move backward. When a field appears with a dark border around it, the text you type appears in the active field. The default button is the one that appears highlighted. You can press the Return key to perform the default button. If you decide not to use options you set in a dialog, you can press the Esc key to perform the Cancel button and disregard the options. Before you can use the keyboard shortcuts, you need to turn on the option. Click the Apple menu, click Preferences, and then click the Keyboard icon. Click the Keyboard Shortcuts tab, select a category in the left pane, and select the check box next to the keyboard shortcut you want to enable. Double-click a shortcut to change it. When you're done, click the Close button.

Working with Icons

OS X uses various icons to graphically represent different items on the desktop, in the Dock, or in a window. The icons represent applications, documents, folders, volumes, and the Trash. **Application icons** are programs you use to create documents. **Document icons** are files you create with applications. **Folder icons** are a storage area for files. **Volume icons** are storage devices, such as hard disks, removable disks, network disks, Internet computers, CDs, DVDs, and iPods. The **Trash icon** (located in the Dock) appears in three different ways: empty, full, and ejecting removable media. On the desktop or within a window, you can select and deselect one or more icons to perform tasks, such as opening, launching, copying, and moving. When you select an icon, the icon graphic and its name become highlighted. Within a Finder window, icons appear in different ways, depending on the window view you select.

Select Icons

◆ **Select an icon.** Click the icon you want to select.

◆ **Select multiple icons by clicking.** Click the first icon you want to select, hold down , and then click the other icons you want to select within the same window.

> **TIMESAVER** *Click the first icon, press the Shift key, and then click the last one to select every icon in between.*

◆ **Select multiple icons by dragging.** Position the mouse pointer to the left of the first icon you want to select, drag diagonally across the adjacent icons you want to select, and then release the mouse button.

> A shaded box appears as you drag to indicate the selection area.

◆ **Select all icons.** Click the Edit menu, and then click Select All.

> **TIMESAVER** *Press* ⌘+A *to select all icons.*

Start dragging here

Selection rectangle

Select multiple icons by dragging

Select multiple icons by clicking

Deselect Icons

◆ **Deselect all icons.** Click a blank area in the window or on the desktop.

◆ **Deselect an icon in a multiple selection.** Press and hold down ⌘, and then click the icon you want to deselect, while keeping the others selected.

Deselect all icons

Move or Copy Icons

1 To move multiple icons, select the ones you want to move; to copy an icon, hold down the Option key.

2 Point to the icons, and then drag them to the new location.

As you drag, a shaded image of the icon moves along with the mouse pointer.

TROUBLE? *Press the Esc key to cancel the move or copy.*

3 Release the mouse button and the Option key, if necessary.

TIMESAVER *Press ⌘+X to move or press ⌘+C to copy selected icons; and then press ⌘+V to paste them.*

Did You Know?

You can change the icon view size. In as Icons view, drag the Zoom control on the Status bar.

For Your Information

Viewing Content in Icons

When you display a multi-page document or a QuickTime movie file in Icon view, you can thumb through the document or watch the movie. When you point to a multi-page document, such as a PDF, or a QuickTime move (.MOV), the thumbnail displays Previous and Next buttons or Play/Pause button, which you can click to view or play it as a thumbnail preview. The icon preview is also available in the Preview pane in Column and Cover Flow views.

Viewing Windows

A window displays icons and other information in the Finder, and content in an application. One of the powerful things about the OS X is that you can open more than one window or application at once. You can identify a window by its name on the title bar at the top of the window. Before you can work with a window, you need to activate it first. The active window is the one in front with the available buttons (red, yellow, and green) in the upper-left corner. When you're done using a window, you can quickly close it to reduce the clutter on the desktop. You can use the View menu in the Finder to show or hide window parts.

Parts of a Window

Windows in OS X consist of the following parts:

- **Close button.** Closes the window.
- **Minimize button.** Shrinks the window to an icon in the Dock.
- **Zoom button.** Toggles the window size between full and a custom size.
- **Title bar.** Displays the name of the window.
- **Toolbar.** Displays buttons and controls for commonly used window commands.
- **Tab bar.** Displays folder tabs (**New!**) along with an Add Tab (+) button (**New!**) in a single window.
- **Full screen.** Displays the window using the full screen (**New!**).
- **Size control.** Allows you to set a custom window size.
- **Zoom control.** Allows you to set a view percentage in as Icons view.
- **Status bar.** Displays information about selected items.
- **Path bar.** Displays path from the hard drive to the current folder.
- **Sidebar.** Displays commonly used volumes and folders.
- **Column heading.** Displays the names of columns and sorts them (in list view only).
- **Search field.** Allows you to find files based on the name.
- **Scroll bar.** Displays the content of the window.

Open and Close a Window

◆ **Open a Finder window.** Double-click a volume or folder icon.

◆ **Open a new Finder window.** Click the **File** menu, and then click **New Finder Window**.

◆ **Close a window.** Click the **Close** button (red) to close the window, or hold down the Option key, and then click the **Close** button (red) to close all windows.

 TIMESAVER *If you see a dot in the center of the Close button, you need to save your changes.*

Activate a Window

◆ **Activate a window.** Click anywhere on the window, or click the **Window** menu, and then click the window name.

◆ **Activate and bring all Finder windows to front.** Click the **Window** menu, and then click **Bring All To Front**. All open Finder windows that are not minimized are moved in front of application windows.

◆ **Activate and bring a specific application window to the front.** Display the Dock, press (click and hold) an application icon to display a menu, and then select the window you want to make active.

◆ **Activate a window by cycling through them.** Click the **Window** menu, and then click **Cycle Through Window**.

 TIMESAVER *Press ⌘+` (accent) to cycle through open windows.*

Click to close window

Double-click to open Finder window

New Finder window

Window menu

Active window

Managing Windows

When you open multiple windows, your desktop can get cluttered with many windows from the Finder and open applications. To organize your desktop, you may need to move windows to a different location or change its size. Each window has resize buttons to minimize or zoom a window, a Full Screen button (**New!**) to toggle to and from full screen, and a size control that you can use to resize the window to a custom size. An icon appears in the Dock for each minimized window, which you can use to quickly switch between windows or redisplay it. You can Control-click the Finder or application icon to switch between open windows or press Control+Up Arrow to activate Exposé in Mission Control.

Switch Among Open Windows

1 If windows are visible, click in the window to make it active.

2 If the windows are not visible, Control-click the Finder or an application icon, and then click a window or press Control+Up Arrow to activate Exposé in Mission Control, and then click a window you want.

See Also

See "Exposing Windows in Mission Control" on page 22 for information on temporarily showing and hiding all windows.

Move a Window

1 Point to the window's title bar.

2 Drag the window to a new location, and then release the mouse button.

> **TIMESAVER** *Hold down the A key while you drag the title bar of an inactive window to move it without making it active.*

Use Buttons to Resize a Window

All windows contain the same sizing buttons:

◆ **Minimize button (active window).** Click the yellow button to shrink a window as an icon in the Dock, or double-click the title bar.

TIMESAVER *Press* ⌘+M *to minimize the active window.*

◆ **Minimize button (all windows).** Hold down the Option key, and then click the yellow button or double-click the title bar to minimize all windows.

◆ **Redisplay minimized window.** Click the window's icon in the Dock or click the Window menu, and then click the window's name.

◆ **Zoom button.** Click the green button to toggle between the smallest possible size that fits on your screen, and the size you set with the size control.

◆ **Full Screen button.** Click the double-arrow button (**New!**) to toggle to and from full screen.

Use the Mouse to Resize a Window

1 Move the mouse over the edge or corner of the window (cursor changes to a double arrow).

An edge resizes up/down or left/right and a corner resizes up/down and left/right.

2 Drag the size control until the window is the size you want.

Minimize button
Zoom button
Full Screen button

Minimized window

Using the Tab Bar

With the Tab bar (**New!**) in the Finder, you can work with multiple windows in a single window to declutter the desktop. It works like the tabs in Safari. The Tab bar displays a tab for each open window and an Add Tab button (+) to open a new tab. You can click a tab to make it active and work with its contents. To move a file between tabs, just drag and drop from one tab to another. If the tabs are not in the position you want, you can change the order by simply dragging the tab. You can also use commands on the File menu to create or close a tab and the Window menu to move a tab to a new window or merge all windows together with tabs. If you want more space for tabs, you can expand a Finder window to full screen (**New!**), just like an app window. If you like using tabs, you can set an option in Finder Preferences to open folders in tabs instead of new windows (**New!**).

Show or Hide the Tab Bar

1. Click in the window to make it active.

2. Click the **View** menu, and then click **Show Tab Bar** (**New!**) or **Hide Tab Bar** (**New!**).

 TROUBLE? *If there are multiple tabs in a window, the Hide Tab Bar command is grayed out. Close until only one remains.*

 TIMESAVER *Press Shift+⌘+T to show/hide the Tab bar.*

 The Tab bar shows or hides in the active Finder window.

Tab bar

Work with Tabs

1. Use any of the following to work with tabs (**New!**):

 ◆ **Add a Tab.** Click the **Add Tab** button (+) on the Tab bar.

 ◆ **Close a Tab.** Point to or click a tab, and then click the **Close** button on the tab.

 ◆ **Switch Between Tabs.** Point to a tab, and then click it.

 ◆ **Move Files Between Tabs.** Select the files, and then drag them onto the destination tab. To copy, hold the Option key.

 ◆ **Change Tab Order.** Drag a tab to another position or window.

 ◆ **Move Tab to New Window.** Click the tab, click the **Window** menu, and then click **Move Tab to New Window**.

 ◆ **Merge All Windows to Tabs.** Click the **Window** menu, and then click **Marge All Windows**.

Open New Windows in Tabs

1. Click the **Finder** menu, and then click **Preferences**.

2. Click **General**.

3. Select the **Open folders in tabs instead of new windows** check box (**New!**).

4. To select a default folder to open in the new tab, click the **New Finder windows show** pop-up, and then select a folder..

5. Click the **Close** button.

Close tab Active tab Inactive tab

Add Tab button

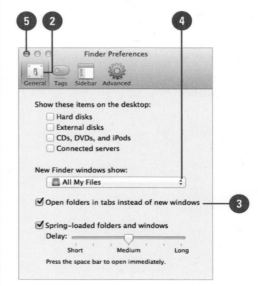

Using the Sidebar

The Sidebar is a panel which appears in the left column of Finder windows, that you can use to quickly access commonly used locations on your computer. The panel appears with areas or sections, including Favorites, Shared, Devices, and Tags (**New!**). The Favorites section contains for folders, including your All My Files, AirDrop, Applications, Desktop, Documents, Downloads, Movies, Music, Pictures, and any Smart Folders. The Shared section contains shared and networked computers. You can use the Sidebar to move and copy documents to disks and folders on or connected to your computer, eject removable disks, and burn a CD or DVD. The Devices section contains items for volumes attached to your computer. To show or hide items in a section, point to the section name, and then click Show or Hide. The Tags section (**New!**) contains tags for displaying or assigning tagged items.

Use the Sidebar

◆ **Display icons.** Click icons in the Sidebar to display contents.

◆ **Move or copy icons.** Drag the folder or document icons from the Contents pane to the Sidebar icon in order to move or copy them.

◆ **Add a file, folder or application.** Drag its icon to Favorites (display line) or select it, click the **File** menu, and then click **Add to Sidebar**.

◆ **Remove icon.** Control-click its icon, and then click **Remove from Sidebar**.

◆ **Change column width.** Position the mouse pointer over the divider, and then drag to change the width.

◆ **Hide or show sidebar.** Click the **View** menu, then click **Hide Sidebar** or **Show Sidebar**.

◆ **Eject a disk.** Click the **Eject** button next to any removable disk.

◆ **Burn a CD.** Insert a blank CD or DVD, drag files and folders to it, and then click the **Burn** button.

◆ **Display tagged items.** Click a tag name (**New!**).

◆ **Assign tags to items.** Drag a selection to a tag in the Sidebar (**New!**).

Sidebar

Eject button Drag here to change width.

Using Toolbars

The toolbar, in a Finder window, provides easy access to commonly used window commands. You can use commands on the View menu to hide the toolbar and sidebar, to display more information in the window, or to show the toolbar to display tools and navigational controls. The Toolbar Control button is no longer available on the toolbar. When you hide the toolbar, the Finder also hides the Sidebar panel and window borders, and moves the status bar to display under the title bar.

Parts of a Toolbar

Toolbars in the Finder consist of the following parts:

◆ **Back and Forward buttons.** Displays the content from the previous or next window.

◆ **View buttons.** Displays the window in different views.

◆ **Arrange by button.** Displays the window contents by attributes.

◆ **Action pop-up menu.** Displays window or item commands.

◆ **Edit Tags button.** Allows you to assign and edit tags (**New!**).

◆ **Share selected items.** Allows you to share selected items.

◆ **Search field.** Allows you to search for a file by name.

Show or Hide the Toolbar and Sidebar

1 Click the **View** menu, and then click **Hide Toolbar** or **Show Toolbar**.

TIMESAVER *Press ⌥+⌘+T to hide/show the toolbar.*

If a double arrow appears at the right side of the toolbar, the window is too small to show all the icons. You can either resize the window, or click the double arrow, and then select a toolbar item.

To customize the toolbar, click the **View** menu, and then click **Customize Toolbar**.

Displaying and Using the Dock

The Dock is a bar at the bottom of the screen that you can use to open frequently used applications and utilities, system preferences, web sites and the Trash, as well as redisplay minimized applications and Finder windows. If you don't see the Dock at the bottom of your screen, then it's automatically hidden. You can change an option in the Dock pane of System Preferences to always display the Dock. The Dock has two sides with a divider line separating the two. The left side is for applications and the right side is for everything else: stacks, files, documents, folders, and disks. When you point to an icon, its name appears above it. Document and folder icons in the Dock actually display an image of the contents to make it a little easier to distinguish between them. When you click an icon, it launches or opens it. When you launch an application, its icon appears in the Dock with a shiny image below it; when an option is set in preferences. When you press and hold an icon, a list of commands appears on a menu. When you quit an application or window not permanently placed in the Dock, its icon is removed from the Dock. In addition to the predefined icons in the Dock, you can also quickly and permanently add your own icons in the Dock.

Display and Use the Dock

◆ **Display a hidden Dock.** Move the mouse pointer to the bottom or side of the screen.

◆ **Open, launch or redisplay a minimized item.** Click its icon.

◆ **Choose commands for an item.** Press and hold or Control-click the icon in the Dock, and then click a command.

◆ **Choose commands for an open item.** Press and hold or Control-click the open icon in the Dock, and then click a command.

Did You Know?

You can turn Dock hiding off and on. Click the Apple menu, point to Dock, and then click Turn Hiding Off or Turn Hiding On.

You can quickly switch between applications in the Dock. Hold down ⌘, and then repeatedly press the Tab key. Release the keys to switch.

Open item Stacks Minimized item

Applications Divider All others

Press and hold or Control-click an icon in the Dock

Displaying and Using Stacks on the Dock

Folders in the Dock are called **stacks**. You can use stacks to reduce clutter and quickly access folders of documents, applications, downloads, and other folders. When you click a stack in the Dock, it springs open to display an arc or a grid of icons for the items in the stack. You can scroll through stacks, open folders, and navigate back. The Dock comes with two stacks, the Documents and Downloads folders, which stores your documents and downloaded items from the Internet. You can create more stacks by dragging the folder you want to the Dock and modify stacks by Control-clicking it in the Dock.

Work with Stacks on the Dock

◆ **Display a stack.** Click a folder in the Dock.

◆ **Open the stack folder.** Control-click the folder in the Dock, and then click **Open "name"** or point to **Options**, and click **Show in Finder**.

◆ **Open an item in a stack folder.** Click the folder in the Dock, and then click the item. If you click a folder in Grid view, you can click the return path icon in the upper left of the stack to return.

◆ **Add a stack to the Dock.** Drag the folder to the Dock.

◆ **Remove a stack from the Dock.** Control-click the folder in the Dock, point to **Options**, and then click **Remove from Dock**.

◆ **Change the stack display.** Control-click the folder in the Dock, and then click **Automatic**, **List**, **Grid**, or **Fan**. Automatic displays in a fan or grid depending on available space.

◆ **Change stack icon in the Dock.** Control-click the folder or stack in the Dock, and then click **Folder** or **Stack**.

◆ **Sort items in a stack.** Control-click the folder in the Dock, and then select the sort type (under Sort by) you want.

Fan stack for Documents folder

Stack options for the selected folder

Exposing Windows in Mission Control

When you have multiple windows and applications open at the same time, the screen can get cluttered and make it difficult to work. Mission Control with Exposé let you quickly view all your open windows to make it easier to locate and work with them. Mission Control expands to make it quick and easy to determine what's running on your computer. It displays the Dashboard, desktop workspaces, and all open windows (grouped by application), even ones in full screen view (as separate thumbnails). In Mission Control, you can click the Dashboard, a desktop ,or a window to bring it to the front. With Exposé, you can also quickly show all open windows in the current application at the same time (press the Mission Control key (F3) or Control+Up Arrow) or hide all the open windows to see your desktop (F11 or portable Fn-F11).

Use Exposé in Mission Control

◆ **Show all open windows at once with Mission Control.** Click the **Mission Control** icon or Mission Control key (F3) or press the Control+Up Arrow or three finger swipe on a trackpad to start/exit.

 For temporary use, hold down the Mission Control key, and then release.

◆ **Show all open windows in the current application.** Press the Control+Down Arrow key or Option+click an app in the Dock, and then click **Show All Windows** or **Show Recents**. Press Tab to cycle through open and recent documents.

◆ **Hide all open windows (show desktop).** Press the F11 key to start/exit.

 For temporary use, hold down the F11 key, and then release.

◆ **Activate a window.** Click the **Mission Control** icon to open all windows, point to a window to highlight it, and then click to activate it.

◆ **Activate an application window.** Press and hold the ⌘ key, and then press Tab. Continue to press Tab, and then release to activate the one you want.

Mission Control spaces

Shows all open windows at once

Click to open window

Mission Control icon Shows all open windows in current application

Grouping Windows in Mission Control

Spaces works in Mission Control to help you group windows on a desktop or full screen apps into unique spaces, named Desktop 1, Desktop 2, Calendar, etc to reduce desktop clutter. You can spread out your work in different spaces by assigning (opening) a window (Finder or app) or full screen app to a space. You can quickly view and switch between spaces, rearrange spaces, and move windows between spaces. Each space displays only the windows or full screen app for that space. To work with Spaces, you open Mission Control by clicking the Mission Control icon in the Dock, pressing the Mission Control key (typically F3) or Control+Up Arrow, or swiping up using three or four fingers on a trackpad; see the Track pane in System Preferences for options.

Use Spaces in Mission Control

◆ **Switch between spaces.** Hold down the Control key and then press the left or right arrow keys to scroll the spaces or swipe left or right using three or four fingers on a trackpad.

◆ **View all spaces in Mission Control.** Click the Mission Control icon, or press the Mission Control key (F3) or Control+Up Arrow, or swipe up using three or four fingers on a trackpad.

◆ **Add a space.** Open the Mission Control icon, point to right corner or press Option key and then click the **Add** (+) button.

◆ **Delete a space.** Click the Mission Control icon, point a space or press Option key to display **Delete** (x) button, and then click it. You can't delete full screen apps, Dashboard, or Desktop 1.

◆ **Rearrange space order.** Click the Mission Control icon, and then drag a space. You can't order the Dashboard or Desktop 1.

◆ **Move a window between spaces.** Click the Mission Control icon, and then drag the window to a space or the **Add** (+) button to create a new space.

◆ **Preferences for spaces.** See "Customizing Mission Control" on page 92 for details.

Selected space Full screen app Delete space Add space

Mission Control icon

Open windows in the selected space; drag a window to another space to move it.

Switching Users

Many users can use the same computer. Individual OS X accounts allow users to keep their files private and to customize the operating system with their own preferences. OS X manages these separate accounts by giving each user a unique user name and password. When a user selects an account and types a password (if necessary), OS X starts with that user's configuration settings and network permissions. When you want to change users, you can logout, which lets you either restore your workspace—known as Resume—or save and close all files and running applications before it signs you off the computer. Or, switch users, which quickly switches between users without having to logout, close applications, and save your current settings. With fast user switching, the name of the current user appears (by default, which you can customize in Users & Groups preferences) in the status menu area, where you can quickly switch to a new user. If you leave your computer unattended for any period of time, you can set additional security logout options to protect your information.

Fast User Switching

1 Click the *user name* in the upper-right corner of the menu bar.

2 Click the user account to which you want to switch.

The name grayed out is the current user, and a check mark next to a name indicates that the user is logged in.

If required, a Login window opens, requesting a password.

3 If necessary, type your password.

4 Click **Log In**.

The computer switches to the new user's desktop (like a box switching sides), which includes the user's home folder, mail, and personal settings.

See Also

See "Setting Fast User Switching" on page 406 for information on enabling Fast User Switching.

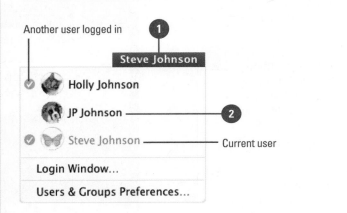

Another user logged in

Current user

Logout of Your Computer

1 Click the **Apple** menu, and then click **Log Out** *user name*.

 TIMESAVER *Press Shift+⌘+Q to log off. If you press the Option key while you select the Log Out menu command, OS X skips the confirmation dialog.*

2 Select the **Reopen windows when logging back in** check box to use Resume.

3 Click **Log Out** or wait 60 seconds to close all your applications, save your settings, and sign off.

 A Login window appears.

4 Click your name.

5 If required, type your password, and then click **Log In**.

Counts down from 60 seconds until automatic log out.

Set Logout Security Options

1 Click the **System Preferences** icon in the Dock, and then click the **Security & Privacy** icon.

2 Click the **General** tab.

3 Select or clear the **Require password *X* after sleep or screen saver begins** check box, and then specify a time delay before the password is required.

4 Click **Advanced**, select or clear the **Log out after *X* minutes of inactivity** check box, and then enter the number of minutes you want, and then click **OK**.

 IMPORTANT *If any Save dialogs appear, your computer will not log you out.*

5 Click the **Close** button.

Sleeping, Restarting, and Shutting Down

When you finish working on your computer, you can put it to sleep for a little while or shut it down for longer periods. If you install a software update or have a problem, you can restart—shutdown and start—your computer. Sleeping causes your computer screen to go blank and halt the spinning of your hard disk. Restarting or shutting down your computer allows you to restore—known as Resume—your workspace including applications to the exact place you left it or return to a clean desktop, which closes all open files and windows, and quits all open applications, before it turns off. Avoid pushing the power switch to shutdown, so you don't lose important data and cause system problems.

Sleep, Restart, or Shut Down

When you're done working on your computer, do one of the following:

◆ **Sleep.** Click the **Apple** menu, and then click **Sleep**.

> **IMPORTANT** *When your computer is inactive for a time set in Energy Saver preferences, OS X puts your computer to sleep.*

To wake up your computer, click the mouse button or press any keyboard key.

◆ **Restart or Shutdown.** Click the **Apple** menu, and then click **Restart** or **Shut Down**.

 ◆ Select the **Reopen windows when logging back in** check box to use Resume.

 ◆ If other users are logged in, type the administrator name and password, and then click **Restart** or **Shut Down**.

 ◆ Click the **Restart** or **Shut Down** button or wait 60 seconds.

> **IMPORTANT** *If you press the Option key while you select the Restart or Shut Down command, OS X skips the dialog.*

> **IMPORTANT** *If your computer has a power key, you can press it to display a dialog with Sleep, Restart, and Shut Down buttons.*

Sleep, Restart, and Shut Down commands

Resume setting during a restart

Understanding Your Options

Option	Shortcut	When to use it
Sleep	⌘+Alt+Eject	When you want to stop working for a little while, save computer memory, and conserve power.
Shut Down	⌘+Alt+Ctrl+Eject	When you finish working on your Mac and you want to turn off the power to the computer.
Restart	⌘+Ctrl+Eject	When you have problems and want to reset your computer (clear memory and reload system files).

Managing Files and Folders

2

Introduction

File management involves organizing and keeping track of files and folders. It helps you stay organized so information is easy to locate and use. A **folder** is a container for storing applications and files, similar to a folder in a file cabinet. As with a file cabinet, working with poorly managed files is like looking for a needle in a haystack—it's frustrating and time-consuming to search through irrelevant, misnamed, and out-of-date files to find the one you want.

Finder allows you to organize folders and files in a file hierarchy, imitating the way you store paper documents in real folders. Just as a file cabinet contains several folders, each containing related documents with dividers grouping related folders together, so the Finder file hierarchy allows you to organize your files in folders, and then place folders in other folders. At the top of each hierarchy is the name of the hard drive or main folder. This drive or folder contains several files and folders, and each folder contains related files and folders.

Using the file management tools, you save files in folders with appropriate names for easy identification, quickly and easily create new folders so you can reorganize information, delete files and folders that you no longer need, search for a file when you cannot remember where you stored it, create shortcuts to files and folders for quick and easy access, and compress files and folders to save space.

What You'll Do

Open and View Disks

View and Open Documents

Change the Window View

Arrange Files and Folders in Icons View

Work with Files and Folders in List View and Columns View

View Files with Cover Flow View

View Files Using Quick Look

Go to Common or Recent Places

Organize Files and Folders by Tags

Create and Rename Files and Folders

Copy and Move Files and Folders

Use Spring-Loaded Folders

Share Files Using Online Services

Delete and Restore Files and Folders

Get and Set File Information

Create a CD or DVD Using the Finder

Mount and Eject Disks

Opening and Viewing Disks

The desktop is the starting point to access every disk, folder, and file on your computer. When Finder Preferences are appropriately set to display desktop icons, the desktop displays several types of local, removable, and network drives. Drives and folders are represented by icons on the desktop. Each icon graphic represents a different type of disk. Disks are devices that store information used by the computer. The disk with the OS X installed on it is called the **startup disk**, which is typically the hard disk inside your computer. The files related to OS X are stored in the **System folder** on your startup disk. You should not move this folder or make any changes to its contents. Additional OS X related files are stored in the **Library folder**, which stores system and application preference settings and files. Also on your startup disk is an **Applications folder** that contains the complete collection of OS X programs on your computer. Lastly, the **Users folder** stores contents for individual user accounts on a shared computer. You double-click a disk icon, such as your hard disk or a removable disk, on the desktop to open a Finder window, displaying the contents of the disk. Once you open more than one drive or folder, you can use buttons on the toolbar to help you move quickly between folders.

Open and View Disks

1. If you want to view a disk, insert it in your drive.

 The removable disk appears on the desktop (if set in Finder Preferences) along with your other drivers, such as your hard disk or a network disk.

2. Double-click the drive icon on the desktop to open it.

 TIMESAVER *Press Shift+⌘+C or click the Go menu, and then click Computer to display disks.*

3. Double-click a folder icon in the Finder window to open it.

4. Click the **Back** or **Forward** buttons on the toolbar to return or move to a previously visited window.

 TIMESAVER *Hold down A and click a window's title bar to display a folder hierarchy menu.*

5. When you're done, click the **Close** button.

Drives on Computer

Did You Know?

You can display disk icons on the desktop. Click the Finder menu, click Preferences, click General, select the check boxes for the disk icons you want to show, and then click the Close button.

You can display icons in the Sidebar. Click the Finder menu, click Preferences, click Sidebar, select the check boxes for the icons you want to show, and then click the Close button.

You can open a disk or folder in a separate window. Click the Finder menu, click Preferences, click General, select the Always Open New Folders In A New Window check box, and then click the Close button.

You can encrypt a drive for security from the Finder. Control-click the drive icon, click Encrypt *drive name*, enter password information, and then click Encrypt Disk. You can't undo this operation and you won't be able to access the drive without the password.

See Also

See "Changing the Window View" on page 32 for information on changing the display of a folder's contents.

See "Mounting and Ejecting Disks" on page 56 for information on using disks, CDs, and DVDs.

Typical Disks on a Computer

Icon	Type Description
	Local A hard magnetic disk (or hard disk) located inside your computer on which you can store large amounts of data. The disk stores all the files on your computer.
	External A hard magnetic disk (or hard disk) connected to your computer using a FireWire or USB plug. The disk provides extra storage.
	Network A hard magnetic disk (or hard disk) connected to your computer over a network. The disk provides extra storage and file sharing.
	iPod A portable hard magnetic disk that plays music and works with iTunes, which you can also use as a hard disk. The disk provides a compact, bootable hard drive.
	Removable A soft removable magnetic disk on which you can store 1 GB or more of computer data. USB drives are standard on all computers.
	Compact Disc-Read-Only Memory (CD-ROM) An optical disk on which you can read or copy up to 1 GB (typical size is 650, 700, or 740 MB) of data. The disc cannot be erased or burned with new data.
	Compact Disc-Recordable (CD-R) A non-reusable disc on which you can burn up to 1 GB (typical size is 650, 700, or 740 MB) of data in multiple sessions. The disc can be burned again with new data until full, but cannot be erased.
	Compact Disc-Rewritable (CD-RW) A reusable disc on which you can read, write, and erase data. Discs come in normal and high-speed formats (typical size is 650, 700, or 740 MB).
	Digital Video Disc (DVD) A disc that holds a minimum of 4.7 GB, enough for a full-length movie. The disc cannot be erased or burned with additional data.
	Digital Video Disc-Recordable (DVD-R) A non-reusable disc on which you can burn up to 4.7 GB of data in multiple sessions. The disc can be burned again with new data until full, but cannot be erased.
	Digital Video Disc-Rewritable (DVD-RW) A reusable disc on which you can read, write, and erase data. The disc holds up to 4.7 GB on each side.
	Flash A memory card the size of a large stamp that holds 128, 256, 512 MB, or greater. Flash drives connect directly into a USB plug and work on any Mac or Windows PC (no software required).

Viewing and Opening Documents

When you open a disk, the Finder window displays the contents of the disk, which includes files and folders containing information and software on your computer. OS X creates a **Users folder** that contains a set of personal folders, known as the **Home folder**, for each user on a shared computer. The Home folder makes it easy to manage the personal and business files and folders you work with every day. The Home folder contains these folders: Desktop, Documents, Downloads, Movies, Music, Pictures, and Public. Depending on your previous installation, devices installed, or other users, your personal folders might differ. You can quickly access your personal folders from the Favorites section of the Sidebar, including all files on your hard disk with the All My Files option. You can view file information, organize files and folders, and open files and folders. Once you open more than one folder, you can use buttons on the toolbar to help you move quickly between folders.

View and Open Documents

① Double-click the Hard Disk icon on the desktop or in the Computer window.

TIMESAVER *Press Shift+⌘+C or click the Go menu, and then click Computer to display disks.*

② In the Favorites section of the Sidebar, select from the following:

- ◆ All My Files
- ◆ AirDrop
- ◆ Applications
- ◆ Desktop
- ◆ Documents
- ◆ Downloads
- ◆ Movies
- ◆ Music
- ◆ Pictures

③ To open a folder, double-click it.

④ If available, drag the scroll box, or click the scroll arrows to view additional documents.

⑤ To open a document, double-click the file to open its associated application and the document.

⑥ When you're done, click the **Close** button.

View All My Files

1. In the Finder, click the **Go** menu, and then click **All My Files**.

 TIMESAVER *Press Shift+⌘+F to open All My Files.*

 ◆ In the Favorites section of the Sidebar, you can also click **All My Files**.

 The Finder displays all your personal files by kind (default).

2. To change the display, click the **Arrange by** button on the toolbar, and then select an option.

3. To display more files, click the grayed out icons on either side of the category rows.

4. To show all files in a category, click **Show All**. The number next to it indicates the total number of files.

 ◆ To show only a single row of files, click **Show Less**.

Did You Know?

You can quickly open the Home folder from the desktop. Press Shift+⌘+H. You can also click the desktop background, and then press ⌘+Up Arrow, which is the Enclosing Folder command on the Go menu. Since your Desktop folder is actually in your Home folder, using the command takes you back one folder level.

Your Favorites folder still exists. The Favorites folder from previous versions of the Mac OS is located in the Library folder of your Home folder. The Favorites folder contained links to your favorites files, folders, and web sites in Microsoft Internet Explorer. If you want to use it, drag the Favorites folder to the Sidebar for quick and easy access.

Folders in the Home Folder

Folder	Type Description
Desktop	Each user's desktop is mirrored in this folder to keep one separate and maintain the unique custom look and feel.
Documents	A folder designated to store your personal documents and folders.
Downloads	A folder designated to store your items downloaded from the Internet.
Movies	A folder designated to store your movie files; programs, iMovie, use this folder.
Music	A folder designated to store your music files; programs, iTunes, use this folder.
Pictures	A folder designated to store your picture files; programs, iPhoto, use this folder.
Public	A folder where you can place documents and folders that you can share with other users on your computer or a network.

Changing the Window View

OS X displays the contents of a drive or folder in different ways to help you find the information you're looking for about a file or folder. The available views include Icons, List, Columns, and Cover Flow. You can change the window view from the View menu, or you can click the View buttons on the Finder window toolbar.

Icons view displays icons, sorted alphabetically in horizontal rows, with the name of the file or folder below each icon. You can also customize the display to include information about the file next to each icon, or a miniature representation of the file or folder. A picture file displays a thumbnail preview of the image. A multi-page document or a QuickTime movie file allows you to thumb through the document or watch the movie. When you point to a multi-page document, such as a PDF, or a QuickTime move (.MOV), the thumbnail displays Previous and Next buttons or Play/Pause button, which you can click to view or play it as a thumbnail preview. The icon preview is also available in the Preview pane in Column and Cover Flow views. In

Icons view, you can drag the Zoom control slider on the Status bar to adjust the view percentage.

List view displays small icons, sorted alphabetically in a single vertical column with the name of the file or folder and additional information, such as date and size, in columns to the right.

Columns view displays icons, sorted alphabetically into vertical panes, or frames, which allows you to view information from two different locations. This arrangement enables you to view the file hierarchy of your computer and the contents of a folder simultaneously, making it easy to copy, move, delete, and rename files and folders.

Cover Flow view displays a flip through screen with a large preview of a documents first page at the top and displays list view at the bottom. This enables you to page through multipage documents or play movies. You can also display search results in an easy-to-read format.

Icons View

Point to icon to display buttons

Multi-page document QuickTime movie

Customize Views

Every window remembers its view settings independently. You might prefer to look at your Documents folder in List view, but your Applications folder in Columns view.

However, you can set view specific options to permanently customize the way you view icons in each view. In Icons view, you can change icon size, show item informa-tion or icon preview, tag (**New!**), position, arrangement, and background. In List and Cover Flow views, you can change file size, date, and status related information. In Columns view, you can show icons and the preview column (summary information in the right column). See "Customizing Finder Window Views" on page 82 for more informa-tion about the specific options.

List View

Columns View

Cover Flow View

Arranging Files and Folders in Icons View

When you select a folder view to display your files and folders, you can change the way individual files and folders are sorted by using the Arrange By button on the toolbar (all views) or Arrange By menu options on the View menu (Icons view only). You can sort the files by name, kind, application, date (several ways), size, or tag (**New!**). In Icons view, you can have OS X help you clean up your windows by automatically aligning icons to an invisible grid in rows and columns—which icons snap to when called to line up—by using Clean Up menu options on the View menu. The Arrange By button and menu options and the Clean Up commands are only temporary until you make changes to the window. If you want OS X to automatically keep icons arranged or cleaned up, you need to select appropriate options using the Show View Options command on the View menu or use the Keep Arranged By menu options on the Action button.

Arrange or Clean Up Items in Icons View

1. Display the desktop or open the folder you want to arrange.

2. To arrange icons, click a view icon, click the **Arrange By** button on the toolbar, and then click the view you want to use:

 ◆ **Name**
 ◆ **Kind**
 ◆ **Application**
 ◆ **Date Last Opened**
 ◆ **Date Added**
 ◆ **Date Last Modified**
 ◆ **Date Created**
 ◆ **Size**
 ◆ **Tags** (**New!**)
 ◆ **None**

 TIMESAVER *Press Control+ ⌘+1 (Name) thru 9 (Tags) and Control+ ⌘+0 (None).*

3. Click the **Icons View** button on the toolbar.

4. To clean up icons, select the icons you want or deselect all, click the **View** menu, and then click **Clean Up** or **Clean Up Selection**.

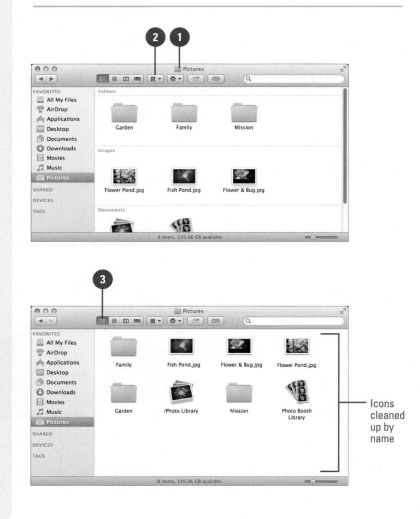

Icons cleaned up by name

Did You Know?

You can override the grid settings as you drag. When the Snap To Grid setting is turned on (in Show View Options), pressing ⌘ lets you drag the icon freely; when the Snap To Grid setting is turned Off, pressing ⌘ snaps the icon to the grid. When you perform this operation, begin the drag before you press the ⌘ key.

You can use gestures in Icons view. In Icons view, you can swipe through rows of icons quickly using your Multi-Touch trackpad or Magic Mouse.

You can keep a folder arranged by a specified attribute. Open the folder in the Finder, click the Icons View button on the toolbar, click the Action button on the toolbar, point to Keep Arranged By, and then click the view you want: Name, Date Modified, Date Created, Last Opened, Date Added, Size, Kind, and Tags.

You can clean up folder icons by a specified attribute. Open the folder in the Finder, click the Icons View button on the toolbar, select icons as desired, click the View menu, point to Clean Up By, and then click the view you want: Name, Date Modified, Date Created, Last Opened, Date Added, Size, Kind, and Tags (**New!**). You can also use shortcut keys: Option+⌘+1 (Name) thru 9 (Tags).

See Also

See "Customizing Finder Window Views" on page 82 for information on setting options in Show View Options.

Options for Arranging Files and Folders

Option	Arranges Files and Folders
Name	Alphabetically
Kind	By type, such as all documents created using the TextEdit program.
Application	Chronologically by application type.
Date Last Opened	Chronologically by their last opened date.
Date Added	Chronologically by their last added to folder date.
Date Last Modified	Chronologically by their last modification date, with the latest modification date listed last.
Date Created	Chronologically by their creation date.
Size	By size, with the largest folder or file listed first.
Tags (**New!**)	By tags, such as a color or name
None	Not arranged by attribute.

For Your Information

Compressing Files and Folders to Save Space

You can compress files and folders into a single file using Stuffit compression software to decrease their size. Compressed folders are useful for reducing the file size of one or more large files, thus freeing disk space and reducing the time it takes to transfer files to another computer over the Internet or network. When a file is compressed, a copy is used in the compression, and the original remains intact. You can uncompress, or extract, a file from the compressed file and open it as you normally would. See "Compressing and Uncompressing Files and Folders" on page 449, and "Opening Compressed Files" on page 448 for more information about compressing and uncompressing files and folders.

Working with Files and Folders in List View

You can display files and folders in a variety of different ways, depending on what you want to see and do. When you view files and folders in List view, a default list of file and folder information appears, which consists of Name, Date Modified, Size, and Kind. If the default list of file and folder details doesn't provide you with the information you need, you can add and remove any file and folder information using Show View Options. If you need to change the way OS X sorts your files and folders, you can use the column header buttons. Clicking on one of the column header buttons (such as Name, Date Modified, Size, or Kind) in List view, sorts the files and folders by the type of information listed in the column. If the columns are not organized in the order you want, you can use the mouse to quickly rearrange columns. If you see an ellipsis in a column, it is too small to display all the information in it. You can drag the column divider to change column sizes all at once or individually.

Show and Hide Folders in List View

1️⃣ Open the folder you want to view.

2️⃣ Click the **List View** button on the toolbar.

3️⃣ Click the triangle (pointing right) next to a folder in the list.

TIMESAVER *Select the folder, and then press ⌘+Right Arrow.*

The folder expands to display an indented list of folders and files from within the folder.

4️⃣ Click the triangle (pointing down) next to a folder in the list.

TIMESAVER *Select the folder, and then press ⌘+Left Arrow.*

The folder collapses.

Did You Know?

You can quickly show the full text with ellipsis. Point to the icon's name without clicking for a moment to display a balloon. Hold down the Option key to display it immediately.

Sort Files and Folders by Column in List View

1. Open the folder you want to view.

2. Click the **List View** button on the toolbar.

3. Click the column header name to sort the file and folder in ascending or descending order.

4. To reverse the column sort, click the column header name again.

Did You Know?

You can add and remove columns in List view. Click the View menu, click Show View Options, select or clear the check boxes you want to add or remove, and then click the Close button.

Rearrange and Widen Columns

1. Open the folder you want to view.

2. Click the **List View** or **Cover Flow View** button on the toolbar.

3. To rearrange columns, drag the column header to a new position.

4. To change the width of columns, drag the column divider.

 The width of the column changes and all the columns to the right shift based on the change.

Viewing Files with Cover Flow View

Just as you use Cover Flow to flip through album art in iTunes, now you can use it to flip through your files. Cover Flow view displays a flip through screen with a large preview of a documents first page at the top and displays List view at the bottom. Cover Flow enables you to page through multipage documents or play movies. You can also display search results in an easy-to-read format. List view at the bottom of Cover Flow displays a default list of file and folder information, which consists of Name, Date Modified, Size, and Kind.

View Files with Cover Flow

① Open the folder you want to view.

② Click the **Cover Flow View** button on the toolbar.

③ Use either one of the following methods to display a file in Cover Flow.

◆ **Top pane.** Click the item, either side of slider, or drag the slider to display the file you want.

◆ **Bottom pane.** Click the triangle (pointing right) next to a folder in the list to display an indented list of folders and files from within the folder, and then select the file you want to display.

Top pane

Drag to collapse/expand top pane

Drag to scroll through cover flow

Bottom pane

See Also

See "Working with Files and Folders in List View" on page 36 for information on using List view.

Working with Files and Folders in Columns View

Columns view makes is easy to display several levels of folders in alphabetical order at the same time within the same window. Columns view displays the window in panes, which allows you to view information from different locations making it easy to copy, move, delete, and rename files and folders. When you click a disk or folder in the first pane, the second pane shows a list of all the folders in it. Each time you click a folder in one pane, the pane to its right shows its contents. The other panes slide to the left, in some cases, out of view, which you can scroll back to display them. When you find and click the file you want, the next pane to the right, the **Preview column**, shows a file icon and information about it. If the file is a picture or PDF, the Finder displays the picture or PDF miniature. If the file is a sound or movie, you can play it in the Finder window.

View Folders in Columns View

1. Open the folder you want to view.

2. Click the **Columns View** button on the toolbar.

3. Double-click the folder you want to open in a pane.

 The contents of the folder appears in the next pane to the right.

4. To resize a column, drag its right-side handle.

5. Click the file you want to view in the Preview column.

Preview column

Keyboard Options for Columns View	
Option	**Description**
Left or Right Arrow	Jumps one pane to the left or right
Up or Down Arrow	Within a pane, moves up or down to select an item

Viewing Files Using Quick Look

Quick Look allows you to view the contents of a file or folder without opening it or starting an application. Quick Looks work almost everywhere you use files. It only takes a simple key stroke, the Spacebar. Content types include web pages in e-mail, addresses as Google Maps, Contacts, and Spotlight results. If you select a single or multipage text document, you can read the text and scroll through it; if you select a video, you can play it. When you select more than one image or item, you can display a slide show and use arrow buttons to move from slide to slide. If you like to use gestures on a Multi-Touch trackpad, you can three-finder tap on the trackpad to preview files or swipe to navigate between images and pages in a PDF or iWork document.

View Files Using Quick Look

1. Open the folder you want to view.

2. Select the one or more files or folder you want to view.

3. Press the Spacebar.

 ◆ You can also click the **Action** button on the toolbar, and then click **Quick Look** (if you select items, a number appears), or click the **Quick Look** button on a customized toolbar.

 TIMESAVER *Press ⌘+Y or three-finger tap to display and exit Quick Look.*

4. If you selected more than one item or image, use the follow buttons to navigate through the items.

 ◆ **Previous and Next**. Navigate from slide to slide.

 ◆ **Index**. Display a pictorial index of the selected images or items. Click an index item to display it.

 ◆ **Plus**. Open the file in a matching application.

5. To open the selected item, click the **Open with Preview** button.

6. To view the selected item in full screen, click the **Full Screen** button. To exit back, click the **Exit Full Screen** button.

7. When you're done, click the **Close** button or press the Spacebar.

Use a swipe gesture to navigate between images, and pages in a PDF or iWork document.

Going to Common or Recent Places

OS X keeps a list of your most recently used files, folders, and network computers. Instead of navigating through a long list of folders to open a recently used file, you can use the Recent Folders list to find it quickly. If you want to go to a common location, such as your computer, network connections, AirDrop, All My Files folder, Documents folder, Desktop folder, Downloads folder, Home folder, Applications folder, Utilities folder, or one you specify, the Go menu makes it quick and easy. If you want to go to the Library folder, press the Option key. After you have opened several folders, you can use the folder hierarchy menu in a window's title bar to quickly go back through the folders.

Go Places

 Click the **Go** menu.

 Select any of the following:

- ◆ **Common locations.** Click the location name. Press the Option key to display the Library.

- ◆ **Recent folders.** Point to **Recent Folders**, and then click the name of the folder.

- ◆ **Specific folder.** Click **Go to Folder**, type a path location, and then click **Go**. You can use the tilde (~) to indicate the Home folder, "~/Documents/".

 To go back through the folders, hold down ⌘, click the window's title bar, and then click a location from the folder hierarchy menu.

TIMESAVER *Press ⌘+[to go Back a folder; press ⌘+] to go Forward a folder.*

 When you're done, click the **Close** button.

Did You Know?

You can quickly open recent applications and documents. Click the Apple menu, point to Recent Items, and then click the recently used application or document you want to open.

Specific folder

Common locations

Recent folders

Organizing Files and Folders by Tags

Assigning an icon or folder a tag, such as a color or name, can help you organize and find it later. OS X provides 10 default tags (**New!**), either colors or names (Work, Home, and Important). However, you can add your own, rename or delete them to suit your own needs and preferences. You can assign one or more tags to items using the Edit Tags button (**New!**) on the toolbar or tags in the Sidebar (**New!**). When you save a document, you can also assign one or moret tags to it. You can tag files wherever they are located, including in an iCloud, local or network drive. After you tag items, you can select a tag in the Sidebar to quickly display them. You can also use tags with the Find command in a Finder window to search for files and folders with a particular tag. Tags are integrated with apps, so you can search for files more quickly or group related items together.

Tag or Untag Items

1. Open the folder window with the file or folder icons you want to tag.

2. Select the icons you want to apply tags.

3. Use any of the following to tag a file or folder.

 ◆ **Toolbar.** Click the **Edit Tags** button on the toolbar, and then click one or more tags from the list (click **Show All** to view all tags) or enter one or more new tags (separated by spaces) in the Tags box.

 TIMESAVER *You can also use the File or Action menu, or Control-click to access the tags.*

 ◆ **Sidebar.** Point to Tags in the Sidebar, click **Show**, and then drag the selection to a tag in the Sidebar.

4. To remove a tag from a selection, click the **Edit Tags** button, select the tag in the Tags box, and then press Delete.

5. When you're done, click the **Close** button.

Select tags

Blue tag for icons

View Items by Tags

① Open a folder window.

② Point to Tags in the Sidebar, and then click **Show** to display the list of tags.

③ Click a tag in the Sidebar or click **All Tags**, and then click a tag.

 All the items associated with a tag appear in the Finder window.

④ When you're done, click the **Close** button.

Did You Know?

You can sort by tags in List view. In List view, click the View menu, click Show View Options, select the Tags check box, and then click the Close button.

Manage Tags

① Click the **Finder** menu, and then click **Preferences**.

② Click **Tags**.

③ To show or hide tags in the Sidebar, select or clear the check box across from the tag.

④ To rename a tag, click the tag name to select it, and then enter another name.

⑤ To delete a tag, Control-click the tag, click **Delete Tag** "***name***", and then click **Delete Tag** to confirm.

 TIMESAVER *You can also rename and delete in the Sidebar.*

⑥ To use tags in Finder menus, drag tags to the area below. Drag a tag out to remove it.

⑦ Click the **Close** button.

All tags

Fish Pond.jpg Flower & Bug.jpg

Flower on Pond.jpg

Items with Blue tags

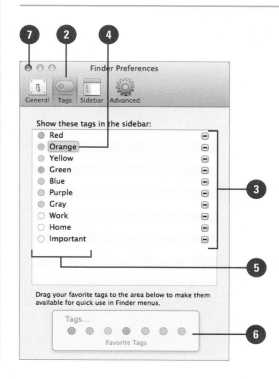

Creating and Renaming Files and Folders

The keys to organizing files and folders effectively within a hierarchy are to store related items together and to name folders informatively. Creating a new folder can help you organize and keep track of files and other folders. In order to create a folder, you select the location where you want the new folder, create the folder, and then lastly, name the folder. You can also select files first, and then create a folder. You should name each folder meaningfully, so that just by reading the folder's name you know its contents. After you name a folder or file, you can rename it at any time.

Create a Folder

1 Open the drive or folder where you want to create a folder.

 ◆ To create a folder with a selection, select the files you want to use.

2 Click the **File** menu, and then click **New Folder** or **New Folder with Selection (# Items)**.

 TROUBLE? *If the New Folder command is grayed out, you don't have permission to create a folder in the folder. Click the File menu, and then click Get Info to change permissions.*

3 With the new folder name selected, type a new name.

4 Press Return.

Untitled new folder

Did You Know?

File names can be up to 255 characters. You can use spaces and underscores in names, but you can't use a colon (:). If you are going to use these files on a Windows PC, then don't use the following characters: * : < > | ? " \ or /. It's probably best to keep the name descriptive, but short. This allows you to view the file name in all view settings.

Rename a File or Folder

1. Open the drive or folder with the file or folder you want to rename.

2. Click the file or folder to select it.

3. To erase the entire current name, press Return.

 TROUBLE? *If you can't change the name of a file or folder, you may not have permission to make changes to the item. Click the File menu, and then click Get Info to change permissions.*

4. With the name selected, type a new name, or click to position the insertion point, and then edit the name.

 IMPORTANT *If extensions are showing, changing the name doesn't change the extension as long as the extension stays the same. If you change the extension, the file type changes and you may not be able to open the file with the application in which it was created.*

5. Press Return.

 The file may move to a location based on sort and view.

See Also

See "Showing or Hiding File Extensions" on page 81 for information on file extensions.

For Your Information

Correcting Your Most Recent Action in the Finder

Everyone makes mistakes and changes their mind at some point, especially when you make changes in the Finder. You can instantly correct your most recent action by using the Undo command (⌘+Z) on the Edit menu. If you change your mind about undoing an action, you can just as easily use the Redo command (⌘+Y) to restore the action you reversed.

Copying and Moving Files and Folders

Sometimes you'll need to move a file from one folder to another, or copy a file from one folder to another, leaving the file in the first location and placing a copy of it in the second. If the file or folder and the location where you want to move it are visible in a window or on the desktop, you can simply drag the item from one location to the other. When you drag multiple items, they flock together; the cursor indicates how many files. Moving a file or folder on the same disk relocates it, whereas dragging it from one disk to another copies it so that it appears in both locations. When the destination folder or drive is not visible, you can use the Cut (to move), Copy, and Paste commands on the Edit menu to move or copy the items.

Copy or Move a File or Folder

1. Open the drive or folder containing the file or folder you want to copy or move.

2. Select the files or folders you want to copy.

3. Click the **Edit** menu, and then click **Cut** (to move) or **Copy**.

 TIMESAVER *Press ⌘+X to move or press ⌘+C to copy.*

4. Navigate to the drive or folder containing the folder where you want to copy or move the items.

5. Click the **Edit** menu, and then click **Paste**.

 TIMESAVER *Press ⌘+V to paste.*

 TROUBLE? *If you can't copy a file or folder, click the File menu, and then click Get Info to change permissions.*

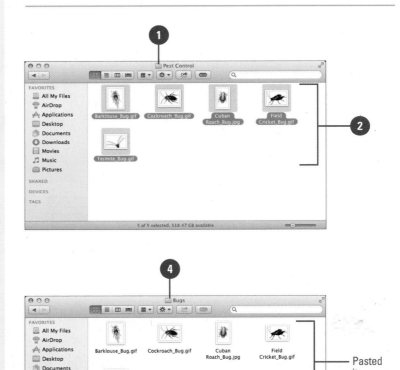

Pasted item copied to another folder.

Did You Know?

You need certain permissions to move or copy a file. You need Read Only or Read & Write permissions to the item you want to move or copy. You need Read & Write Only access to the location where you want to place it.

Copy or Move a File or Folder Using Drag and Drop

 Open the drive or folder containing the files and folders you want to move or copy.

 Drag the selection onto a folder, an icon in the Sidebar, a tab (**New!**), or the desktop.

To copy files and folder, hold down the Option key while you drag.

When you drag multiple items, they flock together; the cursor indicates how many files.

IMPORTANT *If you pause for a few moments on the destination folder (when spring-loaded folders is turned on) the destination folder automatically opens.*

 Release the items.

 If you add a file to a folder that contains a file of the same name, click **Keep Both Files**, **Stop**, or **Replace**. Keeping both add "copy" to the end of the name.

 If you add a folder to a folder that contains a folder of the same name, click **Stop** or **Replace**.

See Also

See "Using Spring-Loaded Folders" on page 48 for information on copying and moving items using spring-loaded folders.

See "Using the Tab Bar" on page 16 for information on using tabs in a Finder window.

Flocking files

For Your Information

Moving and Copying Items Using Mission Control

Exposé in Mission Control can make it easier to move and copy files and folders using drag and drop. To move or copy items between open windows, start to drag the items (hold down the Option key to copy or hold down ⌘+Option to create an alias), press Control-Up Arrow (show all open windows) or Control-Down Arrow (show all open windows in the same application), point to the window where you want to move or copy the item, release Control-Up Arrow or Control-Down Arrow, and then drag some more or release the items. A similar process works moving or copying items to the desktop using F11. The Mission Control shortcut keys can be changed, so check System Preferences if they are not working properly.

Using Spring-Loaded Folders

When you are moving or copying files and folders around, it can be tiresome to drag a selection to a folder, open the folder, and then continue to drag it to another folder. Spring-loaded folders allow you to drag a file or folder on top of another folder and it springs open to let you continue dragging the selection to another location in one continuous motion. When you drag a selection onto a folder (or even an icon in the Sidebar) and pause for a moment (with the mouse pressed), the window for the folder opens, so you can continue to drag to another folder as desired. You can use Finder Preferences to turn spring-loaded folders on and off, and set the delay setting for the amount of time you want to pause. If you set a long delay or turn off spring-loaded folders, you can press the Spacebar while you drag a selection to open the window immediately. The Spacebar method is useful because windows don't automatically open when you don't want them to, yet you still have the option to use spring-loaded folders when you need it.

Use Spring-Loaded Folders

1. Open the drive or folder containing the files and folders you want to move or copy.

2. To move, drag the selection onto a folder or an icon in the Sidebar. To copy, hold down the Option key while you drag.

3. Press the Spacebar, or pause for a few moments.

 The folder window automatically opens centered on your cursor:

 - **In Icons view**, the new window replaces the previous window.

 - **In List view**, a new window opens.

 - **In Columns view**, a new column opens, displaying the new folder's contents.

Drag continues in spring-loaded folder.

Did You Know?

You can set the spring-loaded delay.
Click the Finder menu, click Preferences, click General, drag the Delay slider, and then click the Close button.

Sharing Files Using Online Services

The Finder and many applications in OS X, such as Safari, Contacts, Preview, Photo Booth, and QuickTime, include a Share button on the toolbar or a menu item that allows you to share files and information using online services including Email, Message, AirDrop, Facebook, Twitter, Flickr, and Vimeo. For example, you can tweet links from Safari, post photos and videos to Flickr or Vimeo, post information to Facebook, and share notes with Mail and Messages. The available sharing services vary depending on the selected file or information.

Share Files Using Online Services

1. Open the Finder or application with the file or information you want to share.

2. Select the files or folders in the Finder or information in the application you want to share.

3. Click the **Share** button on the toolbar, and then select an available service.

 TIMESAVER *You can also Control-click or tap with two fingers an item, point to Share, and then select a service.*

 IMPORTANT *The list of available services vary depending on the selected file or information.*

4. If prompted, click **Log In** to access a message application or click **Add Account** to configure an account.

5. Enter or specify any related information you want to include, and then send or post it using the service.

 ◆ The instructions vary depending on the service.

See Also

See "Using Application Services" on page 450 for more information on sharing information using online services.

Deleting and Restoring Files and Folders

When you organize the contents of a folder, disk, or the desktop, you might find files and folders that you no longer need. You can delete these items or remove them from the disk. If you delete a file or folder from the desktop or from the hard disk, it goes into the Trash. The **Trash**, located on the right side of the Dock, is a temporary storage area for deleted files. The Trash stores all the items you delete from your hard disk so that if you accidentally delete an item, you can remove it from the Trash to restore it. You can use the Put Back command to restore a deleted item to it's original folder. Be aware that if you delete a file from a removable disk, it is permanently deleted, not stored in the Trash. The files in the Trash do occupy room on your computer, so you need to empty it to free up space.

Delete Files and Folders

1. Select the files and folders you want to delete.

 TROUBLE? *If an item is locked, you can't put it in the Trash. Click the File menu, and then click Get Info to unlock it.*

2. Drag the selection to the Trash in the Dock.

 TIMESAVER *Press ⌘+Delete key to delete selected items.*

3. Click the **Finder** menu, and then click **Empty Trash**.

 TIMESAVER *Click the Trash icon in the Dock, and then click Empty Trash, or press Shift+⌘ +Delete to empty the trash.*

4. Click **Empty Trash** to confirm the deletion.

 TIMESAVER *Press Shift+⌘ Option+Delete to empty the trash and skip the warning dialog.*

Restore Files and Folders

① In the Dock, click the **Trash** icon.

② Select the item or items you want to restore.

③ Click the **File** menu, and then click **Put Back** or drag the items back to their original folder or any other location.

 The items are restored to their original location with the Put Back command or to a dragged location.

④ When you're done, click the **Close** button for the Trash window.

Did You Know?

You can uninstall software using the Trash. There's no uninstall program for OS X. To uninstall a software, drag its folder from the Applications folder to the Trash icon in the Dock.

You can undo a deletion. If you accidentally delete a file, click the Edit menu, and then click Undo Delete. OS X remembers your last three actions.

You can still recover deleted files after you empty the Trash in some cases. If you install special data recovery software, you still may be able to recover deleted files.

You can turn off the empty Trash warning. Click the Finder menu, click Preferences, click Advanced, clear the Show Warning Before Emptying The Trash check box, and then click the Close button.

For Your Information

Deleting Files Securely and Forever

When you delete files by emptying the Trash, OS X deletes the access information used to locate the files, but doesn't actually delete the files. The disk space used by the deleted files is marked as free space, however the deleted files remain on your disk until new data is written over them. As a result, deleted files can be recovered. You can use the Secure Empty Trash command on the Finder menu to securely delete files and folders from your hard disk without any possibility of recovery by writing over the space. This can be useful if you are selling or giving away your computer. To delete files and folders securely forever, drag them into the Trash, click the Finder menu, click Secure Empty Trash, and then click Secure Empty Trash to confirm the deletion. Files securely deleted are completely overwritten by meaningless data, which may take a few moments or minutes to complete depending on the size of the files. You can also use the Disk Utility to securely erase files. See "Formatting and Copying a Disk," on page 452 for more details.

Getting and Setting File Information

You can get information about a hard disk, removable disk, network disk, application, folder, or file using the Info window. The Info window displays information about the kind, size, location, date created, and date modified. If you select a disk, the Info window also includes information about format, capacity, available space, and used space. In addition to displaying information, you can also use the Info window to add tags (**New!**) for identification and enhance searches, create a stationery file, lock an item, change a files name and extension, determine which application to open a file with, change its ownership and permissions, and write a comment. When you set a file as stationery, the file opens as an untitled copy of the original, so the original file doesn't get changed. If you want to see information for different items without having to close the Info window, you can use Show Inspector to keep the Info window open while you select different items.

Display Info Window

1. Select the files, disks, folders, applications, or alias; don't select anything to get desktop info.

2. Use one of the following methods:

 ◆ **Separate window for each item**. Click the **File** menu, and then click **Get Info**.

 A separate Info window appears for each selected item. This is useful for comparing settings and information.

 ◆ **Single window for all items**. Hold down the Option key, click the **File** menu, and then click **Show Inspector**.

 A single Info window appears, displaying statistics (by type and size) about the selected items and options common to all the selected items. This is useful for setting the same option for a lot of items, such as locking or unlocking files.

3. Click the expand button (triangle) to display category options, or the collapse button (down arrow) to hide them.

4. When you're done, click the **Close** button.

Add tags (**New!**) for use in identification and searches.

Separate window for each item.

Expanded pane

Single window for multiple items.

Collapsed pane

Set Info Window Options

① Select the files, disks, folders, or applications you want to set.

② Click the expand button (triangle) for a category.

③ Change the options you want:

- ◆ **Tags**. Add your own tags (**New!**), which you can display in a Finder window and use in searches.

- ◆ **General**. View information about the selected items; create a Stationery Pad (a file opens as untitled); and lock or unlock a file.

- ◆ **More Info**. View information (varies) about the selected item.

- ◆ **Name & Extension**. Read and edit item name and extension; and hide extensions.

- ◆ **Content Index**. Index a disk or folder for better search results.

- ◆ **Memory**. Set memory options for Classic applications only.

- ◆ **Open With**. Specify which application opens when you double-click an icon.

- ◆ **Preview**. Display magnified picture thumbnails or play sounds and movies.

- ◆ **Languages**. Add or remove languages for an application.

- ◆ **Sharing & Permission**. Set read and write access privileges.

④ When you're done, click the **Close** button.

See Also

See "Setting File Access Permissions" on page 400 for information on setting file permissions and ownership.

③

— Tags
— General
— Name & Extension
— Open With

④

— Sharing & Permissions

Creating a CD or DVD Using the Finder

The low cost and large storage size of CDs or DVDs (getting cheaper), and the popularity of recording hardware make using CDs and DVDs an effective approach to some file management tasks. For example, CDs or DVDs are an effective way to back up information or transfer information to another computer without a network or to a Microsoft Windows computer. Before you can create a CD or DVD, you must have blank CDs or DVDs and a CD-RW or DVD-RW drive (also known as a writer or burner) installed on your computer. You can copy or write files and folders to either CD-Rs or DVD-Rs (recordable) or CD-RWs or DVD-RWs (rewritable). With recordables, you can write files and folders only once and read them many times, but you can't erase them. With rewritables, you can read, write, and erase files and folders many times, just like a removable disk. When you write to, or **burn**, a CD or DVD, OS X needs disk space on your hard disk to temporarily store files during the process, so make sure you have free hard disk space available for the size of the CD or DVD. Do not copy more files and folders to the CD or DVD than it will hold; anything beyond the limit will not copy. When the burn is complete, you can use the CD or DVD on a Macintosh or Windows PC appropriately equipped. You can also use other OS X applications with disc burning features, such as iTunes, iPhoto, iDVD, or Disk Utility, to create specialized CDs or DVDs.

Prepare to Burn a CD or DVD

1. Insert a blank CD-R, CD-RW, DVD-R, or DVD-RW disc into your drive.

 If you insert a CD-RW disc that you previously recorded, the dialog doesn't appear; you need to erase the disc with Disk Utility before you can burn data on it again.

 TROUBLE? *If the dialog doesn't appear, click the Apple menu, click Preferences, click CDs & DVDs, select the options you want, and then click the Close button.*

2. Click the **Action** pop-up, and then click **Open Finder**.

3. Select or clear the **Make this action the default** check box.

4. Click **OK**.

 The blank disc appears on the desktop, where you can add and remove files and folders.

Click to eject CD.

Click to ignore action.

Add and Remove Files and Folders to a CD or DVD

1. Open a Finder window.

2. Navigate to and select the files and folders you want to add to the CD or DVD disc.

3. Drag the files and folders to the CD or DVD disc in the Sidebar, and then organize them.

 IMPORTANT *If you're using these files on a Windows PC, make sure the file names don't include \ / : * ? " < > |, otherwise you can't open them.*

4. To remove files and folders, click the CD or DVD disc in the Sidebar, or double-click the disc on the desktop, and then drag out the items you don't want.

Create a CD or DVD

1. If you want, rename the CD or DVD disc just like any other file.

2. Use any of the following methods to create a CD or DVD:

 ◆ **Drag to Trash.** When you drag a disk icon onto the **Trash** icon, it changes to a Burn icon.

 ◆ **Burn command.** Select the disk icon, click the **File** menu, and then click **Burn** or click the **Burn** button in the Burn folder.

 ◆ **Sidebar Burn button.** Click the **Burn** button in the Sidebar.

3. Type a name for the disc.

4. Click the **Burn Speed** pop-up, and then select a speed.

5. Select the **Save Burn Folder To** check box, and then type a name to create a burn folder.

6. Click **Burn**.

Burn command on File menu Burn button **2** CD to burn

Sidebar Burn button Drag to Trash

Mounting and Ejecting Disks

When you insert a disk (such as a removable, CD, or DVD), its icon appears, or **mounts**, in the Computer window, in the Sidebar, and on the desktop (unless you've changed Finder Preferences) for you to open and use. When you no longer need a disk, you eject, or dismount, it from the drive. OS X provides several different ways to eject a disk: drag the disk icon to the Trash (only happens for disks; a little strange, but its old time Mac functionality), use the Eject menu (if available), select the Eject command, use the Sidebar, or hold down the Eject key. You can also use these methods to remove, or **unmount**, a network or FireWire drive, an iPod, or a disk image from your desktop.

Mount and Eject Disks

1. Insert the disk into the appropriate drive to mount the disk.

2. Use any of the following methods to eject a disk:

 ◆ **Drag to Trash.** When you drag a disk icon onto the **Trash** icon in the Dock, it changes to an Eject icon.

 ◆ **Eject command.** Select the disk icon, click the **File** menu, and then click **Eject**. You can also Control-click the disk icon, and then click **Eject**.

 ◆ **Eject menu.** Click the **Eject** menu (if available on the right side of the menu bar), and then click **Eject** "*disc name*" or press F12.

 ◆ **Sidebar Eject button.** Click the **Eject** button in the Sidebar.

 ◆ **Eject key.** Press and hold down the Media Eject key in the upper-right corner of your keyboard (if available) for a moment, or press F12.

 TROUBLE? *If a CD or DVD doesn't eject, insert a straightened paper clip into the small hole on the front of the drive, or click the Apple menu, click Restart, and hold down the mouse button until it ejects before the restart.*

Eject button

Finding What You Want with Spotlight

Introduction

If you're looking for specific content on your computer or network and you don't know where to find it, you can use Spotlight to help you locate it. Spotlight not only searches the names of your files and folders, it also searches their content. In addition, Spotlight searches other information stored in files, known as **metadata**, which describes how and when and by whom a particular set of data was collected, or how the data is formatted. Examples of metadata include authors, page size, creation and modification dates, duration of music and movies, dimensions of graphics or PDF documents, exposure time of a camera lens for photographs, and names of layers in Photoshop.

Spotlight is conveniently located on the right side of the menu bar on your Mac screen. You can identify Spotlight by the blue icon with a magnifying glass. Spotlight performs a live search of your Home folder on your computer using the information you know. As you type in Spotlight, a menu appears displaying a list of everything Spotlight can find to match what you've typed so far. As you continue to type, the list changes. Spotlight searches for everything on your computer that matches what you've typed, which includes every file, folder, program, e-mail message, address book entry, calendar appointment, picture, movie, PDF document, music file, web bookmark, Microsoft Office document, and System Preferences panel, and lists the 20 best matches divided into categories, which you can customize later.

When you start OS X for the first time, Spotlight automatically starts collecting search information about your Home folder, known as **indexing**. The indexing process initially takes about 15 to 30 minutes to perform (the Spotlight icon pulses) and then updates take place as needed. Indexing the information on your computer reduces the time it takes to perform a search.

What You'll Do

Find Information Using Spotlight

Find Information in the Spotlight Window

Filter Spotlight Results

Group and Sort Spotlight Results

Work with Spotlight Results

Set Spotlight Preferences

Search for Files Using the Find Window

Search for Hard to Find Information

Work with Find Window Results

Create and Use Smart Folders

Get Help While You Work

Get Help Using Spotlight

Finding Information Using Spotlight

If you're looking for specific content on your computer and you don't know where to find it, you can use Spotlight to help you find it. Even if you can only remember part of the content. Spotlight performs a live search of your Home folder on your computer using the information you know. As you type in Spotlight, a menu appears displaying a list of everything Spotlight can find to match what you've typed so far. As you continue to type, the list changes. If you type two words, Spotlight finds items that contain both words. Spotlight searches for everything on your computer that matches what you've typed, which includes every file, folder, program, e-mail message, address book entry, calendar appointment, to-do item, picture, movie, PDF document, music file, web bookmark, document, and System Preferences panel, and lists the 20 best matches divided into categories, which you can customize later. Spotlight not only searches the names of your files and folders, it also searches their content, and displays a preview of the material from the menu. In addition, you can drag items from the Spotlight menu for use in folder or on the desktop. You can search by typing phrases or metadata attributes, and using boolean operators.

Find Information Using Spotlight

1. Click the **Spotlight** (magnifying-glass) icon on the menu bar.

 TIMESAVER *Press* ⌘+Space bar to open Spotlight.

2. In the Spotlight field, type what you want to find. To find a specific phrase, place quotes around it.

 As you type, a menu begins to display a list of everything Spotlight can find to match what you've typed so far. As you continue to type, the list changes.

3. To preview an item, point to the item in the list.

 TIMESAVER *Press and hold* ⌘ to display more information.

4. To copy an item, drag the item off the Spotlight list.

5. To open an item, click the item or use the arrow keys to scroll down the list, and then press Return.

6. To clear or stop a search, click the **Close** button (x) in the Spotlight field.

Wikipedia

Preview of search item

Find Information with Metadata Using Spotlight

1 Click the **Spotlight** (magnifying-glass) icon on the right side of the menu bar.

TIMESAVER *Press* ⌘+Space bar to open Spotlight.

2 In the Spotlight field, type *code:keyword*. Use quotation marks around text to search for an exact phrase.

Where the code is a category, such as *kind*, *date*, *modified*, or *author*, and keyword is a specific type of category.

Here are some examples:

◆ **kind:preference network** displays the network system preference on your computer.

◆ **kind:contact steve** displays all the contacts with the name steve on your computer.

◆ **kind:music by:"Bruce Springsteen"** displays all music by Bruce Springsteen.

◆ **date:today kind:email** displays all the email for today on your computer.

Did You Know?

You can quickly cancel a Spotlight search. Press the Esc key to close the Spotlight menu and erase what you've typed. Now, you can type a new search. Press the Esc key again to cancel the entire search. To cancel the entire search in one step, press ⌘+Space bar again, ⌘+period, or ⌘+Esc.

Find Code and Keywords

Find	Code:Keyword
Program	kind:app, kind:application
Address book contact	kind:contact
Folder	kind:folder
Mail message	kind:email, kind:mail message
iCal appointment	kind:event
iCal task	kind:to do, kind:todo
Image, picture	kind:image
Movie	kind:movie
Music or Sound	kind:music, kind:audio
PDF file	kind:pdf
System Preference	kind:preference, kind:system preference
Safari bookmark	kind:bookmark
Font	kind:font
Presentation	kind:presentation
Week	date:this week, date:next week
Month	date:this month, date:next month
Year	date:this year, date:next year
Today	date:today
Tomorrow	date:tomorrow
Yesterday	date:yesterday

For Your Information

Using Boolean Operators to Help Your Search

If you can't find the information you are looking for using the Spotlight field or Search field, you can use boolean operators (AND, OR, NOT, and dash (-) for AND NOT to exclude items) to refine your help search. For example, typing **report AND proposal** finds both words, typing **report OR proposal** finds either *report* or *proposal*, while typing **report NOT proposal** finds *report*, but excludes *proposal*. If you type **report - proposal**, Spotlight finds *report* but not *proposal*. You can also use keywords in your search with boolean operators. For example, typing **kind:pdf report AND kind:presentation proposal**, finds PDF documents with *report* and presentation files with *proposal*.

Finding Information in the Spotlight Window

If you can't find what you're looking for on the Spotlight menu with the 20 most likely matches, you can click the Show All in Finder command at the top of the Spotlight menu to open the Spotlight window and view the complete list of matches organized by category. The Show All in Finder command displays the results of your search by retrieving content on your entire computer that matches the criteria. The Search bar, located below the toolbar, indicates the search location and type, which is "This Mac," folder or disk name, such as "Documents" or "All My Files," and "Shared" by default. You can search your entire computer (This Mac), your Home folder (All My Files), or shared network computer by the file name and the contents of a file.

Open and View the Spotlight Window to Locate Information

1 Click the **Spotlight** (magnifying-glass) icon on the right side of the menu bar.

TIMESAVER *Press* Option+⌘+Space bar to open Spotlight window directly.

2 In the Spotlight field, start to type what you want to find.

3 Click **Show All in Finder** on the Spotlight menu.

The Spotlight window opens, displaying the results of your search by category.

If a search is currently in progress, a sprocket icon whirls around in the upper-left window corner.

4 To narrow or change the search, type the text you want to find in the Search field.

5 To open an item, double-click the item or use the arrow keys to scroll down the list, and then press Return.

6 To clear or stop a search, click the **Close** button (x) in the Search field.

7 When you're done, click the **Close** button.

Narrow Results in the Spotlight Window

1. Press Option+⌘+Space bar or click **Show All in Finder** on the Spotlight menu to open the Spotlight window.

 The Spotlight window opens, displaying the results of your search by category.

 If a search is currently in progress, a sprocket icon whirls around in the upper-left corner of the window.

2. In the Search bar, click the button with the search location you want:

 ◆ **This Mac.** Searches all the disks on your computer.

 ◆ **All My Files.** Searches your Home folder.

 ◆ **Server, Volume** or **Folder Name.** Searches only the currently opened server, volume, or folder. The item name appears in quotes in the Search bar.

 ◆ **Shared.** Searches shared folders on disks and computer.

3. To narrow or change the search, type the text you want to find in the Search field.

4. To open an item, double-click the item or use the arrow keys to scroll down the list, and then press Return.

5. To clear or stop a search, click the **Close** button (x) in the Search field.

6. When you're done, click the **Close** button.

For Your Information

Searching Made Easy

You can add text to the Spotlight Comments field in the Get Info dialog for a specific file or folder that you can quickly search for using Spotlight later. Control-click a file or folder, click Get Info, and then type the text you want in the Spotlight Comments field.

Filtering Spotlight Results

If the list of Spotlight results is too long to find the results you want, you can revise your search text in the Search field or use the Search bar to filter, or narrow down, the list. The Search bar allows you to filter down the Spotlight results by location and type. The left side of the Search bar provides buttons to filter the search results by where the information is stored, such as This Mac (your entire computer), All My Files (your Home folder), or Shared (your networked computers), if available. After you select where, you can select how. You can filter the result by whether the search criteria is in the content of a file or the file name of the results. If you want to further narrow down the Spotlight results, you can add other search criteria using file attributes.

Filter Spotlight Results

1. Press Option+⌘+Space bar or click **Show All in Finder** on the Spotlight menu to open the Spotlight window, and then perform or narrow a search.

 The Spotlight window displays the results of your search by category.

2. In the Search bar, click the button with the search location you want:

 ◆ **This Mac.** Searches all the disks on your computer.

 ◆ **All My Files.** Searches your Home folder.

 ◆ **Server, Volume** or **Folder Name.** Searches only the currently opened server, volume, or folder. The item name appears in quotes in the Search bar.

 ◆ **Shared.** Searches shared folders on disks and computer.

3. To clear a search, click the **Close** button (x) in the Search field.

4. When you're done, click the **Close** button.

Filtered results

Change Spotlight Criteria in the Spotlight Window

1 Press Option+⌘+Space bar or click **Show All in Finder** on the Spotlight menu to open the Spotlight window.

The Spotlight window opens, displaying the results of your search by category.

If a search is currently in progress, a sprocket icon whirls around in the upper-left corner of the window.

2 Click the **Action** button, and then click **Show Search Criteria**.

The Spotlight items option appears in the first Search pop-up, indicating Spotlight results in the window.

3 Click the **Add** (+) button, and then specify the criteria you want.

4 Click the first **Search** pop-up of the second criteria item, and then select or type the search criteria.

◆ Select **Other** on the pop-up to display a complete list of searchable attributes.

5 Click the second **Search** pop-up of the second criteria item, and then select or type more specific search criteria.

6 To remove search criteria, click the **Remove** (-) button.

7 Click the **Action** button, and then click **Hide Search Criteria**.

8 To clear or stop a search, click the **Close** button (x) in the Search field.

9 When you're done, click the **Close** button.

Other available search criteria

Grouping and Sorting Spotlight Results

After you perform a search using the Spotlight window, you can use the Arrange By button, Arranged By submenu on the Action menu or the column header button in List or Cover Flow view to group and sort the results of your search to make it easier to find what you're looking for. Clicking on one of the column header buttons—such as Name, Kind, or Last Opened (default options)—in the search result window in either List or Cover Flow view, sorts the files and folders by the type of information listed in the column. If the columns are not organized in the order you want, you can use the mouse to quickly drag a column header to rearrange them.

Group and Sort Spotlight Results

1. Press Option+⌘+Space bar or click **Show All in Finder** on the Spotlight menu to open the Spotlight window, and then perform or narrow a search.

 The Spotlight window displays the results of your search by category.

2. Click the **List View** or **Cover Flow** button on the toolbar to display the search results in list form.

3. Click a column header name (default shown) to sort the file and folder in ascending or descending order:

 - **Name.** List in alphabetical order by element name.

 - **Kind.** List by kind of item, including applications, documents, or images.

 - **Last Opened.** List by the date you last opened it.

4. To change the view options, click the **Action** button, click **Show View Options**, select options, and then click the **Close** button.

5. When you're done, click the **Close** button.

Select view options for Spotlight search results

Working with Spotlight Results

After you perform a search using the Spotlight window, you can Control-click an item to display a shortcut menu and get more information about an item in the Spotlight results. When you Control-click an item, the shortcut menu allows you to open the item, get information about the item from the Get Info dialog box, locate the item in the Finder, display a slide show for graphic items, or create an e-mail with attachments using Mail.

Work with Spotlight Results

1 Press Option+⌘+Space bar or click **Show All in Finder** on the Spotlight menu to open the Spotlight window, and then perform or narrow a search.

The Spotlight window displays the results of your search by category.

2 Select the item(s) you want.

3 Click the **Action** button, and then click the option you want:

TIMESAVER *Control-click or right-click the items(s) you want.*

- **Open.** Opens the selected item(s).

- **Open With.** Opens the selected item(s) with a specified application. Point to Open With, and then select an available application.

- **Open Enclosing Folder.** Displays the selected item(s) in a Finder window.

- **Get Info.** Opens the Get Info dialog box with basic file information for the selected item(s).

- **Quick Look.** View the contents of a file or folder without opening it.

4 When you're done, click the **Close** button.

Setting Spotlight Preferences

You can change Spotlight preferences to customize the way you use Spotlight. You can specify the categories, such as Applications, Documents, Folders, and so on, you want or don't want to include in a Spotlight search. In addition, you can change the order of the categories to prioritize the way the results appears. If you prefer different shortcut keys to display the Spotlight menu or open the Spotlight window, you can change them. When Spotlight performs a search, it looks everywhere on your computer (except for someone else's Home folder). If you want to keep certain disks, partitions, or folders private, you can add them to your privacy settings in Spotlight preferences. When you add an item to the privacy list, Spotlight removes them from the Spotlight index.

Set Spotlight Search Results Preferences

1. Click the **System Preferences** icon in the Dock, and then click the **Spotlight** icon.

 TIMESAVER *Click Spotlight preferences at the bottom of the Spotlight menu (after you've started a search).*

2. Click the **Search Results** tab.

3. Select the check boxes you want to include in the search results or clear the check boxes you don't want to include in the search results.

4. To change the order to the search results categories, drag the categories to the location you want.

5. Click the **Close** button.

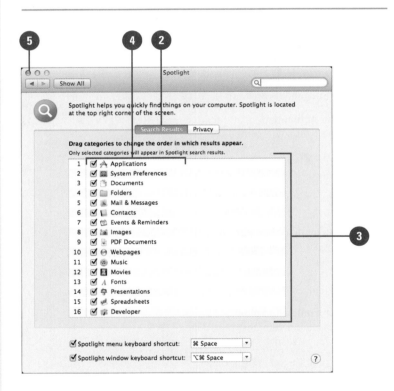

Did You Know?

You can use Spotlight everywhere (almost). The Spotlight Search field is also available in the Finder, Mail, System Preferences, and Open and Save dialogs to name a few.

For Your Information

Selecting the Default Search Location

You can specify the default search location for Spotlight. Click the Finder menu, click Preferences, click Advanced, click the When performing a search pop-up, then click Search This Mac, Search the Current Folder, or Use the Previous Search Scope.

Set Spotlight Privacy Preferences

1. Click the **System Preferences** icon in the Dock, and then click the **Spotlight** icon.

2. Click the **Privacy** tab.

3. Drag the items (disks, partitions, or folders) to the list of non-searchable items from the desktop, or click the **Add** (+) button, navigate to the item, and then click **Choose**.

4. To delete an item, click the item, and then press Delete or click the **Remove** (-) button.

5. Click the **Close** button.

Set Keyboard Shortcuts for Spotlight

1. Click the **System Preferences** icon in the Dock, and then click the **Spotlight** icon.

2. Select the **Spotlight menu keyboard shortcut** check box, click the list arrow, and then select the shortcut you want.

3. Select the **Spotlight window keyboard shortcut** check box, click the list arrow, and then select the shortcut you want.

4. Click the **Close** button.

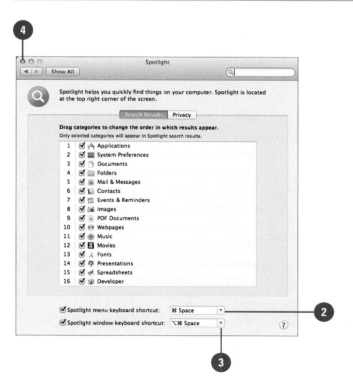

Searching for Files Using the Find Window

Spotlight provides a quick and easy way to search for files, but if you need to perform a more specific search, the Find window can help you search for what you need. The Find window lets you specify where and how you want to search—This Mac, All My Files or "folder or disk name," or Shared—with either file contents or name and make relevant suggestions as you type. You can narrow your search by selecting or typing a specific list of criteria—such as name, location, size, kind, or tag (**New!**)—available in the Find window. For example, you can search for all graphic files with the *.jpg* extension you created last month that contain *web*. After you complete a search, a separate results window opens. Unlike the Spotlight, you can change the criteria and perform a new search, and then compare the results.

Search for Files Using the Find Window

1. Open a Finder window.

2. Click the **File** menu, and then click **Find**.

 TIMESAVER *Press* ⌘+*F to open the Find window.*

3. In the Search field, type the text in which you want to search.

4. On the Search menu, select a suggestion, such as Filename contains "text" or a tag (**New!**), to narrow the search as desired.

5. Click the button with the search location you want:

 ◆ **This Mac.** Searches all the disks on your computer.

 ◆ **All My Files.** Searches your Home folder.

 ◆ **Server, Volume** or **Folder Name.** Searches only the currently opened server, volume, or folder. The item name appears in quotes in the Search bar.

 ◆ **Shared.** Searches shared folders on disks and computer.

6. To change the search, click the drop-down button, and then click **Filename** or **Everything**.

Narrow Search for Files Using the Find Window

1 Click the **File** menu, and then click **Find**.

2 In the Search field, type the text in which you want to perform an initial search.

3 Click the first **Search** pop-up, and then select or type the search criteria; options vary depending on the criteria.

- ◆ **Kind**. Finds files that are or aren't a certain kind.

- ◆ **Last Opened Date**. Finds files that you last opened.

- ◆ **Last Modified Date**. Finds files according to the date modified.

- ◆ **Created Date**. Finds files according to the date created.

- ◆ **Name**. Finds all or part of a file name (capitalization doesn't matter); select another option, such as Contains, Starts With, Ends With, or Is.

- ◆ **Contents**. Finds words inside your file; handy if you don't remember the name.

- ◆ **Other**. Finds files based on other selected attributes, such as Tags (**New!**).

4 Click the second **Search** pop-up, and then select or type more specific search criteria.

5 To add search criteria, click the **Add** (+) button, and then specify the criteria you want.

6 To remove search criteria, click the **Remove** (-) button.

The search results appear in the window.

7 To pause or stop a search in progress, click the **X** button.

For Your Information

Setting a Search Location Preference

In the Finder Preferences dialog, you can specify a search location preference. You can select any of the following options: Search This Mac, Search the Current Folder, or Use the Previous Search Scope. Click the Finder menu, click Preferences, click Advanced, click the When performing a search pop-up, and then select the option you want.

Searching for Hard to Find Information

In addition to searching for typical information, such as name, location, size, or kind, you can also search for file specific metadata, such as visibility (visible files, not hidden one used by OS X), duration, dimensions, pixel height and width, device make, layers, and tags (**New!**). There are over 115 different metadata search attributes from which to choose. For example, you can select search attributes to find visible files (not hidden ones used by OS X), the duration of music and movies, the dimensions of graphics or PDF documents, the device used to acquire a document, and the names of layers in Photoshop.

Search for Hard to Find Information

1. In the Finder, click the **File** menu, and then click **Find**.

 TIMESAVER *Press* ⌘+F *to open the Find window.*

 ◆ You can also use the Search field located in every Finder window.

2. In the Search field, type the text in which you want to search.

3. To display only matches with filename, select **Filename contains "text"** on the Search menu.

4. At the top of the window, click the button with the search location you want: **This Mac, All My files** or "folder or disk name," or **Shared**.

5. Click the first **Search** pop-up, and then click **Other**.

6. Select the search attribute you want to find, such as Tags (**New!**).

7. Click **OK**.

Working with Find Window Results

Work with Find Window Results

After you perform a search with the Find window, you can use the following options to work with the results:

◆ **Find the location of a file.** Click a file to display the location in the Path bar at bottom of the window.

◆ **Open the location of a file.** Click the **File** menu, and then click **Open Enclosed Folder**.

◆ **Open a file.** Double-click the file icon.

◆ **Move or delete a file.** Drag the file to a new location or the Trash.

◆ **Rename a file.** Click its name, select the text, and then type a new name.

◆ **Copy a file.** Use the **Copy** and **Paste** commands on the **Edit** menu.

◆ **Get file information.** Click the File menu, and then click **Get Info**. Add criteria to Spotlight Comments for use in Spotlight searches.

◆ **Sort the result by category.** Click the column header.

◆ **Start a new search.** Change the text in the Search field, or click the Close (x) button in the Search field and type a new search.

◆ **Close the search.** Click the **Close** button or press ⌘+W.

After you perform a search with the Find window, you can perform a variety of file management operations directly with the Find window results, which are similar to the ones you can perform in the Finder. For example, you can get file information, and move, copy, rename, or delete a file directly in the search results window. In addition, you can display the location of a file in the search results window, and then open its folder location or open the file.

Double-click to open Click column to sort

Path bar

Tags for the file

Creating and Using Smart Folders

A Smart folder is a self-updating folder that performs a search based on the search criteria you set and save in the Search dialog box. You can create a Smart folder by specifying a search in the Search dialog box and then saving it as a saved search. For example, if you set up a search for *Last Opened* and *This week*, and saved it as a Smart folder. In the Sidebar, you can click the Smart folder to perform the smart search, or Control-click it and click Show Search Criteria to edit it.

Create and Use a Smart Folder

1. Click the **File** menu, and then click **New Smart Folder**.

2. Use the **Add** (+) button to specify the search criteria you want to save as a Smart folder.

3. Click the **Save** button.

4. Type a name for the Smart folder.

5. Specify the location where you want to save the Smart folder.

 The default location is the Saved Searches folder.

6. Select or clear the **Add To Sidebar** check box to either add or not add the Smart folder to the sidebar.

7. Click **Save**.

8. To use a Smart folder, click the Smart folder icon on the Sidebar, or navigate to the Saved Searches folder, and then double-click it.

 ◆ The Saved Searches folder is located in the Library folder, which is located in the Home folder.

Did You Know?

You can open a recent item. Click the Apple menu, point to Recent Items, and then click the recently used document you want to open.

Smart folder

Edit a Smart Folder

① Navigate to the Smart folder you want to edit; you can click Smart folder in the Sidebar to select to display it.

② Click the **Action** menu, and then click **Show Search Criteria**.

③ Change the search criteria you want to modify.

④ Click **Save**.

⑤ Click the **Action** menu, and then click **Hide Search Criteria**.

Did You Know?

Where's the Smart folder? The Smart folder is located in the Saved Searches folder in the Library folder, which is located in the Home folder.

You can delete a Smart folder. Control-click the smart folder in the Sidebar, click Open Enclosing folder, and then drag the Smart folder you want to delete to the Trash icon.

You can remove a Smart folder from the Sidebar. Control-click the smart folder in the Sidebar, and then click Remove from Sidebar. The folder is removed from the sidebar, however it remains in the Save Searches folder.

You can add a Smart folder or other folder to the Sidebar. Select the folder in a Finder window or desktop, click the File menu, and then click Add To Sidebar.

Saved Searches folder

Items grayed out, not accessible.
Drag to trash to delete.

Getting Help While You Work

When you have a question about how to do something in OS X, you can usually find the answer with several clicks of your mouse. Mac OS X Help is a resource of information to help you use OS X. The Mac OS X Help Center is like an online book with a table of contents, complete with a search feature, and additional links to the Internet to make finding information a little bit easier. You can access help from the Help menu in the Finder as well as many other OS X applications, such as Safari and Messages; you can even switch between the different help libraries using the Home button. If you see the Help button (question mark) in a window or dialog, you can click it to get feature related help. If you have an Internet connection, Help retrieves online updates to Mac OS X Help content as necessary. For additional help and support information, visit the Apple web site at *www.apple.com*.

Browse for Help Information

1. In the Finder, or any other application, click the **Help** menu, and then click **Help Center** or **<application name> Help**.

2. To select another Help, click the **Help for all your apps** link, and then click a help library.

3. Click a link in the Help window until you find the topic with the information you're looking for.

4. Use the Help toolbar to navigation help topics:

 ◆ Click the **Back** and **Forward** button to view previously viewed topics.

 ◆ Click the **Action** button to change text size, find and highlight text on current page, or print current topic.

 ◆ Click the **Home** button to return to the first page of the help.

 ◆ Click the **Add Bookmark** button to add the current help topic to bookmarks. Click **Bookmarks** button to display the bookmark list to open, remove or email.

5. Click the **Close** button to quit Help.

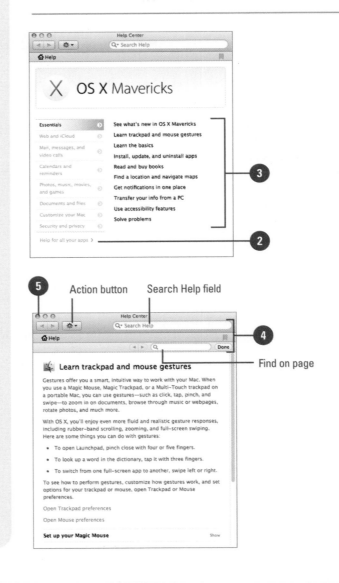

Search for Help Information

1. In the Finder, or any other application, click the **Help** menu, and then click **Help Center** or **<application name> Help**.

2. Click the magnifying glass in the Search field, and then click **Include Product Support Results** to check or uncheck it.

3. Click in the Search field.

 TIMESAVER *Press the Tab key to quickly go to the Search field.*

4. Type the words you want to find in the help topics, and then press Return.

 A list of matches appears with a Relevance column ranking the results by percentage.

5. Click the topic you want to read in the search results list.

6. Use the navigation buttons (**Back** and **Forward**) on the Help toolbar to move between help topics.

7. Click the **Close** button to quit Help.

Did You Know?

You can start a new search in a new window. Click the File menu, click New, and then perform a new search.

You can print a help topic. Display the help topic in the Help window, click the Action button on the Help toolbar, click Print, and then click Print again.

You can change the size of Help text. Click the Action button on the Help toolbar, click Make Text Smaller or Make Text Bigger.

Possible matches to search criteria

Getting Help Using Spotlight

In addition to using Spotlight to find files and other information on your computer, you can also use Spotlight to quickly find help information. When you click the Help menu, the Spotlight Search field appears at the top, where you can type the help information you want to find and display. You can access help from the Help menu in the Finder as well as many other OS X applications, such as Safari and Messages. When you select a help topic from the Help menu, the Help window appears displaying the topic. If you want to display all the related help topics, click Show All Help Results. A complete search results appears, where you can double-click a topic to display it. If available, menu items appear on the Help menu, where you can select it to display an blue arrow pointing to the location of the menu.

Get Help Using Spotlight

1. Click the **Help** menu.

2. In the Spotlight Search field, start to type what you want to find. To find a specific phrase, place quotes around it. For example, "Preferences"

 As you type, a menu begins to display a list of everything Spotlight can find in Help to match what you've typed so far. As you continue to type, the list changes.

3. On the Help menu, select one of the following options:

 ◆ **Display a Help Topic**. Click the Help topic item or use the arrow keys to scroll down the list, and then press Return to open the Help window.

 ◆ **Show All Help Results**. Click **Show All Help Results** to display the search results for help topics, and then double-click the topic you want to open the Help window.

 ◆ **Display a Menu Item**. Point to the Menu item name to display a blue arrow pointing to the location of the menu item.

4. Click the **Close** button to quit Help.

Display menu item

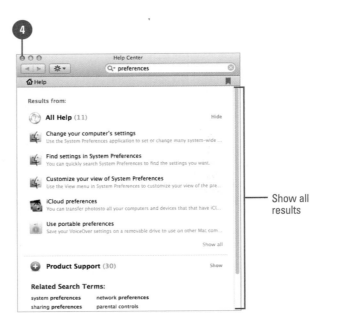

Show all results

Customizing the Finder

Introduction

Finder Preferences allow you to control how you interact with your desktop, windows, and icons. You can access Finder Preferences from the Finder menu. Finder Preferences are grouped into four main areas: General, Tags, Sidebar, and Advanced. The Finder Preferences window is a central location to set Finder related options. However, you can customize the Finder and the desktop in other places too.

In each of the Finder window views (Icon, List, and Column), you can set view specific options to customize the way you view icons. In addition to the predefined items in the Sidebar (the left pane in a Finder window), you can add your own items, including folders, documents, Web Internet Location files, to name a few. The Finder toolbar comes with a few standard buttons, and you can customize to add more. You can use the Customize Toolbar dialog to quickly drag button icons on and off the toolbar. You can set Dock preferences to adjust the Dock size and icon magnification (when you point to one), change the Dock position on the screen, apply a bounce effect to an icon when you launch an application, select a minimization special effect, and make it disappear when not in use.

To save some time, you can create shortcuts to the files, folders, or disks you use frequently, known as Aliases. An **alias** allows you to access the original folder or file from several different places. Mission Control with Spaces and Exposé let you view what's running on your computer and quickly move between windows to make it easier to work with windows in order to find, move, or copy files. If you have novice users who want to use your computer, you can set up a shared user account with Simple Finder, which is a simplified version of the OS X Finder with fewer menus and icons. It's a great way for them to explore, yet keep your data safe.

What You'll Do

Understand Finder Preferences

Show Icons on the Desktop

Customize the Way Windows Open

Show or Hide File Extensions

Customize Finder Window Views

Customize the Toolbar

Customize the Sidebar

Customize the Dock

Create Aliases

Customize Mission Control

Use Simple Finder

Understanding Finder Preferences

Finder Preferences allow you to control how you interact with your desktop, windows, and icons. Finder Preferences are grouped into four main areas: General, Tags (**New!**), Sidebar, and Advanced. You can open Finder Preferences by selecting Preferences from the Finder menu.

The **General preferences pane** allows you to display icons for local and network disks on the desktop, select options for opening new Finder windows, and enable spring-loaded folders and windows. The **Tags prefer-** ences pane (**New!**) allows you to manage tags—colors and names—for Finder items, which you can use as search criteria in Spotlight or the Find window. If you accidentally remove a Sidebar icon, you can use the **Sidebar preferences pane** to redisplay Finder specific icons, such as computer, hard disks, iDisk, network, desktop, and applications. The **Advanced preferences pane** provides options to show file extensions, a change file extension warning, an empty the Trash warning, empty the Trash securely, and where to perform a Spotlight search.

General

Sidebar

Tags

Advanced

Showing Icons on the Desktop

When you insert a removable disk, a CD, or DVD, or connect to a network server, an icon for the disk automatically appears on the desktop. Depending on your work style, you may or may not want icons to simply appear. You can use Finder Preferences to specify whether icons for hard and external disks, CDs, and network servers appear on your desktop. Having the icons on the desktop makes dragging them to the Eject icon in the Dock quick and easy, but the icons also add clutter to the desktop.

Show Volume Icons on the Desktop

1. Click the **Finder** menu, and then click **Preferences**.

2. Click **General**.

3. Select or clear the checkmarks for the icons you want to show or hide on the desktop.
 - ◆ Hard disks
 - ◆ External disks
 - ◆ CDs, DVDs and iPods
 - ◆ Connected servers (computers attached to a network)

4. Click the **Close** button.

Customizing the Way Windows Open

When you create a new Finder window, you can specify options to open folders in tabs instead of new windows (**New!**) or use spring-loaded folders and windows. Spring-loaded folders allows you to drag a file or folder on top of another folder, and it springs open to let you continue dragging the selection to another location. Instead of starting and stopping when you move or copy items from one folder to another, you can drag items continuously from folder to folder.

Customize the Way Finder Windows Open

1. Click the **Finder** menu, and then click **Preferences**.

2. Click **General**.

3. Click the **New Finder windows open** pop-up, and then select the window you want to open when you open a new Finder window.

4. Select or clear the **Open folders in tabs instead of new windows** check box (**New!**).

5. Select or clear the **Spring-loaded folders and windows** check box. If you select it, drag the slider to adjust the delay.

 TIMESAVER *When you drag an item to a folder with a spring-loaded folder, you can press the Spacebar to open the window immediately without the delay.*

6. Click the **Close** button.

Showing or Hiding File Extensions

A **file extension** is a three-letter suffix at the end of a document's file name that identifies the file type. For Windows operating system users, a file extension determines which application can open a file; the Mac doesn't use it. You might never have seen a document's file extension because your system might be set up to hide it. The file extension for simple text files is ".txt" (pronounced "dot t-x-t"), and many graphic files have the extension ".bmp" or ".jpg". This means that the full name for a text file named Memo is Memo.txt. If you double-click a document whose file name ends with the three-letter extension ".txt," Finder automatically opens the document with TextEdit, a word processing application. If you plan to exchange files with the Windows operating system, then show the file extensions, so Windows recognizes them. As a precaution, you can also set an option to display a warning before allowing a file extension change.

Show or Hide File Extensions

1. Click the **Finder** menu, and then click **Preferences**.

2. Click **Advanced**.

3. Select or clear the **Show all file extensions** check box.

4. Select or clear the **Show warning before changing an extension** check box.

5. Click the **Close** button.

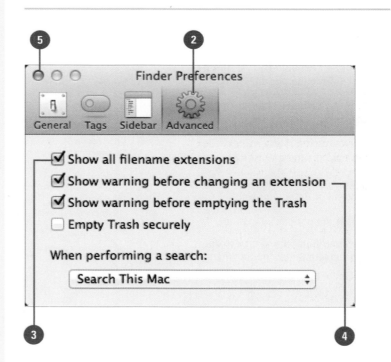

Did You Know?

You can hide or show extensions one icon at a time. Select the icons you want to show or hide, click the File menu, click Get Info, select or clear the Hide Extension check box, and then click the Close button.

You can set an option to show a warning before emptying the Trash. Click the Finder menu, click Preferences, click Advanced, select the Show Warning Before Emptying The Trash check box, and then click the Close button.

Customizing Finder Window Views

In each of the Finder window views (as Icons, as List, as Columns, and as Cover Flow, you can set view specific options to customize the way you view icons. For Icon, List, and Cover Flow views, you can select to apply your changes to the current window or to all Finder windows (a personal default). In Icon view, you can change icon size, label position, arrangement, and background. In List and Cover Flow views, you can change file size, date, and status related information. To make the display easier to view, you can display relative dates, such as "Today" and "Yesterday." In Column view, you can show icons and the preview column (summary information in the right column).

Change Icon View Options

1. In a Finder window, click the **View** menu, and then click **As Icons**.

2. Click the **View** menu, and then click **Show View Options**.

3. Select an **Arrange By** and **Sort By** option from the pop-ups.

4. Drag the slider to change the icon size or the grid spacing.

5. To change the icon text size, click the pop-up, and then select a size.

6. Click the label position option (Bottom or Right) you want.

7. Select the options you want:

 ◆ **Show item info**. Check to show item info under the icon name.

 ◆ **Show icon preview**. Check to show a preview in the icon.

8. Click the **Background** option you want, and any related settings.

9. Click **Use as Defaults** to apply view changes to all windows.

10. Select the **Always open in icon view** check box to apply changes to the window; select the **Browse in icon view** check box to set default style to the view.

11. Click the **Close** button.

Change List View or Cover Flow Options

1. In a Finder window, click the **View** menu, and then click **As List** or **Cover Flow**.

2. Click the **View** menu, and then click **Show View Options**.

3. Select an **Arrange By** and **Sort By** option from the pop-ups.

4. Select an Icon size, and then select an icon text size.

5. Select or clear the check boxes you want to display in list form.

6. Click **Use as Defaults** to apply view changes to all windows.

7. Select the **Always open in <view>** check box to apply changes to the window; select the **Browse in <view>** check box to set default style to the view.

8. Click the **Close** button.

Change Column View Options

1. In a Finder window, click the **View** menu, and then click **As Columns**.

2. Click the **View** menu, and then click **Show View Options**.

3. Select an **Arrange By** and **Sort By** option from the pop-ups.

4. Click the **Text size** pop-up, and then select a point size.

5. Select or clear the check boxes you want to show previews.

6. Select the **Always open in column view** check box to apply changes to the window; select the **Browse in column view** check box to set default style to the view.

7. Click the **Close** button.

Customizing the Toolbar

The Finder toolbar comes with a few standard buttons, but you can add more. You can use the Customize Toolbar dialog to quickly drag button icons on and off. The buttons include Path (navigation pop-up), Eject, Burn, Customize, Separator (designates groups), Space (adds a gap), Flexible Space (adds a gap that expands), New Folder, Delete, Connect, Get Info, iDisk, Search, and Quick Look. If you want the simple look again, you can drag the Default Set of buttons onto the toolbar to reset it. In addition to the button icons in the dialog, you can also drag icons, such as favorite folders, disks, or applications, from the desktop or any Finder folder onto the toolbar. You can also use the A key to cycle through size combinations of large and small icons and text labels.

Customize the Finder Toolbar

1. Click the **View** menu, and then click **Customize Toolbar**.

2. Click the **Show** pop-up, and then select a display option of **Icon Only**, **Icon & Text**, or **Text Only**.

 TIMESAVER *Control-click the toolbar (without the dialog open), and then click a display option.*

3. To add icons to the toolbar, drag them into place from the gallery.

4. To remove icons, drag them up or down off the toolbar.

5. To rearrange icons, drag them horizontally on the toolbar.

6. To reset the toolbar, drag the default set of items onto the toolbar.

7. When you're finished, click **Done**.

Did You Know?

You can access buttons that don't fit on a narrow window. You can either resize the window, or click the double arrow, and then select a toolbar item.

Add, Remove, or Rearrange Icons to the Toolbar

① Display the icons you want to add to the Finder toolbar in the desktop or any folder window.

② Hold down ⌘, and then drag icons from the desktop, or any folder window, directly onto the toolbar, and then pause before releasing the icon.

 TROUBLE? *If pausing doesn't work, use A while you drag.*

③ To remove an icon from the toolbar, hold down ⌘, and then drag the icon off the toolbar.

④ To rearrange an icon on the toolbar, hold down ⌘, and then drag the icon horizontally on the toolbar.

Change Toolbar Styles

① Control-click a blank area of the toolbar, and then click **Icon and Text**, **Icon Only**, or **Text Only**.

> ### Did You Know?
>
> **You can change toolbar styles in some applications too.** You can also use ⌘ in OS X applications, such as Mail, and many other applications.

Icon added to toolbar

Other toolbar styles

Customizing the Sidebar

In addition to the predefined items in the Sidebar, you can add your own items, including folders and documents, to name a few. When you click a volume or folder in the Sidebar, the Finder displays its contents in the window. When you click an application, document, or Web Internet Location file, the item opens in its own application window. You can remove or rearrange items and categories—including Favorites, Shared, Devices and Tags (**New!**)—on the Sidebar to customize it. However, when you remove a Sidebar icon, you can't undo it, but you can redisplay OS X specific items using Finder Preferences. Unfortunately, you have to recreate the ones you added.

Customize the Sidebar

◆ **Add items.** Drag the items to the lower section of the Sidebar.

> **TIMESAVER** *Select an item, and then press* ⌘+T, *or use the Add To Sidebar command on the File menu.*

◆ **Remove items.** Control-click the item, and then click **Remove from Sidebar**.

◆ **Rearrange items.** Drag the items up or down in the list.

◆ **Rearrange categories.** Drag the category name up or down in the list.

◆ **Change the column width.** Position the mouse pointer over the divider between the Sidebar and the window contents, and then drag to change the width.

◆ **Hide and show the Sidebar.** Click the **View** menu, and then click **Hide Sidebar** or **Show Sidebar**.

Add item to Sidebar

Drag to change column width

Remove item from Sidebar

Change Sidebar Preferences

1 Click the **Finder** menu, and then click **Preferences**.

2 Click **Sidebar**.

3 Select or clear the check boxes with the items you want or don't want to see in the Sidebar.

◆ The items in Sidebar Preferences include icons for the categories Favorites, Shared, Devices, and Recent Tags (**New!**).

4 Click the **Close** button.

4 **2**

Finder Preferences

General Tags Sidebar Advanced

Show these items in the sidebar:

FAVORITES
☑ 🖥 All My Files
☑ 📡 AirDrop
☑ 🅰 Applications
☑ 🖥 Desktop
☑ 🗐 Documents
☑ ⬇ Downloads
☑ 🎬 Movies
☑ 🎵 Music
☑ 📷 Pictures
☐ 🏠 stevejohnson

SHARED
☑ ☁ Back to My Mac
☑ 📨 Connected servers
☑ 🐾 Bonjour computers

DEVICES
☐ 💾 Steve's Mac mini
⊟ 💽 Hard disks
☑ 🖥 External disks
☑ 💿 CDs, DVDs, and iPods

TAGS
☑ ◯ Recent Tags

3

Customizing the Dock

After you have worked with the Dock for a while, you probably want to customize it to better suit your needs. You can set Dock Preferences to adjust the Dock size and icon magnification when you point to one, change the Dock position on the screen, apply a bounce effect to an icon when you launch an application, select a minimization special effect, and even make it disappear when not in use.

Customize the Dock

1. Click the **Apple** menu, point to **Dock**, and then click **Dock Preferences**.

 TIMESAVER *Control-click the divider in the Dock to quickly display the Dock submenu.*

2. Select the Dock options you want:

 ◆ **Dock Size**. Drag slider to change the Dock size.

 TIMESAVER *Point to the divider in the Dock (double-headed arrow), and then drag to size it.*

 ◆ **Magnification**. Select to enable it, and then drag the slider to magnify the icons when you point to them in the Dock.

 ◆ **Position on screen**. Click the Left, Bottom, or Right option.

 ◆ **Minimize windows using**. Select an animation effect.

 ◆ **Double-click a window's title bar to minimize**. Select to use double-click method.

 ◆ **Minimize windows into application icon**. Select to minimize windows into the application icon on the dock.

 ◆ **Animate opening applications**. Select to have the application icon bounce when you launch it.

 ◆ **Automatically hide and show the Dock**. Select to auto hide/show the dock when not pointing or pointing to it.

 ◆ **Show indicator lights for open applications**. Select to show lights under dock icon.

3. Click the **Close** button.

Magnifying icons

For Your Information

Displaying the Genie Effect

You can slow down the minimization of a window or application (a cool genie effect). Shift-click a window's Minimize button. The window collapses into the Dock about one-fifth the usual speed. You can also Shift-click the icon in the Dock to slowly unminimize the window. Unfortunately, you can't speed it up.

Add, Remove, and Rearrange Items in the Dock

Add an item

- ◆ **Add an item.** Drag an icon from a Finder window to the Dock, and then position application icons to the left of the divider line and all other icons to the right.

- ◆ **Add an open application item.** Open the application to display the icon in the Dock, press and hold or Control-click the application icon, point to **Options**, and then click **Keep In Dock**.

Add an open application

- ◆ **Open a document using an application item.** Drag the document icon to the application icon in the Dock.

- ◆ **Move an item.** Drag the icon to the position you want in the Dock.

Open a document

- ◆ **Remove an item.** Drag an icon out of the Dock.

 TROUBLE? *If you delete an application or document from your computer with an icon in the Dock, the Dock icon changes to a question mark, which you can remove.*

Remove an item

- ◆ **Open a folder stack.** Click a folder icon to display the stack list, and then click an item.

- ◆ **Customize a folder stack.** Control-click a folder icon to display a shortcut menu, and then click an option.

Did You Know?

You can use the Dock submenu to quickly change dock options. Click the Apple menu, point to Dock, and then select an option: turn Hiding On/Off, Turn Magnification On/Off, or Position on Left, Bottom, or Right,

Customize a folder stack

Creating Aliases

It can take you a while to access a file or folder buried several levels down in a folder. To save some time, you can create shortcuts to the items you use frequently. **Aliases** are shortcuts that point to a folder or file. An alias allows you to access the original folder or file from several different places. When you create an alias to a folder or file, the icon includes a little arrow in the lower-left corner. You can't make an alias for an application. However, you can add an application into the Dock, which acts like an alias. When you double-click an alias icon, a folder opens with the contents of the original folder or a document opens using its associated application. If you delete an alias of a folder or file, the original folder or file is not deleted, just the alias.

Create an Alias

1. Open the Finder window with the icon in which you want to create an alias.

2. Select the icon.

3. Click the **File** menu, and then click **Make Alias**.

 TIMESAVER *Hold down ⌘+Option, and then drag a file or folder to create an alias.*

 The alias icon appears in the Finder window.

4. If you want, rename the alias icon, and then press Return.

5. Drag the alias icon to the desktop or another folder.

Did You Know?

You can quickly find the original file or folder of an alias. Select the alias file or folder, click the File menu, and then click Show Original. You can also press ⌘+R.

Create an Alias with the Title Bar

1. Open the application and document in which you want to create an alias.

2. Position the mouse pointer on the icon next to the document title in the title bar.

3. Drag the icon to the desktop, or on a folder or disk.

Did You Know?

You can drag the Title bar icon onto an application Dock icon. If you want to open a document created in one program (say TextEdit), and you want to open it up in another program (say Microsoft Word), you can drag the Title bar icon of a document in TextEdit to the Microsoft Word icon in the Dock to open it.

You can drag an alias icon into the Dock. Drag the alias icon into the Dock on the right side. When you release the mouse, the icon appears in the Dock.

Alias for TextEdit document

Customizing Mission Control

In Mission Control preferences you can customize Exposé, Spaces, and Dashboard options. Exposé in Mission Control lets you quickly move windows out of the way temporarily to make it easier to work with windows to find, move, or copy files. The default way to move windows with Exposé is to use keyboard function keys. You can customize them to move windows in three ways: screen corners, keyboard, and mouse. Use Hot Corners, you can trigger an operation when you point to one of the screen corners. Using the keyboard pop-ups, you can change the shortcuts. When you display the pop-ups, you can press other modifier keys, such as Shift, Option, Control, or ⌘ to create a new shortcut. If you have a mouse with two or three buttons, you can change options to trigger them. With Spaces, you can group and arrange windows to reduce desktop clutter, organize materials into Spaces, and have separate Spaces for multiple displays (**New!**). You can also set options to show the Dashboard as a space, switch to a space with open windows for an application, and automatically reorder spaces.

Customize Exposé in Mission Control

① Click the **System Preferences** icon in the Dock, and then click the **Mission Control** icon.

② Click the pop-ups for each item, press a keyboard modifier (Shift, Control, Option, or ⌘) if you want, and then select a shortcut key, and then set a mouse button.

 ◆ **Mission Control**. Set to toggle between show/hide all open windows at once; default set to Shift+Up Arrow.

 ◆ **Application Windows**. Set to toggle between show/hide all open windows in the current application; default set to Shift+Down Arrow.

 ◆ **Show Desktop**. Set to toggle between hide/show all open windows and show/hide desktop; default set to F11.

③ To set active screen corners to activate operations, click **Hot Corners**, select corner operations, and then click **OK**.

④ Click the **Close** button.

Customize Spaces in Mission Control

1. Click the **System Preferences** icon in the Dock, and then click the **Mission Control** icon.

2. Select or clear check boxes for the following Spaces options:

 ◆ **Automatically reorder Spaces based on most recent use.**

 ◆ **When switching to an application, switch to a Space with open windows for the application.**

 ◆ **Group windows by application.**

 ◆ **Displays have separate Spaces. (New!)**

3. Click the **Close** button.

Customize Dashboard in Mission Control

1. Click the **System Preferences** icon in the Dock, and then click the **Mission Control** icon.

2. To show the dashboard as a space in Mission control, select the **Show Dashboard as a space** check box.

3. In the Keyboard and Mouse Shortcuts area, click the Show Dashboard pop-up, press a keyboard modifier (Shift, Control, Option, or ⌘) if you want, and then select a shortcut key and/or a mouse button.

 ◆ **Show Dashboard**. Set to toggle between show/hide the dashboard.

4. Click the **Close** button.

Using Simple Finder

If you have novice users who want to use your computer, you should set up a user account with the Simple Finder in Parental Controls preferences. **Simple Finder** is a simplified version of the OS X Finder with fewer menus and icons, and allows limited access to the items on your hard disk. The Dock contains only three folders: Documents, My Applications, and Shared. The Documents folder provides a place for users to save their documents, while the My Applications folder provides access to the applications you select for them in Parental Control preferences. If you want to share documents with them, they can access the items in the Shared folder.

Set Up the Simple Finder

1. Click the **System Preferences** icon in the Dock, and then click the **Parental Controls** icon.

2. Click the user account for the person you want to set up the Simple Finder. If necessary, click the **Lock** icon and enter user name and password, first. Also, click the **Enable Parental Control** button as needed.

3. Click the **System** tab.

4. Select the **Use Simple Finder** check box.

5. Select or clear the **Limit Applications** check box, and then select an **Allow App Store Apps** option to a specified limit.

6. Select or clear the applications you want to enable or disable for the account.

7. Click the **Close** button.

Did You Know?

You can get administrative access while logged in to Simple Finder. Click the Finder menu, click Run Full Finder, and then type your name and password. When you're done, click the Finder menu, and then click Return To Simple Finder.

Simple Finder

Setting System Preferences

Introduction

System Preferences allows you to customize various parts of OS X, such as the appearance of your desktop, your computers' date and time, the way CDs and DVDs start up when you insert them, or use speech recognition to convert a spoken voice into commands or electronic text. For those of you with a Mac laptop, you can manage power usage for your computer. Accessibility preferences make it easier for a person with a disability, such as difficulty seeing or hearing or controlling a mouse or trackpad, to use a computer. If you have an ink device attached to your computer, you can use Ink Preferences to improve the recognition of ink to text.

You can access System Preferences from the Dock or the Apple menu. Many applications also have their own preferences, which you can access from the application menu within the application. System Preferences are organized into categories by default. Each category contains a set of icons, which you can open to set customization options in preference panes for different aspects of the Macintosh operating system.

Some System Preference panes are locked for security reasons. If preference settings are all grayed out, the preference pane is locked to prevent non-administrators from making changes. Check the Lock icon at the bottom of System Preferences. If the Lock icon is locked, you need an administrator name and password to unlock it and make changes. If you log in as an administrator, the Lock icon is unlocked, unless you set a security option to have the preference panes stay locked. When you close the preference pane, it locks automatically.

What You'll Do

Understand System Preferences

View System Preferences

Lock and Unlock Preference Settings

Change Appearance Options

Set Up the Desktop

Set Up Screen Savers

Set the Date and Time

Change Language & Region Options

Change Text Substitution Options

Save Energy and Manage Power

Select a Startup Disk

Change the Way a CD & DVD Starts

Control Sound

Dictate Your Speech

Let Mac Do the Talking

Set Accessibility Options

Recognize Your Speech

Explore and Use VoiceOver

Set Ink Preferences

Understanding System Preferences

System Preferences allow you to customize system wide settings for various aspects of OS X and your computer. The System Preferences window is organized alphabetically or by categories: Personal, Hardware, Internet & Network, and System. Each category contains preference areas that you can change to customize the way OS X works. Only an administrator can change system settings that affect every account.

Personal

General. Change the look and feel of buttons, selected items, and scroll bars. See page 100.

Desktop & Screen Saver. Change the desktop background or select a visual screen effect to hide your desktop. See pages 102-103 (**New!**).

Dock. Change the location of the Dock, adjust the size of icons, set magnification, or hide the Dock. See pages 88-89 in Chapter 4.

Mission Control. Set keyboard shortcuts or mouse positions to show or hide all your windows at one time, or create unique spaces for projects. See page 92-93 in Chapter 4 (**New!**).

Language & Region. Change your computer to read or write with other languages (**New!**) and substitute text. See pages 106-109.

Security & Privacy. Protect your computer and the information on it, and adjust firewall settings to protect your computer from access over the Internet. See pages 407-408 in Chapter 15.

Spotlight. Select the categories and priority order you want used in Spotlight searches. See pages 66-67 in Chapter 3.

Notifications. Change general and application specific options for the Notification Center (**New!**). See pages 390-391 in Chapter 14.

Hardware

CDs & DVDs. Set startup options when you insert a CD/DVD. (Available only if a CD/DVD player is installed.) See pages 113 and 328.

Displays. Set the screen size, resolution, color settings, and arrange multiple screens. See page 470-473 in Chapter 18 (**New!**).

Energy Saver. Set the computer to sleep and conserve power, and schedule shutdown and startup. See page 110-111 (**New!**).

Ink. Set the computer to write text using a graphics tablet and stylus, recognize the ink, and turn it into words. (Available only if a tablet or ink device is installed.) See page 130.

Keyboard. Change the speed of your keyboard, and customize universal keyboard shortcuts or application shortcuts. See page 467 in Chapter 18.

Mouse. Change the speed of your mouse, primary mouse button, or scroll wheel zoom. See pages 468 in Chapter 18.

Trackpad. Change the options related to using your internal or external trackpad. See pages 469 in Chapter 18.

Printers & Scanners. Add a printer, print jobs, set up to receive scans and faxes, and share printers and fax modems with other users. See pages 208-212 in Chapter 8 (**New!**).

Sound. Change computer sound volume, effects, and sound input or output devices. See pages 114-115.

Internet & Wireless

iCloud. Create an online iCloud account and set access options. See pages 356-369 in Chapter 13 (**New!**).

Internet Accounts. Setup and manage accounts for internet services. See page 268 in Chapter 10 (**New!**).

Network. Create and manage network and Internet connection settings. See page 428 in Chapter 16.

Bluetooth. Control how to send and receive files between your computer and other Bluetooth devices. (Available if Bluetooth is enabled). See pages 429-431 in Chapter 16.

Sharing. Set sharing services for files, web, printer, internet, and bluetooth with others. See pages 420-423 in Chapter 16.

System

Users & Groups. Set up accounts, access privileges, and log in and out settings to share your computer with others. See pages 397-401 in Chapter 15.

Parental Controls. Set limits on computer use, including content, Mail and Messages, and time, and create logs. See pages 402-403 in Chapter 15.

App Store. Set options (**New!**) to check for software updates automatically on the Internet. See pages 446-447 in Chapter 17.

Dictation & Speech. Set the computer to take dictation as typed text, speak the text on the screen, or use spoken commands to control your computer. See pages 116-119 (**New!**).

Date & Time. Set your computer's date, time, and time zone, or use a network time server. See pages 104-105.

Startup Disk. Select the disk or drive you want to use to start up your computer. See page 112.

Time Machine. Set options to back up everything on your computer. See page 494 in Chapter 20.

Accessibility. Set options (**New!**) for the visual or hearing impaired to make it easier to use the computer keyboard, mouse & trackpad, and screen. See pages 120-129.

Adding or Removing Third-Party System Preferences

You can also add other System Preferences developed by third-party companies. To install a third-party preference, download the preference, double-click its icon, and then follow the on-screen instructions. To uninstall a third-party preference, use the method provided by the developer, or hold down the Control key, click the Preference icon, click the Remove or Uninstall command, and then follow the on-screen instructions.

Categories

Viewing System Preferences

System Preferences are organized into categories by default. Each category contains a set of icons, which you can open to set customization options in preference panes for different aspects of the Mac OS. You can view the icons in the System Preferences window alphabetically, depending on your preference, or search for the one you want. Simply click a preference icon to open it, and then make the changes you want. The preferences take effect when you quit or close System Preferences.

View System Preferences

① Click the **Apple** menu, and then click **System Preferences** or click the **System Preferences** icon in the Dock.

② To change preference organization, click the **View** menu, and then click **Organize By Categories** or **Organize Alphabetically**.

③ To find a preference, enter a name in the Find box.

④ To open a preference, click the icon.

> **TIMESAVER** *Press the first letter of the preferences name to select the icon, and then press the Spacebar to open it.*

⑤ To switch to another preference, click the **View** menu, and then click the one you want to open.

> **TIMESAVER** *Click the Show All button on the toolbar to show all the preference icons.*

⑥ When you're done, click the **Close** button.

Other third-party preferences

Did You Know?

You can customize the System Preferences toolbar. Open System Preferences, click the View menu, click Customize, select or clear a check box, and then click Done.

Locking and Unlocking Preference Settings

Some preference panes are locked for security reasons. If preference settings are all grayed out, the preference pane is locked to prevent non-administrators from making changes. Check the Lock icon at the bottom of System Preferences. If the Lock icon is locked, you need an administrator name and password to unlock it and make changes. If you log in as an administrator, the Lock icon is unlocked, unless you set a security option to have the preference panes stay locked. When you close the preference pane, it locks automatically.

Unlock a Preference Pane

1. Click the **System Preferences** icon in the Dock.

2. Click the preference pane icon (such as Security) that you want to lock settings.

3. Click the **Lock** icon.

4. To unlock, type an administrator name and password.

5. Click **Unlock**.

6. Click the **Close** button.

Set Preference Panes to Lock

1. Click the **System Preferences** icon in the Dock.

2. Click the **Security & Privacy** icon, and then click the **General** tab.

3. If grayed out, click the **Lock** icon, type an administrator name and password, and then click **Unlock**.

4. Click **Advanced**.

5. Select the **Require an administrator password to access system preferences with lock icons** check box.

6. Click **OK**.

7. Click the **Close** button.

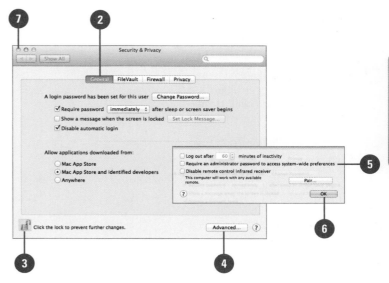

Changing Appearance Options

The General pane in System Preferences allows you to change the look and feel of OS X in a few areas. You can change the color scheme for buttons, menus, and windows, and the highlight color for text and lists. Or if you're not comfortable using the scroll bars, you can change the way scroll bars work and the placement of the scroll arrows. If your text looks blurry or jagged, you can adjust the font smoothing, known as **anti-aliasing**, style to fix it (after you log out and back in). As you open files and applications, OS X keeps a list in the Recent Items submenu in the Apple menu. In the Appearance pane, you can set the number of recent items that appear in the menu.

Change the Appearance Color and Scroll Bars

1 Click the **System Preferences** icon in the Dock, and then click the **General** icon.

2 Click the **Appearance** pop-up, and then select a color. If you select Other, the Color Picker palette appears so you can select a color.

3 Click the **Highlight Color** pop-up, and then select a color.

4 Click the **Sidebar icon size** pop-up, and then select a size.

5 Click the **Automatically based on mouse or trackpad**, **When scrolling**, or **Always** option to select an how you want to show/hide overlay scroll bars as needed.

6 Click the **Jump to the next page** or **Jump to here** option to select an operation when you click in the scroll bar.

7 Click the **Close** button.

Smooth Fonts

 Click the **System Preferences** icon in the Dock, and then click the **General** icon.

2 Select the **Use LCD font smoothing when available** check box to enable font smoothing, which reduces jagged edges for some fonts.

3 Click the **Close** button.

Change Number of Recent Items

1 Click the **System Preferences** icon in the Dock, and then click the **General** icon.

2 Click the pop-ups for the **Recent Items**, and then select a number.

◆ **Clear Recent Items Submenu.** Click the **Apple** menu, point to **Recent Items**, and then click **Clear Menu**.

3 Select the **Ask to keep changes when closing documents** check box to display an alert.

4 Deselect the **Close windows when quitting an application** check box to restore windows when quitting and re-opening apps.

5 Click the **Close** button.

Setting Up the Desktop

The desktop **background**, or wallpaper, is a picture that serves as your desktop's backdrop, the basic surface on which icons and windows appear. You can select a background picture from the ones provided with OS X (which includes Desktop Pictures (**New!**), such as the Mavericks wave, or Solid Colors, which allows you to create custom colors) or select one of your own in the Desktop & Screen Saver pane in System Preferences. You can select pictures in a variety of formats (such as JPEG, PICT, GIF, TIFF, PDF, or PSD) from your own Pictures folder, another folder you select, or even an iPhoto folder (Photo Library, Last Import, or iPhoto album), and then select options to display them on the screen. When you select a picture from a folder, you can display all the pictures at certain intervals in alphabetical or random order. In addition, you can turn on or off the translucent menu bar effect.

Select a Desktop Background

1. Click the **System Preferences** icon in the Dock, and then click the **Desktop & Screen Saver** icon.

2. Click the **Desktop** tab.

3. Click an image category folder in the left column.

4. Select a thumbnail (**New!**).

5. If you want to use your own folder of pictures, click the **Add** (+) button, select the folder, and then click **Choose**.

 ◆ To remove one of your own added folders, select the folder, and then click the **Remove** (-) button.

6. To show all the pictures in a folder, select the **Change picture** check box, select an interval from the pop-up, and then select the **Random order** check box or clear it for random order.

7. Select the the **Translucent menu bar** check box to enable the menu effect or clear the check box disable it.

8. Click the **Close** button.

Setting Up Screen Savers

In the past, you needed a screen saver (a continually moving display) to protect your monitor from screen burn in. With new technology, those days are gone. Screen savers are more for entertainment than anything else. When you leave your computer idle for a specified wait time, a screen saver displays a continuous scene, such as an aquarium, until you move your mouse to stop it. If a security option is set in the Security & Privacy pane in System Preferences, your computer requires a password when you wake from a screen saver. You can select a slide show or screen saver from the ones provided with OS X, such as Sliding panels or Photo Wall, or select a source, such as National Geographic or a folder on your computer with pictures (all saved in the same format). With iTunes Artwork, you can turn screen saver into a jukebox; just click an album. With iPhoto, you can use onscreen controls to pause or flip through photos in an album.

Set Up a Screen Saver

1. Click the **System Preferences** icon in the Dock, and then click the **Desktop & Screen Saver** icon.

2. Click the **Screen Saver** tab.

3. Click a slideshow or screen saver.

 ◆ Select **Random** to use different screen savers each time.

4. Select from the available options for the selected item:

 ◆ Click the **Source** pop-up, select a default source or **Choose Folder**, and then select one.

 ◆ Select the **Shuffle slide order** check box to shuffle order.

 ◆ Click **Screen Saver Options**, select the option you want, and then click **OK**.

5. Click the **Start after** pop-up, and then select a time when the screen saver starts or **Never**.

6. Select the **Show with clock** check box to show the clock.

7. To activate the screen saver with your mouse pointer, click **Hot Corners**, specify the options you want in the corner you want it, and then click **OK**.

8. Click the **Close** button.

Activate screen hot corners

Select the option you want in the corner you want it.

Setting the Date and Time

The date and time you set on your computer is very important. When you save a file or send and receive an e-mail, your computer uses the date and time you set in the Date & Time preference pane. You can set the date and time manually, or if your computer is connected to the Internet, you can have a time server set it automatically. If you have an Internet connect, such as DSL or cable, use the time server, otherwise you should set it manually. To make sure your files and e-mail times are not off by a few hours, you need to set your time zone, either manually or automatically. When you travel, OS X can automatically change your time zone using Wi-Fi. You can also set the date and time to display as a digital (12:05 PM) or analog (round face with hands) clock in the menu bar, or have the computer speak, announcing the time at certain intervals.

Set the Date and Time

1 Click the **System Preferences** icon in the Dock, and then click the **Date & Time** icon.

2 Click the **Date & Time** tab.

3 To set the time automatically over the Internet, select the **Set date & time automatically** check box, and then use the pop-up to select a time server.

4 To set the date and time manually, use any of the following methods:

◆ Select the individual date and time fields, and then enter a number, or use the up and down arrows.

◆ Click a date in the calendar and drag the hands on the clock.

5 Click the **Time Zone** tab.

◆ To automatically set the time zone, select the **Set time zone automatically using current location** check box.

6 Click the part of the map closest to your location.

7 Click the **Closest City** pop-up, and then select the closest city to your location.

8 Click the **Close** button.

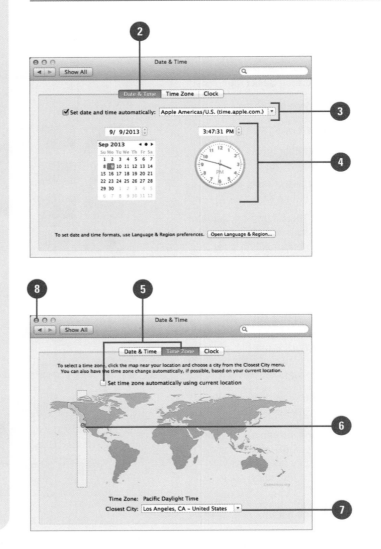

Set Date and Time Options

1 Click the **System Preferences** icon in the Dock, and then click the **Date & Time** icon.

2 Click the **Clock** tab.

3 Select the **Show date and time in menu bar** check box.

4 Select the view as (**Digital** or **Analog**) option you want.

5 Select or clear the following check boxes:

◆ **Display the time with seconds**. Check to add seconds to the time (Menu bar).

◆ **Flash the time separators**. Check to show a blinking colon.

◆ **Use a 24-hour clock**. Check to show military time (18:00 instead of 6:00 PM).

◆ **Show AM/PM**. Check to show AM or PM.

◆ **Show the day of the week**. Check to show the day of the week (Menu bar).

◆ **Show the date**. Check to show the date (Menu bar).

6 To speak the time, select the **Announce the time** check box, click the pop-up, and then select an interval.

To change the computer voice, click **Customize Voice**.

7 Click the **Close** button.

Menu bar

Sun 4:29 PM
Sunday, July 1, 2013

View as Analog
✓ View as Digital

Open Date & Time Preferences...

For Your Information

Using the Menu Bar Clock

When you display the clock in the menu bar, the time appears in analog form or as a clock icon with the current time. If you want to know the date, click the clock. A menu drops down displaying the complete date. The menu also allows you to switch between digital and analog clock types and open the Date & Time pane in System Preferences.

Changing Language & Region Options

The Language & Region pane (**New!**) in System Preferences gives you options to use different languages for menus, dialogs, and the keyboard, as well as write text in other languages. The language you write can be different from the language for menus, dialogs, and the keyboard. You can select international regions, calendars, and formats for dates, times, numbers, and measurement units. In Keyboard Preferences, you can use the Input Sources tab to select a keyboard layout, which lets you type in other languages. If you're not familiar with the keyboard layout, you can use the Keyboard Viewer to show you what keys to press to display the keys you want in the input menu language. To make language selection easier, you can add the Input menu to the menu bar.

Set Language and Formats

1. Click the **System Preferences** icon in the Dock, and then click the **Language & Region** icon.

2. To add a language, click the **Add** (+) button, select a language, click **Add**, and then click the button for the primary language you want (**New!**).

 ◆ **Reorder languages.** Drag a language in the list (**New!**).

3. To remove a language, select it, and then click the **Remove** (-) button.

4. Select the following Language & Region options (**New!**):

 ◆ **Region.** Select a region whose formats are used for dates, times, and currencies.

 ◆ **First day of week.** Select a day to start your week.

 ◆ **Calendar.** Select a calendar type to display dates, times, and currencies.

 ◆ **Time format.** Select or clear the **24-Hour Time** check box to use 24-Hour or 12-Hour time.

 ◆ **List sort order.** Select the way to sort items by name in Finder.

5. To customize date, time, and number formats, click **Advanced**, select the options you want, and then click **OK**.

6. Click the **Close** button.

Languages in use

Advanced options to customize date, time, and number formats

Set Input Sources Options

① Click the **System Preferences** icon in the Dock, click the **Language & Region** icon, and then click **Keyboard Preferences**.

◆ You can also click **Keyboard** icon in System Preferences.

② Click the **Input Sources** tab.

③ To add an input source, click the **Add** (+) button, select a language, select an input source, and then click **Add**.

◆ To locate an input source, enter a name in the Search field.

④ To remove an input source, select the input source, click the **Remove** (-) button.

⑤ To preview a keyboard for an input source, select it in the language list.

⑥ Select or clear the **Automatically switch to a document's input source** check box to use the same or different input sources.

⑦ To change input menu languages from the menu bar, select the **Show Input menu in menu bar** check box.

◆ **Character Viewer.** Click the Input menu on the menu bar, and then click **Show** or **Hide Character Viewer**.

◆ **Keyboard Viewer.** Click the Input menu on the menu bar, and then click **Show** or **Hide Character Viewer**.

⑧ Click the **Close** button.

TIMESAVER *Press ⌘+ Spacebar to switch between the two most recent keyboard layouts. Press Option+⌘+Spacebar to cycle down the list of keyboards.*

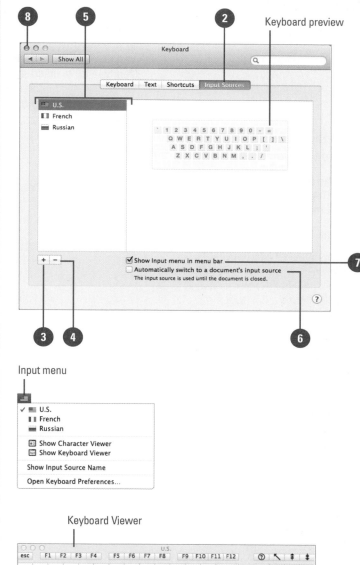

Keyboard preview

Input menu

Keyboard Viewer

Changing Text Substitution Options

The Language & Region pane (**New!**) in System Preferences gives you options to automatically correct common spelling errors and insert symbols as you type. You can add words and phrases that you misspell, or add often-typed words and save time by just typing their initials. You can use text substitution to quickly insert symbols. For example, you can type (c) to insert ©. You can also set options to check spelling and select text by language, and automatically change double or single quotation marks.

Set Symbol and Text Substitution Options

1. Click the **System Preferences** icon in the Dock, and then click the **Keyboard** icon.

2. Click the **Text** tab (**New!**).

 ◆ You can also click **Keyboard Preferences** in the Language & Region pane in System Preferences.

3. Select language and selection settings for the following options:

 ◆ **Correct Spelling.** Select the **Correct spelling automatically** check box to enable spell checking.

 ◆ **Spelling.** Select **Automatic by Language** or a specific language to spell check.

4. Select the **Use smart quotes and dashes** check box (**New!**), and then select options when you type double or single quotation marks.

5. Click the **Close** button.

Add, Edit. or Remove a Text Substitution Entry

① Click the **System Preferences** icon in the Dock, and then click the **Keyboard** icon.

② Click the **Text** tab (**New!**).

③ Do one of the following:

 ◆ **Add.** Click the **Add** (+) button, type a misspelled word or an abbreviation, press Tab, type the replacement text, and then press Return.

 ◆ **Edit.** Double-click an entry, make a change, and then press Return.

 ◆ **Remove.** Select an entry, click **Remove** (-) button.

④ Click the **Close** button.

Add (+) and Remove (-) buttons

Replace Text as You Type

 ◆ To correct spelling errors or insert symbols automatically, continue typing until text substitution makes the required correction.

 ◆ **Enable Correct Spelling.** Click the **System Preferences** icon in the Dock, click the **Keyboard** icon, click the **Text** tab, and then select the **Correct spelling automatically** check box to enable automatic spell checking as you type.

See examples of text substitution in the following table.

Examples of Text Substitution

Type of Correction	If You Type	AutoCorrect Inserts
Common typos	can;t	can't
Common typos	windoes	windows
Superscript ordinals	2nd	2nd
Stacked fractions	1/2	½
Smart quotes	" "	" "
Em dashes	Madison--a small city in Wisconsin--is a nice place to live.	Madison—a small city in Wisconsin—is a nice place to live.
Symbols	(c)	©
Symbols	(r)	®

Saving Energy and Managing Power

When you're not using your computer, you can save energy by putting it to sleep. When you put your computer to sleep, the power mode is set to low and the screen goes black to save energy. Your computer is still running, so it takes less time for it to wake up. While your computer sleeps, you can use Power Nap, if your Mac supports it, when AC plugged in or batter powered to download OS X and app updates and perform Time Machine backups to Time Capsule, so your computer is always up-to-date. You can use the Sleep command on the Apple menu to put your computer right to sleep, or you can put your computer and display to sleep automatically when it has been idle for a specific amount of time or when you schedule it at a regular time interval. You can also set the hard disk to sleep whenever possible to save more energy. If you have a Mac laptop, such as a MacBook, it automatically goes to sleep when you close the lid. You move your mouse or press a key to wake it up. If a security option is set in System Preferences, your computer requires a password when it wakes from a sleep.

Set Sleep Options

1. Click the **System Preferences** icon in the Dock, and then click the **Energy Saver** icon.

2. To enable or disable Power Nap, click the **Battery** or **Power Adapter** tab, and then select or clear the **Enable Power Nap while on battery power** or **Enable Power Nap while plugged into a power adapter** check box.

 TROUBLE? *If Power Nap settings are not available, check Apple for compatibility or perform a firmware update using Software Update on the Apple menu.*

3. Drag the slider to set a time interval for Computer sleep and Display sleep. Drag to **Never** to prevent sleeping.

4. To conserve energy, select the **Put the hard disk(s) to sleep when possible** check box.

5. On the Battery tab, select or clear the **Slightly dim the display while on battery power** check box.

6. Click the **Close** button.

For Your Information

Putting Apps to Sleep with App Nap

App Nap (**New!**) looks at which apps are not doing anything in the background, or which have their windows out of view, and puts them to sleep, just like when you close the lid of your MacBook. When App Nap puts apps to sleep, it provides better performance for other running apps and saves battery life on laptops. When a sleeping app is activated or needed, it immediately wakes up and is ready to go. This is done all behind the scenes. You don't have to do anything.

Set a Sleep, Startup, or Shut Down Schedule

1. Click the **System Preferences** icon in the Dock, and then click the **Energy Saver** icon.

2. Click the **Battery** or **Power Adapter** tab, if available.

3. Click **Schedule**, and then click **Details**, if necessary.

4. Select or clear the **Start up or waker** check box. If so, select an interval from the pop-up, and then set a time.

5. Select or clear the bottom check box. If so, select an operation from the first pop-up menu, select an interval from the second pop-up, and then set a time.

6. Click **OK**, and then click the **Close** button.

Set Wake and Power Failure Restart Options

1. Click the **System Preferences** icon in the Dock, and then click the **Energy Saver** icon.

2. Click the **Power Adapter** tab, if available.

3. Select or clear the **Wake for network access** check box.

4. Select or clear the **Start automatically after a power failure** check box.

5. Click the **Close** button.

Selecting a Startup Disk

Instead of starting from your local hard disk, you can start your computer from a CD or DVD, a network volume, another disk or disk partition (a single hard disk separated into two distinct areas), or another operating system, such as Microsoft Windows. Starting your computer with Windows is useful when you want to use applications that are not compatible with OS X. When you start your computer in Windows, you need to use the Startup Disk Control Panel in the Apple menu to switch back to your OS X startup disk. If Windows is not available in the Startup Disk preference pane, you need to have an Intel-based Mac and use Boot Camp Assistant to set up your computer. You can also restart you computer in Target Disk Mode, which allows you to connect to another computer using a FireWire cable and use it as a hard disk.

Select a Startup Disk

1. Click the **System Preferences** icon in the Dock, and then click the **Startup Disk** icon.

2. Click the icon of the system folder you want to use as the startup disk.

3. To restart your computer, click **Restart**.

 TIMESAVER *Hold down the Option key while you restart your computer, select a startup disk, and then click Restart.*

4. To restart your computer in order to connect to another computer using a FireWire cable, click **Target Disk Mode**, read the dialog for instructions, and then click **Restart**.

See Also

See Chapter 19,"Working with OS X Along with Windows," on page 481 for information on starting your computer with Microsoft Windows 7 or later.

Changing the Way a CD or DVD Starts

When you insert a CD or DVD into your computer, OS X automatically performs an operation, such as opening iTunes and playing an audio CD. You can change what happens when you insert a CD or DVD in the CDs & DVDs preference pane in System Preferences. You can have OS X open a dialog to ask you what to do, ignore it, run a script, or open an application, such as iTunes, iPhoto, iDVD, or Finder, to burn or play a disc. If you ignore a CD or DVD, the disc doesn't show up on the desktop or in a Finder window.

Change CD or DVD Start Settings

1. Click the **System Preferences** icon in the Dock, and then click the **CDs & DVDs** icon.

 TROUBLE? *TIf the device doesn't have a CD or DVD writer/player, the CDs& DVDs icon doesn't appear.*

2. Click the pop-ups for each type of CD or DVD, and then select a startup option:

 ◆ **Ask what to do**. A dialog appears that asks you what to do with the disc.

 ◆ **Open an application**. Select Open Finder, Open application name or click Open An Application to select one.

 OS X automatically opens the application you select.

 ◆ **Run Script**. Select and schedule a script to run.

 ◆ **Ignore**. Nothing happens.

3. Click the **Close** button.

Did You Know?

You can change Finder preferences to show CDs or DVDs on the desktop. Click the Finder menu, click Preferences, click General, select the CDs, DVDs, and iPods check box, and then click the Close button.

Controlling Sound

The Sound pane in System Preferences allows you to adjust input, output and alert volumes, change input and output sound devices, change alert sounds, and play Front Row, an entertainment system, and user interface sound effects, such as when you drag an icon to the Trash. You can use an input device, such as a microphone, to record your voice or give spoken commands on an output device, such as built-in or external speakers, to play music, words, and other sounds. If your computer has two stereo speakers, you can adjust the sound balance between them. If you don't want to hear sound from your speakers, you can turn on Mute, just like on your TV or stereo. If you use applications with volume controls, such as iTunes, the volume can only be equal to or less than the computer's output volume. To make volume control easier, you can add output volume to the menu bar.

Change Sound Effects

① Click the **System Preferences** icon in the Dock, and then click the **Sound** icon.

② Click the **Sound Effects** tab.

③ To change an alert sound, click a sound from the list.

④ Drag the **Alert volume** slider to adjust the alert volume, which is relative to the output volume.

> **TIMESAVER** *Hold down the Option key while you drag the main volume on the status menu bar to adjust the alert volume.*

⑤ To play Finder related sounds, select the **Play user interface sound effects** check box.

⑥ If you have volume keys on your keyboard, clear the **Play feedback when volume keys is changed** check box to disable the feedback option and use the volume keys.

⑦ To change output volume from the menu bar, select the **Show volume in menu bar** check box.

⑧ Click the **Close** button.

 Volume on menu bar

Set Sound Output Options

1. Click the **System Preferences** icon in the Dock, and then click the **Sound** icon.

2. Click the **Output** tab.

3. Select a device for sound output.

 Options vary depending on the output sound device.

4. Drag the **Balance** slider to adjust the sound for the left and right speakers.

5. Drag the **Output volume** slider to increase or decrease the volume, or select the **Mute** check box to turn speaker sound off.

6. Click the **Close** button.

Set Sound Input Options

1. Click the **System Preferences** icon in the Dock, and then click the **Sound** icon.

2. Click the **Input** tab.

3. Select a device for sound input.

 Options vary depending on the input sound device.

4. Drag the **Input volume** slider to increase or decrease the volume.

 The Input level meter displays the sound level coming from the selected sound device.

5. Click the **Close** button.

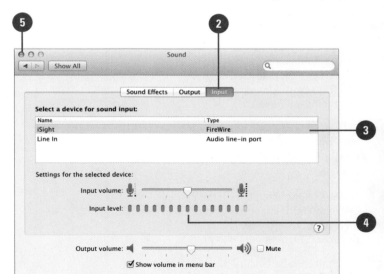

Dictating Your Speech

The Dictation & Speech pane in System Preferences allows you to dictate the text you type using the language you want in OS X or an application, including TextEdit, Preview, and Contacts. When you use the dictation option, the information you dictate is recorded and sent to Apple to convert what you say into text. It also sends other information, such as your first name and nickname and those in your address book for better recognition and conversion. You can click About Dictation and Privacy to find out more details about what gets sent. Before you get started, make sure a microphone available on or connected to your computer, and then enable the option in preferences. You can start the dictation in a place that accepts text by selecting the Start Dictation command from the Edit menu or specifying a keyboard shortcut for easy access when you need it. After you start, a Dictation box appears at the insertion point. At this point, dictate your text, and then click Done to convert it to type. Dictation understands basic commands, such as new line or punctuation (period, comma, etc.) in the current language. If you don't want it converted or it's taking to long, click Cancel. If you want to control the use of dictation for specific users, you can set parental controls in System Preferences.

Setup Dictation Options

1. Click the **System Preferences** icon in the Dock, and then click the **Dictation & Speech** icon.

2. Click the **Dictation** tab.

3. To find out about the information sent to Apple for the dictation conversion, click **About Dictation and Privacy**, read the information, and then click **Done**.

4. Click the **Microphone** pop-up, and then select a microphone attached to your computer, Line In, or Automatic.

5. To set a shortcut to start dictation, click the **Shortcut** pop-up, and then select a default key option, or **Customize** to enter a new key.

6. Click the **Language** pop-up, and then select the language you to use for the conversion.

7. Click the **Close** button.

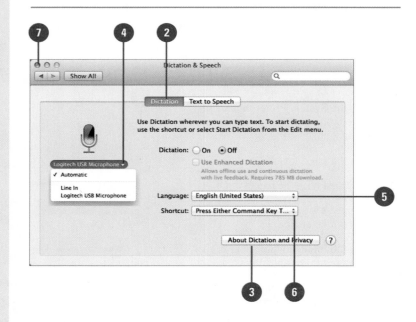

Enable or Disable Dictation in System Preferences

1. Click the **System Preferences** icon in the Dock, and then click the **Dictation & Speech** icon.

2. Click the **Dictation** tab.

3. To enable dictation, click the **On** option, and then click **Enable Dictation** to confirm.

 To disable dictation, click the **Off** option.

4. Click the **Close** button.

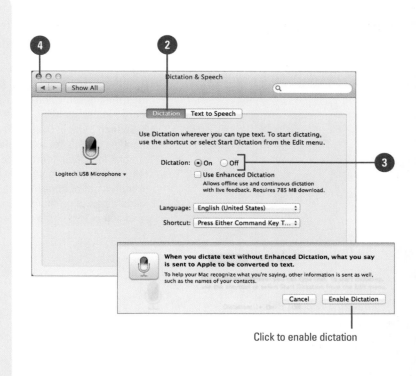

Click to enable dictation

Start and Use Dictation

1. Position the insertion cursor in a place where you want to dictate text, such as an application or Finder.

2. Start the dictation using any of the following:

 ◆ Use the shortcut specified in Dictation preferences; the default is ⌘ ⌘ (**New!**).

 ◆ Click the **Edit** menu, click **Start Dictation**.

 If prompted, click **OK**, and then click **Enable Dictation**.

3. Dictate the text you want converted into type on the screen.

4. Click **Done** in the Dictation box.

 ◆ To stop the conversion, click **Cancel** in the Dictation box.

 The text is converted to type.

Letting Mac Do the Talking

Your Macintosh can speak to you as well as listen. OS X can read aloud what appears on your screen, such as typed text, alert messages, window items, menus, and other interface items. It speaks using a synthesized voice, such as Pipe Organ, Cellos, or Junior. Some voices, such as Pipe Organ, are based on a song and sing the voice. Alex is a new synthesized English voice that uses advanced Apple synthesis to deliver a more natural speaking voice at a faster rate. You can use the Dictation & Speech pane in System Preferences to select a default voice, set talking alert options for when alerts appear on the screen, and other spoken options for the user interface. Instead of just showing you, the Mac can tell you when an application needs your attention, such as when your printer is out of paper, or read buttons, icons, tabs, dialog options, and selected text in e-mails and documents when you point to it as well as read select text when you press a keyboard shortcut.

Set the Default Speaking Voice

1 Click the **System Preferences** icon in the Dock, and then click the **Dictation & Speech** icon.

2 Click the **Text to Speech** tab.

3 Click the **System Voice** pop-up, and then select one of the voices from the list.

◆ Click **Show More Voices** at the bottom of the pop-up to display more voices from which to choose. Click **Show Fewer Voice** at the bottom of the pop-up to reduce the list.

The computer speaks so you can hear the voice, and a description of the voice appears on the right.

4 To change the speed at which the voice speaks, drag the **Speaking Rate** slider.

5 To hear the select speaking voice at the current rate, click **Play**.

6 Click the **Close** button.

Set Spoken User Interface Options

1 Click the **System Preferences** icon in the Dock, and then click the **Dictation & Speech** icon.

2 Click the **Text to Speech** tab.

3 Select the **Announce when alerts are displayed** check box, click **Set Alert Options**, specify the following alert options, and then click **OK**.

◆ **Voice.** Reads the contents of an alert dialog. Use the pop-up to select an alert voice.

◆ **Phrase.** Speak a certain phrase when an alert appears. Use the pop-up to select a phrase.

◆ **Delay.** Drag to set the delay between the alert and the computer speaking.

◆ **Play.** Click to display a sample of the alert.

4 Select the other spoken items option you want:

◆ **Speak selected text when the key is pressed**. Check to read any text you select when you press a key combination.

To change the key combination, click **Change Key**, press a keyboard shortcut or stop speaking selected text, and then click **OK**.

5 Click the **Close** button.

Setting Accessibility Options

The Accessibility pane in System Preferences makes it easier for a person with a disability, such as difficulty seeing or hearing, to use a computer. You can set options to switch the screen to grayscale for more visual contrast, zoom in on the screen in a separate window to make it larger and easier to see, use VoiceOver so you can hear descriptions of screen items, have the screen flash when alert sounds occur, use audio to flash the screen when an alert sound occurs, and use captions (**New!**) to define and select styles for screen subtitles and captions or enable Closed Captions and SDH (subtitles for the deaf and hard of hearing). If you're not sure where to find an option, you can use the Search field. You can set an option to show Accessibility status in the menu bar, where you can also quickly open Accessibility preferences. You can also open the Accessibility pane anywhere on your Mac with the ⌘+Option+F5 keyboard shortcut.

Set Seeing Options

1. Click the **System Preferences** icon in the Dock, and then click the **Accessibility** icon.

2. Click the **Display**, **Zoom**, or **VoiceOver** category.

3. Specify the options you want for the selected category.

 ◆ Display. Select or clear check boxes for the **Invert colors** or **Use grayscale** options. Use the sliders to adjust contrast and cursor size.

 ◆ Zoom. Select or clear check boxes for the **Use keyboard shortcuts to zoom**, **Use scroll gesture with modifier keys to zoom**, **Smooth images**, or **Zoom follows the keyboard focus** options. Set the **Zoom style** to Fullscreen or Picture-in-picture. Click **More Options** to customize the way zoom works.

 ◆ VoiceOver. Select or clear the **Enable VoiceOver** check box.

4. Click the **Close** button.

Search field

Select to show the Accessibility menu in the menu bar

Set Hearing Options

1. Click the **System Preferences** icon in the Dock, and then click the **Accessibility** icon.

2. Click the **Audio** category.

3. Select or clear the any of the following check boxes:

 ◆ **Flash the screen when an alert sound occurs**. To test the screen flash, click **Test Screen Flash**.

 ◆ **Play stereo audio as mono**.

4. Click the **Caption** category (**New!**).

5. Select a style for subtitles and captions. The defaults include Default, Classic and Large Text.

 ◆ **Add or Remove Styles.** Click the **Add** (+) or **Remove** (-) button for the selected style.

6. If you prefer using closed captions and subtitles for the deaf and hard of hearing (SDH), select the **Prefer Closed Captions and SDH** check box.

7. Click the **Close** button.

Search field

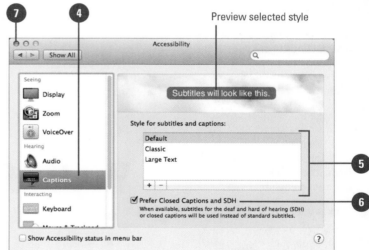

Preview selected style

Setting Accessibility Interacting Options

The Accessibility pane in System Preferences makes it easier for a person with a disability, such as difficulty controlling a mouse or using a keyboard, to use a computer. You can set options to use speech recognition to control your computer, such as using menus, using spoken commands, use switch control (**New!**) to auto scan panels and UI elements—such as Keyboard, Pointer, App, Dock, Menu bar, System, Custom, and Location—to make it easy to select and use them, use Sticky Keys or Slow Keys to help control the keyboard, and use Mouse Keys to make mouse functionality available on the numeric keypad.

Set Keyboard and Mouse Options

1 Click the **System Preferences** icon in the Dock, and then click the **Accessibility** icon.

2 Click the **Keyboard** category.

3 To press a group of modifier keys as a sequence, select the **Enable Sticky Keys** check box, and then click **Options** to set options to **Beep when a modifier key is set** or **Display pressed keys on screen**.

4 To make the keyboard respond more slowly, select the **Enable Slow Keys** check box, and then click **Options** to set options to **Acceptance delay** or the **Use click key sounds** options.

5 Click the **Mouse & Trackpad** category.

6 To use the keyboard number pad to control the mouse, select the **Enable Mouse Keys** check box.

Press 5 on the numeric keypad to click an item on the screen. Press 0 to press and hold, and then press 5 again to release, press and hold.

7 Click **Options** to set the **Initial Delay** for the pointer when you press the mouse or the **Maximum Speed** for the pointer.

8 Click the **Close** button.

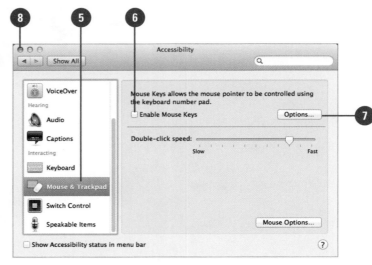

Set Switch Control and Speech Recognition Options

1 Click the **System Preferences** icon in the Dock, and then click the **Accessibility** icon.

2 Click the **Switch Control** category (**New!**).

3 To enable switch control, select the **Enable Switch Control** check box on the General tab.

The Home row of the Switch Control menu appears. With auto scan on (the default), Switch Control steps through the panel.

4 Click the **Switches** tab.

5 To add, remove, or change a selected switch, use the **Add** (+), **Remove** (-), or **Action** buttons.

6 Click the **Navigation** and **Timing** tabs to customize switch control options.

7 To use Switch Control, press the Select Item switch (default set to Space bar) to start auto scan. Continue to press the Select Item to select and work with items.

8 Click the **Speakable Items** category.

9 To use spoken commands, click the **Settings** tab, select the **On** option, and then select and calibrate a microphone.

10 Click the **Listening Key** tab to set the start listening key and method.

11 Click the **Commands** tab to select groups of commands to use.

12 Click the **Close** button.

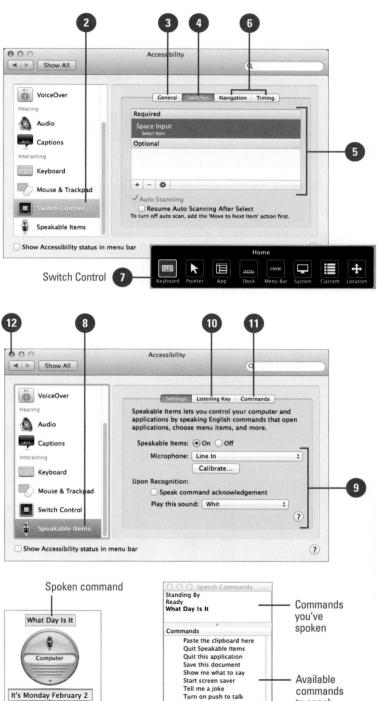

Switch Control **7**

Spoken command

Computer response

Commands you've spoken

Available commands to speak

Having VoiceOver Read from the Screen

VoiceOver is a screen reader utility for OS X that speaks the text in documents and windows. When you open accessible applications in VoiceOver, the application automatically speaks text. For example, Messages speaks new text messages as they arrive.

When you move around your screen or within documents using VoiceOver, a dark rectangle appears, known as the VoiceOver cursor, to indicate the screen focus area for what to speak. You can use your mouse and keyboard with VoiceOver to move and configure the VoiceOver cursor. You can also let VoiceOver help you drag and drop. Simply mark the item you want to drag, then mark the destination and VoiceOver does the rest. VoiceOver uses Apple synthesis to deliver a more natural speaking voice at a faster rate. OS X includes built-in voices that speak 23 languages, which you can customize to suit your needs. You can also download higher-quality versions of the languages from VoiceOver Utility.

VoiceOver also supports **Braille** (with greater display device support, including Bluetooth) and note-takers. If you have a supported Braille display connected to your computer, VoiceOver detects and configures it and can translate output into standard, Grade 2 contracted Braille for use in supported devices. A Braille display shows one line of screen content in a row of Braille cells. You can specify the default level at which you receive the content, known as the braille verbosity level, as well as specific levels for individual controls, such as applications, check boxes, headings, images, and links. In addition, it supports more than 80 braille tables in a wide range of languages.

Getting Started with VoiceOver

Before you can use VoiceOver, you need to turn it on in the Accessibility pane of System Preferences or use the keyboard shortcut ⌘+Option+F5. In addition to turning on VoiceOver, it's a good idea to use the VoiceOver utility to customize VoiceOver so it works the way you want. You can set options in the following areas: General, Verbosity, Speech, Navigation, Web, Sound, Visual,

General

Speech

Commanders, Braille, and Activities. If you have want to use your VoiceOver preferences on all your Macs, you can set up and enable Portable Preferences in the VoiceOver Utility under General settings.

Working with VoiceOver

The easiest way to use VoiceOver is to use the VoiceOver keys, the Control and Option keys together. These are known as VO keys. When used together, the Control and Options keys allows you to control VoiceOver and move the VoiceOver cursor. However, it's easy to get lost. If you do get lost in VoiceOver and you're not sure where the focus is located, you can use the F1 through F6 keys with the VO keys to hear information about items where the VoiceOver cursor, keyboard, or mouse pointer is focused. If you are not sure what a key on the keyboard does in VoiceOver, you can use **keyboard help** to learn the names of the keys. After you start keyboard help, simply, press any key to hear its name. If you like to use the numeric pad on your extended keyboard, you can use **NumPad** and **Keyboard Commanders** using drag and drop to program the keys with

VoiceOver commands. If you prefer using menus instead of VO keyboard shortcuts, you can use one of the VoiceOver menu's to get help with or execute a command. The over-sized white-on-black menu makes it easy to use.

In VoiceOver, you can navigate sequentially through a document or application or skip through by object. You can also create **hot spots** using drag and drop to monitor an object or area in a window and get notification when something changes. If you can't find what you're looking for, you can perform **smart searches** for objects and text in the current window.

When you're browsing the web, VoiceOver can begin reading a web page immediately when it's loaded. It also allows you to intelligently navigate around web pages, including tables to important parts using web spots.

If you use a trackpad, you can control VoiceOver by touching the pad. The surface of the trackpad acts as the active window with each corner representing absolute window coordinates. VoiceOver guides you through the process using voice commands.

Braille

Commanders

Setting VoiceOver Preferences

Before you can use VoiceOver, you need to turn it on in the Accessibility pane of System Preferences. When you turn VoiceOver on, you can configure output over AirPlay or the default audio. In addition to turning on VoiceOver, you can also open the VoiceOver utility, which you can use to set a variety of different options. You can set options in the following areas: General, Verbosity, Speech, Navigation, Web, Sound, Visual, Commanders, Braille, and Activities.

Set VoiceOver Preferences

1 Click the **System Preferences** icon in the Dock, and then click the **Accessibility** icon.

2 Click the **VoiceOver** category.

3 Select or clear the **Enable VoiceOver** check box.

◆ If prompted with the Welcome dialog, click **OK** to continue.

◆ If prompted with a VoiceOver Audio dialog, click **Continue** or **Revert** to configure output.

TIMESAVER *Press* ⌘*+F5 to turn VoiceOver on and off.*

4 Click **Open VoiceOver Utility**.

TIMESAVER *Double-click the VoiceOver Utility icon in the Utilities folder.*

5 Select a category on the left, and then select the options you want.

◆ **General.** Enter a login greeting and select a portable preference option.

◆ **Verbosity.** Specify text and announcement options. Also includes general and instructional hint options. In the Braille tab, you can specify the default level (amount of information you want to receive) for use with a refreshable braille display. You can also set levels for specific controls, such as headings, images, and links.

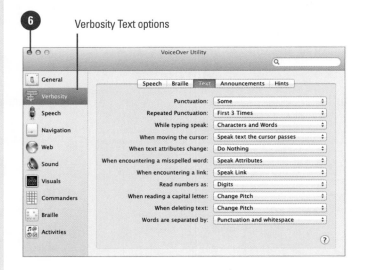

Verbosity Text options

- **Speech.** Specify voice and pronunciation options. You can mute speech or customize the voice rate, pitch, or volume.

- **Navigation.** Specify mouse and keyboard options. You can change VoiceOver cursor tracking options.

- **Web.** Specify web navigation options, either DOM (Document Object Model) or Group (such as paragraph to paragraph).

- **Sound.** Mute sounds and enable positional audio.

- **Visuals.** Specify VoiceOver cursor, Caption and Braille panel, and menu options.

- **Commanders.** Enable NumPad Commander and Keyboard Commander, and customize commands. You can enable, assign, and use Quick Nav to navigate web pages and applications using only the arrow keys and navigate web pages using single keys.

- **Braille.** Specify display and input options.

- **Activities.** Set up activities and customize VoiceOver settings for specific users. You can set up different voices, rates, and hot spots for different situations and applications. You can switch activities manually or have VoiceOver switch them for you based on the application in use.

6 Click the **Close** button for the VoiceOver Utility.

7 Click the **Close** button.

Verbosity Announcements options

Navigation options

Visuals VoiceOver Cursor options

Using VoiceOver Commands

The easiest way to use VoiceOver is to use the VoiceOver keys, the Control and Option keys together. These are known as VO keys. When used together, the Control and Option keys allows you to control VoiceOver and move the VoiceOver cursor. If you're not sure what a keyboard key does, you can enable keyboard help, where you can press any key to hear its name as well as the name of the VoiceOver command. In addition to the VO keys, you can also use the standard keyboard shortcuts that work within OS X. You can quickly turn VoiceOver on and off using a keyboard shortcut, ⌘+F5. If you're using a menu instead of a VO keyboard shortcut, you can use one of the VoiceOver menu's to get help with or execute a command. The oversized white-on-black menu makes it easy to use. In VoiceOver, you can create up to 10 hot spots to monitor an object or area in an accessible window and get notification when something changes.

Use VoiceOver Commands

1 To start or stop VoiceOver, press ⌘+F5.

2 Use the following keyboard shortcuts for help with VoiceOver.

> **IMPORTANT** *On a portable computer where function keys are used of other things, you need to press the Fn key first.*

- ◆ **VoiceOver menu.** VO+F7; use arrow keys to navigate
- ◆ **Item Chooser menu.** VO+I
- ◆ **Windows Chooser menu.** Lists all open windows: VO+F2 twice
- ◆ **Program Chooser menu.** Lists all open programs: VO+F1 twice.
- ◆ **VoiceOver Help.** VO+?; Help for an item: VO+H
- ◆ **Command menu.** Command menu for an item: VO+H+H
- ◆ **Select a menu.** Return
- ◆ **Stop an action or close a menu.** Esc
- ◆ **Keyboard help.** Hear key names on keyboard: VO+K
- ◆ **VoiceOver Utility.** VO+F8

VoiceOver Menu

For Your Information

VoiceOver Keyboard Commands

Using VoiceOver means learning a lot of keyboard commands. You can get a list of the VoiceOver keyboard shortcuts along with the OS X keyboard shortcuts on the web at *www.perspection.com*.

3 Use the following common commands for VoiceOver.

◆ **What's on the screen.** Under mouse: VO+F5; keyboard highlight: VO+F4; VoiceOver cursor box: VO+F3

◆ **Read everything.** VoiceOver cursor: VO+A; In window, Dock, or desktop, VO+Shift+W

◆ **Pause/resume speech.** Press and release Control; press again to resume. Repeat phrase: VO+Z

◆ **Show/Hide caption panel.** VO+Command+F10

◆ **Show/Hide Braille panel.** VO+Command+F9

◆ **NumPad Commander on/off.** VO+Clear

◆ **Navigation.** VO+arrow keys; visible area top or bottom: VO+Home or VO+End

◆ **Links on a web page.** VO+U

◆ **Text in a document.** Read all text: VO+A; read sentence: VO+S; read line: VO+L

◆ **Search.** Find text: VO+F; find hyperlink: VO+Command+L; find graphic: VO+Command+G

4 Use the following commands to create and use hot spots.

◆ **Create Hot Spot.** Select item, and then press VO+Shift+ [number key]

◆ **Go to Hot Spot.** Press VO+ [number key]

◆ **Hear Hot Spot.** Press VO+ Command+[number key]

◆ **Watch for Hot Spot Changes.** Press VO+ Command+Shift+ [number key]

VoiceOver Navigation menu

VoiceOver Commands menu

Setting Ink Preferences

If you have an ink device on your computer, you can use System Preferences to improve the recognition of ink to text. You can adjust Ink Preferences to your writing style, either widely or closely spaced, and to see how quickly your writing pen cursor changes back into a clicking device. You can improve recognition by adding words it may not know, such as names (like a custom dictionary for spell checking). As you write, Ink recognizes certain gestures or shapes, which get performed as commands, such as Undo, or pressed as keys, such as Delete or Space. The Gestures tab provides a list of gestures that you can turn on and off.

Set Ink Preferences

1. Click the **System Preferences** icon in the Dock, and then click the **Ink** icon.

2. Click the **On** or **Off** option to turn handwriting recognition on or off.

3. Click the **Settings** tab.

4. Specify the options you want:

 ◆ **My handwriting style is**. Drag slider to set spacing.

 ◆ **Allow me to write anywhere**. Check to use Anywhere mode.

 ◆ **Language**. Click to select a ink writing language.

 ◆ **Ink pad font**. Click to select a default recognition font.

 ◆ **Show ink window**. Check to use Ink Pad mode.

 ◆ **Show ink in menu bar**. Check to add the Ink menu commands to the menu bar.

5. Click the **Gestures** tab.

6. Select or clear the check boxes to turn gesture actions on and off.

7. Click the **Word List** tab.

8. Use the buttons to add or change uncommon words you use.

9. Click the **Close** button.

Click to adjust additional writing and mouse usage options.

Using OS X Applications

Introduction

Now that you know how to work with the graphical elements that make OS X work, you're ready to work with applications. An **application**, also known as **app**, is software you use to accomplish a specific task, such as word processing or managing files on your computer.

OS X comes with several built-in applications that are useful for creating written documents, creating and organizing contacts, managing calendars, sending and receiving email or instant messaging, browsing the web, communicating online face to face, previewing and marking up images and PDFs, reading and managing iBooks, and viewing and navigating maps. If you need a break, you can also play games as an individual or with other using the Game Center.

Along with the built-in applications, OS X comes with several utilities that are extremely useful for completing basic tasks, such as performing basic calculations, creating sticky notes, capturing screen shots and images from a digital camera, and displaying information with daskboard and widgets. If you deal with a lot of fonts, OS X comes packaged with a font management system second to none.

In addition to the applications and utilities that come with OS X, you also have a multitude of applications developed by third-party developers. You can quickly access, purchase, download, and install these applications using the Mac App Store. If an app is not currently available at the App Store, you can also purchase it directly from the developer over the Internet using the company web site or other retail locations.

What You'll Do

Get Apps from the App Store

Download and Install Other Apps

Use OS X Apps

Launch and Quit Apps

Open Applications and Files

View Full Screen Apps

Switch Between Apps

Play Chess

Play Games with the Game Center

Create and Edit a Contacts List

Manage a Contacts List

Perform Calculations and Conversions

Get and Manage iBooks

Read and Mark Up iBooks

View and Navigate Maps

Capture Images with a Digital Camera

Capture Screen Shots with Grab

Preview Images and PDF's

Use Apps with Auto Save

Create Sticky Notes

Manage Fonts with Font Book

Work with Dashboard and Widgets

With the App Store, you can quickly buy (many are free too!) and download apps to your computer. When an update is available for an app, the developer can use the Apple Push Notification service to let you know. When you start an update, the App Store delivers only the data that is different from the previous version, so it uses Internet bandwidth more efficiently. Before you can start using the App Store to make purchases and download software, you need to sign in with an Apple ID (email and password), which can be the same one used for iCloud, iTunes Store, or Apple Support. If you don't have one, you can click the Sign In link in the App Store, and then click Create Apple ID to create one. After you purchase an app, you can install it free on every Mac or Apple device you own. You can also update an app from Updates or delete an app from a computer or device or remove it from Purchases in the App Store.

Find, Buy, Download, and Install an Application at the App Store

1. Click the **App Store** icon in the Dock, or click the **Apple** menu, and then click **App Store**.

2. Click **Sign In** in Quick Links, enter your Apple ID and password, and then click **Sign In**.

3. If you want to make a purchase using an iTunes gift card or other credit, click **Redeem**, enter your code, and then click **Redeem**.

4. Locate the application you want.
 - Click the **Featured**, **Top Charts** or **Categories** button on the toolbar and then browse.
 - Swipe left or right on the trackpad or mouse to browse.
 - Enter a name in the Search box on the toolbar, and then select an item from the list.

5. Click the app's icon or name, and then click a price or **Free**, and then click **Buy App** or **Install App**.

6. To get download and install status, click the **Purchases** button on the toolbar, or click the **Launchpad** icon in the Dock, and then view the app's icon and progress bar.

Click to view app updates

Sign In link

Click the arrow to share the app link on Twitter or in Messages

Work in the App Store

◆ **Pause or resume a download.** Click the **Purchases** button, find the app in the list, and then click **Pause**, or **Resume**. In Launchpad, click the application icon.

◆ **Cancel a download.** Click the **Purchases** button, find the app in the list, and then click **Cancel**.

◆ **Check for unfinished downloads.** Click the **Store** menu, and then click **Check for Unfinished Downloads**.

◆ **Download and install a purchased app on another Mac.** On the other Mac, open App Store, sign in using the Apple ID that purchased the app, click the **Purchases** button, find the app in the list, and then click **Install**.

◆ **Update an app.** Click the **Updates** button, and then download and install the updates all at once, or individually from the list. All of the updates are free unless specified.

To update all apps, click **Update All** or click the **Update All** arrow, and then click an option: **Install Now**, **Try in an Hour**, **Try Tonight**, or **Remind Me Tomorrow**.

◆ **Uninstall an app from the App Store.** In Launchpad, click and hold down the app icon until all th e icons start to wiggle, and then click the app's **Delete** button (x).

◆ **Remove an app from Purchases.** Click the **Purchases** button, point to the app, and then click the **Delete** button (x).

◆ **Review and change account information.** When signed in, click the **Store** menu, and then click **View Account**, or click **Account** in Quick Links.

Apps purchased Purchases button Status

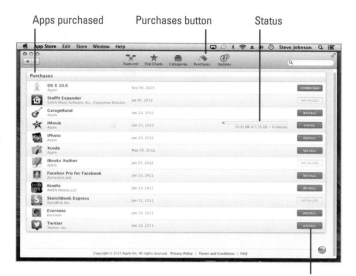

Install an app purchased on another Mac

Updates button Update All options

Delete app from the App Store Launchpad

Downloading and Installing Other Apps

OS X comes with a set of applications automatically loaded during the installation of the operating system, and appear on the hard drive within the Applications folder. All other third-party applications need to be installed separately. You can download applications using the App Store. If an application is not currently available there, you can install a third-party application by inserting the software installation CD or DVD and following the instructions, or by downloading the software from the web in your browser, such as Safari, to your hard disk, uncompressing the file if necessary, starting the installer (typically in a disk image file, .dmg, which mounts as a disk icon), and following the instructions. In some cases, an installer application is not used to perform an installation. In that case, all you need to do is simply drag the software files to your hard disk, typically in the Applications folder. To uninstall an application, simply drag the icon (or its folder) to the Trash.

Install Third-Party Applications Downloaded from the Internet

1 Download the software application from the web.

 When you download or copy a file from a server or connected drive, a progress bar appears in the icon along with a Close button (x) to cancel it.

 Compressed files use these file extensions: **.sit** (standard Mac), **.zip** (standard Windows), **.tar** (tape archive Unix), **.gz** (standard Unix), **.tar.gz**, or **.tgz**

2 If the file is compressed, use the StuffIt Expander application (available at *www.download.com*) to uncompress the file.

 Safari uncompresses it for you into a disk image file (.dmg).

3 Double-click the disk image file (**.dmg**).

 A disk icon from the disk image mounts on your desktop.

4 Double-click the mounted disk icon and the installer (as needed) to start the installer program, and then follow the instructions.

5 Drag the disk image file into the Trash to remove and eject it.

1 Use the Download button in Safari to displays downloads

Download progress bar; click the Close button to cancel it.

Installer app icon

Using OS X Apps

OS X comes with several accessories, built-in applications that, while not as feature-rich as many applications sold separately, are extremely useful for completing basic tasks. A frequently used list of OS X applications is provided here. However, you can view a complete list of installed applications in Launchpad or in the Applications folder. The Applications folder also contains a Utilities folder with additional applications you can use to perform specialized functions, which are detailed more in later chapters.

Frequently Used OS X Applications

Program	Description
App Store	Provides a place to buy, download, and install applications
Automator	Automates tasks using workflows and no programming
Calculator	Performs arithmetic calculations
Calendar (**New!**)	Keeps track of calendar appointments
Contacts	Stores names, addresses, and other contact information
Dashboard	Provides a screen for mini-program called widgets
Dictionary	Provides an illustrated dictionary and thesaurus
DVD Player	Plays sound, music, and video
FaceTime	Makes video calls to other Intel-based Mac computers, iPads, iPhones, or iPod touchs
Game Center	Provides a place to play online games with your friends, wherever they are
Image Capture	Transfers images from your camera to your computer
iTunes (**New!**)	Plays digital sound files
iBooks (**New!**)	Stores, organizes and displays online books for reading and studying
Mail	Provides e-mail, newsgroup, and directory services
Maps (**New!**)	Displays maps and directions for locations and services around the world
Messages	Sends and receives instant messages to online contacts
Mission Control	Shows everything running on the computer and organizes windows into spaces
Notes	Creates and manages notes
Photo Booth	Takes pictures and adds visual effects
Preview	Views, rotates, resizes, crops, and converts image files
QuickTime Player	Plays and edits media located on your computer, a CD, or Internet
Reminders	Creates and manages a reminder list
Safari (**New!**)	Displays web (HTML) pages
Stickies	Creates notes for reminders, lists, and messages
TextEdit	Creates, edits, and displays text, Rich Text Format, and Word documents
Time Machine	Backs up everything on your computer

Launching Apps

All OS X applications are automatically loaded during the installation of the operating system, and appear on your computer within the Applications folder. All other third-party applications need to be installed using the Mac App Store or separately with third-party installer. You can open, or launch, an application several ways. The quickest way is to use Launchpad, which is a full-screen home page for all your applications (now with larger icons. Launchpad is conveniently available in the Dock. Launchpad can contain multiple pages, where you can rearrange or move Apps, organize Apps into folders, and search for Apps. If you no longer want an app in Launchpad (that's not part of OS X), you can uninstall it. In addition to Launchpad, you can also open Apps available in the Dock and the Applications folder.

Open, Find, Move, or Delete an Application from Launchpad

1. Click the **Launchpad** icon in the Dock.

 TIMESAVER *Pinch three fingers and your thumb on the trackpad to start Launchpad.*

2. To move to the next page of Apps, swipe left or right using two fingers, click the gray dots above the Dock (white is the current page), or press the arrow keys.

3. To search for an app, enter the criteria in the Search box. Click the **Close** button (x) to cancel.

4. To open an app, click its icon.

5. To rearrange Apps, drag its icon to a new location.

 ◆ If the location is on another page, drag to the right edge of the screen, pause, let the next page appear, and then release it.

 ◆ To add an app to the Dock, drag it to a Dock location.

6. To uninstall an app, click and hold an app's icon until all apps wiggle, and then click the app's **Delete** button (x). If you want an app back, you need to download it again.

7. To close Launchpad, press Esc or click a blank area in Launchpad.

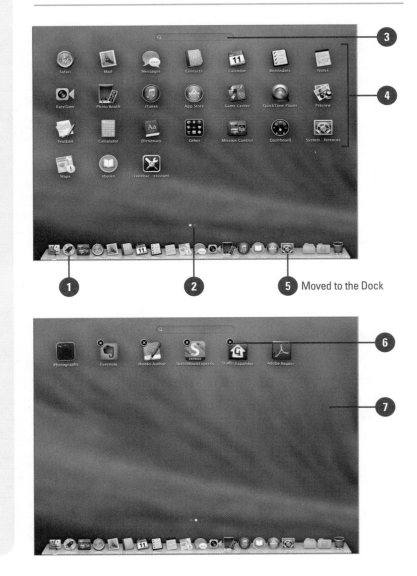

5 Moved to the Dock

Work with Folders in Launchpad

1 Click the **Launchpad** icon in the Dock.

2 Use any of the following folder operations.

◆ **Open a folder.** Click a folder icon.

◆ **Create a folder.** Drag one app's icon over another. Launchpad creates a folder and suggests a name.

◆ **Change a folder's name.** Click to open the folder, click the folder name, and then type a new name.

◆ **Move an app into a folder.** Drag the app onto the folder. Each folder can hold as many as 32 Apps.

◆ **Move an app out of a folder.** Click to open the folder, and then drag the app out of the folder.

Open folder Selected folder name

Folder contents

Open an Application from a Finder Window

1 Double-click the hard drive icon on your desktop.

2 To change views, click a view button, such as View By Columns.

3 Click the **Applications** folder or navigate to the application folder.

4 Double-click on the application name, or application icon, to launch.

Application details are displayed

Opening Apps and Files

As you open applications and files, their names are kept in the Recent Items submenu in the Apple menu for easy access the next time you want to open a specific application or file. The Mac OS has always allowed you to double-click a document icon to launch the application used to create it and the document itself. If the Mac OS doesn't know what application created it (and gives you an error message), you can use drag and drop in the Dock to help you open the document. You can drag a document icon in the Dock onto an application icon. If a document is stored in the Documents folder, you can click the Documents folder in the Dock and then click the document in the stack to open it.

Open Recently Used Applications and Files

1. Click the **Apple** menu, and then point to **Recent Items**.

2. Click the recent application or file under the **Applications** or **Documents** listing.

3. To clear the recent list, click the **Apple** menu, point to **Recent Items**, and then click **Clear Menu**.

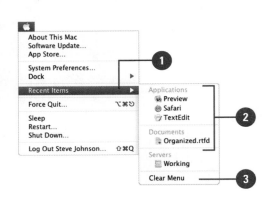

Open Applications and Files

◆ Double-click the document icon.

◆ Drag the document icon to the application icon in the Dock, either the one that created the document or one that will accept it. If the application can possibly open it, the application icon becomes highlighted. Release the icon to open the application and the document.

 NOTE Hold down Option+⌘ while you drag a document icon into the Dock to force all applications to accept the icon. However, an error message may result.

◆ Click the Documents folder in the Dock, and then click a document in the stack list.

Double-click to open Blank icon; no association

Drag icon onto an accepting application icon to open Documents folder

Viewing Full Screen Apps

OS X provides support for full screen Apps, such as Calendar, Mail, Safari, Photo Booth, and QuickTime, and Finder windows (**New!**). Apps and Finder windows (**New!**) built to take advantage of the full screen have a Full Screen button (diagonal double-arrows) in the window title bar. You can have multiple full screen Apps and windows open at the same time. A swipe of the trackpad takes you from full screen to another or back to the desktop. When an app or window is full screen, the menu bar is hidden, which you can access by pointing to the top of the screen, where you can close it.

Work with Full Screen Applications or Finder

◆ **Open full screen.** Click the **Full Screen** button in the right-corner of the window title bar.

◆ **Open full screen on secondary display.** Drag the window to the desired display, and then click the **Full Screen** button in the right-corner of the window title bar.

◆ **Unhide menu bar.** Point to the top of the screen.

◆ **Close full-screen.** Point to the top of the screen to display the hidden menu, and then click the **Full Screen** button.

◆ **Move between full screen Apps.** Swipe left and right, or press the arrow keys.

Click the Full Screen button to expand.

Point to top of the screen to display hidden menu.

Click the Full Screen button to collapse.

Switching Between Apps

The Dock is initially located at the bottom of the desktop and is most often used to launch an application or switch from one application to another. When you launch an application, its icon appears in the Dock with a black arrow below it (when a General preference option is set). If an application is not available in the Dock, you can hide any open applications to display the desktop, open your hard disk, and then launch the application you want. If you arrange open application windows so that they are visible, you can switch among them simply by clicking in the window in which you want to work.

Hide and Show an Application

1 Click the application menu.

In this case, the Chess menu.

2 Click **Hide *application name*** to hide the application.

TIMESAVER *Press ⌘+H to hide the application.*

3 Point to the bottom of the screen to display the Dock. You'll see the hidden application in the Dock.

4 To show the application, click the application icon in the Dock.

Hide Other Applications

1 Click the application menu, and then click **Hide Others**.

TIMESAVER *Press Option+ ⌘+H to hide all other applications.*

Did You Know?

You can bring forward an application and its windows and hide all other applications. Hold down Option+ ⌘, and then click the program icon in the Dock.

Switch Between Applications

OS X provides several ways to switch between applications:

◆ Click a visible window in the other application.

◆ Display the Dock, and then click an application icon to show or launch the application.

◆ Press and hold down ⌘, and then repeatedly press the Tab key to highlight the Dock icon of an open application. (Use Shift+⌘+Tab to move backwards) Release both keys when you reach the one you want to open.

To leave without switching applications, press the Esc key.

TIMESAVER *Press ⌘+Tab once to open the application you used most recently. This is very useful when you are switching between two applications.*

◆ Press F11 (use Exposé) to hide all open windows, double-click the hard disk icon, open the Applications folder, and then double-click an application icon.

Did You Know?

You can quickly switch between windows within an application (including the Finder). Repeatedly press ⌘+~ (the Tilde key to the left of the number 1 key) to cycle through open windows in the application. Release both the keys to display the window you want.

Click menu to hide application Click window to switch

Active window Click icon in the Dock to switch

For Your Information

Opening a Document with a Different App

Most documents on your computer are associated with a specific application. For example, if you double-click a document whose file name ends with the three-letter extension ".txt," OS X automatically opens the document with TextEdit, a word processing application. There are situations, though, when you need to open a document with a program other than the one OS X chooses, or when you want to choose a different default program. For example, you might want to open a text document in Microsoft Word rather than TextEdit so that you can take advantage of advanced features. To do this, Control-click the document icon you want to open, point to Open With, and then click the application you want to use to open the document, or drag the file onto the application icon in the Dock.

...ps

When you're done working with an application, you should exit, or close it, to conserve your computer's resources. If an application stops responding while you work, OS X provides you with the option to end the task. When you end a task, you'll probably lose any unsaved work in the problem application. If the problem persists, you might need to reinstall the application or contact product support to fix the problem.

Quit an Application

1. Click the application menu.

 In this case, the Chess menu.

2. Click **Quit** *application name.*

 TIMESAVER *Press ⌘+Q to quit an application.*

3. If necessary, click **Save** to save your changes.

Quit an Application That is Not Responding

1. Click the **Apple** menu, and then click **Force Quit**.

 TIMESAVER *Press ⌘+ Option+Esc to force a quit.*

2. Click the application name you want to force a quit.

3. Click **Force Quit**.

4. Click **Force Quit** again to confirm you want to force a quit.

5. Click the **Close** button.

Playing Chess

CHECKMATE, oh how I love to hear that word, or at least when I'm the one saying them. Computers aren't just for business, worksheets, and documents. We all know that there are thousands of games available, but one of the most challenging games in the world is available as soon as you load OS X. Chess gives you more options, and even makes it quite a challenge to those who have moved beyond the beginner stage. After you start Chess, you can sign in to the Game Center with your Apple ID and password to play with others online, save high scores, and view chess achievements.

Play Chess

1. Click the **Launchpad** icon in the Dock, click the **Other** folder, and then click the **Chess** icon.

 ◆ If prompted, enter your Apple ID and password, and then click **Sign In** to use the Game Center for online gaming, or click **Cancel** to disable it.

2. Click and drag a piece.

3. Black responds with a move.

4. Click the **Moves** menu, and then click **Take Back Move**, **Show Hint**, **Show Last Move**, **Game Log** (toggle on/off), or **Achievements**.

5. Click the **Chess** menu, and then click **Preferences**. Select from the following options:

 ◆ Click the **Board** pop-up to select a new playing surface.

 ◆ Click the **Pieces** pop-up to select different playing pieces.

 ◆ Select the check boxes for Speech to use voice recognition to call your moves.

 ◆ Drag the **Computer Plays** slider to increase or decrease the computer's playing skills.

6. Click **OK**.

7. Click the **Game** menu, and then select a game option, such as New Game or Save Game.

8. Quit Chess.

Playing Games with the Game Center

The Game Center is a social gaming network you can use to play games by yourself or with your friends all over the world on a Mac, iPad, iPhone, or iPod touch. You can quickly buy (many are free too!) and download games from the App Store that work with Game Center. Before you can start using the Game Center, you need to sign in with an Apple ID (email and password) or create one. You can add your friends by making a request, or by accepting a request from another player. With Parental Controls preferences, you can allow or restrict others from joining games and adding friends. With Notifications preferences, you can specify Game Center alerts. You can check out leaderboards and see how you high score ranks against scores around the world. The Game Center also recommends games and players, so you can start a multiplayer game with others you know or don't know, as well as have an in-game voice chat to talk with opponents or team members.

Get Started with Game Center

1. Click the **Launchpad** icon in the Dock, and then click the **Game Center** icon.

2. Enter your Apple ID and password, and then click **Sign In** or click **Create Apple ID** to create one.

3. If prompted, review the terms and conditions, select the check box, and then click **Accept**.

4. Enter a nickname.

5. Select or clear the **Public Profile** check box to make your profile visible, and use your nickname on public leaderboards.

6. Select or clear the **Use Contacts for Friend Suggestions** check box to upload your contacts.

7. Click **Continue**.

8. To add photo, click **Change Photo**, and then choose or take a picture.

9. To edit account information, click **Account: *email address***, and then click **View Account**, modify options, and then click **Save**.

10. To sign out, click **Account: *email address***, and then click **Sign Out**.

Play Games with Friends

1. Click the **Launchpad** icon in the Dock, click the **Game Center** icon, and then sign in.

2. To add games, click the **Games** tab, click **Find Game Center Games** to open the App Store, click the app you want, and then follow the instructions to download and install it.

3. To add friends, click the **Friends** or **Request** tab, click **Add Friends**, enter your friend's email address or nickname, and then click **Send**.

 ◆ To respond to a request, click the **Requests** tab, click the request, and then click **Accept** or **Ignore**.

4. To play a game, select one:

 ◆ **Yourself.** Click the **Games** tab, click a game, and then click **Play Game**.

 ◆ **With Friends.** Click the **Friends** tab, click a friend, click a game, and then click **Play**.

 ◆ **With Challengers.** Click the **Challengers** tab, click a challenger, and then click **Play**.

5. To view games, scores, and achievement levels, select one:

 ◆ **Scores.** Click the **Games** tab, click a game, and then click **Leaderboard**.

 ◆ **Achievement.** Click the **Games** tab, click a game, and then click **Achievements**.

 ◆ **For Friends.** Click the **Friends** tab, click a friend, and then click **Games** or **Points**.

6. To sign out, click the **Me** tab, click **Account:** *email address*, and then click **Sign Out**.

7. Quit Game Center.

Creating a Contacts List

When you work with Contacts, you have the ability to create cards of information. Each card can hold all the information you want to keep on a contact, no matter how many phone numbers and e-mail addresses a particular friend or company might have. In addition, you can add a picture with a drag and a drop. Contacts comes packaged with a bunch of features such as: label generation, change of address notification, synchronization with Apple iCloud or iTunes (across Mac and Windows computers and iOS5 or later devices including iPhone, iPad, or iPod touch), Google Contacts, or Yahoo! Address Book, view Messages Buddy status, and even the ability to use speech recognition to look up and search the Contacts.

Create a Contacts List

1. Click the **Contacts** icon in the Dock.

2. Click the **View** menu, and then click **Show Groups**.

3. To create a group, click the **File** menu, and then click **New Group**, give the new group a descriptive name, and then press Return.

4. Click a group or **All Contacts** you wan to use .

5. To add an existing contact to a group, drag it to the group name.

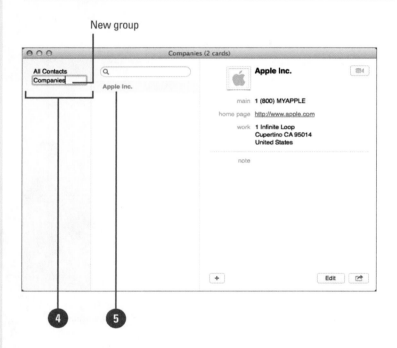

New group

Did You Know?

You can select and update your "me" card. Contacts automatically creates an address "me" card for you with information you entered during set up. Other applications, such as Calendar, Messages, and Mail, use information from your "me" card. You can keep some or all of the information private and exclude it when you send your card to contacts. To display your "me" card, click the Card menu, and then click Go to My Card. To use another card as a "me" card, select the card, click the Card menu, and then click Make This My Card.

For Your Information

Importing Contacts from Twitter and Facebook

When you're set up for Twitter and Facebook in the Internet Accounts pane of System Preferences, you can have OS X automatically add your Twitter and Facebook friends, including profile and contact information, to Contacts. If a Twitter or Facebook friend updates any information, it automatically gets updates in Contacts too.

6 Click the **New Card** (+) button to add a new card.

7 Type a Name, and then using the Tab key, type a Company Name (if necessary). If so, select the **Company** check box.

8 Press Tab or click in card fields to add information such as: Phone number, e-mail address, home address, Internet home page, and Instant Messaging user name, such as a Facebook, Google Talk, Skype, or AIM screen name.

If you enter an IM or AIM user name, you can view Messages Buddy status while browsing contacts.

9 To change a field name, click on the **Field** pop-up, and then select a field or click **Custom**.

10 To add a field, click the **Card** menu, point to **Add Field**, and then select a field type.

11 If a field is not needed, click the **Remove** button (-) to remove it.

12 Click **Done**.

13 Quit Contacts.

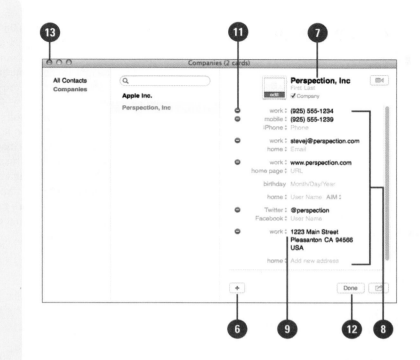

Did You Know?

You can archive your Contacts data. If your Contacts data is important, you can back up the data in case of a catastrophic failure. Open Contacts, click the File menu, point to Export, and then click Contacts Archive. The file name comes with the date of the archive. All you have to do is select where you'd like to save the archive, and then click Save. To restore the data, click the File menu, and then click Import. Select the archive file with the correct date, and then click Open.

For Your Information

Importing Contacts from Yahoo!

Contacts lets you import and sync Yahoo! contacts by simply adding a Yahoo! account using the Add (+) button on the Accounts tab in Contacts Preferences. When you add a Yahoo! account, all your Yahoo! contacts are imported into Contacts. When you make a change to a Yahoo! contact in Contacts, the change is updated on your Mac and Yahoo! Address Book. You can view Yahoo! contacts separately from groups or with all contacts.

Importing Addresses into Contacts

Contacts creates and reads vCards, the standard method of exchanging data between applications. If you have vCards in another application, such as an e-mail application, you can import or export addresses with Contacts. To create a vCard, drag an address card out of the Contacts window. You can drag individual vCards in and out of the Contacts window. To import a set of vCards, click the File menu, click Import, select the vCards file that contains the exported addresses, click Open, and then click OK (if you're updating contact information, click Review Duplicates to reconcile conflicts).

Editing a Contacts List

Once a contact is placed within Contacts, it's a simple matter to edit or add information concerning a contact. Editing or updating a contact involves the same skills learned in creating a contact, with the exception that the information is already there, so all you need to do is edit, add, or delete the contact. You can add, change, and remove fields—including yearless birthdays—as well as put a face with a name by inserting an existing or capture a new iPhoto picture. In addition, you can also use the information in Contacts to start other operations: click an address to see a Google map of the location, click a URL to open the website, click an email address to send an email or start a FaceTime video call, press and hold an email to access social network profiles, such as Facebook, or click the green circle (which indicates online status) next to a contact picture to invite a contact to text chats in Messages, AIM, or other chat application.

Edit a Contact List

1. Click the **Contacts** icon in the Dock.

2. Click the **View** menu, and then click **Show Groups**.

3. Click the group or **All Contacts** you want to modify.

4. Select the Name from the available cards in the Group.

5. Click **Edit**.

 IMPORTANT *The Edit button is a toggle button, and once it's clicked, the name changes to Done.*

Did You Know?

The Address Book application remembers your location. When you open the Contacts, it loads the Group that you had last used.

You can delete a group. Select the group, click the Edit menu, click Delete Group, and then click Delete to confirm.

Search bar

⑥ Click in any of the fields to edit the existing information.

◆ **Change a field name.** Click on the **Field** pop-up, and then select a field or click **Custom**.

◆ **Add a field.** Click the **Card** menu, point to **Add Field**, and then select a field type.

◆ **Remove a field.** Click the **Remove** button (-) next to it.

⑦ To add or change a picture, double-click the picture frame, select a picture (Defaults, Recents, or Camera), adjust zoom, or Apply an effect), and then click **Done**.

⑧ Click **Done**.

⑨ To remove a contact from the list, select a contact, press the Delete key, and then confirm your delete.

⑩ To use information to start other tasks, click the label next to the field, and then select a command (varies based on field type), such as Map this Address, Send Email, FaceTime, Search with Spotlight, or Open URL.

⑪ Quit Contacts.

Did You Know?

You can let the Contacts read a contact to you. Control-click an item in the contact window, point to Speech, and then click Start Speaking. To end the audio, Control-click, point to Speech, and then click Stop Speaking.

You can search for Contacts info in Google or Spotlight. Control-click a searchable item (such as name or phone) in the contact window, and then click Search with Google or Search with Spotlight.

Editing field

For Your Information

Printing from Contacts

Contacts makes it easy to print a mailing list or print labels. The expanded Print dialog provides options to select a printing style and specify the specific fields from Contacts you want to include in the printing. To print a mailing list or labels from Contacts, click the File menu, click Print, select a printer from the pop-up, select Lists or Mailing Labels from the Style pop-up, select a paper size from the pop-up, select an orientation, select or clear the attributes (fields) to display the information you want (such as phone, e-mail, address, Instant Messenger, photo, job title, etc.), select a font size from the pop-up, specify the number of copies, preview the results in the left pane, and then click Print.

Managing and Sharing a Contacts List

Unlike paper address books, Contacts in OS X can create a very organized system... if you know what to do. You can create individual contacts and then put them in groups. With Contacts, you can manage your groups and the contacts, and then share them with others. You can even use the vCard format to exchange contact information between various programs or set up synchronization and sharing with iCloud, iTunes, Google Contacts, or Yahoo Address Book. With iCloud or iTunes, you can sync across multiple computers (Mac and Windows) and devices using iOS5 or later, including iPhone, iPad, or iPod touch. With Google, you can import and sync contacts in Contacts with their online accounts. In Contacts preferences, you can add accounts and search for contacts and addresses using CardDAV, Microsoft Exchange 2007 or later, LDAP (Lightweight Directory Access Protocol) servers, iCloud, or Yahoo!.

Manage a Contacts List

1. Click the **Contacts** menu, and then click **Preferences**.

2. Click **General** to organize the viewable screen.

3. Make any of the following changes: Display Order, Sort By, Address Format, and Font Size.

4. Click **Accounts** to create and synchronize your Contacts.

5. To create an account, click the **Add** (+) button, fill in the account information, and then click **Create**.

 ◆ **Account type.** Select an account type: CardDAV, Exchange, LDAP, iCloud, or Yahoo!.

 Yahoo! imports all contacts in the account into Contacts.

 ◆ **User name and password.** Enter a username and password.

 ◆ **Server address.** Enter the server address.

6. To enable or disable accounts, select the account, and then click the **Enable this account** check box.

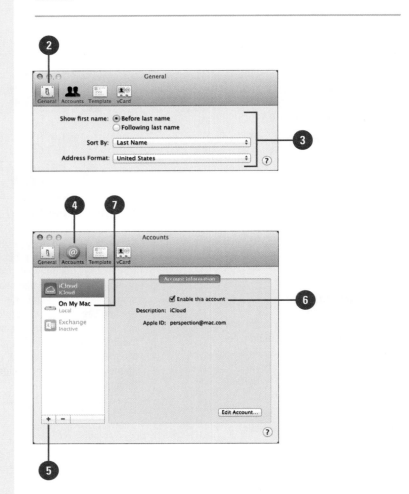

7 To synchronize a Google account, click **On My Mac**, click the check box for the account you want, click **Configure**, and then follow the on-screen instructions.

- ◆ **iCloud.** You can enable/disable synchronization in iCloud preferences.

- ◆ **iTunes.** You can enable/disable synchronization in iTunes (see page 341 for details).

8 Click **Template** to organize the card data screen.

9 Make changes to the template. Use the **Add Field** pop-up or **Add** (+) button to add fields; use the **Delete** (-) button to remove fields.

10 Click **vCard** to set the preferences for vCards.

11 Make any of the following changes: vCard Format, vCard 2.1 Encoding, Enable Private 'Me' Card, Export Notes in vCards, and Export Photos in vCards.

12 Quit Address Book.

Click to add additional contact fields.

Did You Know?

You can share my card with Email, Message, or AirDrop. Click the Card menu, point to Share My Card, and then click Email My Card, Message My Card, or AirDrop My Card.

You can exchange contacts in Contacts with other Mac users. Select a contact, click the File menu, point to Export, and then click Export vCard.

For Your Information

Using Directory to Share Information

Directory is an application, located in the Utilities folder, that allows you to share information about people, groups, locations, and resources within your organization. If you have access to your organization's directory server or Active Directory, you can configure Directory and authenticate your personal information using the Directory Utility in the Utilities folder. You can create shared contacts from your Contacts, use e-mail addresses to send e-mail using Mail, use names to chat in Messages, or load group web services in Safari.

Performing Calculations and Conversions

OS X comes with a great tool to help you perform common calculations and to do complex conversions. The Calculator application has been around for a long time, however, OS X gave it a few powerful features, that just might make you want to reacquaint yourself with an old friend. If you're like most people, you probably have a dozen calculators laying about your home and office. If you're tired of all the mess, then take a look at the Mac's idea of a calculator. Not only does it help you add 2 + 2; it helps you convert miles into kilometers or the Euro dollar into American currency. The Calculator application gives you the ability to perform conversions on everything from currency to volume, from temperature to speed, and more.

Work with the Calculator

1. Click the **Launchpad** icon in the Dock, and then click the **Calculator** icon.

2. Click the buttons on the calculator to perform standard calculations.

3. Click the **Window** menu, and then click **Show Paper Tape** to display a Paper Tape dialog, which shows all of your calculations.

4. Click **Clear** to clear the tape, or click **Recalculate Totals** to have the calculator refigure the total.

5. Click the **File** menu, and then click **Print Tape** to have a paper copy of your calculations.

6. Click the **View** menu, and then click **Scientific** to have access to a scientific calculator.

7. Quit Calculator.

Did You Know?

You can use the keypad with the Calculator. If you have a 10-keypad, instead of trying to click the calculator buttons, just use the keypad. The Calculator automatically reads the keypad objects, and display the results in the calculation window.

Work with Conversions

1. Click the **Applications** folder in the Dock, and then click the **Calculator** icon.

2. Enter a value into the calculation window.

3. Click the **Convert** menu, and then click **Currency**.

4. Click the **Convert** pop-up, and then click **Currency**. If you need to change the convert type, click the Convert pop-up and make your change.

5. Click the **From** and **To** pop-ups to select currency countries.

6. If available, click **Update** to access the latest exchange rate (requires an Internet connection).

7. Click **Convert**.

 The conversion results display in the calculation window.

8. Quit Calculator.

Conversion results

Did You Know?

You can save calculation results in memory. Click the M+ (memory add) button to save a calculation result or to add a calculation result to the value residing in memory. At any time during the calculation, if you want to use that result, click the MR (Memory Recall) button and the number reappears. In addition, you can use the M- (memory subtract) to subtract a displayed result from the value in memory, or the MC (Memory Clear) button to clear out the memory.

Getting and Managing iBooks

The iBooks app is an electronic bookshelf that allows you to purchase, organize, read, and mark up online books. If you already use iBooks on your iPad, iPhone, or iPod touch, the books in your Apple ID account are available in iBooks on your Mac (**New!**) with the use of iCloud. iCloud syncs your iBooks to all your devices, and even remembers which page you're on, so you can continue reading on any device. You can purchase (many are free too) and download books from the iBook Store, which works very much like the App Store, where you can get almost any book under the sun. You can use the Store menu to sign in or out and view your Apple ID account information.

Get Started with iBooks

1. Click the **Launchpad** icon in the Dock, and then click the **iBooks** icon.

2. If prompted, do the following:
 - Click **Agree** to the license agreement.
 - Click **Get Started** in the Welcome screen.
 - Click **Sign In**, and then enter your Apple ID.

3. If you're in the iBooks Store, click **Library** on the toolbar.

4. To view books, click a view tab: **All Books**, **Collections**, **Authors**, **Categories**, or **List**.

5. To find a book, enter a name in the Search box, and then select a suggestion from the list.

6. To change the sort by, click the **Sort By** button arrow, and then select an option or click a heading column in Lists view, and then click the Sort arrow.

7. To enable syncing, click the **iBooks** menu, click **Preferences**, click **General**, select the **Sync bookmarks, highlights, and collections across devices** check box, and then click the **Close** button.

8. Quit iBooks.

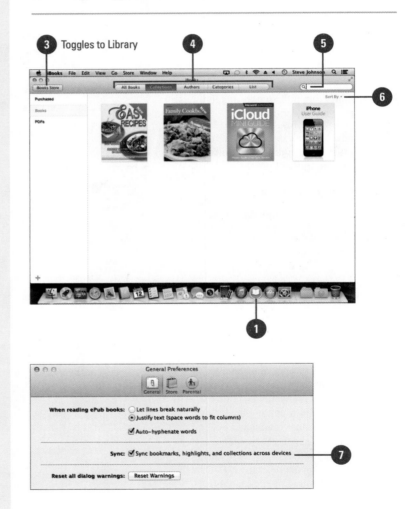

Toggles to Library

Get Books from the iBooks Store

1. Click the **Launchpad** icon in the Dock, and then click the **iBooks** icon.

2. Click **iBooks Store** on the toolbar.

3. Locate the book you want.

 ◆ Click the **Featured, Top Charts NY Times**, or **Top Authors** button on the toolbar and then browse.

 ◆ Swipe left or right on the trackpad or mouse to browse.

 ◆ Enter a name in the Search box, and then select an item from the list.

4. To view more details about a book, click the book's icon or name. To return to the book list, click the **Back** button on the toolbar.

5. To get a book, click **Free**, or click **Buy Book**, and then click **Buy**.

 ◆ To read the book, click **Read**.

6. To view downloads and install status, click the **Downloads** button on the toolbar.

 ◆ To check for available book updates and downloads, click the **Store** menu, click **Check for Available Downloads**, and then click **OK**.

7. To return to the library, click **Library** on the toolbar.

8. Quit iBooks.

Did You Know?

You can show purchases in iCloud. In iBooks, click the View menu, and then click Show Purchases in iCloud to select it with a check mark.

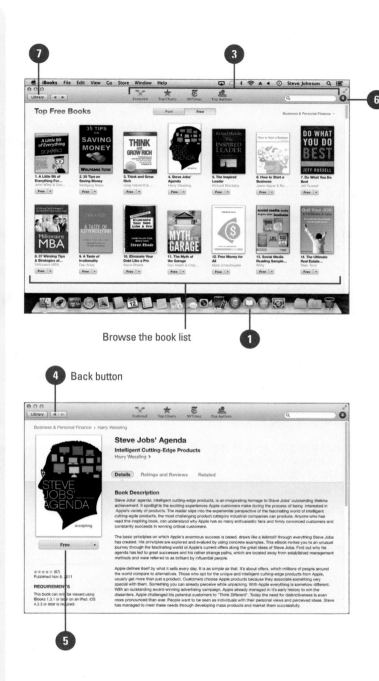

Browse the book list

Back button

Reading and Marking Up iBooks

With iBooks (**New!**), you can read and work with books using the same techniques as other touch devices, such as turning a page with a swipe, zooming in on image with a pinch, or scrolling from cover to cover. You can open as many books as you like and search through them to help you find what you need. When you quote a passage from a book while writing a report or paper, iBooks adds a citation for you. When you take notes, highlight passages, or add a bookmark, iCloud syncs them to all your devices. iCloud also remembers which page you're on, so you can continue reading on any device.

Open and Read iBooks

1 Click the **Launchpad** icon in the Dock, and then click the **iBooks** icon.

2 Locate the book you want.

◆ Click the **All Books**, **Collections**, **Authors**, **Categories**, or **List**. button on the toolbar and then browse.

◆ Swipe left or right on the trackpad or mouse to browse.

◆ Enter a name in the Search box.

3 Double-click a book to open it.

4 To navigate pages, point to the right or left side of the page, and then click the **Arrow** button, or swipe right or left.

5 To use the toolbar, point to the book title to display it.

◆ **iBooks Library.** Click to return to the iBooks library.

◆ **Table of Contents.** Click to display and navigate a TOC.

◆ **Show Notes.** Click to work with highlight and notes.

◆ **Appearance.** Click to change the look and font.

◆ **Search.** Use to find content.

◆ **Bookmarks.** Click to add or remove bookmarks.

6 To close a book, click the **Close** button.

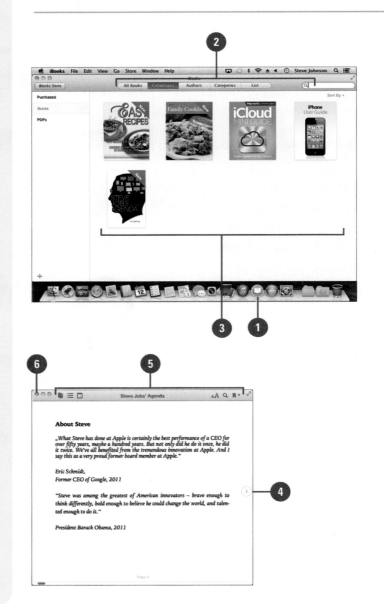

Mark Up Books

1. Click the **Launchpad** icon in the Dock, and then click the **iBooks** icon.

2. Double-click the book you want to open.

3. To find specific content, click the **Search** button on the toolbar, and then enter a work or page number.

4. Select the text you want to use or mark up, and then use the menu:

 ◆ **Highlight.** Click a highlight color or underline.

 ◆ **Add a Note.** Click **Add Note**, and then enter a note in the sticky note.

 ◆ **Share.** Point to **More**, and then click **Facebook**, **Twitter**, **Messages**, or **Email**.

 ◆ **Search.** Point to **More**, and then click **Search Book**, **Search Web**, or **Search Wikipedia**.

5. To bookmark a page, go to the page, and then click the **Bookmark** button on the toolbar.

 ◆ **Navigate to a Bookmark.** Click the **Bookmark** button arrow on the toolbar, and then click a bookmark.

 ◆ **Remove a Bookmark.** Go to the bookmark, click the **View** menu, and then click **Remove Bookmark**.

6. To view or hide notes and highlights, click the **Show Notes** button on toolbar.

 ◆ **Navigate.** Click an item in the Notes panel to display it.

7. When you're done, click the **Close** button to save and exit the book.

8. Quit iBooks.

Highlighted text

Highlights and notes in the Notes panel

Viewing and Navigating Maps

With the Maps app (**New!**), you can view map locations and get directions. You can view maps three different ways: standard (illustrated), hybrid (satellite with street illustrations), and satellite (flyover with photo-realistic images). With Location Services, you can always keep track of your current location. Maps makes it easy to get information on points of interest, like restaurants and hotels, showing you phone numbers, photos, and even Yelp reviews. Once you find a place, you can get directions, real-time traffic conditions, and suggested alternate routes. If you like a place, you can bookmark it or drop a pin. When you're ready to go, you can send your map to your iPhone via Email, Messages, AirDrop, Twitter, or Facebook for voice navigation. Whenever you see an address in Mail, Contacts, and Calendar, you can display a map for its location.

View and Navigate Maps

1. Click the **Launchpad** icon in the Dock, and then click the **Maps** icon.

2. If prompted, click **OK** or **Don't Allow** to use your current location.
 - You can enable or disable Location Services for Maps in Privacy preferences.

3. To find a street address or point of interest, enter it in the Search box, and then select a suggestion from the list as desired.

4. To go to the current location, click the **Go to Current Location** button on the toolbar.

5. To change the view, click the **Standard**, **Hybrid**, or **Satellite** button on the toolbar.

6. To zoom in and out, click the **Zoom In** (+) and **Zoom Out** (-) in the lower-right corner of the screen.

7. To switch to 3D, click the **3D** button on the toolbar. To adjust the camera angle, hold down the pointer on the **Compass**, while you drag up and down. You may need to zoom in to see 3D objects.
 - **Flyover views.** In Hybrid or Satellite view, drag the map with the mouse or two fingers.

8. Quit Maps.

Location Services on menu bar

Current location

Compass

Location Services menu

Use to enable or disable Location Services for Maps

Get Directions

1. Click the **Launchpad** icon in the Dock, and then click the **Maps** icon.

2. Click the **Directions** button on the toolbar to open the Directions sidebar.

3. In the Start and End box, enter a location, and then select a suggestion as desired.

 ◆ **Scale for Map.** Click the **View** menu, and then click **Show Scale** or **Hide Scale**.

4. Click the **Car** or **Walk** button to select a mode of transportation, and then click **Directions**.

5. To zoom in on a direction, click it in the Directions sidebar.

6. To display traffic conditions, click the **Traffic** button on the toolbar.

 ◆ Orange dots show slow downs, and red dots show stop-and-go traffic.

7. If a marker or pin appears on the map, click it for more details. Click the **Info** icon for more options.

8. To mark a location with a pin, click the **View** menu, click **Drop Pin**, and then drag the pin.

 ◆ To remove a pin, select it, click the **View** menu, and then click **Remove Pin**.

9. To share a map or add a bookmark, click the **Share** button on the toolbar, and then click a method or click **Add Bookmark**.

 ◆ To go to a bookmark, click the **Bookmark** button, and then click the bookmark name.

10. To cancel the directions or start over, click **Clear**. To close the sidebar, click **Close**.

11. Quit Maps.

Traffic marker

Bookmarks button

Display and options from Info icon

Dropped pin/bookmark

Capturing Images with a Digital Camera

OS X has provided you a way to directly access your digital camera and organize your images and even sounds. Just plug in your digital camera or scanner directly, and import your pictures or sounds from any application that supports Services and Rich Text Format (most digital cameras and scanners). Image Capture lets you download all or selected contents from your digital camera, rotate images, and even delete unwanted pictures from your camera. You can even use Image Capture to take a picture using the Take Picture command on the File menu or scan an image when a compatible device with a camera or scanner—with an automatic document-feeder or flatbed—is connected to your computer. In addition, you can use the images to create a slideshow or format them for printing.

Capture Images with a Digital Camera

1 Plug a digital device into your computer.

2 If necessary, click the **Launchpad** icon in the Dock, click the **Other** folder, and then click the **Image Capture** icon.

3 If necessary, select the device you want to use.

4 Click the **Import To** pop-up, and then select a location to download the images.

5 To select some images to import or modify, hold down ⌘, and then click the individual images you want or hold down the Shift key and then click a start and end image to select a range.

6 To rotate or delete selected images, click **Rotate Left**, **Rotate Right**, or **Delete** buttons.

7 To delete images after import, select the **Delete after import** check box.

8 Click **Import** to move only selected images or click **Import All** to move all the images from the digital device to your destination.

9 Quit Image Capture.

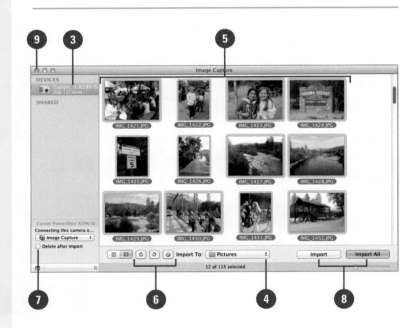

Capturing Screen Shots with Grab

If there is something on your computer screen, such as an error dialog, window, or desktop, that you want to capture as a picture to show someone, you can use a built-in utility called Grab to get the job done. Grab is useful for taking pictures of different parts of the screen, like the ones in this book. This may not be a tool you'll use everyday (unless you are a computer trainer or book author), but it may come in handy one day.

Capture Screen Shots with Grab

1. Display the screen you want to capture.

2. Click the **Launchpad** icon in the Dock, click the **Other** folder, and then click the **Grab** icon.

3. Click the **Capture** menu, and then select the command with the method you want to use:

 - ◆ **Selection.** Drag to select a capture area.

 - ◆ **Window.** Click the **Choose Window** button, and then click a window.

 - ◆ **Screen.** Click a screen.

 - ◆ **Timed Screen.** Click the **Start Timer** button, display a screen, and then wait 10 seconds.

4. Click the **File** menu, and then click **Save**.

5. Select the drive and folder in which you want to save the file.

6. Type a name for the file, and then click **Save**.

7. Quit Grab.

Did You Know?

You can show a pointer in a screen capture. Click the Grab menu, click Preferences, click a pointer type or the blank one for no pointer, and then click the Close button.

Grab app in Applications folder

Selection method

Window method

Screen method

Timed Screen method

Previewing Images and PDF's

Need a quick way to view images, or possibly a Portable Document File (PDF)? No problem, the built-in PDF viewer, Preview, lets you quickly view graphics and PDF files as a full screen app. Preview works to open images or documents, which are not identified by another program, regardless of type. You can open iWork documents and most Microsoft Office documents. When you open a PostScript or EPS (Encapsulated PostScript) file, Preview converts the file into the PDF format. You can open multiple PDFs in a single document window or import scan images in Preview. When you've opened a PDF file, Preview lets you perform an improved indexed search with a sidebar display, select text and embedded images and copy it to the clipboard, and even view FAX documents. In the Sidebar, you can view by thumbnails, table of contents, highlights and notes, and bookmarks (**New!**) for easy access. You can also open and view multiple image files as a contact sheet. If you want to add text or outlined text (**New!**) comments, annotations (such as speech and though bubbles, highlights and notes, or a strikethrough), or even signatures—using a camera from a handwritten signature—to a PDF, you can get easy access to these tools by using the Edit toolbar (**New!**). With the Smart Magnify tool, you can focus on a specific part of an image or PDF. If you want to adjust image size or color levels, you can use the Adjust Size or Adjust Color commands on the Tools menu for high-quality results. As you make changes to a file, Preview periodically saves it as you work, however, you can also explicitly save snapshot versions.

Set Preview Preferences

1. Click the **Launchpad** icon in the Dock, and then click the **Preview** icon.

2. Click the **Preview** menu, and then click **Preferences**.

3. Click any of the following icons:

 ◆ **General.** Sets options to open files in a single or separate windows.

 ◆ **Images.** Sets options for scaling images.

 ◆ **PDF.** Sets options for scaling PDFs, opening and viewing documents, and annotations.

 ◆ **Signatures.** Allows you to scan a signature with an iSight or FaceTime camera.

4. Click the **Close** button.

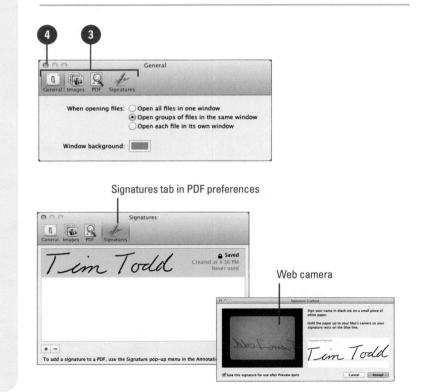

Signatures tab in PDF preferences

Web camera

Preview Images and PDF's

1. Click the **Launchpad** icon in the Dock, and then click the **Preview** icon.

2. Click the **File** menu, click **Open**, select one or more document or image files, and then click **Open**.

3. To view/change the Sidebar display, click the **View** button, and then click **Content Only**, **Thumbnails**, **Table of Contents**, **Highlights and Notes**, **Bookmarks (New!)**, or **Contact Sheet**.

4. To move between pages in a PDF or images, click an item in the Sidebar.

5. To increase or decrease the view size, click the **Zoom In** or **Zoom Out** buttons. To use Smart Magnify, click the **Tools** menu, and then click **Show Magnifier** or **Hide Magnifier**.

6. To select a portion of a document or image, click the **Show Edit Toolbar** button, click a selection tool button (**Text** or **Rectangle**) (**New!**), and then drag to select it.

7. To modify a selected image, click the **Tools** menu, and then click **Adjust Size** or **Adjust Color**.

8. To draw or add notes, text, outlined text (**New!**), speech or thought bubble, signatures on the document, click the **Show Edit Toolbar** button, and then use the toolbar buttons.

 ◆ To create or insert a signature, click the **Signature** button, and then click **Create Signature from <device>** or a signature.

9. To print, display the document or select a portion of it, click the **File** menu, and then click **Print**.

10. To save a version, click the **File** menu, and then click **Save**.

11. Quit Preview.

Smart Magnify tool

Show/Hide Edit Toolbar button Search bar

Search results in Sidebar Added signature Highlighted search results in document

Using Apps with Auto Save

Some Apps—including Preview, TextEdit, and Automator—in OS X come with Auto Save, which automatically saves document changes as you work. Auto Save works in the background to save only your changes, so you don't need to do anything unless you want to. Auto Save adds only the changes directly into the file, so there's only one file to manage. If you don't want your changes, you can revert to a previous version using a Time Machine timeline. Saved versions get pruned as needed to keep them manageable. If you need a copy of a document, you can make a duplicate. If you don't want others to make changes to a document, you can lock it. If you don't make changes to a document for two weeks, OS X automatically locks the document for you. When you open it again, it asks if you want to unlock it.

Use Auto Save and Versions

1 Open the app with Auto Save, and then open or create a document.

2 Click the **File** menu, and then click **Save**. To force a Save As, press ⌘+Shift+Option+S.

3 If a document is locked, click **Unlock**. To duplicate a locked document, click **Duplicate**.

4 To tag, lock, or duplicate a document, use the following:

◆ **Tag a document.** Click the document name arrow, and then specify tags (**New!**).

◆ **Lock/Unlock a document.** Click the document name arrow, and then select or clear the **Locked** check box (**New!**).

◆ **Duplicate a document.** Click the **File** menu, and then click **Duplicate** or press ⌘+Shift+D.

5 To revert to or delete a version, click the **File** menu, point to **Revert To**, click a version (for a revert), or click **Browse All Versions**, and then use the following:

◆ **Revert to saved.** Display the version, and then click **Restore**. To cancel, click **Done**.

◆ **Delete a version.** Click the document name arrow, and then click **Delete This Version**.

Assign tags **4**

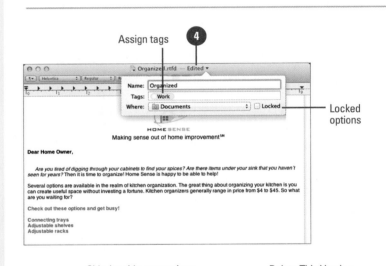

Locked options

Side-by-side comparison Delete This Version

Current version **5** Use to select versions

Creating Sticky Notes

The Sticky Notes application is not new to OS X, however it does give you the ability to tack notes onto your desktop; where they stay until removed. Just think, no longer do you need to worry about the sticky note on your monitor losing its "stick" and falling off. You can use your desktop the way Apple intended—to help with everyday life. Once you create a sticky note, you can change the color of the note, change the color and size of the text, or even have your sticky note talk to you by turning on the speech mode through the Edit menu.

Create Sticky Notes

1. Click the **Launchpad** icon in the Dock, click the **Other** folder, and then click the **Stickies** icon.

 When you first open the Stickies application, you'll see 3 pre-written stickies notes.

2. Click the **File** menu, and then click **New Note**.

3. Type the text into the note area.

4. To increase or decrease the note size, drag the lower-right corner of the sticky note.

5. Click the **Font** menu, and then select from the font options.

6. Click the **Note** menu, and then select between **Floating Windows** or **Translucent Windows**.

7. To change the color of the selected note, click the **Color** menu and make your change.

8. Click the **File** menu to import or export notes, archive your notes, and to print or save your notes.

9. Click the **Close** button to quit without saving.

10. Quit Stickies.

It's easy to customize your notes.

Make your notes stand out and get noticed.

- Format text using different **fonts** and font sizes
- Add emphasis with **bold** and *italic* text styles or color.
- Include graphics ⬚.

Stickies has lots of other great features, including a spell checker, import and export features, and other ways to arrange and customize your notes. Plus, you'll find a "Make New Sticky Note" service in many applications.

Look in Help to find out more about

Make a note of it!

Stickies lets you keep notes (like these) on your desktop. Use a Stickies note to jot down reminders, lists, or other information. You can also use notes to store frequently used text or graphics.

- To close this note, click the close button.

- To collapse this note, double click the title bar.

Your current notes appear when you open Stickies.

Make plans for the family vacation for this summer.

Managing Fonts with Font Book

Most of us have fonts...a whole lot of fonts. OS X organizes fonts into main folders: User and Computer. Fonts in the User folder reside in your Home folder for private use, while fonts in the Computer folder are available for all users. Besides these folders, you can also organize your fonts into specific user-defined folders, known as collections, and then activate those folders, or specific fonts within the folder without having to restart your application. To automate a collection, you can create an Smart Collection based on a search criteria. In addition, Font Book gives you a window to view the font, and change its viewing size.

Manage Fonts with Font Book

1. Click the **Launchpad** icon in the Dock, click the **Other** folder, and then click the **Font Book** icon.

2. Click the **Add Collections** (+) button, type a name, and then press Return.

3. Click the **Add Fonts** (+) button.

4. Select the fonts you want to add to the New Collection (active folder).

5. Click **Open**.

6. Select a collection from the Collection column, and then click on a font to view a sample.

7. To increase or decrease the view of the font in the window, drag the view slider up or down.

8. To copy a font, click and drag a font from the Font window into another Collection.

9. If necessary, type search criteria to locate specific fonts.

10. To remove a font from a Collection (this does not delete the file from the hard drive), select a font, and then press the Delete key.

11. To create a Smart Collection, click the **File** menu, click **New Smart Collection**, enter a name, specify a search criteria, and then click **OK**.

12. Quit Font Book.

Type collection here

Activating, Deactivating, and Customizing Fonts

Once you've created a series of font collections, it'll be necessary to instruct the Font Book application as to what fonts you want to use, and what fonts you want to turn off. It's important to understand that fonts consume memory on your computer. For example, if you have hundreds of fonts active (and that's not unusual), it takes more RAM memory to maintain those fonts; even if you're not using them. That's where font management comes into play. Using Font Book, you can decide what fonts you need, and what fonts can be retired, or disabled, for the remainder of the work session.

Activate and Deactivate Fonts

1. Click the **Launchpad** icon in the Dock, and then click the **Font Book** icon.

2. To deactivate a collection or a font, select the collection or font, click **Disable**, and then click **Disable** to confirm.

 IMPORTANT *The Enable button is a toggle, when a font is active, it displays the word On, and when a font is disabled it displays the word Off.*

3. To activate selected fonts, select one of more fonts from the Font column, and then click **Enable**.

 If a font is disabled, it says Off to the right of the font.

4. Quit Font Book.

Disabled Font window

2 Selected font

3

Did You Know?

You can find duplicate fonts. If a dot appears next to a font family, it means you have a duplicate. You can correct the problem by disabling the one you don't want. Select the version you want, click the Edit menu, and then click Resolve Duplicates.

You can locate a font on your computer. Select the font, click the File menu, and then click Reveal In Finder.

Working with Dashboard

Dashboard is a OS X screen that gives you quick access to widgets, such as news headlines and updates, slide shows, weather information, traffic maps, Internet radio streams, and slide shows of online photo albums. The Dashboard is a full screen oriented app, which is available to the left of your desktop and in Launchpad. **Widgets** are mini-applications that can connect to web services, such as an RSS feed (which automatically delivers web content to your desktop), or integrate with many of your applications, such as viewing your calendar. OS X comes with a set of widgets to get you started, which includes the Calculator, Weather, World Clock, and Calendar widgets by default. However, you can easily download more widgets online. You can quickly open Dashboard by pressing the F12 key. If you prefer a different shortcut key, you can select one in the Mission Control pane of System Preferences.

Work with Dashboard

◆ **Show or Hide Dashboard.** Press F12.

◆ **Move a Widget.** Drag it to another location.

◆ **Add Widgets.** Click the **Add** (+) button in the lower-left corner, and then click a widget on the Widget screen. Click a blank area to cancel.

◆ **Create Folders for Widgets.** Drag a widget icon onto another icon, just like Launchpad.

◆ **Search for Widgets.** Click the **Add** (+) button in the lower-left corner, click in the Search box on the Widget screen, and then type the keyword you want to find.

 As you type the results that match your criteria appear. Click the **Close** (x) button to cancel the search.

◆ **Remove Widgets.** Click the **Remove** (-) button in the lower-left corner, and then click the **Close** (x) button in the lower-left corner of the widget. Click the Remove (-) button to exit.

 TIMESAVER *Point to an individual widget, press Option, and then click the Close (x) button.*

Dashboard widgets

Click to remove a widget

Click to add a widget

Click to exit the Dashboard

Change Dashboard Preferences

① Click the **Apple** menu, and then click **System Preferences**.

② Click the **Mission Control** icon.

③ Select the **Show Dashboard as a space** check box or clear it to hide the Dashboard in Mission Control.

④ Click the **Show Dashboard** pop-up, press a keyboard modifier (Shift, Control, Option, or ⌘) if you want, and then select the shortcut key you want.

 If you want to see more shortcut options, hold down the Shift, Control, Option, or Command keys, or a combination of the keys, while you view the pop-up menu.

⑤ If you have a Mighty Mouse, Magic Mouse, or other multi-button mouse, you can use the other pop-up to set mouse button shortcuts.

⑥ Click the **Close** button.

Did You Know?

You can add pre-installed widgets to the Dashboard. Press F12, click the Add (+) button, and then click a widget, which includes Contacts, Dictionary, ESPN, Flight Tracker, Movies, Ski Report, Stickies, Stocks, Tile Game, Translation, Unit Converter, and Web Clip. In fact, you can add more than one of the same widget, such as two World Clocks for two different times around the world.

⑥

Mission Control

◄ ► Show All

Mission Control gives you an overview of all your open windows, thumbnails of your full-screen applications, and Dashboard, all arranged in a unified view.

☑ Show Dashboard as a Space ─── ③

☑ Automatically rearrange Spaces based on most recent use

☑ When switching to an application, switch to a Space with open windows for the application

☑ Group windows by application

☑ Displays have separate Spaces

Keyboard and Mouse Shortcuts

With a single keystroke, view all open windows, windows of the current application, or hide windows to locate an item on the desktop that might be covered up.

Mission Control:	^ ↑	–
Application windows:	^ ↓	–
Show Desktop:	F11	–
Show Dashboard:	F12	–

(for additional choices press Shift, Control, Option, or Command)

Hot Corners... ⑦

④ ⑤

Adding and Removing Dashboard Widgets

Even though OS X comes with a wide range of commonly used widgets, there is always room for more. Developers are continually creating new widgets, which you can download from the Internet and install onto your computer. If you no longer use a widget on the Dashboard, you can remove a pre-installed widget from the Widget screen, or remove a widget you installed from your computer.

Install a Dashboard Widget

1. Press F12 to open Dashboard.

2. Click the **Add** (+) button in the lower left corner to display the Widget screen with the installed widgets.

3. Click **More Widgets**.

4. Browse the widget web site to find the widget you want to download and install.

5. Click the widget's Download button.

 The installer should automatically start. If it doesn't, double-click the downloaded file. If the file is compressed, you need to uncompress it first.

6. Click **Install**.

7. Click **Keep** to keep the widget or click **Delete** if you decide not to keep it.

8. Press F12 to exit Dashboard.

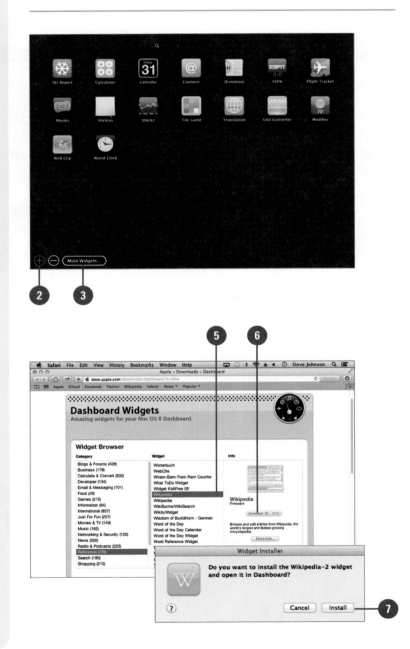

Did You Know?

You can make widgets available to all users. Move or copy the widget into the Widgets folder in the Library folder for your computer from the similar Library folder in your Home folder. All the OS X pre-installed widgets are stored in the Widgets folder for your computer.

Remove an Installed Dashboard Widget

1 Press F12 to open Dashboard.

2 Click the **Add** (+) button in the lower left corner to display the Widget screen with the installed widgets.

3 Click the **Remove** (-) button in the lower left corner.

A Close (x) button appears on icons for widgets you installed; the ones pre-installed cannot be removed.

4 Click the **Close** (x) button in the lower-left corner of the widget.

5 Click **Delete** to confirm the removal.

6 Press F12 to exit Dashboard.

Did You Know?

You can customize a widget. When you point to a widget on the Dashboard and a small info (i) button appears, you can customize the widget. Click the small info (i) button to display the settings you can change. The available options vary depending on the widget.

Creating a Web Clip Dashboard Widget

You can also create your own widgets by using Web Clips or Dashcode. A Web Clip widget is a container for a web page you can add to the Dashboard. When you open the Web Clip widget in Dashboard, the web page associated with it opens. If you're a developer with a basic knowledge of HTML, JavaScript, and CSS, you can create your own Dashboard widget using Dashcode. Dashcode is out of the scope of this book. For more information on Dashcode, go to the Apple Developer Connection web site.

Create a Web Clip Dashboard Widget

1. Launch Safari, and then display the web page you want to make into a Web Clip widget.

2. Click the **File** menu, and then click **Open in Dashboard**.

3. Move the page to highlight the area you want to use, and then click the mouse button.

4. To reposition the highlighted area, drag the area. To resize it, drag the circular handles on the edges of the box.

5. Click **Add**.

6. To customize the widget, point to it, click the small info (i) button, and then specify the options you want:

 ◆ **Edges.** Displays thumbnails of different edge styles. Click the style you want.

 ◆ **Only Play Audio in Dashboard.** Select or clear the check box to play or not play audio in Dashboard.

 ◆ **Edit.** Click to select a different highlighted area.

7. When you're finished, click **Done**.

Working with Documents

Introduction

OS X comes with a word processing application, called TextEdit, you can use to create basic documents. TextEdit is designed especially for working with text, so it's a snap to create and edit letters, or any other word-based communication. TextEdit contains all the tools and features you need to produce interesting documents that say exactly what you mean, and have the look to match.

TextEdit is a versatile word-processing application. You can use TextEdit to view, create, and edit documents containing multi-lingual text, graphics, movies, and other document files. If you are working with HTML code (document as they appear in a web browser), TextEdit makes the perfect editor. If you have speakers connected to your Macintosh, you can hear documents read aloud by your computer. When you're done working with a document, you can save it in multiple formats, such as plain text, Rich Text Format (RTF), Microsoft Word, and Portable Document File (PDF).

Tools, such as the Spelling Checker and Dictionary, help you present your thoughts accurately, clearly, and effectively. When your text is complete, you can quickly add formatting elements, such as bold type and special fonts, to make your documents look professional. Each document contains simple styles that have common design elements. Apply the existing styles for headings, titles, body text, and so forth. Then modify the styles, or create your own to better suit your needs. Make sure you get the look you want by adding emphasis using italics, boldface, and underline, changing text alignment, adjusting line and paragraph spacing, setting tabs and indents, creating bulleted or numbered lists, and adding tables. When you're done, your document is sure to demand attention and convey your message in its appearance.

What You'll Do

Create and Open a Document

Edit Text

Recognize Handwriting Ink

Make Corrections

Make Text Substitutions

Check Spelling and Grammar

Look Up Words with Dictionary

Find and Replace Text

Format Text

Display Rulers

Set Paragraph Tabs and Indents

Change Character Spacing

Change Line Spacing

Add Lists and Tables

Apply and Create a Style

Insert Special Characters

Add Pictures, Movies, or Files to a Document

Save and Close a Document

Set TextEdit Preferences

Creating and Opening a Document

A **document** is a file you create using a word processing program, such as a letter, memo, or resume. When you start TextEdit, a blank document appears in the work area, known as the document window. You can type information to create a new document and save the result in a file, or you can open an existing file (using the Sidebar and List or Column view) in various formats, and save the document with changes. You can also add pictures, movies, and files in your documents. If iCloud is enabled, the iCloud Document Library opens, where you can create or open documents on iCloud or on your Mac (On My Mac).

Create a Document

① Click the **Launchpad** icon in the Dock, and then click the **TextEdit** icon.

If the iCloud Document Library dialog opens, click **iCloud** or **On My Mac**, and then click **New Document**. See page 365 for more details on using the dialog.

If TextEdit is already open, click the **File** menu, and then click **New**.

② To change the file format, click the **Format** menu, and then click **Make Plain Text** or **Make Rich Text**.

③ Type your text.

◆ **Character picker.** To quickly use an accented letter, hold down the letter to display a dialog, and then press a number with the one you want.

④ Press Return when you want to start a new paragraph.

⑤ When you're done, save and close the document.

Document window

Character picker

Press and hold "e" to display the character picker.

Did You Know?

You can set the file format for all new documents. Click the TextEdit menu, click Preferences, click the Plain Text or Rich Text option, and then click the Close button.

For Your Information

Understanding Document Formats

You can open and edit plain text, HTML (HyperText Markup Language, which displays web pages in a browser), Rich Text Format (RTF), Rich Text Format Directory (RTFD), and Microsoft Word files in TextEdit. However, you can only save files in the plain text, RTF, and Word format. Plain text files use the file extension **.txt**, RTF files use **.rtf**, and Word files use **.doc**. If you add graphics to an RTF file, the file extension changes to **.rtfd**. The RTF and Word formats can include formatting, pictures, and other embedded files, while the plain text format can only include nonformatted text. In a plain text document, you cannot change preset tabs and font styles and colors are not saved. Since Microsoft Word is a full featured word processing application, not all Word features, such as tables, are supported in TextEdit.

Open an Existing Document from Within an Application

1. Click the **File** menu, and then click **Open**.

 If iCloud is turned on, the iCloud Document Library dialog opens, click **iCloud** or **On My Mac**. See page 365 for more details on using the dialog.

2. Select the folder location folder in which you want to open the file.

3. Click the document you want to open.

4. If the document contains one or more languages, click the **Plain Text Encoding** pop-up, and then select **Unicode** (for multiple languages) or a specific language.

5. If you want to open a HTML document or create a plain text document, select the **Ignore rich text commands** check box.

6. Click **Open**.

iCloud disabled

Where pop-up

Open a Recent Document

1. Click the **File** menu, and then point to **Open Recent**.

2. Click the recently opened document you want to re-open.

Did You Know?

You can remove all recently used documents from the Open Recent sub-menu. Click the File menu, point to Open Recent, and then click Clear Menu.

Editing Text

One of the advantages of using a word processing program is that you can edit a document or change the contents without re-creating it. In the TextEdit work area, the mouse pointer changes to the I-beam pointer, which you can use to reposition the insertion point (called navigating) and insert, delete, or select text. Before you can edit text, you need to highlight, or select, the text you want to modify. Then you can delete, replace, move (cut), or copy text within one document or between documents even if they're different programs. When you cut or copy an item, it's placed on the Clipboard, which stores only a single piece of information at a time. You can also move or copy selected text without storing it on the Clipboard by using drag-and-drop editing.

Select and Edit Text

1. Open a document, and then move the I-beam pointer to the left or right of the text you want to select.

2. Click, and then drag the pointer to highlight the text.

 TIMESAVER *Double-click a word to select it; triple-click a paragraph to select it.*

3. Perform one of the following editing commands:

 ◆ To replace text, type your text.

 ◆ To delete text, press the Delete key.

Insert and Delete Text

1. Click in the document to place the insertion point where you want to make the change.

 ◆ To insert text, type your text.

 ◆ **Character picker.** To quickly use an accented letter, hold down the letter to display a dialog, and then press a number with the one you want.

 ◆ To delete text, press the Delete key.

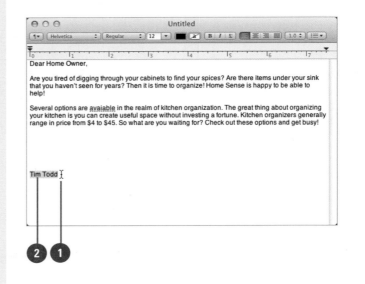

Move or Copy Text

1. Select the text you want to move or copy.

2. Click the **Edit** menu, and then click **Cut** or **Copy**.

 TIMESAVER *Press ⌘+X to cut or press ⌘+C to copy.*

3. Click where you want to insert the text.

4. Click the **Edit** menu, and then click **Paste**.

 TIMESAVER *Press ⌘+V to paste.*

Move or Copy Text Using Drag and Drop

1. Select the text you want to move or copy.

2. Point to the selected text, and then click and hold the mouse button.

 If you want to copy the text to a new location, also press and hold the Option key. A plus sign (+) appears in the pointer box, indicating that you are dragging a copy of the selected text.

3. Drag the selected text to the new location, and then release the mouse button (and the Option key, if necessary).

4. Click anywhere in the document to deselect the text.

Untitled

Dear Home Owner,

Are you tired of digging through your cabinets to find your spices? Are there items under your sink that you haven't seen for years? Then it is time to organize! Home Sense is happy to be able to help!

Several options are avaiable in the realm of kitchen organization. The great thing about organizing your kitchen is you can create useful space without investing a fortune. Kitchen organizers generally range in price from $4 to $45. So what are you waiting for? Check out these options and get busy!

Tim Todd
Home Sense, Inc.

Dear Home Owner,

Are you tired of digging through your cabinets to find your spices? Are there items under your sink that you haven't seen for years? Then it is time to organize! Home Sense is happy to be able to help!

Several options are avaiable in the realm of kitchen organization. The great thing about organizing your kitchen is you can create useful space without investing a fortune. Kitchen organizers generally range in price from $4 to $45. So what are you waiting for? Check out these options and get busy!

Check out these options and get busy!

Tim Todd
Home Sense, Inc.

Dear Home Owner,

Are you tired of digging through your cabinets to find your spices? Are there items under your sink that you haven't seen for years? Then it is time to organize! Home Sense is happy to be able to help!

Several options are avaiable in the realm of kitchen organization. The great thing about organizing your kitchen is you can create useful space without investing a fortune. Kitchen organizers generally range in price from $4 to $45. So what are you waiting for?

Check out these options and get busy!

Tim Todd
Home Sense, Inc.

Recognizing Handwriting Ink

Although typing information into an document or e-mail through the keyboard is fast and efficient, you may find that you need to enter information in handwritten form, known as **ink**. Programs that accept ink, such as TextEdit or Mail, provide handwriting recognition to help you convert handwriting into text. Before you can insert handwritten text into a document, you need to have an ink device, or a handwriting tablet, such as Wacom, attached to and installed on your computer. With handwriting recognition turned on in the Ink pane in System Preferences, you can write in two ink modes: Anywhere or Ink pad. Anywhere mode is useful for writing in a word processing document. As you write in Anywhere mode, your ink strokes appear in a yellow lined translucent overlay. As the Mac recognizes the writing, it converts the ink to text, inserts it in the open document, and erases it from the overlay. When you need to use the mouse, you need to turn off Anywhere mode. Ink pad provides a floating window in which you can use the stylus to write ink and to perform commands as the mouse. Using ink can be tricky at first, but over time you'll get the hang of it.

Insert Handwritten Text Anywhere into a Document

1 Open a program, such as TextEdit, that accepts ink.

2 Turn on handwriting recognition (Ink icon in System Preferences).

The Ink toolbar appears.

3 Write your text in the yellow lined overlay. After recognition, the text that you write appears in the document.

4 To turn Anywhere mode off to use the mouse, click the **On/Off** button on the Ink toolbar.

5 When you're done, turn off handwriting recognition, and close any open documents.

See Also

See "Setting Ink Preferences" on page 130 for information on turning hand-writing recognition on and off, as well as other options.

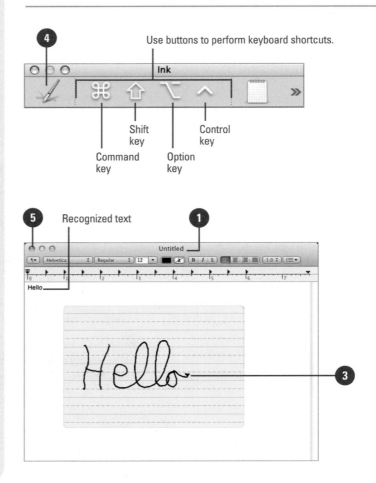

Use buttons to perform keyboard shortcuts.

Shift key

Control key

Command key

Option key

Recognized text

Hello

Insert Handwritten Text Using the Ink Pad

1 Open a program, such as TextEdit, that accepts ink.

2 Turn on handwriting recognition (Ink icon in System Preferences).

The Ink toolbar appears.

3 Click the **Show Ink Pad** button on the Ink toolbar.

4 Click the **A** button to input text, or click the **Star** button to create a drawing.

5 Write your text or draw with the pen in the Ink Pad window.

> **TROUBLE?** *If Ink makes a mistake, hold down the Option key, tap the word, and then select a transcription option.*

6 Use the Ink toolbar buttons (Command, Shift, Option, or Control) to perform keyboard shortcuts.

7 Click **Send** to have your text or drawing pasted into the open document behind it.

8 When you're done, turn off handwriting recognition, and close any open documents.

Ink drawing

Click to clear Ink pad.

Did You Know?

You can recognize gestures in Ink pad.
As you write, Ink recognizes certain gestures, or shapes, which get performed as commands, such as Undo, or pressed as keys, such as Delete or Space. A list is available on the Gestures tab in the Ink pane in System Preferences.

For Your Information

Handwriting in Chinese and Other Languages

OS X supports displaying and typing vertical text used by Chinese and Japanese languages. If you have a Multi-Touch trackpad on your Mac, you can draw Chinese characters in your documents. When you draw on the trackpad, the Chinese characters appear in an input window, which recommends closely matched characters from an extended Simplified Chinese recognizer with Roman symbols, punctuation, and a small set of additional characters and allows you to choose the one you want. The input window—which is movable—also provides suggestions for subsequent characters based on what you chose. It supports filtering by tones, ordering and filtering by radical or stroke count and improved pinyin-had conversion accuracy.

Making Corrections

Everyone makes mistakes and changes their mind at some point, especially when creating or revising a document. With TextEdit you can instantly correct typing errors by pressing a key. You can also reverse more complicated actions, such as typing an entire word, formatting a paragraph, or creating a chart. If you need to undo several actions, you can use the Undo command multiple times. With the Undo command, if you change your mind, you can just as easily use the Redo command to restore the action you reversed.

Undo or Redo an Action

◆ Click the **Edit** menu, and then click **Undo** to reverse your most recent action, such as typing a word or formatting a paragraph.

 TIMESAVER *Press ⌘+Z to undo.*

◆ Click the **Edit** menu, and then click **Redo** to restore the last action you reversed.

 TIMESAVER *Press ⌘+Shift+Z to redo your undo.*

 NOTE *The Undo and Redo commands may change based on the action that was last performed (such as typing or dragging).*

Did You Know?

You can zoom in and out in TextEdit. In TextEdit, click the View menu, and then click Zoom In (or press Shift+⌘+. (period)) or Zoom Out (or press Shift+⌘+, (comma)). If you have a trackpad, you can also pinch to zoom in and out. To view the actual size, click the View menu, and then click Actual Size (press ⌘+0 (zero)).

Click to undo

Click to redo

Edit	
Undo Typing	⌘Z
Redo Drag	⇧⌘Z
Cut	⌘X
Copy	⌘C
Paste	⌘V
Paste and Match Style	⌥⇧⌘V
Delete	
Complete	⌥⌝
Select All	⌘A
Insert	▶
Attach Files...	⇧⌘A
Add Link...	⌘K
Find	▶
Spelling and Grammar	▶
Substitutions	▶
Transformations	▶
Speech	▶
Start Dictation	⌘⌘
Special Characters...	⌥⌘T

Correct Typing Errors Using the Keyboard

To Delete	Press
One character at a time to the left of the insertion point	Delete
One word at a time to the left of the insertion point	Option+Delete
Selected text	Delete

Making Text Substitutions

Text substitution allows you to correct words and phrases that you misspell or insert symbols. For example, you can type "teh" to change to "the" or type (c) to insert ©. Suggested words for text substitution appear below the word, where you can press Return to accept the change or click the X to keep the current spelling. You can add words, phrases, and symbols to the Symbol and Text Substitution list in Keyboard preferences (**New!**). In TextEdit, you can use Smart Copy/Paste to adjust text formatting during a copy and paste, Smart Dashes to automatically replace a sequence of dashes to typographical dashes, Smart Quotes to replace quotes and apostrophes to typographical ones, and Smart Links to convert URLs into links. TextEdit also uses **data detectors** to analyze what you type to detect specialized text, such as dates and addresses, so you can take smart actions, such as create a contact, create an Calendar event, or map an address depending on the type of information.

Select Substitution Options

1. Click the **Edit** menu, point to **Substitutions**, and then select or deselect any of the following options:

 ◆ **Show Substitutions.** Opens the Substitutions dialog where you can enable or disable text substitution options (*ones listed below*), open the Keyboard preferences (**New!**) dialog, or make text replacements.

 ◆ **Smart Copy/Paste.** Adjusts the formatting for text when you copy and paste.

 ◆ **Smart Quotes.** Replaces quotes and apostrophes with typographical ones

 ◆ **Smart Dashes.** Replaces a sequence of dashes with typographical dashes

 ◆ **Smart Links.** Converts URLs into links

 ◆ **Data Detectors.** Analyzes text, such as dates and addresses, in order to take smart actions.

 ◆ **Text Replacement.** Replaces text using the list in Keyboard preferences (**New!**).

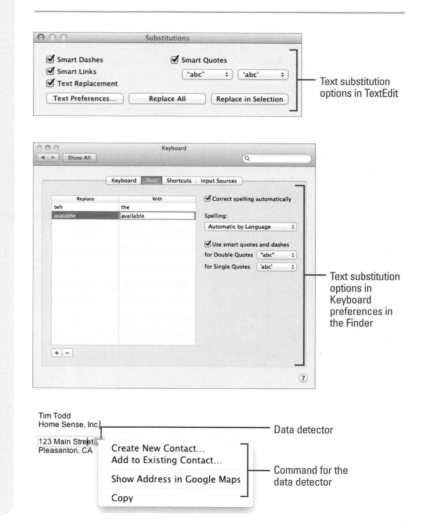

Text substitution options in TextEdit

Text substitution options in Keyboard preferences in the Finder

Data detector

Command for the data detector

Checking Spelling and Grammar

As you type, a red wavy line appears under words not listed in TextEdit's dictionary (such as misspellings or names) or duplicated words (such as the the). You can correct these errors as well as grammatical problems as they arise or after you finish the entire document. For common spelling errors, such as "teh," TextEdit can automatically correct the mistake as you type. TextEdit uses symbol and text substitution options in Language & Text preferences to make the correction. Before you print your final document, use the Spell and Grammar Checker to ensure that your document is error-free.

Correct Spelling and Grammar as You Type

1 Select the spelling and grammar commands to enable the options.

◆ **Check Spelling.** Click the **Edit** menu, point to **Spelling and Grammar**, and then click **Check Spelling While Type**.

◆ **Correct Spelling.** Click the **Edit** menu, point to **Spelling and Grammar**, and then click **Correct Spelling Automatically**.

◆ **Check Grammar.** Click the **Edit** menu, point to **Spelling and Grammar**, and then click **Check Grammar With Spelling**.

2 Control-click a word with a red dotted underline.

3 Click a substitution, or click **Ignore Spelling** to skip any other instances of the word.

Did You Know?

You can add a familiar word to your dictionary. Control-click the wavy line under the word in question, and then click Learn Spelling. The wavy line disappears and you've added the word or name to the dictionary.

Correct Spelling and Grammar

1. Click at the beginning of the document or select the text you want to correct.

2. Click the **Edit** menu, point to **Spelling and Grammar**, and then click **Show Spelling and Grammar**.

 As it checks each sentence in the document or your selection, TextEdit selects misspelled words or problematic sentences and provides appropriate alternatives.

3. If necessary, click the **Language** pop-up, and then select a language.

4. To check grammar, select the **Check grammar** check box.

5. Select an option:

 ◆ Click a suggestion, and then click **Change** to make a substitution.

 ◆ If no suggestion is appropriate, click in the document and edit the text yourself. Click **Find Next** to continue.

 ◆ Click **Ignore** to skip the word.

 ◆ Click **Learn** to add the word to the dictionary.

 ◆ Click **Define** to look up the word in the dictionary.

 ◆ Click **Guess** to suggest possible corrections.

 The Spell Checker will beep when the process is done.

6. Click the **Close** button to return to the document.

Spelling and Grammar dialog

Suggestion window

Looking Up Words with Dictionary

The Dictionary application, located in the Applications folder, gives you the ability to search for words and definitions as a stand-alone program or from any application, such as TextEdit. Within an application, you can view words in a Quick Look Dictionary panel or open the Dictionary application. You can also use the Dictionary widget in Dashboard to look up and find the definitions you need. Dictionary provides several different sources for you to reference, including English and other language dictionaries, an Apple terms dictionary, a thesaurus (second edition), and Wikipedia, which is a free online encyclopedia. You can select which sources you want to use as well as set parental controls to limit access to some works for specific users.

Look Up Words with Dictionary

1. Start the Dictionary application as a stand-alone program or in another application:

 ◆ **Stand Alone.** Click the **Launchpad** icon in the Dock, and then click the **Dictionary** icon.

 ◆ **In an Application.** Hold down the Control key and click the word you want, click **Look Up "word"** from the menu to display the word in the Dictionary panel.

2. In an application, view the Quick Look Dictionary panel, and then click an item to find out more. Click the **Return** (arrow) button to go back.

 To open the Dictionary app and expand the search, click **Dictionary**, **Thesaurus**, or **Wikipedia** in the Quick Look.

3. Select the source you want to search: **All**, **Dictionary**, **Thesaurus**, **Apple**, or **Wikipedia**.

4. Type the search word or phrase you want, if necessary.

5. Click a link to find out about an item.

6. Click the **Close** button.

Thesaurus for selected text

Set Dictionary Preferences

1 Click the **Launchpad** icon in the Dock, and then click the **Dictionary** icon.

2 Click the **Dictionary** menu, and then click **Preferences**.

3 Select or specify the various options you want to use:

◆ **Sources.** Select the check boxes for the dictionaries and thesaurus' you want to use, and then select the reference resource you want to set additional options.

◆ **Pronunciation.** If available, select the pronunciation option you want.

4 Click the **Close** button.

5 Quit Dictionary.

4

Preferences

Drag reference sources into the order you prefer:

☑ New Oxford American Dictionary (American English)
☑ Oxford American Writer's Thesaurus (American English)
☑ Apple Dictionary
☑ Wikipedia
☐ 现代汉语规范词典 (Simplified Chinese)
☐ Diccionario General de la Lengua Española Vox (Spanish)
☐ Duden Dictionary Data Set I (DDDS-I) (German)
☐ ウィズダム英和・和英辞典 (Japanese-English)
☐ スーパー大辞林 (Japanese)
☐ Oxford Dictionary of English (British English)
☐ Oxford Thesaurus of English (British English)

3

New Oxford American Dictionary 3rd edition © 2010 by Oxford University Press, Inc.

Pronunciation:
◉ US English (Diacritical)
◯ US English (IPA)

Did You Know?

You can look up information with a gesture. Double-tap with three fingers to select a word or phrase in any OS X app to look it up. Results from dictionary, thesaurus, and web are displayed inline under the selected item. In the Dictionary app, you can also swipe through your history.

You can set parental controls for dictionary use. Click the System Preferences icon in the Dock, click the Parental Control icon, enter your administrator password, select the user you want to set limits, click Other, select the Hide profanity in Dictionary check box, and then click the Close button.

You can view recent dictionary searches. To see previously viewed words, use the Back and Forward buttons. To skip to a specific word, hold down the Back or Forward buttons to see a menu of recent words.

For Your Information

Speaking Text in a Document

TextEdit can speak all or part of the text in a document. To speak text in a document, deselect all text to speak the entire document or select the text you want to hear, click the Edit menu, point to Speech, and then click Start Speaking. To make the speaking stop, click the Edit menu, point to Speech, and then click Stop Speaking. The voice you hear is set in the Speech pane of System Preferences. To change the sound of the computer's voice, click the Apple menu, click System Preferences, click Speech, click the Default Voice tab, select a voice, and then click the Close button.

Finding and Replacing Text

The Find and Replace commands make it easy to locate or replace specific text or formulas in a document using the Find and Replace toolbar. For example, you might want to find each reference to an individual or company name in a long report to verify that it's properly used. Or you might want to replace all references to a special character in your document with another one. If you only know part of a word you want to find, you can use the Contains option—with the Search bar arrow—to help you locate what you're looking for. If you are looking for a case sensitive text with upper and lower case characters, turn off the Ignore Case option. To make sure you check the entire document no matter where you start, turn on the Wrap Around option. When you search for text in a document, all occurrences of the text are highlighted in yellow for easy identification.

Find Text

1. Click at the beginning of the document, or select the text you want to find.

2. Click the **Edit** menu, point to **Find**, and then click **Find**.

3. Type the text you want to find.

 Inline find highlights all word occurrences in yellow.

4. Click the **Search bar** arrow, and then select other options:

 ◆ **Ignore Case.** Check to ignore upper and lower case letters.

 ◆ **Wrap Around.** Check to wrap back to the beginning or end of the document.

 ◆ **Contains.** Select a search option: **Contains**, **Starts With**, or **Full Word**.

 ◆ **Insert Pattern.** Select to search for special characters.

5. Click **Previous** or **Next** on the Find toolbar until the text you want to find is highlighted.

6. To clear the search, click the **Close** button (x) in the Search bar.

7. When you're done, click the **Done** button on the Find toolbar.

Replace Text

1. Click at the beginning of the document, or select the text you want to replace.

2. Click the **Edit** menu, point to **Find**, and then click **Find and Replace**, or click **Find**, and then click the **Replace** check box.

3. Type the text you want to find.

 Inline find highlights all word occurrences in yellow.

4. Type the text you want to replace.

5. Click the **Search bar** arrow, and then select other options:

 ◆ **Ignore Case.** Check to ignore upper and lower case characters.

 ◆ **Wrap Around.** Check to wrap back to the beginning or end of the document.

 ◆ **Contains.** Select a search option: **Contains**, **Starts With**, or **Full Word**.

 ◆ **Insert Pattern.** Select to search for special characters.

6. Click one of the Replace buttons:

 ◆ **All.** Click to substitute text throughout the entire document.

 ◆ **Replace.** Click to substitute the replacement text and find the next occurrence.

7. Click **Previous** or **Next** on the Find and Replace toolbar until the text you want to find is highlighted.

8. To clear the search, click the **Close** button (x) in the Search bar.

9. When you're done, click the **Done** button on the Find and Replace toolbar.

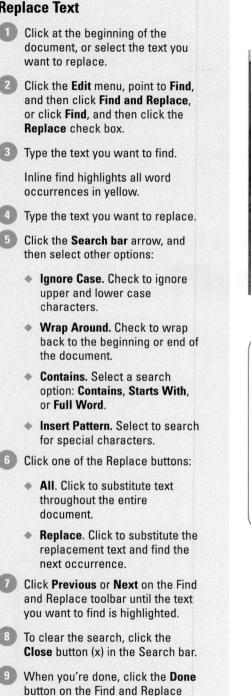

For Your Information

Using Bidirectional Text

If you use different languages in the same document, the mixing of the text can sometimes cause problems. For example, if you use one language, such as Hebrew or Arabic, written from right to left and another language, such as English, written from left to right, the flow of text between the two may not look right. With bidirectional text, you can mix languages with the results you want. You can also use a split-cursor to help show you the right direction of the text at the boundary between right-to-left and left-to-right text.

Formatting Text

When you are working with Rich Text Format (RTF) and Word Format documents, you can change the format or the appearance of text and graphics in a document so that the document is easier to read and more attractive. A quick and powerful way to add emphasis to parts of a document is to format text using bold, italics, underline, or color. For special emphasis, you can combine formats, such as bold and italics. In addition, you can change the font style and size. A **font** is a set of characters with the same typeface or design that you can increase or decrease in size, such as Arial or Times New Roman. Font size is measured in points; one point is 1/72 of an inch high. You can quickly access these formatting options on the Formatting toolbar.

Format Text

1 Select the text or click in the paragraph you want to format.

2 Select any of the formatting options on the Formatting toolbar:

- ◆ **Font Family, Typeface, and Size.** Click a pop-up, and then select a font family, typeface, or size. Click **Show Fonts** to make multiple options at once.

- ◆ **Font Color and Background Color.** Click the **Color** box, and then select a color. Click **Show Colors** to select a specific or custom color.

- ◆ **Bold, Italic, and Underline Text.** Click the **Bold**, **Italic**, or **Underline** button.

3 Click an alignment button: **Left**, **Center**, **Justify**, and **Right**.

4 Click in the document to unselect the newly formatted text.

Did You Know?

You can make text upper case, lower case or capitalize. Select the text, click the Edit menu, point to Transformations, and then click Make Upper Case, Make Lower Case, or Capitalize.

Color palette

Fonts dialog

Colors dialog

Select options for font, typeface, and size.

Select a text color

Displaying Rulers

The TextEdit ruler does more than just measure. The horizontal ruler above the document shows the length of the typing line and lets you quickly adjust left and right margins, indents, and set tabs. You can hide the ruler to get more room for your document. When you press Return to start a new paragraph, TextEdit continues to use the same ruler settings. As you work with a document, ruler settings change. Instead of resetting ruler settings each time, you can copy and paste them.

Show and Hide the Ruler

1. Click the **Format** menu, point to **Text**, and then click **Show Ruler**.

 TIMESAVER *Press ⌘+R to show or hide the ruler.*

 A check mark next to the command indicates the ruler is shown. A non check mark indicates the ruler is hidden.

Copy and Paste the Ruler

1. Click in the line to place the insertion point or select the lines with the ruler settings you want to copy.

2. Click the **Format** menu, point to **Text**, and then click **Copy Ruler**.

 TIMESAVER *Press Control+⌘+Z to copy ruler.*

3. Click in the line to place the insertion point or select the lines in which you want to paste the ruler.

4. Click the **Format** menu, point to **Text**, and then click **Paste Ruler**.

 TIMESAVER *Press Control+⌘+Z to paste ruler.*

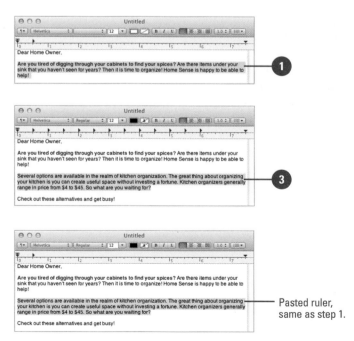

Pasted ruler, same as step 1.

Setting Paragraph Tabs

Tabs set text or numerical data alignment in relation to the edges of a document. A **tab stop** is a predefined stopping point along the document's typing line. Default tab stops are set every half-inch on the ruler, but you can set multiple tabs per paragraph at any location. Each paragraph in a document contains its own set of tab stops. The default tab stops do not appear on the ruler, but the manual tab stops you set do appear. Once you place a tab stop, you can drag the tab stop to position it where you want. If you want to add or adjust tab stops in multiple paragraphs, simply select the paragraphs first.

Create and Clear a Tab Stop

1. Select the text or click in the paragraph you want to format.

2. Click a position on the ruler to insert a tab stop.

3. To change the tab stop, Control-click the tab stop, and then select a tab style: **Left tab**, **Center tab**, **Right tab**, or **Decimal tab**.

 TIMESAVER *Double-click a tab stop to cycle through the different types.*

4. To move a tab, drag the tab stop to position it where you want.

5. To clear a tab stop, drag it off the ruler.

See Also

See "Setting Up Page Options" on page 214 for information on changing the paper size.

Tab Stops		
Tab Stop	**Name**	**Description**
▶	Left tab stop	Aligns tab text to the left
◆	Center tab stop	Aligns tab text to the center
◀	Right tab stop	Aligns tab text to the right
●	Decimal tab stop	Aligns numbers to the decimal point

Setting Paragraph Indents

When you indent a paragraph, you move its edge in from the left or right margin. You can indent the entire left or right edge of a paragraph or just the first line. The markers on the ruler control the indentation of the current paragraph. The ruler has three markers. The top rectangle, called the **paragraph indent marker**, controls where the first line of the paragraph begins. The bottom triangle, called the **left indent marker**, controls where the remaining lines of the paragraph begin. The triangle on the right side of the ruler, called the **right indent marker**, controls where the right edge of the paragraph ends.

Change Paragraph Indents

Select the text or click in the paragraph you want to format.

◆ To change the left indent of the first line, drag the Paragraph Indent marker.

◆ To change the indent of the second and subsequent lines, drag the Left Indent marker (under the Paragraph Indent marker).

◆ To change the left indent for all lines, drag the Left Indent marker, and the Paragraph Indent marker to the same point.

◆ To change the right indent for all lines, drag the Right Indent marker.

As you drag a marker, the dotted guideline helps you position the indent accurately.

Paragraph Indent marker Right Indent marker

Left Indent marker

Dear Home Owner,

Are you tired of digging through your cabinets to find your spices? Are there items under your sink that you haven't seen for years? Then it is time to organize! Home Sense is happy to be able to help!

Several options are available in the realm of kitchen organization. The great thing about organizing your kitchen is you can create useful space without investing a fortune. Kitchen organizers generally range in price from $4 to $45. So what are you waiting for?

Check out these alternatives and get busy!

Tim Todd
Home Sense, Inc.

Did You Know?

You can set your text to be hyphenated. Hyphenation prevents ugly gaps and short lines in text. Click the Format menu, and then click Allow Hyphenation. To turn hyphenation off, click the Format menu, and then click Disallow Hyphenation.

For Your Information

Changing Text Wrap

By default, TextEdit wraps lines of text based on the width of the window. If you change the width of the window, the lines of text get shorter or longer. If you widen the window, the text gets smaller. When you print the document, TextEdit reduces the font size of the text to match the printed document to what you see on the screen, which might not be the results you want to achieve. To avoid this, you can change the text to wrap to the paper size. TextEdit uses the paper size and orientation you set in Page Setup, to determine the point in which the text line wraps. To change text wrap, click the Format menu, and then click Wrap to Page or Wrap to Window. When you change the text wrap to Wrap To Page, a rectangle appears in the window indicating the margins of the document.

Changing Character Spacing

Kerning is the amount of space between each character that you type. Sometimes the space between two characters is larger than others, which makes the word look uneven. You can expand or condense the spacing to create a special effect for a title, or re-align the **baseline**, which is the position of characters to the bottom edge of the text—this is helpful for positioning the copyright or trademark symbols.

Change Character Spacing

1. Select the text you want to format.

2. Click the **Format** menu, point to **Font**, and then point to **Kern**.

3. Click any of the following options:

 ◆ **Use Default**. Uses default kerning.

 ◆ **Use None**. Removes kerning.

 ◆ **Tighten**. Moves the characters together slightly; you can repeat the command.

 ◆ **Loosen**. Moves the characters slightly apart; you can repeat the command.

Change Character Baseline

1. Select the text you want to format.

2. Click the **Format** menu, point to **Font**, and then point to **Baseline**.

3. Click any of the following options:

 ◆ **Superscript**. Moves the text above the level of normal text.

 ◆ **Subscript**. Moves the text below the level of normal text.

 ◆ **Raise**. Moves the text up only a little bit; you can repeat the command.

 ◆ **Lower**. Moves the text down only a little bit; you can repeat the command.

Changing Line Spacing

The lines in all TextEdit documents are single-spaced by default, which is appropriate for letters and most documents. But you can easily change your document line spacing to double or you can specify to allow extra space between every line. This is useful when you want to make notes on a printed document. Sometimes, you'll want to add space above and below certain paragraphs, for headlines, or indented quotations to help set off the text. To set specialized line spacing settings, use the Other command on the Spacing pop-up. You can select options for line height, inter-line spacing, and paragraph spacing. **Line height** is the distance from the top of a line to the top of the line below it; **inter-line spacing** is the distance from the bottom of a line to the top of the line below it; and **paragraph spacing** is the distance from the bottom of a paragraph to the top of the first line in the paragraph below it.

Change Line Spacing

1. Select the text you want to change.

2. Click the **Spacing** pop-up on the Formatting toolbar, and then select a spacing option:

 ◆ Click an available line spacing option from 0.5 (half a line) to 1.0 (single line) to 2.0 (double line).

 ◆ Click **Show More**, specify the exacting options you want, and then click **OK**.

Specify exacting line spacing options

Did You Know?

You can insert and remove a page break. Click the Format menu, and then click Wrap To Page (if necessary) so the page break can be visible. Click to place the insertion point where you want the page break, press Control+Q, and then press Control+L. To remove a page break, place the insertion point below the page break, and then press Delete.

Adding Lists and Tables

The best way to draw attention to a list is to format the items with bullets or numbers. You can even create multi-level lists. For different emphasis, change any bullet or number style to one of TextEdit's many predefined formats. For example, switch round bullets to check boxes or Roman numerals to lowercase letters. You can also customize the list style or insert a picture as a bullet. If you move, insert, or delete items in a numbered list, TextEdit sequentially renumbers the list for you. A **table** neatly organizes information into rows and columns. The intersection of a column and row is called a **cell**. Enter text into cells just as you would anywhere else in TextEdit, except that pressing the Tab key moves you from one cell to the next. You can format a table just like you format any other text in TextEdit.

Create a Numbered or Bulleted List

1. Select the text you want to change or click to place the insertion point where you want to start a list.

2. Click the **Lists** pop-up on the Formatting toolbar, and then select the numbered or bulleted list option you want.

3. For a new list line, type a list item, and then press Return.

 ◆ To add to an existing list, place the insertion point at the end of the line, and then press Return.

4. To indent a list, place the insertion point at the beginning of the line, and then press Tab.

 ◆ To go back to the previous indent level, hold down the Shift key and press Return.

5. To finish a list, press Return twice.

Add a Table

1. Place the insertion point where you want to insert a table.

2. Click the **Format** menu, and then click **Table**.

3. Type the number of rows and columns you want or use the arrow buttons.

4. Set any of the following table options:

 ◆ Alignment. Left, Center, Justified, Right, or Top, Baseline, Middle, or Bottom.

 ◆ Cell Border. Use the arrow button to set the pixel border.

 ◆ Cell Background. Click the pop-up to select **None** or **Color Fill**. Click the color box, click a color, and then click the **Close** button.

5. Click the **Close** button in the Table dialog box.

6. To adjust the height or width of a row or column, position the pointer over a cell border, and then drag the border.

Did You Know?

You can merge cells in a table. Select the cells you want to merge, click the Format menu, point to Text, click Table, click Merge Cells, and then click the Close button.

You can create a table in a table. Select the cell you want to insert a table, click the Format menu, point to Text, click Table, click Nest Table, and then click the Close button.

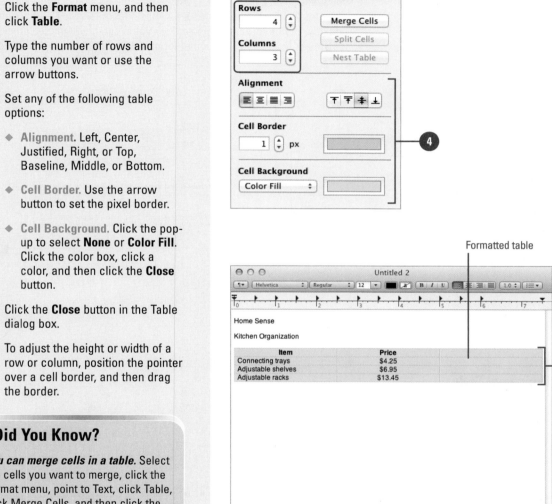

Applying and Creating a Style

When you want to apply multiple groupings of formatting, such as font type, size and color, use a style. A **style** is a collection of formatting settings saved within a document or favorites list that you can apply to text. TextEdit keeps track of all the styles in the current document. If you want to save a style for use in all documents, you can add it to a favorites list. TextEdit provides a few basic favorite styles. But you can add your own to create the exact look you want. If you need a quick way to apply a single instance of formatting, you can copy and paste it.

Apply a Favorite Style

1. Select the text you want to apply a style.

2. Click the **Styles** pop-up on the Formatting toolbar.

3. Click the style you want to apply.

Apply a Document Style

1. Select the text whose formatting you want to save as a style.

2. Click the **Format** menu, point to **Font**, and then click **Styles**.

3. If necessary, click the **Document Styles** option.

4. Click the arrow buttons to select the style you want to apply.

5. Click **Apply**, and then when you're done, click **Done**.

Add a Style to Favorites

1. Select the text whose formatting you want to save as a style.

2. Click the **Format** menu, point to **Font**, and then click **Styles**.

3. Click **Add To Favorites**.

4. Type a name for the style.

5. Select or clear the check boxes to include the font or ruler as part of the style.

6. Click **Add**.

Did You Know?

You can remove a style favorite. Click the Format menu, point to Font, click Styles, click the Favorite Styles option, click the pop-up, select the style favorite, and then click Remove From Favorites.

Copy and Paste Formatting

1. Select the text in which you want to copy the formatting.

2. Click the **Format** menu, point to **Font**, and then click **Copy Style**.

 TIMESAVER *Press Option+⌘+Z to copy ruler.*

3. Select the text to which you want to apply a style.

4. Click the **Format** menu, point to **Font**, and then click **Paste Style**.

Inserting Special Characters

When you need to insert special characters such as ©, ™, or ® that don't appear on your keyboard, you can use a special accessory called Special Character to do the job. Special Character is available in Mac applications and displays all the characters that are available for each of the fonts on your computer. You can insert special characters in a variety of symbol fonts, including arrows, punctuations, currency symbols, pictographs, bullets/stars, math symbols, letter like symbols, emoji (emoticons), and latin. Each one of the fonts also includes style variations.

Insert a Special Character

1. Click in the text to place the insertion point where you want to insert a special character.

2. Click the **Edit** menu, and then click **Special Characters**.

3. Select a category, click **Recently Used**, or click **Favorites** to select from your favorites.

4. Click a subcategory, if necessary, and then click the special character you want to insert.

5. Click a font variation, if desired.

6. To add the character to a favorites list, click **Add To Favorites**.

7. To insert a special character into a document, double-click the character.

8. Click the **Close** button.

> ### See Also
>
> *See "Making Text Substitutions" on page 191 for information on quickly inserting symbols using text substitution while you type.*

List of favorites

Adding Pictures, Movies, or Files to a Document

If you have a picture, movie, or another file, (such as another text file, spreadsheet, or PDF), you can place them within a TextEdit document. Before you can add a picture, movie, or files to a TextEdit document, the file needs to be converted to the Rich Text Format (RTF). Pictures and movies appear in the document as embedded graphics, while files appear as embedded icons. With embedding, a copy of the file becomes part of the TextEdit file. If you want to edit the embedded file, you make changes in the TextEdit file, and the original file remains intact. You can double-click the embedded graphics or icons to open and view the files.

Add a Picture, Movie, or File to a Document

1 Click the **Format** menu, and then click **Make Rich Text**.

2 Switch to the Finder, and then open the folder containing the picture, movie, or file you want to add.

3 Display the picture, movie, or file icon in the Finder and the TextEdit document on the screen where you can view them both.

4 Drag the picture, movie, or file icon from the Finder to the document window where you want to place it.

The image is placed in your document.

◆ To insert a file, you can also click the **Edit** menu (**New!**), click **Attach Files**, browse and select the file and then click **Open**.

5 Close the Finder window.

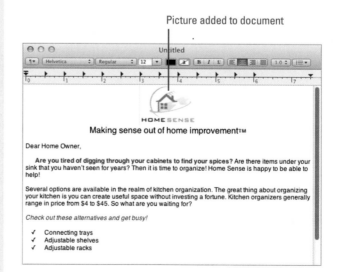

Picture added to document

Saving and Closing a Document

Saving your files frequently ensures that you don't lose work during an unexpected power loss. With TextEdit you don't have to worry, because the program automatically saves your work with Auto Save. Even though TextEdit saves your work, it's important to name your Untitled document. With the Save... command, you specify a file name and folder, one or more tags (**New!**), and a file format in the Save As dialog, which appears in a compact view (useful for saving in the same place) and an expanded view (useful for saving in a different location or creating a new folder). If you want to change a file's name or location, you can use the Rename or Move To commands on the File. If you want to copy the original file, you can use the Duplicate command on the File menu; which along with the Rename command acts like Save As.

Save an Untitled Document as Rich Text or Microsoft Word

1. For plain text only, click the **Format** menu, and then click **Make Rich Text**.

2. For an Untitled document, click the **File** menu, and then click **Save...**.

 ◆ To save a version, click the **File** menu, and then click **Save**. To force a Save As dialog, press ⌘+Shift+Option+S.

3. Type a name for the file, or use the suggested name.

4. Click in the Tags box, select or enter one or more tags (**New!**).

5. Select the hard drive and folder in which you want to save the file.

6. To change the format of a file, click the **File Format** pop-up, and then click **Rich Text Format** or one of the Word formats.

7. Click **Save**.

Compact view

Click to expand dialog to show Sidebar and file list.

3

Save As: Untitled.rtfd

Tags: Important — 4

Where: Letters — 5

File Format: Rich Text Format with Attachments — 6

Cancel Save

7

Did You Know?

TextEdit can save documents as a PDF file. Click the File menu, click Save As PDF, type a name, navigate to a folder, and then click Save.

For Your Information

Protecting Documents

If you have content in your TextEdit document that you don't want users to change, you can make the document read-only. This is useful for documents, such as "read me" files, contracts, and any other document you want users to read, but not accidentally change. To prevent others from changing your TextEdit documents, click the Format menu, and then click Prevent Editing. To allow users to make changes to a read-only document, click the Format menu, and then click Allow Editing. Another way to protect a document is to lock it. When you lock a file, users can make changes to the file, but the application prevents them from saving it. To lock a file, click the document name arrow in the title bar in TextEdit, and then click Lock; to unlock it, click the document name arrow, and then click Unlock.

Save an Untitled Document as Plain Text

1. For plain text only, click the **Format** menu, and then click **Make Plain Text**.

2. For an Untitled document, click the **File** menu, and then click **Save....**

 ◆ To save a version, click the **File** menu, and then click **Save**.

3. Type a name for the file, or use the suggested name.

4. Click in the Tags box, select or enter one or more tags (**New!**).

5. Select the hard drive and folder in which you want to save the file.

6. Click the **Plain Text Encoding** pop-up, and then select an encoding format.

7. Click **Save**.

Compact view 3 Click to expand dialog

Save As:	Untitled.txt	
Tags:	Important	4
Where:	Letters	5
Plain Text Encoding:	Unicode (UTF-8)	6

☑ If no extension is provided, use ".txt".

Cancel Save

7

Close a Document

1. Click the **Close** button.

2. If the document is Untitled, type a name, select a location, select a format, and then click **Save**.

3. Quit TextEdit.

Did You Know?

You can revert to a previously saved document. Before you save, click the File menu, point to Revert To, and then click a previous saved document or Browser All Versions. *See "Using Apps with Auto Save" on page 164 for more information on working with Auto Save and restoring document.*

Using TextEdit for Web Design

You can use TextEdit to create and edit HTML code documents. You can open an existing HTML file or create a new one using plain text or RTF Rich Text Format. If you want to add graphics to your RTF document, you cannot save it as an HTML file. However, you can save it as a web archive file. In addition, you can insert a link to an URL address into a document.

Create Plain HTML Code Files

1. For plain text only, click the **Format** menu, and then click **Make Plain Text**.

2. Write the HTML code.

3. For an Untitled document, click the **File** menu, and then click **Save...**.

 ◆ To save a version, click the **File** menu, and then click **Save**.

4. Add the .html extension at the end of the file name.

5. Click **Save**.

6. Click **Use .html**.

Did You Know?

You can set preferences to save HTML files. Click the TextEdit menu, click Preferences, click the Open and Save tab, select a document type, a setting for cascading style sheets (CSS), and an encoding. If you want to include code to preserve blank areas, select the Preserve White Space check box, and then click the Close button.

Open an HTML Document

1. Click the **File** menu, and then click **Open**.

 If iCloud is turned on, the iCloud Document Library dialog opens, click **iCloud** or **On My Mac**. See page 365 for more details on using the dialog.

2. Select the hard drive and the folder in which you want to open the file.

3. Click the document you want to open.

4. Select the **Ignore rich text commands** check box.

5. Click **Open**.

Add a Link

1. Select the text you want for the link.

2. Click the **Edit** menu, and then click **Add Link**.

3. Type or paste the URL link address in the Link Destination box.

4. Click **OK**.

> ### Did You Know?
>
> *You can edit or remove a link.* To edit a link, select the link, click the Edit menu, click Edit Link, edit the link text, and then click OK. To remove a link, select the link, click the Edit menu, click Edit Link, and then click Remove Link.

Setting TextEdit Preferences

TextEdit preferences help you configure some of the more common features of the program. You can set preferences for new documents, default fonts, rich text processing, default plain text encoding, editing, and saving. These preference areas allow you to turn features on and off as well as customize the way TextEdit works.

Set General Preferences

1 Click the **TextEdit** menu, and then click **Preferences**.

2 Click the **New Document** tab.

3 Select or specify the various options you want to use:

- ◆ **Format.** Select options for document format and text wrapping.

- ◆ **Window Size.** Specify the width and height you want.

- ◆ **Font.** Click **Change** to select the default fonts you want.

- ◆ **Properties and Options.** Enter document properties and check or clear to enable or disable the editing options.

4 Click the **Open and Save** tab.

5 Select or specify the various options you want to use:

- ◆ **When Opening a File.** Check or clear to ignore or allow rich text commands.

- ◆ **When Saving a File.** Check or clear the options you want.

- ◆ **Plain Text File Encoding.** Click the Open or Save pop-ups to select a text encoding default.

- ◆ **HTML Saving Options.** Click the pop-ups to select a default HTML type, styling, and encoding.

6 Click the **Close** button.

Printing, Scanning and Faxing

Introduction

Let's face it, you work all day on a computer, but sooner or later, you're going to have to get your one-of-a-kind project, text document, or photograph off the computer. Computer data finds itself in the most unlikely places. For example, you could save a text document onto a CD, DVD, or removable drive, and then store it away; never to be seen again. Probably the most common place you find computer data is on paper. It might be nice to talk of a paperless society, however, many people still prefer the satisfying feel of paper in their hands, as opposed to a computer monitor. That's where OS X steps in and makes your life easy. Not only does OS X give you all the standard ways to print to paper or fax, it also gives you hundreds of printer drives; supporting the vast majority of printers and scanners in the market. In addition, you can save paper by previewing your jobs—using OS X's print preview feature—which shows you a color-accurate on-screen version of your print job.

If you have a scanner or a printer with a scanner, you can scan images and documents to your computer, typically without any other special software. Simply, plug-in and play. If you're in an application, like Preview, you can import from a scanner; click the File menu, point to Import from Scanner, and then select a scanner.

If you fax documents, then OS X is an operating system tailor-made expressly for your needs. OS X integrates its faxing features with a state-of-the-art printing system. Just open the Printers & Scanners pane in System Preferences, and you can set up your computer to receive faxes. Then, when you go to print a document from virtually any application, you'll see a Fax button in the Print dialog. In addition, if you have a large print job that you would rather print after work, or a fax that has to be sent at a specific time; OS X lets you schedule a time to print a document, or fax with the click of a button.

What You'll Do

Understand Printers

Understand Printer Drivers

Add or Remove a Printer

Set Print Settings

Share a Printer

Set Up Page Options

Set Basic Print Options

Preview Documents

Save Documents as PDF Documents

Manage Print Queues

Create a Cover Page

Scan Documents

Send Fax Documents

Receive Faxes Automatically

Understanding Printers

Although there are many different kinds of printers, there are two main categories: ink-jet and laser. An **ink-jet printer** works by spraying ionized ink on a sheet of paper. Ink-jet printers are less expensive and considerably slower than laser printers, but they still produce a good quality output. A **laser printer** utilizes a laser beam to produce an image on a drum, which is rolled through a reservoir of toner and transferred to the paper through a combination of heat and pressure. Laser printers are faster and produce a higher quality output than ink-jets, but they are also more expensive. Ink-jet and laser printers are combined with other hardware devices, such as a copier and scanner, into a multi-function device. A **multi-function device** provides common device functionality at a lower cost than purchasing each device separately. Printers are classified by two main characteristics: resolution and speed. Printer resolution refers to the sharpness and clarity of a printed page. For printers, the resolution indicates the number of dots per inch (dpi). For example, a 300-dpi printer is one that is capable of printing 300 distinct dots in a line one-inch long, or 90,000 dots per square inch. The higher the dpi, the sharper the print quality. Printer speed is measured in pages per minute (ppm). The speed of printers varies widely. In general, ink-jet printers range from about 4 to 10 ppm, while laser printers range from about 10 to 30 ppm. The speed depends on the amount of printer memory (the more the better) and the page's contents: if there is just text or the page has only one color, the ppm is in the high range, but when a page contains graphics and/or has multiple colors, the ppm rate falls to the low range.

Laser printer installed

Understanding Printer Drivers

Printer drivers are lines of code designed to help an operating system communicate with a specific printer. No two printer models are created equal: Some have two paper trays, while others have one; some are ink-jet, while others are laser; some are color and some black and white. Although there are generic printer drivers available, most printers have a driver program, designed specifically for that make and model. OS X installs all of the printer drivers onto your hard drive when you run the OS X installation program.

The drivers become available when you attach your printer and run the Printer Setup Utility. The good news is that the process of hooking up your printer, and being able to print is easy to do. OS X comes bundled with almost every conceivable printer driver; however, new printers and updates are being released all the time. When you plug in a new printer, OS X downloads the appropriate

driver. Periodically, it checks to make sure it has the lastest driver using Software Update as needed. It's always a good idea to keep the CD or DVD that came with your printer handy; it contains a driver for that particular model of printer. In addition, the web sites for the printer companies such as *www.epson.com* or *www.hp.com*, contain the latest updates and patches for their printers. You can visit them to see if any updates are available.

Since you'll only need one or two printer drivers, you can delete the others. All those unused drivers take up over a gigabyte of space on your hard drive. Once you've installed the necessary printers, select the Library folder (located on the main hard drive), click Printers folder, and then delete the unused drivers. If necessary, you can always reinstall them from the OS X install disks.

Printer options

Printer driver options

| General | Driver | Supply Levels |

Name: HP LaserJet 3050

Location: Steve's Mac mini

Queue Name: HP_LaserJet_3050

Driver Version: 17.5

Cancel OK

| General | Driver | Supply Levels |

Print Using: HP LaserJet 3050

To take full advantage of your printer's options, confirm that they are accurately shown here. For information on your printer and its optional hardware, check the printer's documentation.

Fit to Page: Prompt User

Cancel OK

Printer driver version

Adding or Removing a Printer

Setting up a printer use to be a difficult and time-consuming process. There were all kinds of questions to answer, driver files to find, and after all that time, you might still have problems. With OS X, setting up a printer is easy. Adding a printer can be as simple as plugging it into your computer. In most cases that's all you need to do. OS X automatically tries to autoconfigure almost any USB, FireWire, or Bluetooth connection. If you want to install a network printer, such as Bonjour, or your printer doesn't appear in the printer list, you can add it manually in the Printers & Scanners pane in System Preferences. If you no longer use a printer, you can quickly remove it while you're in Printers & Scanners preferences.

Add or Remove a Printer

1. To add a printer, follow the printer setup instructions to install any necessary software, and then connect it to your computer using a USB or FireWire connection.

 OS X automatically tries to install the printer. In most cases, the printer is available in any Print dialog box.

 If the printer is not available, continue.

2. Click the **System Preferences** icon in the Dock, and then click the **Printers & Scanners** icon (**New!**).

 The printer appears in the left column. If your printer doesn't appears in the list, follow the instructions to add a printer manually on the next page.

3. To remove a printer, select the printer you want to remove, click the **Remove** (-) button, and then click **OK**.

4. Click the **Close** button.

For Your Information

Using AirPrint

If you have an AirPrint compatible printer on your network, OS X automatically adds it to the printer list (just like a USB printer) without having to download a printer driver. The printer appears in the Nearby Printers list in the Print dialog.

Add a Printer Manually

1. Click the **System Preferences** icon in the Dock, and then click the **Printers & Scanners** icon.

2. Click the **Add** (+) button.

 TIMESAVER *In a Print dialog box, click the Printer pop-up, and then click Add Printer.*

3. Use the toolbar buttons to specify the information required to display (if necessary) and select the printer you want to add:

 ◆ **Default.** Displays available autoconfigured printers

 ◆ **Fax.** Displays available autoconfigured faxes.

 ◆ **IP.** Provides options to setup a network printer using an IP (Internet Protocol) address, such as 192.160.1.170.

 Also can provide options to setup special-case printers, such as Canon IJ Network, Epson FireWire or TCP/IP, or HP IP Printing.

 ◆ **Windows.** Displays network printers using Windows and an Ethernet connection.

4. Click **Add**, and then click **Continue**, if necessary.

5. Click the **Close** button in the Add Printer window.

6. Click the **Close** button.

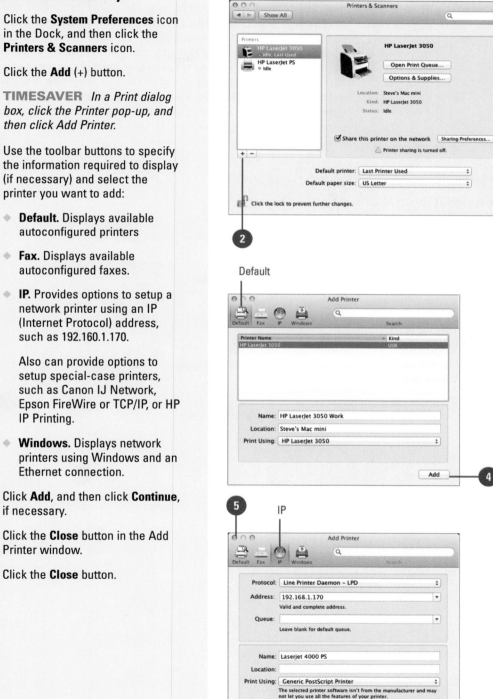

Default

IP

Setting Print Settings

Using your Mac to print and fax is an obvious extension of the normal, everyday computing process. You write and create documents, and send them to paper; you take a photograph using a digital camera and send it to a photo-quality printer. You can use the Printers & Scanners pane in System Preferences to modify many of the aspects of printing. For example, you can set the default printer, the one that automatically appears when you want to print, and the default paper size. If you want to find out the available options for a specific printer, you can use Options and Supplies, where you can find printer information, change a printer name, select a different driver, and check out printer supplies available online, such as ink and toner.

Set Default Printer Settings

1. Click the **System Preferences** icon in the Dock, and then click the **Printers & Scanners** icon.

2. Click the **Default Printer** pop-up, and then click **Last Printer Used** or select a default printer to appear first in the Print dialogs of all your applications.

3. Click the **Default Paper Size in Page Setup** pop-up, and then select a paper size to be used as a default in the Print dialogs of all your applications.

4. Click the **Close** button.

Set Printer Specific Settings

1 Click the **System Preferences** icon in the Dock, and then click the **Printers & Scanners** icon.

2 Select the printer you want to change print settings.

3 Click **Options & Supplies**.

4 Click the tab for the area in which you want to change settings, such as General, Driver, or Supply Levels. The tabs vary depending on the printer.

◆ **General.** Displays printer information (queue and host name, and driver version). You can change the name and location of the printer.

◆ **Driver.** Allows you to select a different driver.

◆ **Supply Levels.** Allows you to access a web site that lets you order more supplies, such as ink or toner. Click **Supplies** to open the web site.

5 Click **OK**.

6 Click the **Close** button.

See Also

See "Using Network Sharing Services" on page 420 for more information on setting Sharing Preferences.

4

| General | Driver | Supply Levels |

Name: HP LaserJet 3050

Location: Steve's Mac mini

Queue Name: HP_LaserJet_3050
Driver Version: 17.5

Cancel OK **5**

For Your Information

Selecting a Printer's PPD File

A PostScript Printer Description (PPD) file specifies a printer's options and features. When you add a printer to your computer, OS X selects a PPD for you. If you have another PPD for your printer (typically provided by the printer manufacturer), you can use it instead. Click the System Preferences icon in the Dock, click the Printers & Scanners icon, select your printer, click Options & Supplies, click the Driver tab, click the Print Using pop-up, click Other, select the PPD file you want, click OK or Open, and then click OK.

Sharing a Printer

If you have a printer connected to your computer and your computer is connected to a network, you can share your printer with other network users. Before you can share a printer, you need to turn on printer sharing in the Sharing pane in System Preferences and then enable sharing for each printer in the Printers & Scanners pane. After you share a printer, other users—with OS X, UNIX, or Windows computers—connected to your network can use your printer; you can also connect to other shared printers—including an AirPort base station— available on your network. For security purposes, if you want to share your printer with a Windows user via SMB/CIFS, you need to set Firewall options to allow all incoming connections on the Firewall tab of Security preferences. If a Windows user has Bonjour installed, the user can use the Bonjour wizard to connect to your printer on a Mac. After you share your printer, if a user connected to your network still cannot access your printer, you can provide them with your Mac IP address (available in Network preferences for the network connection, such as Ethernet) and queue name (available in Printers & Scanners preferences in Options & Supplies) to make the connection to the shared printer.

Share a Printer

1. Click the **System Preferences** icon in the Dock, and then click the **Printers & Scanners** icon.

2. Select the printer you want to change print settings.

3. Select the **Share this printer on the network** check box.

4. If printer sharing is turned off, click **Sharing Preferences**, select the **Printer Sharing** check box, and then click the **Close** button.

 ◆ You can also click the **System Preferences** icon in the Dock, and then click the **Sharing** icon.

5. To share your printer with Windows users via SMB/CIFS, click **Show All**, click the **Security** icon, click **Firewall**, click **Start**, click **Advanced** (if you want to set other options), and then click the **Back** button.

6. Click the **Close** button.

Click to add a shared printer

Access a Shared Printer

1. Click the **System Preferences** icon in the Dock, and then click the **Printers & Scanners** icon.

2. Click the **Add** (+) button.

3. Use the toolbar buttons to specify the information required to display and select the printer you want:

 ◆ **IP.** Provides options to setup a network printer using an IP (Internet Protocol) address, such as 192.160.1.170.

 Also can provide options to setup special-case printers, such as Canon IJ Network, Epson FireWire or TCP/IP, or HP IP Printing.

 ◆ **Windows.** Displays network printers using Windows and an Ethernet connection.

4. Click **Add**.

5. Click the **Close** button in the Printers & Scanners Browser window.

6. Click the **Close** button.

For Your Information

Using AirPort Base Station to Share a Printer

If you have an AirPort Extreme or AirPort Express base station, you can share a USB printer with other computers on your network. When you use an AirPort Express base station, you may not see error or status messages, such as *Out of Paper*. To use the AirPort base station, you need to follow setup instructions to install any software, connect the printer to your computer, print a test page, and then connect the printer to the AirPort base station. You can also print to shared Windows printers over a network or share your own printer with Windows users.

Setting Up Page Options

With few exceptions, Mac applications give you the ability to print a document to paper. Programs, such as TextEdit—Mac's proprietary word processing application—give you the option to print what you have committed to type. When you select the Print option (located under the File menu), you're instructing the application to use an output device (the printer) to place your words on paper. Since all printers have options, it's important to be able to set those options before printing. You might be using a specific size paper or printing orientation. For this operation, you'll use the Page Setup command, located within the File menu of most applications.

Set Up Page Options

1. Open a document, such as a text document.

2. Click the **File** menu, and then click **Page Setup**.

3. Click the **Settings** pop-up, and then select from the following options:

 ◆ **Page Attributes**. This option lets you select a printer, specific paper size, orientation, and print scale.

 ◆ **Custom Paper Size**. Click **New** to create a customized paper size by entering height, width, and margin values into the appropriate input fields.

 ◆ **Document Specific Option**. This option gives you specific options for the current application.

 ◆ **Summary**. Click **Summary** to see an outline of your options.

 ◆ **Save As Default**. Click this option to save your current settings as default for future printing operations.

4 Click the **Format for** pop-up, and then select a printer from the available options.

5 Click the **Paper Size** pop-up, and then select a paper size from the available options.

6 Click the **Orientation** buttons, and then select from the following:

- ◆ **Portrait**
- ◆ **Landscape**

7 Enter in a printing scale percentage.

8 Click **OK**.

9 If necessary, save the file and close the application.

Settings:	Page Attributes ◆
Format For:	Any Printer ◆
Paper Size:	US Letter ◆
	8.50 by 11.00 inches
Orientation:	[icons]
Scale:	100 %

(?) Cancel OK

Did You Know?

You can send two different print jobs to two different printers. Suppose you're printing a large job (50 pages), and you need another job (2 pages) printed right away. Just open the second job, click the File menu, and then click Print. Click the Printer pop-up, select another printer for the second job, and then click Print. OS X processes both jobs on both printers at the same time.

For Your Information

Using Page Setup

The Page Setup command changes the page properties within each application. Therefore, you can use the Page Setup command to generate individual defaults for each of your applications. To change the default settings for all applications at the same time, go to your Dock and click System Preferences, click the Printers & Scanners icon, and then change the default paper size and printer in the pop-ups.

Setting Basic Print Options

All applications that allow you to send a document to a printer, give you the ability to set up specific printing parameters. Some print options are generic, such as how many pages to print, and some are more specific, such as what paper tray to use (in a multi-tray printer). Regardless of the options, they're all located in one specific location, the Print command of the opened application. When you select the Print command, a dialog opens displaying a preview of the pages with all the options associated with the default printer; including the ability to change the default printer, and any other printing values.

Set Basic Print Options

1. Open a document.

2. Click the **File** menu, and then click **Print**.

3. Click the **Printer** pop-up, and then select a printer from the available options.

 The Print dialog displays a preview of the page. You can click buttons below the print preview to scroll through pages.

4. Click **Show Details**, if necessary, to expand the Print dialog box.

5. Click the **Presets** pop-up, and then select a user-defined print setting.

6. Specify the following standard print options:

 ◆ Preview Image. Click the arrows below the preview image to view the document.

 ◆ Copies. Type the number of copies you want. Select or clear the **Collated** check box. Selected prints 1, 2, 3, 1, 2, 3. Cleared prints 1, 1, 2, 2, 3, 3.

 ◆ Pages. Click the **All** option or the **From** option, and then enter the print range you want.

 ◆ Paper Size. Select the paper size you want.

 ◆ Orientation. Select the portrait or landscape option you want.

Print preview

7 Click the **Options** pop-up, and then select from the available options:

- ◆ **Application Specific Options.** If you're using Microsoft Word, this option lists specific options for that specific application.

- ◆ **Layout.** When printing large documents, allows you to select how many pages per sheet, the layout direction, border options, and two-sided printing.

- ◆ **Color Matching.** Gives you access to Mac's ColorSync management system, and the ability to apply the new Quartz Filters to the printed document.

- ◆ **Paper Handling.** Select to print in reverse order (page 1 prints last), whether to print all, odd, or even pages, and scale a document to fit the paper.

- ◆ **Paper Feed.** Select the paper tray for all pages or a different paper tray for the first and remaining pages.

- ◆ **Cover Page.** Lets you select options to print a cover page, such as standard, classified, unclassified, or confidential.

- ◆ **Color/Quality Options.** Lets you set printer resolution options.

- ◆ **Finishing**. Let you set printing to different media types, such as paper weight.

IMPORTANT *The print settings on the Options pop-up vary depending on the selected printer.*

8 To save your print settings, click the **Presets** pop-up, click **Save Current Settings as Presets**, type a name, and then click **OK**.

9 Click **Print**.

For Your Information

Using the Desktop to Print

The typical method for printing a document goes something like this: You open an application, open a document, click the File menu, and then click Print. While the majority of the time that's exactly what you want to do; especially if you need to make minor corrections to the document before printing, there is an easier way to go from document to printer: Desktop printers. Desktop printers give you the ability to create an icon of a printer, and with a drag and a drop, print a document using any connected printer. Not only is this method fast, it gives you the ability to print from two or more connected printers at a time. Printer icons can be located on the desktop, inside a folder, or even placed in the Dock. Click the System Preferences icon in the Dock, and then click the Printers & Scanners icon. Drag the printer you want to the desktop. To print a document, drag a file over the desktop printer icon. If the application opens, make any changes to your print options, and then click Print. You can instantly check on the status of a particular printer. Double-click a desktop print icon to check the status of the printer, including items waiting to print.

Previewing Documents

One of the most frustrating things is looking at a document on your monitor, clicking the Print command, and then deciding that what you see on the paper is not what you wanted. Unfortunately, a monitor is not a piece of paper, and the term What You See is What You Get (WYSIWYG), is a phrase that most computer users do not take very seriously. Once again, Mac comes to the rescue with a preview in the Print dialog and a more detailed display in Preview utility that targets your default printer. If you see what you like, you can print a single copy directly from the Preview dialog, or you can close the preview, and then print using the standard Print option.

Preview Documents

1. Open or create a document in an application.

2. Click the **File** menu, and then click **Print**.

 The Print dialog display a preview of the document. You can click buttons below the print preview to scroll through pages.

3. To open in Preview, click the **PDF** button, and then click **Open PDF in Preview**.

4. In Preview, select from the following options:

 ◆ **View**. Click to display a view: Content Only, Thumbnails, Table of Contents, Highlight and Notes, or Contact Sheet.

 ◆ **Zoom In or Zoom Out**. Click to increase or decrease the viewing size of the image.

 ◆ **Share**. Click to share the file using an online services.

 ◆ **Markup**. Click to highlight parts of the page.

 ◆ **Rotate**. Click to rotate the page.

 ◆ **Show Edit Toolbar**. Click to display the Edit toolbar. Select text, image, or page and add annotation.

5. Click **Cancel** to close or **Print** to print the document.

6. Quit Preview.

Print preview

Click to scroll thru pages

Saving Documents as PDF Documents

The PDF (Portable Document File) format is undoubtedly the most successful multi-platform format ever created by any company. Designed by Adobe, it has become the standard for transferring text and graphics documents, spreadsheets; even creating interactive forms, that can be filled out by a visitor, and then sent back to the owner for processing. The reason for the success of the PDF format is Adobe's tight control over the Adobe Acrobat application (used to create PDF's), and the Acrobat Reader application (used by visitors to read PDF's). Once a PDF document is properly saved, it can be opened by virtually anyone that has Acrobat Reader, regardless of computer or operating system. And the good news is that the Reader application is a free download, just point your browser to *http://www.acrobat.com*, and then click Download Reader to obtain the latest version of the Acrobat Reader application, tailored for your specific operating system.

Save Documents as a PDF

1. Open or create a document in an application.

2. Click the **File** menu, and then click **Print**.

3. Click **PDF**, and then select the type of PDF you want to create:

 ◆ **Save as PDF.** Creates a PDF document. Enter a name, assign tags (**New!**), specify a location, and then click **Save**.

 ◆ **Fax PDF.** Creates and faxes a PDF document.

 ◆ **Add PDF to iTunes.** Creates and adds a PDF document to iTunes.

 ◆ **Mail PDF.** Creates and attaches a PDF document in an e-mail.

 ◆ **Save PDF to Web Receipts Folder.** Creates and stores a PDF document in your Web Receipts folder; great for saving web site receipts.

3 → Specify PDF settings; options vary

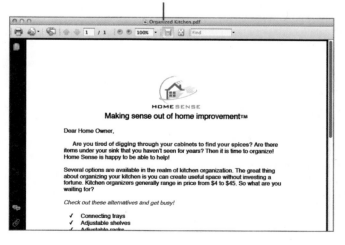

A PDF document viewed in Acrobat Reader.

Managing Print Queues

The definition of a queue is a line. In Great Britain the term is used to describe a line of people waiting to get into a movie or restaurant. In printing terms a **queue** is a group of documents all waiting to be printed on the same printer. OS X handles the queue like a master conductor; keeping everything in order, as it smoothly instructs the printer to print each document in turn. However, sometimes problems can occur that the Print Queue utility doesn't quite know how to handle. For example, it's possible that you want to place a job on hold while other jobs print (preferably yours), or you many want to delete a job. In fact, you can even instruct the printer to stop printing altogether.

Manage Print Queues

1. Open the Printer window with the print jobs you want to manage:

 ◆ Click the **System Preferences** icon in the Dock, click the **Printers & Scanners** icon, select the printer, and then click **Open Print Queue**.

 ◆ Double-click the printer's icon in the Dock while the document is printing.

 ◆ Double-click the printer's icon as a desktop printer.

2. Select a job, and then click one of the following:

 ◆ **Delete**. Deletes the job from the queue.

 ◆ **Hold/Resume**. Stops or resumes the printing of the selected job.

 ◆ **Info**. Opens the Options & Supplies dialog box.

 ◆ **Pause/Resume Printer**. Pauses or resumes the printer.

3. To view information about completed print jobs, including the print time and date, click the **Jobs** menu, and then click **Show Completed Jobs**.

4. Click the **Close** button.

Click to change printer setup options

Current print job

Paused printer

Creating a Cover Page

When you print a document, OS X allows you to create a cover page. When you work with secure information, you can print a cover page that indicates the private nature of a document. For example, you can add a cover page with the following tags: classified, confidential, secret, top secret, and unclassified. Many companies require a cover page to be sent with sensitive documents. Since the decision to use a cover sheet is dependent on the document, OS X gives you the choice to add a cover sheet each time you print a document.

Create a Cover Page

1. Open a document that you want to print a cover page.

2. Click the **File** menu, and then click **Print**.

3. Click the **Printer** pop-up, and then select a printer from the available options.

4. Click the **Options** pop-up, and then click **Cover Page**.

5. Click the print cover page option you want: **None, Before document,** or **After document**.

6. Click the **Cover Page Type** pop-up, and then select the print cover page option you want.

7. Click **Print**.

Scanning Documents

If you have a scanner or a printer with a scanner, you can scan images and documents to your computer, typically without any other special software. Simply, plug-in and play. If you have a flatbed scanner, you can scan many images at once (make sure there is empty space between the images), store each one in it's own file, and straighten any images that were crooked on the scanner bed. If you have a scanner with an automatic feeder, you can scan multiple pages at once. If you're in an application, like Preview, you can import from a scanner; click the File menu, point to Import from Scanner, and then select a scanner.

Scan Documents

① Click the **System Preferences** icon in the Dock, and then click the **Printers & Scanners** icon.

② Select the printer/scanner or scanner device you want to use, and then click the **Scan** tab, if necessary.

③ Click **Open Scanner**.

④ Place the document or image you want to scan in the scanner.

⑤ Select from the following options:

 ◆ **Scan Size.** Select a specific size, or let the scanner do it: click **Detect Separate Items** or **Detect Enclosing Box**.

 ◆ **Scan To.** Select the program you want to use to open and display the scan.

⑥ Click one of the from the following buttons:

 ◆ **Scan.** Scans and creates the document using the default settings.

 The scanned document is stored in the Pictures folder.

 ◆ **Show Details.** Performs an overview prescan to show you the initial scan. You can set the scan options you want before actually scanning the documents.

7 Select from the available options (setting may vary depending on the scanner):

◆ **Kind.** Select a document type: Text, Black & White, or Color.

◆ **Colors.** Select the range of colors: Millions or Billions.

◆ **Resolution.** Specify the dpi (dots per inch).

◆ **Use Custom Size.** Select to specify a custom size and use auto selection.

◆ **Size and Rotation Angle.** Specify a scan size and any rotation.

◆ **Orientation.** Select Portrait or Landscape.

◆ **Scan To.** Select the program you want to use to open and preview the scan.

◆ **Name.** Enter a name for the scan document.

◆ **Format.** Select a file format.

◆ **Image Correction.** Set to manual to specify brightness, tint, temperature, or saturation.

◆ **Descreen.** Select to remove screen moire patterns.

◆ **Color Restoration.** Select to restore faded color.

◆ **Adaptive Lighting.** Select to auto-adjust exposure levels.

◆ **Sharpen.** Select to increase sharpness.

8 Click **Overview** to perform a prescan with the current settings or click **Scan** to perform a scan and create the document using the current settings.

The scanned document is opened in the specified application. The scanned document is stored in the Pictures folder.

Adjust resize handles to change scan area

Scanned document in Preview

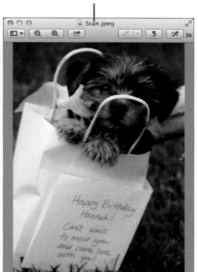

Sending Fax Documents

Using your Mac to print and fax is an obvious extension of the normal, everyday computing process. You have a document, and you need to fax it to a co-worker or friend. Once you've decided whom the fax is to be sent to, and what the fax number is, the next step is to send the fax. When you fax a document, OS X allows you to create a cover page. A cover page indicates to the person receiving the fax, the number of pages in the fax, who is sending the fax, the date and time the fax was sent, and a short text paragraph. Since the decision to use a cover sheet is dependent on the document, OS X gives you the choice to add a cover sheet each time you generate a fax.

Send Fax Documents

1. Open a document that you want to fax.

2. Click the **File** menu, and then click **Print**.

3. Click the **PDF** button, and then click **Fax PDF**.

4. If necessary, click the **Printer** pop-up, and then select your fax modem.

5. Specify the specifics for the fax job (copies, pages, paper size, and orientation).

6. Click the **Options** pop-up, and then select from the following options:

 ◆ **Fax Information**. Type the fax number in the To field. Enter any prefixes into the Dialing Prefix field, such as 9 to get an outside line. Select the **Use Cover page** check box to add a fax cover sheet, and then type the subject and message text you want to display on the Cover Page.

 IMPORTANT *You cannot create a new paragraph while typing the cover page text. The Return key only sends the fax prematurely. To get around this, create the cover page text in another application, and then copy and paste it into the field.*

For Your Information

Addressing Faxes from the Address Book

When you send a Fax, you need a document, and a fax number to send it. Do you need to open the Address Book, and write that number down? No. OS X gives you the ability to pull that information directly from the address card. Remember that in order for an address card to be used for faxing, it must first have a fax number entered into the card. In the Print dialog, click the PDF button, click Fax PDF, click the Options pop-up, and then click Fax Information. Click the Address Book button, select a name from your address list, click the To button to add the name and fax number to the current fax request, select a name, and then click the Close button.

- ◆ **Fax Modem**. Select between tone or pulse phones, whether to hear the dialing through your computer speakers, and if you want the modem to wait for a dial tone before beginning the fax process.

- ◆ **Layout.** When printing large documents, allows you to select how many pages per sheet, the layout direction, border options, and two-sided printing.

- ◆ **Paper Handling.** Select to print in reverse order (page 1 prints last), and whether to print all, odd, or even pages.

- ◆ **Scheduler**. Lets you schedule a time for faxing the document.

- ◆ **Printer Features**. Select between low and high quality output.

7 Click **Fax**.

8 Close your document.

Fax modem options

7

Did You Know?

You can let other users send faxes through your computer. Click the System Preferences icon in the Dock, click the Printers & Scanners icon, select the fax modem you want to share, select the Share This Fax On The Network check box, and then click the Close button. The fax is now available for others to use.

You can view fax information about completed jobs. Click the System Preferences icon in the Dock, click the Printers & Scanners icon, double-click the fax modem icon in the Fax list, click the Jobs menu, and then click Show Completed Jobs.

For Your Information

Checking the Status of a Fax

You can check the status of a fax. Click the fax modem icon in the Dock while a document is being sent. To pause the printer, click the Pause Printer button; to resume the printer, click the Resume Printer button. To put a fax on hold, select it, and then click the Hold button; to resume the fax, select it, and then click the Resume button.

Saving your Fax Print Options

If you have a combination of faxing options that you frequently use, you can save it as a Preset. After selecting your options, click the Presets pop-up menu, click Save As, and then type a name for the new options. If you want to use the new options to fax a document, click the Presets pop-up, select its name from the Presets pop-up menu, and then click Fax.

Receiving Faxes Automatically

It's actually pretty easy to set up your computer to receive faxes automatically. All you need is a phone line, and your Mac. You can set up the Fax to answer after a certain number of rings, and you don't have to be logged in; however, your Mac needs to be on and not in sleep mode, which you can set in Energy Saver preferences. To make it easier to work with faxes, you can set the option to show the Fax status menu in the menu bar for easy access. After you send and receive some faxes, you can view information about the completed job. You can manage the fax queue just like the print queue. You can also manually receive faxes. Wait for the phone to ring, click the Fax status menu, and then click Answer Now.

Receive Faxes Automatically

1. Click the **System Preferences** icon in the Dock, and then click the **Printers & Scanners** icon.

2. Select the fax modem you want to use.

3. To use the Fax status menu, select the **Show fax status in menu bar** check box.

4. Enter your fax number into the field, exactly as you would dial the number.

5. Click **Receive Options**.

6. Select from the following options:

 ◆ **Receive faxes on this computer**. Select the check box to receive faxes.

 ◆ **When a fax arrives answer After**. Enter how many rings are required before the Fax answers the phone.

 ◆ **Save to**. Select the check box, and then select where to save the faxes.

 ◆ **Email to**. Select the check box, and then select where to e-mail the faxes.

7. Click **OK**.

8. Click the **Close** button.

Exploring the Internet

Introduction

The **Internet** is a global collection of more than a billion computers (and growing) linked together to share information. The Internet's physical structure includes telephone lines, cables, satellites, and other telecommunications media. Using the Internet, computer users can share many types of information, including text, graphics, sounds, videos, and computer programs. The World Wide Web (also known as the web or www) is a part of the Internet that consists of web sites located on different computers around the world.

History of the Internet and the World Wide Web

The Internet has its roots in the Advanced Research Projects Agency Network (ARPANET), which the United States Department of Defense started in 1969. In 1986, the National Science Foundation formed NSFNET, which replaced ARPANET. NSFNET expanded the foundation of the U.S. portion of the Internet with high-speed, long-distance data lines. In 1991, the U.S. Congress expanded the capacity and speed of the Internet further and opened it to commercial use. The Internet is now accessible in almost every country in the world. The World Wide Web was developed in Switzerland in 1991 to make finding documents on the Internet easier. Software programs designed to access the web, known as web browsers, use point-and-click interfaces. The first such web browser, Mosaic, was introduced at the University of Illinois in 1993. Since the release of Mosaic, Microsoft Internet Explorer, Netscape, and AOL have become some of the most popular web browsers.

What You'll Do

Connect to the Internet

Set Up a Modem, Ethernet, or Wi-Fi Wireless Connection

Set Up Multiple Connections

Make an Internet Connection

Understand Web Sites and Browsers

View and Customize Safari

Browse the Web

Work with Shared Links

View Top Sites or History List

Bookmark a Web Page

Work with Bookmarks

Fill Out Forms on the Web

Search the Web

Print and Save a Web Page

Save Pictures or Text from a Web Page

Download Files from the Web

Set Safari Preferences

Block Pop-Up Windows

Change Web Notifications

Select a Default Browser and Search

Connecting to the Internet

Universities and large companies are most likely connected to the Internet via high-speed wiring that transmits data very quickly. Home computer owners usually rely on a modem and the phone lines already in place. In some areas, however, several faster connection options are becoming available and affordable. There are **DSL** (Digital Subscriber Lines), wires that provide a complete digital connection; **cable modems**, which use cable television lines; and **wireless**, which doesn't use wires or phone lines. DSL and cable modems, also known as **broadband** connections, are continually turned on and connected to an Ethernet network so you don't need to establish a connection using a dial-up modem. Data travels more slowly over phone wires than over digital lines and cable modems. Wireless provides a mobile connection to the Internet using a Wi-Fi connection anywhere there is a wireless base station, such as a router or a network hub. Whether you use a phone line, a DSL line, a cable modem, or a wireless device, OS X can help you establish a connection to the Internet.

Before you start the process to set up an Internet connection, you need to select an ISP (Internet Service Provider), which is a company that sets up an Internet account for you and provides Internet access. ISPs maintain servers connected directly to the Internet 24 hours a day. You pay a fee, sometimes by the hour, but more often a flat monthly rate. To connect to the Internet, you need to obtain an Internet account and connection information from your ISP or your system administrator. Each type of Internet connection requires certain connection information, including:

◆ **ISP Phone Number**. A number to create a dial-up connection.

◆ **Account Name**. A user name for the Internet account.

◆ **Password**. A security password for the Internet account.

If your ISP needs it, you may also need the following information:

◆ **IP Address**. An IP (Internet Protocol) address is a unique identifier of your computer on the Internet.

◆ **Subnet Mask**. A filter that helps your computer differentiate between computers on a local network and the Internet.

◆ **Router**. A device address that sends and receives information over the Internet.

◆ **Domain Name Server (DNS)**. A computer that translates a web site name into an IP address.

◆ **Proxy**. A computer your Macintosh uses to access the Internet.

When you have the connection information from your ISP or network administrator, you can use the Network pane in System Preferences to set up, configure, and display status for all your network connections, such as Modem, Ethernet, and Wi-Fi.

Network pane in System Preferences

Get assistance

Getting Internet Connection Assistance

At the bottom of the Network pane is the **Assist Me** button. When you click the Assist Me button, it starts the Network Setup Assistant, which asks you a series of questions to help you set up your Internet Connection.

Creating Multiple Connections

If you have a mobile computer, such as a MacBook, you can set up multiple connections for different locations. Setting up multiple connections allows you to connect to the Internet at home using a dial-up connection, at the office using an ethernet connection, or on the road using a wireless connection.

If you have a dial-up modem or AirPort card, you can use the Internet Connect application located in the Applications folder to help you quickly create an Internet connection to different configurations in your current location.

Protecting your Computer from the Internet

When you connect to the Internet, you can access web sites and information on the Internet, but other users on the Internet can also access information on your computer. You can prevent this by activating a firewall, another security layer of protection. A **firewall** is a security system that creates a protective barrier between your computer or network and others on the Internet. The firewall monitors all communication between your computer and the Internet and prevents unsolicited inbound traffic from the Internet from entering your private computer. The firewall prevents all unsolicited communication from reaching your computer unless you specifically allow it to come through. If your computer is directly connected to the Internet, you should activate a firewall. If you are sharing an Internet connection on your network to provide Internet access on multiple computers, you should activate the firewall on the computer connected to the Internet only to avoid creating network communication problems. For more information and instructions on setting up a firewall, see "Configuring an Internet Firewall," on page 425 in Chapter 16.

Sharing an Internet Connection

If you have an Internet connection and work on a network, you can share the Internet connection with other computers on your local area network. For more information and instructions on sharing an Internet connection, see "Sharing an Internet Connection," on page 424 in Chapter 16.

Setting Up a Modem Connection

If you have a dial-up modem installed on your computer, you can set up and use a modem connection to access the Internet or another computer. You only need to set up a dial-up connection once. After you set up the dial-up connection, you can use the Show Modem Status menu to easily connect and disconnect from the Internet or network, and show modem connection information. When you are connected, the Finder displays a connection icon and connects information in the menu.

Set Up a Modem Connection

1 Click the **System Preferences** icon in the Dock, and then click the **Network** icon.

2 Click **Modem** in the list.

◆ If a modem is not in the list, click the **Add** (+) button, click Modem from the Interface pop-up, and then click **Create**.

3 Click **Advanced**.

4 Click the **PPP** tab, and then specify your user name, password, and ISP phone number.

◆ Specify PPP Options to redial a busy connection, automatically connect when starting TCP/IP applications, and automatically disconnect if you select Log Out from the Apple menu.

5 Click the **TCP/IP** and **DNS** tabs, and then specify any settings provided by your ISP, such as IP Address, Subnet Mask, Router, and DNS Servers.

6 Click the **Proxies** tab, and then specify any settings provided by your ISP.

7 Click the **Modem** tab, and then specify any settings specific to your computer's modem.

8 Click **OK**.

9 Click **Apply**.

Setting Up an Ethernet Connection

If you have a DSL or cable modem, you can set up and use an ethernet connection to access the Internet. In addition to connecting to the Internet, you also use ethernet to connect to a local area network (LAN). When you set up an ethernet connection using a cable modem or on a corporate network, some settings are typically configured automatically by a **BOOTP** (boot protocol) or **DHCP** (Dynamic Host Configuration Protocol). If your network supports ones of these services, you can use the Configure IPv4 pop-up in the TCP/IP area to select a protocol. If your ISP uses **PPPoE** (Point to Point Protocol over Ethernet), you need to specify your account and password. Check with your ISP or network administrator to determine if this applies to you.

Set Up an Ethernet Connection

1. Click the **System Preferences** icon in the Dock, and then click the **Network** icon.

2. Click **Ethernet** in the list.

3. If you want assistance, click **Assist Me**, and then follow the instructions.

4. Click **Advanced**, if needed.

5. Click the **TCP/IP** and **DNS** tabs, and then specify any settings provided by your ISP, such as IP Address, Subnet Mask, Router, and DNS Servers.

 TROUBLE? *If your Internet connection is having problems, click Renew DHCP Lease to refresh your IP address.*

6. Click the **Proxies** tab, and then specify any settings provided by your ISP.

7. Click the **Ethernet** tab, and then select a configuration (automatic or manual) and specify settings.

8. Click **OK**.

9. Click **Apply**.

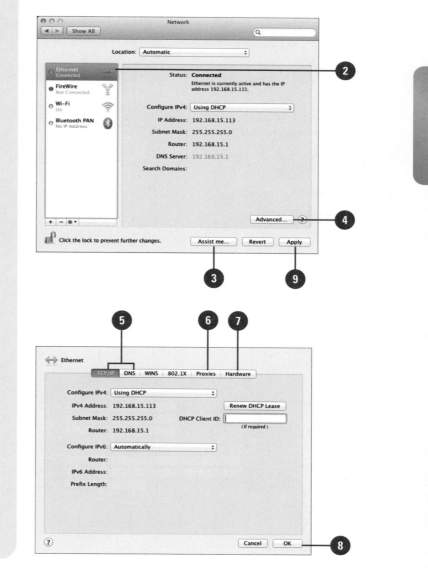

Setting Up a Wireless Connection

If you have an AirPort card on your computer and are within range of a wireless base station, such as a router or network hub, you can set up and use an wireless connection to access the Internet. An AirPort card is Apple's 802.11b-based wireless networking device that enables you to connect to the Internet without using network wires or phone lines. Wireless networks are identified by a network name. You can join a specific network or select one of the detected wireless networks. You can join a wireless network quickly with the Wi-Fi status menu, which includes signal strength for all visible wireless networks.

Set Up a Wireless Connection

1. Click the **System Preferences** icon in the Dock, and then click the **Network** icon.

2. Click **Wi-Fi** in the list.

3. Click **Turn Wi-Fi On**, if needed.

4. Click the **Network Name** pop-up, and then select a wireless network and enter a password.

5. Select or clear the **Ask to join new networks** check box.

6. Click **Advanced**, if needed.

7. Click the **Wi-Fi** tab, and then specify the options you want, such as add or remove a network.

8. Click the **TCP/IP** and **DNS** tabs, and then specify any settings provided by your ISP, such as IP Address, Subnet Mask, Router, and DNS Servers.

9. Click the **Proxies** tab, and then specify any settings provided by your ISP.

10. Click the **Ethernet** tab, and then select a configuration (automatic or manual) and specify settings.

11. Click **OK**.

12. To show the Wi-Fi status menu, select the **Show Wi-Fi status in menu bar** check box.

13. Click **Apply**.

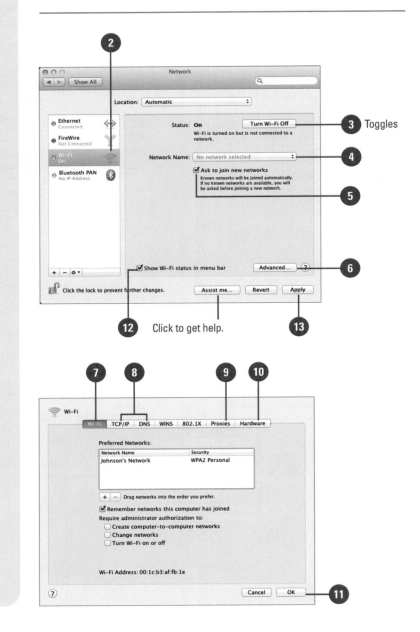

Setting Up Multiple Connections

If you have a mobile computer, such as a MacBook, you can set up multiple connections. For example, you can use a laptop to access the Internet at home using a dial-up modem, go to work and connect to a network using ethernet, or relax at a coffee shop and browse the web using Wi-Fi. Each set of network connections is called a **network port configuration**. You can create different port configurations with unique priorities for different locations, which makes switching from one location to another easier. You can quickly access different locations using the Location submenu on the Apple menu.

Set Network Port Configurations and Locations

1. Click the **System Preferences** icon in the Dock, and then click the **Network** icon.

2. Click the **Location** pop-up, and then select one of the following options:

 ◆ **Automatic**. Default location.

 ◆ **A location name**. Switches to the location name.

 ◆ **Edit Location**. Creates a new location or modifies an existing location.

3. Select the network you want to disable or enable, click the **Action** button, and then click **Make Service Inactive** or **Make Service Action**.

4. Click **Apply**.

For Your Information

Understanding Infrared Wireless Communication

Infrared wireless communication technology allows you to transfer files between computers, typically laptops, with infrared ports even when no formal network is available. IrDA is an infrared wireless communication protocol, a set of rules, that enables computer-to-computer interaction.

Making an Internet Connection

After you set up your connection in the Network Preferences pane, you can also use the pane to connect to the Internet. This is not always convenient, so OS X provides status menus on the right side of the menu bar. The status menus makes it easy to quickly log into different configurations in your current location for dial-up modem, Bluetooth, and Wi-Fi connections. You can use the Network Preferences pane to enable the menus.

Use Status Menus to Connect to the Internet

◆ **Bluetooth.** Click the **Bluetooth** icon on the menu, and then click a command:

　◆ **Turn Bluetooth On or Off.**

　◆ **Discoverable, Send File, Browse Device, Devices** (if connected), **Set Up Bluetooth Device**, or **Open Bluetooth Preferences**.

◆ **Wi-Fi.** Click the **Wi-Fi** icon on the menu, and then click a command:

　◆ **Turn Wi-Fi On or Off.**

　◆ **Join Other Network, Create Network**, or **Open Network Preferences**.

◆ **Modem.** Click the **Modem** icon on the menu, and then click a command:

　◆ **Connect.**

　◆ **Show time connected, Show status while connecting**, or **Open Network Preferences**.

Bluetooth Status menu

Bluetooth: On
Discoverable: Off
Turn Bluetooth Off

Send File...
Browse Device...

Set Up Bluetooth Device...
Open Bluetooth Preferences...

Wi-Fi Status menu

Wi-Fi: On
Turn Wi-Fi Off

No network selected
Johnson's Network
Perspection2

Join Other Network...
Create Network...
Open Network Preferences...

Modem Status menu

Modem: Idle

Connect

✓ Default

✓ Show time connected
✓ Show status while connecting

Open Network Preferences...

Understanding Web Sites and Browsers

A **web site** contains web pages linked together to make searching for information on the Internet easier. **Web pages** are documents that contain highlighted words, phrases, and graphics, called **hyperlinks** (or simply **links**) that open other web pages when you click them. Some web pages contain frames. A **frame** is a separate window within a web page that lets you see more than one web page at a time. **Web browsers** are software programs that you use to "surf the web," or access and display web pages. Browsers make the web easy to navigate by providing a graphical, point-and-click environment. Safari 7.0 or later is a browser from Apple that is built into OS X. Microsoft Internet Explorer and Mozilla Firefox are other popular browsers. With a web browser, you can display web pages from all over the world, use links to move from one web page to another, play audio and video clips, search the web for information, bookmark web pages for easy access, and print text and graphics on web pages.

Web browser Web site

Web page

Links

Viewing and Customizing Safari

Safari is a web browser that you use to search the World Wide Web. When you start Safari from the Dock, your home page appears in the browser pane. If you want a different page to appear when you start Safari and whenever you click the Home button, you can change it at any time. You can also specify a window option when you start Safari (**New!**) and the default page that you want to view when you open a new window or tab. The elements of the Safari window allow you to browse, view, print, and search for information on the Internet. You can customize the Safari window to display the elements you work with the most. The View menu as well as buttons allow you to show and hide display elements, such as the Favorites bar (**New!**) and Sidebar (**New!**) with Bookmarks, Reading List, and Shared Links (**New!**). In order to use Shared Links with Twitter or LinkedIn in Safari, you need to add those accounts in the Internet Accounts pane (**New!**) in System Preferences.

View and Customize Safari

1. Click the **Safari** icon in the Dock.

2. Click the **View** menu, and then click the menu command with the element you want to show or hide in the Safari window.

 - ◆ **Toolbar**
 - ◆ **Customize Toolbar**
 - ◆ **Favorites Bar (New!)**
 - ◆ **Sidebar (New!)**
 - ◆ **Tab Bar**
 - ◆ **Status Bar**
 - ◆ **Bookmarks Sidebar (New!)**
 - ◆ **Reading List Sidebar (New!)**
 - ◆ **Reader**
 - ◆ **One Tab or All Tabs**
 - ◆ **Downloads**
 - ◆ To change the display view, select a zoom commands: **Actual Size, Zoom In, Zoom Out**, or **Zoom Text Only**.

 TIMESAVER *Double-tap to zoom in and double-tap again to return to the original state.*

 - ◆ **Enter Full Screen.** Click the **Full Screen** button. To exit, point to the top of the screen to show the menu bar, and then click the **Full Screen** button or press Esc.

Toolbar 2 Favorites bar Tab bar Reader Full Screen

Sidebar 1 Status bar Browser pane Downloads

Set the Home and Other Pages

① Open the web page you want to be the new home page.

② Click the **Safari** menu, and then click **Preferences**.

③ Click **General**.

④ Click **Set to Current Page**.

 ◆ You can also enter a URL in the Home Page box.

⑤ To specify the option that appears when you do any of the following:

 ◆ **Start Safari**. Click the **Safari open with** pop-up (**New!**), and then select a window option.

 ◆ **New Window**. Click the **New windows open with** pop-up, and then select a page option.

 ◆ **New Tab**. Click the **New tabs open with** pop-up, and then select a page option.

⑥ Click the **Close** button.

Prepare for Share Links

① Click the **System Preferences** icon in the Dock.

② Click the **Internet Accounts** icon.

③ Click **Twitter** or **Linkedin**.

④ Enter your name, user ID, password, and then click **Next**.

⑤ Read the dialog (**New!**) with sign features, and then click **Sign In**.

⑥ Click the **Close** button.

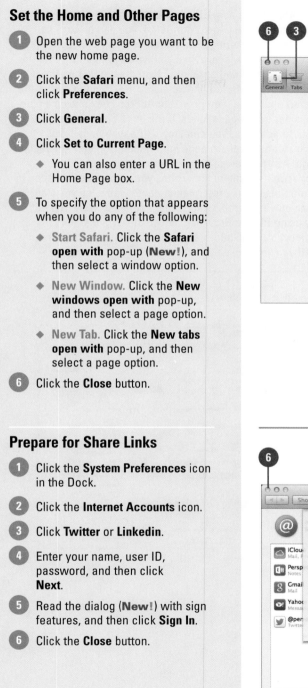

Browsing the Web

A **web address** (also known as a **URL**) is a unique place on the Internet where you can locate a web page. With Safari, you can browse sites on the web with ease by entering a web address or by clicking a link on a web page to access a new site. When you type a web address in the Address box, Safari tries to find a recently visited page that matches what you've typed so far. If Safari finds a match, it fills in the rest of the address. As Safari opens the web page, the Address box shows a blue-shaded progress bar as the page loads. If the page opens too slowly or if you decide not to access it, you can stop it. If a web page loads incorrectly or you want to update page information, you can reload, or refresh the page. As you browse the web, you can move backward or forward one location at a time to show sites you've previously visited in this session. Safari also stores information about web sites you visit and information you've entered, which other users can view. You can prevent this by using Private Browsing, which clears the history list, Downloads window, AutoFill information, searches, and cookies are deleted. It's as if you never used Safari.

Open and View a Web Page

Use any of the following methods to display a web page:

- In the Address box, type the web address, and then press Return.

 If you have recently entered the web page address, Safari remembers it and tries to complete the address for you. The suggested match is highlighted. Click the correct address in a list of possibilities or continue to type until the address you want appears in the Address list.

- Click any link on the web page, such as a picture or colored, underlined text. The mouse pointer changes to a hand when it is over a link.

- Browse Privately. Click the **Safari** menu, click **Private Browsing**, and then click **OK**. To skip the confirmation, Option-click the Private Browsing command.

 - To turn it off, click the **Safari** menu, and then click **Private Browsing**.

Type a web address

Click a link

Navigation Basics

◆ To move back or forward one web page at a time, click the **Back** button or the **Forward** button on the toolbar.

TIMESAVER *To move back, press* ⌘+*[(left bracket). To move forward, press* ⌘+*] (right bracket).*

◆ To stop a page from loading, click the **Stop** button in the Address bar during the load, or click the **View** menu, and then click **Stop**.

TIMESAVER *Press* ⌘+*. (period).*

◆ To reload a page, click the **Reload** button in the Address bar, or click the **View** menu, and then click **Reload**.

TIMESAVER *Press* ⌘+*R.*

◆ To go to the Home page, click the **History** menu, and then click **Home**.

TIMESAVER *Press* ⌘+*Shift+H.*

Did You Know?

You can open a web page on your hard disk or network server. Click the File menu, click Open File, type the complete path and file name of the web page, and then click Open.

You can open a web page from a document in another application. Select the web address, click the application menu (such as TextEdit), point to Services, and then click Open URL.

Back button

Forward button

Reload button

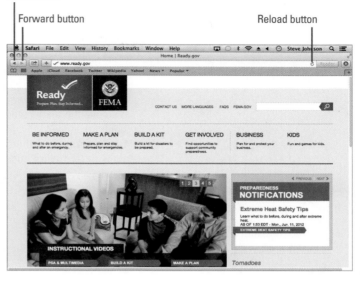

For Your Information

Understanding a Web Address

The address for a web page is called a URL (Uniform Resource Locator). Each web page has a unique URL that is typically composed of four parts: the protocol (a set of rules that allow computers to exchange information), the location of the web site, the name that maintains the web site, and a suffix that identifies the type of site. A URL begins with a protocol, followed by a colon, two slashes, the location of the web site, a dot, the name of the web site, a dot, and a suffix. The web site is the computer where the web pages are located. At the end of the web site name, another slash may appear, followed by one or more folder names and a file name. For example, in the address, http://*www*.perspection.com/downloads/main.htm, the protocol is *http* (HyperText Transfer Protocol), the location of the web site is *www* (World Wide Web), the name of the web site is *perspection*, and the suffix is *com* (a commercial organization); a folder at that site is called */downloads*; and within the folder is a file called *main.htm*.

Browsing the Web Using Tabs

When you open a web page, it opens in the same window you are using. If you want to view more than one page at a time in a single window, you can open web pages in separate tabs or new windows. You can also bookmark a set of tabs for easy access in the future or revert to the tabs that were open the last time you used Safari. Before you start opening web pages in tabs, you can set tab browsing options to specify the way you want to use tabs in Safari. When you open a page in a tab, the Tab bar appears (below the Favorites bar) with the name of the web page along with a box you can use to close the tab. You can also use the View menu to show the Tab bar with all tabs or display each tab individually. If you select a web page from the History or Bookmarks menu, the page opens in the current tab. When you use the Back and Forward buttons on the toolbar, Safari displays web pages previously viewed in the current tab.

Set Tabbed Browsing Options

1. Click the **Safari** menu, and then click **Preferences**.

2. Click **Tabs**.

3. Click the **Open pages in tabs instead of windows** pop-up, and then select an option: **Never**, **Automatically**, or **Always**.

4. Select the ⌘-click opens a link in a new tab check box to open a link in a new tab; clear it to open a link in a new window.

5. Select the **When a new tab or window opens, make it active** check box to open new tabs in front of the current tab.

 IMPORTANT *Some keyboard shortcuts change depending on the tab options you select. The bottom of the Tab Preferences window displays the new shortcuts. The shortcuts change revert back when you disable the options.*

6. Click the **Close** button.

Shortcuts to use when working with tabs.

For Your Information

Using Gestures to Navigate Web Pages

If you have a Multi-Touch trackpad, you can use gestures in Safari to quickly get around the web. You can navigate through the pages of a website by simply swiping. When you swipe to the left, the next page slides into view. When you swipe to the right, you go back to the previous page. You can also zoom in and out with gestures. You can double-tap to zoom in on a column of text or an image. The text and images scale up smoothly, and then text remains sharp. You can double-tap again to zoom out. You can also zoom in and out on text and images more precisely with a pinch.

Open and View a Web Page in a Tab

◆ To show or hide the Tab bar, click the **View** menu, click **Show/Hide Tab Bar**.

◆ To show one tab or all tabs, click the **View** menu, click **Show One Tab** or **Show All Tabs**. In Show All Tabs, click the white dots or swipe to scroll, or click a page to show one tab.

 TIMESAVER *Click the Show All Tabs button on the Tabs bar.*

◆ To open a web page in a tab, click the **File** menu, click **New Tab**, type the web address, and then press Return.

◆ To open a link or bookmark in a tab, hold down ⌘, and then click the item.

◆ To open a bookmark collection in the Favorites bar in tabs, hold down the Control key, click the collection in the Favorites bar, and then click **Open In Tabs**.

◆ To open a folder of bookmarks in the Bookmarks Library in tabs, click the **Bookmarks** menu, click **Show Bookmarks**, hold down the Control key, click the folder in the right pane, and then click **Open In Tabs**.

◆ To switch between web page tabs, click the tab in the Tab bar.

◆ To close a tab, point to the tab, and then click the **Close** box on the tab.

 TIMESAVER *Hold down the Option key and click the Close box to show the web page and close all other tabs.*

One Tab view Close box Active tab

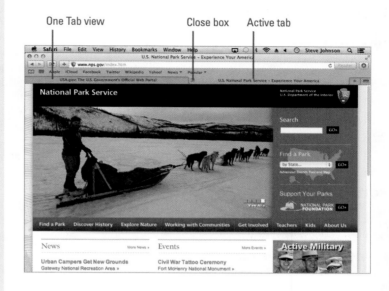

All Tabs view Close box

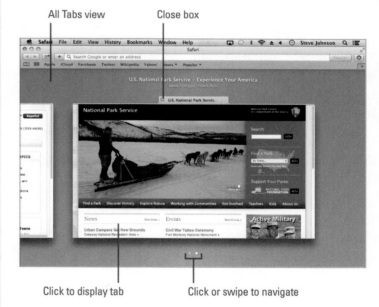

Click to display tab Click or swipe to navigate

Using the Reader and Reading List

Instead of bookmarking articles to read later, you can use Safari's Reading List in the Sidebar (**New!**) to make it easier for you manage and keep track of the information. Safari's Reader allows you to view news stories and other text-based articles in a window that's optimized for easy reading. Reader connects articles that are continued over multiple pages and broken up by ads, graphics, and other elements. When a web page contains a text-based article, the Reading button appears in the Address bar. When you click the Reader button, a viewer appears, similar to a PDF reader, where you can easily read your article without any distractions. If an article contains multiple pages, Safari gets all the pages and stores them, so you can read the entire article offline.

Use the Reader

1. Open a web page with a text-based article, such as a news site.

 A Reading button appears in the Address bar, like the RSS button.

2. Click the **Reading** button in the Address bar.

 ◆ You can also click the **Share** button on the toolbar, and then click **Add to Reading List**.

3. Read and scroll down the article.

4. To navigate the screen, point to the bottom middle of the Reader to display a toolbar.

 ◆ **Zoom in and out.** Click to zoom in and out.

 ◆ **Mail this page.** Click to mail this page using your e-mail program.

 ◆ **Print this page.** Click to print this page.

 ◆ **Close Reader.** Click to close the Reader.

Share button

Use the Reading List

1 Open the web page you want to add to the Reading List.

2 Click the **Sidebar** button (**New!**) on the Favorites bar, and then click the **Reading List** button (**New!**) in the Sidebar.

◆ You can also click the **View** menu, and then click **Show Reading List Sidebar** (**New!**).

3 Click **Add** (+) button (**New!**) in the Address bar. If you down hold, you can click **Reading List**.

◆ You can also Shift-click a link to quickly add it to the list.

◆ You can also click the **Bookmarks** menu, and then click **Add to Reading List**.

4 To view the Reading List in different ways, click **All** or **Unread**.

After you have read an item, it get removed from the Unread reading list, however it remains in the list of all items.

5 To remove a page from the list, point to the item to display a **Remove** button (x), and then click it.

◆ To remove all items in the list, Control-click an item in the list, and then click **Clear All Items**.

6 Click the **Sidebar** button to close it.

Did You Know?

You can change the size of text on a web page. Click the View menu, and then click Zoom Text Only. You can also click the View menu, and then click Zoom In (⌘++) or Zoom Out (⌘+-). To view the page at 100%, click the View menu, and then click Actual Size (⌘+0).

For Your Information

Syncing Reading List and Bookmarks with iCloud

iCloud is a cloud service that stores your content—including bookmarks, reading list items, and more—and wirelessly pushes it to all your devices, such as your iPad, iPhone, iPod touch, Mac, and PC. When you create a bookmark or add to your reading list, all your devices are automatically updated. To enable iCloud, open System Preferences, click the iCloud icon, sign in, if prompted, select the Bookmarks check box, and then click the Close button. That's it.

Working with Shared Links

If you have a Twitter or Linkedin account, you can view and share links (**New!**) from those social networking services directly in Safari. After you setup your Twitter or Linkedin account (**New!**) in the Internet Accounts pane (**New!**) in System Preferences, you can view and work with links in the Sidebar (**New!**). With Twitter, you can view tweets from your Twitter timeline with links, retweet the posts, or visit your Twitter page. With Linkedin, you can view posts with links or visit your Linkedin page. In Safari, you can also update shared links, so you can view the lastest ones at any time.

Work with Shared Links

1. Click the **Sidebar** button (**New!**) on the Favorites bar.

2. Click the **Shared Links** button (**New!**) in the Sidebar.

 ◆ You can also click the **View** menu, and then click the **Show Shared Links Sidebar** or **Hide Shared Links Sidebar**.

3. To search for links, enter a name in the Search box in the Sidebar.

4. To open a linked item, click it from the list.

 A banner appears at the top of the page containing the context for the link.

5. Scroll down the page to view its contents.

6. In Twitter, you can click Retweet on the banner to retweet it.

7. To update your shared links, Control-click the list, and then click **Update Shared Links**.

8. Click the **Sidebar** button to close it.

See Also

See "Viewing and Customizing Safari" on page 236 for information on setting up Twitter or Linkedin accounts for use in Safari.

For Your Information

Sharing Web Pages

Safari provides the ability to share a web page with others using Mail, Messages, AirDrop (**New!**), Twitter, Linkedin, and Facebook. Simply, open the page you want to share, click the Share button on toolbar, and then select the command for the method you want to use. You can also use the Share command on the File menu. In Mail or Messages, address the message, and then send it. You can send the web page in Reader view, or as a web page, PDF, or link from the message window. In AirDrop, select a person, and then click Send. In Twitter, Linkedin, or Facebook, enter a message, and then click Send.

Viewing Top Sites

Top Sites is a visual preview of your favorite web sites. Safari tracks the sites you visit the most and ranks your favorites, displaying up to 24 thumbnail previews. Simply, click the Show Top Sites button on the Favorites bar (**New!**) to view and select a web site to visit. If you don't see a site, you can quickly add one to Top Sites. In Top Sites, you can remove sites (**New!**), mark or unmark sites as permanent (**New!**), and rearrange sites (**New!**). In Safari preferences, you can specify the number of Top Sites shown (**New!**), either 6, 12, or 24.

View and Use Top Sites

◆ **View Top Sites.** Click the **Show Top Sites** button, and then click a thumbnail to visit the page, or use one of the navigation buttons.

 TIMESAVER *To view Top Sites, press Shift+⌘+1.*

◆ **Open a Site.** In Top Sites, click a thumbnail. To open a site in a new tab, ⌘-click a thumbnail.

◆ **Add a Site.** Open the web page, click and hold the **Add** (+) button (**New!**) on the toolbar, and then click Top Sites.

◆ **Remove a Site.** In Top Sites, point to a site (**New!**), and then click the **Never include as top site** button (the X button).

◆ **Mark or Unmark as Permanent Site.** In Top Sites, point to a site (**New!**), click the **Mark as permanent top site** button (the gray Pin button) or **Un-mark as permanent top site** button (the blue Pin button).

◆ **Rearrange Sites.** In Top Sites, drag a thumbnail (**New!**) to another location.

◆ **Change Number of Sites Shown.** Click the **Safari** menu, click **Preferences**, click **General**, click the **Top Sites shows** list arrow, select **6**, **12**, or **24 sites** (**New!**), and then click the **Close** button.

Never include as top site button

Show Top Sites button

Mark as permanent top site button

Use to add a site

Drag to rearrange

Viewing a History List

Sometimes you run across a great web site and simply forget to add it to your Bookmarks list. With Safari there's no need to try to remember all the sites you visit. The History list keeps track of where you've been for a week organized by the date. Safari deletes web pages from the History list older than a week. If you no longer need the pages in the History list, you can clear the entire list. To view the History list, click the History menu, and then point to a day or click Show History. When you show history or bookmarks, you can browse through the list or search sites using the Search box at the bottom of the window.

Open a Web Page from the History List

1. Click the **History** menu, and then click **Show History**.

 ◆ To quickly open a web page, click the **History** menu, point to a date if desired, and then click a web page.

2. Click the **Expand** arrow to display the bookmarks you want to view.

3. Scroll through the list or use the Search box to locate the one you want.

4. Double-click the web page.

Did You Know?

You can delete individual entries in the History list. Click the History menu, click Show History, select the entry you want to remove, press Delete, and then click the Close button.

You can clear the entire History list. Click the History menu, and then click Clear History.

You can clear the entire History list automatically on a regular basis. Click the Safari menu, click Preferences, click General, click the Remove History Items pop-up, select the interval option you want, and then click the Close button.

For Your Information

Emptying the Cache

As you open web pages, Safari saves the page content in a temporary location on your local hard disk, known as the **cache**, to make it faster to open the same pages next time. Anytime you display new content, the cache continues to increase in size, taking up valuable hard disk space. You can empty the cache at anytime to remove the local version of the web page content and free up hard disk space. To empty the cache, click the Safari menu, click Empty Cache, and then click Empty.

Bookmarking a Web Page

Rather than memorizing URLs or keeping a handwritten list of web pages you want to visit, you can use the Bookmarks Library to store and organize the addresses. When you display a web page or a set of tabs that you want to display again at a later time, you can add the web page or tab set to your Bookmarks Library. After you add the bookmark to the Bookmarks Library, you can quickly return to it by using the Favorites bar (**New!**) or Bookmarks menu to select it. If you have bookmarks in other browsers, such as Internet Explorer, Google Chrome, or Mozilla Firefox, you can import the bookmarks in the Bookmarks Library using the Import Bookmarks command on the File menu.

Create Bookmark Pages

1. Open the web site you want to add to your Bookmark list.

2. Click the **Bookmarks** menu, and then click **Add Bookmark** or **Add Bookmark For These Tabs**.

 TIMESAVER *Click the Share or Add (+) (**New!**) button on the toolbar, and then click Add Bookmark, or drag the icon in the Address box to the Favorites bar to quickly add a bookmark.*

3. Click the pop-up, and then select a location: Bookmarks, Top Sites, Favorites Bar (**New!**), Bookmarks Menu, or a folder collection.

4. Type the name for the bookmark, or use the default name supplied.

5. Click **Add**.

6. To quickly return to a bookmark, use the Favorites bar or Bookmarks menu.

Did You Know?

You can drag a bookmark to move or delete it. Drag a bookmark to another place on the Favorites bar to move it, or outside the Safari window to delete it. You can also drag bookmarks and folders from the Bookmarks Library to the Favorites bar.

Share button

Click to open the Sidebar with the Bookmarks Library.

Working with Bookmarks

If your list of bookmarks grows long, you can use the Bookmarks Sidebar (**New!**) or Library to organize bookmarks into folders, rename folder or bookmarks with different or shorter names, delete bookmarks you don't visit anymore, or move bookmarks into folders to make them easier to find. You can use the Sidebar button on the Favorites bar to view the Bookmarks Sidebar. You can use the Edit Bookmarks command to view the Bookmarks Library. The Bookmarks Library shows your folders of bookmarks in the left column, and addresses of bookmarks and folders in the right column. You also use the Bookmarks Library to work with Bonjour web sites. Safari uses Bonjour to find any web sites on your local network or subnet. Before you can work with the Bonjour, you need to enable the options in the Advanced pane of Safari preferences.

Create a Bookmark Folder

1. Click the **Bookmarks** menu, and then click **Add Bookmark Folder**.

 The Sidebar opens (**New!**), displaying the Bookmarks tab with a new untitled folder with the name selected.

2. Type a name for the folder, and then press Return.

3. Display the bookmarks you want to move in the folder.

4. Drag the bookmarks to the folder.

5. Click the **Sidebar** button on the Favorites bar to close it.

 The folder appears on the Favorites bar with a triangle next to the name.

Did You Know?

You can add Rendezvous web sites to the Favorites bar or menu. Click the Safari menu, click Preferences, click Advanced (**New!**), select the Include Bonjour check box where appropriate, and then click the Close button.

You can view a list of Bonjour web sites. Click the Bookmarks Library button on the Favorites bar, and then click Bonjour in the Bookmarks Sidebar.

Organize Bookmarks in the Bookmarks Sidebar or Library

◆ **Show and hide Bookmarks Sidebar.** Click the **Bookmarks** menu, and then click **Show Bookmarks** or **Hide Bookmarks**.

You can also click the **View** menu, and then click the **Show Bookmarks Sidebar** or **Hide Bookmarks Sidebar**.

◆ **Show and hide Bookmarks Library.** Click the **Bookmarks** menu, and then click **Edit Bookmarks (New!)** or **Hide Bookmarks Editor (New!)**.

◆ **Create a folder.** Click the **Add** button (+) at the bottom of the Sidebar or click **New Folder** in the Library, enter a name, and then press Return.

◆ **Rename a folder or bookmark.** In the Bookmarks Sidebar or Library, Control-click the name, click **Rename Folder** or **Rename Bookmark**, type a new name, and then press Return.

TIMESAVER *Click and hold a bookmark or folder in the Favorites bar to rename it.*

◆ **Delete a folder or bookmark.** In the Bookmarks Sidebar or Library, Control-click the name, and then click **Delete**.

◆ **Move or rearrange a folder or bookmark.** In the Bookmarks Sidebar or Library, drag its icon to the location or icon where you want to place it. To copy it, hold down the Option key as you drag the icon.

◆ **Search for a bookmark.** In the Bookmarks Library, click in the Search box, and then enter a bookmark name.

Bookmarks Sidebar Bookmarks Library

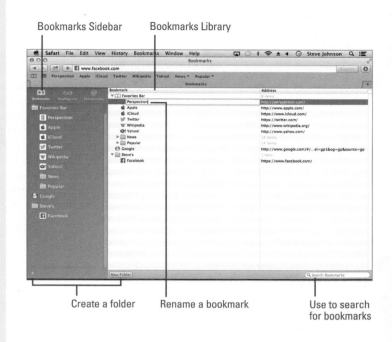

Create a folder Rename a bookmark Use to search for bookmarks

For Your Information

Syncing Bookmarks on Multiple Computers

Using your iCloud account, you can automatically sync your bookmarks on different computers so they are the same. Before you can use the service, you need to create an iCloud account. On each computer, click the System Preferences icon in the Dock, click the iCloud icon, sign-in with your Apple ID, select the Bookmarks check box, and then click the Close button. iCloud automatically syncs your bookmarks to the cloud, and then down to your computer or iOS device.

Filling Out Forms on the Web

Safari can use information in your Contacts or data you previously entered in an online form to automatically complete online forms you need to fill out in the future. AutoFill is a service that helps you complete online forms, credit card information (**New!**), and log in to web sites with a user name and password from Passwords preferences and information from your Contacts. You use the AutoFill pane of the Safari preferences to select, modify, or delete which information AutoFill uses to complete a form or log in. When you use AutoFill to automatically fill in information, Safari highlights the data in yellow so you can see the changes. Safari keeps your information private until you choose to send it. If you no longer need the AutoFill service, you can keep Safari from automatically completing forms and log ins. If you run out of room in a text field, you can now resize text fields on any web page by dragging the corner of the field to make more room and reflow the web page.

Set AutoFill Preferences

1. Click the **Safari** menu, and then click **Preferences**.

2. Click **AutoFill**.

3. Use the following to enable or disable AutoFill options:

 ◆ **Using info from my Contacts card.** Use for information in your Contacts.

 ◆ **User names and passwords.** Use for your web site log in information.

 ◆ **Credit cards.** Use for credit card data (**New!**).

 ◆ **Other forms.** Use based on data from other online forms.

4. For any of the check boxes, click **Edit** to view, add, edit, or remove information stored by AutoFill.

 ◆ **User names and passwords.** Opens the Passwords preferences, where you can remove passwords and set options, including **Allow AutoFill even for websites that request passwords not be saved** (**New!**). Click **AutoFill** to return.

5. Click the **Close** button.

Passwords preferences

User name and password Autofill data

AutoFills for passwords not saved

Contacts Autofill data

Fill Out Forms in Web Pages

① Select AutoFill data and options in the AutoFill pane of Safari preferences; click the **Safari** menu, click **Preferences**, and then click **AutoFill**.

② Use any of the following methods to fill out forms using AutoFill:

◆ **Complete user name and password in a log in.** Display a log in screen, enter a user name and password, and then click **Yes** to save the log in information so you don't have to do it again; click **Not Now** to defer saving the log in information until later; and click **Never for this website** to not save log in information for this web site.

◆ **Complete a web form.** Open the web page, and then click the **AutoFill** button in the Address bar.

◆ **Complete individual boxes in a form.** Open the web page, select a text box, and then start typing. If AutoFill retrieves a match, a menu appears. Select the correct item and then click **AutoFill**. to bypass the menu, press Return.

Did You Know?

You can display an alert before you send a non-secure form. Click the Safari menu, click Preferences, click Security, select the Ask Before Sending A Non-Secure Form To A Secure Website check box, and then click the Close button.

Enter user name and password

Click an AutoFill save option

For Your Information

Checking Spelling and Grammar in Safari

You can't spell check the content of a web page, but you can spell check any text you enter in a text box on a page. For example, if you type a word in a text box on a form or in the Google Search box in the Address bar, you can check its spelling before you complete the form or start the search. To check spelling and grammar, click in a text box, click the Edit menu, point to Spelling and Grammar, and then click Check Document Now. If your computer doesn't recognize a word, a dialog opens, asking you to correct, ignore, or add the word to a dictionary. You can also check spelling as you type, like many word processing programs. When you select the Check Spelling While Typing command on the Spelling and Grammar submenu located on the Edit menu, Safari displays a wavy red line under any term your computer doesn't recognize. You can also select the Check Grammar With Spelling to check grammar on demand.

Searching the Web

You can find all kinds of information on the web. The best way to find information is to use a search engine. A **search engine** is a program you access through a web site and use to search through a collection of Internet information to find what you want. Safari comes with the Google search engine built-in to the program. When performing a search using the Smart Search field in the Address box, the search engine compares keywords with words that it finds as Top Hits. **Keywords** are words or phrases that best describe the information you want to retrieve. If the search engine finds your keywords in the stored database, it lists links to the matched sites. When you open a link from the results, you can use the SnapBack button to quickly return to your search results. In addition, you can search for text that either contains or starts with the text you type within a web page to display the found count and highlight matching terms within a page.

Google Search for Information

1. In the Address box, type a word or phrase you want to find.

 TIMESAVER *Press ⌘+Option+F to select the Address bar content to start a Google search.*

 As you type, suggestions appear in the Top Hit list.

2. In the Top Hit list, select the one you want or press Return.

 Top Hit suggestions improve as you select the results.

3. Click a link in the list of search results to open a web page.

4. To return to the last page of Google search results, click the **SnapBack** button.

 TIMESAVER *Press Option+ ⌘+S to view search results SnapBack.*

5. To repeat a previous search, click the magnifying glass in the Smart Search field, and then select the search term you want.

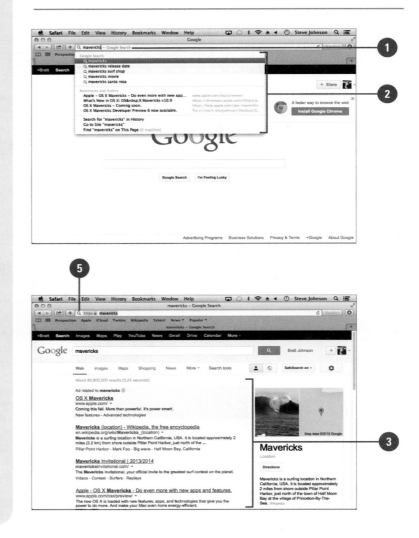

Search Within a Page

1 Click the **Edit** menu, point to **Find**, and then click **Find**.

TIMESAVER *Press ⌘+F.*

2 Click the Find bar arrow, and then click **Contains** or **Starts With**.

3 Click in the Find bar, and then type the word or phrase you want to find on the current page.

Displays the found count and highlights matching terms within the page.

4 Click the left and right arrows on the Find bar to highlight the matching terms.

5 When you're done, click **Done**.

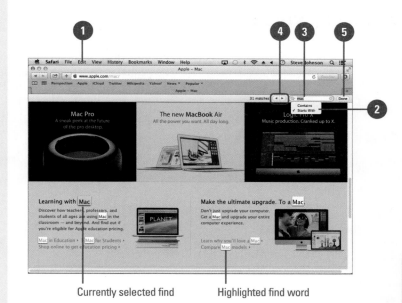

Currently selected find Highlighted find word

Did You Know?

You can revisit search results using SnapBack. Type a search term or phrase in the Search box, press Return, visit some web pages, and then click the SnapBack button in the Search box to return to the search results.

You can open a web page in Dashboard. In Safari, display the web page you want to open in Dashboard, click the Open This Page In Dashboard button on the toolbar, reposition and resize the highlighted area, and then click Add.

You can resize text fields on a web page. Drag the corner of a text field to resize it and reflow the web page.

For Your Information

Opening a Web Page in a Different Window

You can open a web page in a different window. Click the File menu, click New Window, type the web address, and then press Return. To open a web page in a new window using a link, hold down the Control key, click a link or bookmark, and then click Open Link In New Window. To find out the address of a link, point to it, and then view the Status bar. To switch between open windows, use the Window menu.

Printing a Web Page

Web pages are designed for viewing on a computer screen, but you can also print all or part of one. Before you print, you should preview the page to verify that it looks the way you want. When you are ready to print, Safari provides many options for printing web pages. If the web page consists of frames, you can print the specific frame you want to print. You can also use the Print dialog to create a PDF of a web page or send a web page as a PDF fax or PDF mail attachment.

Print a Web Page

1. Open the web page you want to print, click the **File** menu, and then click **Print**.

2. Click the **Printer** pop-up, and then select from the available printers.

3. Click the **Presets** pop-up, and then select from the available preset options.

4. Click the **Show Details** button to expand the dialog.

5. Click the **Print Option**s pop-up, and then select from the available print options, such as Safari.

6. Choose the various print options you want.

7. Click the following options to finalize your print: **PDF**, **Cancel**, or **Print**.

Did You Know?

You can print a frame of a web page. Hold down the Control key, click the frame you want to print, click Print Frame, specify the options you want, and then click Print.

See Also

See Chapter 8, "Printing, Scanning, and Faxing," on page 205 for information on setting up and printing a page.

Viewing PDF Files

In Safari, you can display a PDF file in the browser window along with a toolbar and sidebar to make it easier to view the file. When you point to the middle of an open PDF page, near the bottom, of the Safari window, a toolbar with PDF tools appears. You can use the tools to save the PDF to the Downloads folder, print the PDF, move page to page, zoom in and out to view the screen, and open the PDF in Acrobat or Preview. When you no longer want to use the toolbar, simply move the pointer off it.

View PDF Files in the Browser Window

1. Open the web page with the link to the PDF you want to view.

2. Click the link for the PDF file.

3. Use any of the following PDF tools:

 ◆ **View Toolbar.** Point to the middle of the PDF page, near the bottom.

 If you move the pointer off the toolbar, it disappears.

 ◆ **Save PDF to Download Folder.** Click the button on the toolbar to quickly save the file to the Downloads folder in the Home folder.

 ◆ **Print PDF.** Click the button to print the PDF document.

 ◆ **Move Pages.** Click the arrow buttons in the toolbar or click a page in the sidebar.

 ◆ **Zoom In or Out.** Click the Zoom In (+) or Zoom Out (-) buttons.

 ◆ **Open PDF.** Click the button on the toolbar to open the PDF in Acrobat Reader or Preview.

 ◆ **View Sidebar.** Control-click the document, and then click Show Navigation Pane Buttons.

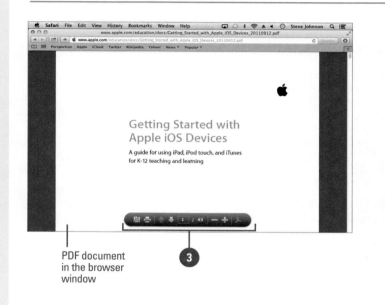

PDF document in the browser window

For Your Information

Saving a Web Page as a PDF

If you visit a web page that you want to reference later, you can export it as a PDF. It's simple and works just like the Save As command. Click the File menu, click Export as PDF (**New!**), specify a name, tags (**New!**), and location, and then click Save.

Saving a Web Page

You can save a web page, and view it later from your local hard drive or use it as source for HTML (HyperText Markup Language) code, which instructs the browser how to display the web page. When you save a web page, Safari can save only the HTML text content of the current page, or all the elements on the page, which includes text and images. When you save, you can also assign one or more tags (**New!**) to the file. Before you save a web page you can view the HTML code to determine if you need it. When you open an HTML file saved from the web, Safari displays only local information and doesn't access remote resources or send data to a remote server.

Save a Web Page

1. Open the web page you want to save, click the **File** menu, and then click **Save As**.

2. Type a name for the file, or use the suggested name.

3. Click in the Tags box, select or enter one or more tags (**New!**).

4. Select the hard drive and folder in which you want to save the file.

5. Click the **Format** pop-up, and then select a web format:

 ◆ **Page Source.** Saves only the source text of this page.

 ◆ **Web Archive.** Saves text, images, and other content on this page.

6. Click **Save**.

Click to expand or collapse.

Export As: Apple – Support – Manuals

Tags: Important

Where: Documents

Format: Web Archive
Saves text, images, and other content of this page.

Cancel Save

Did You Know?

You can view the HTML code of a web page. Open the web page, click the View menu, and then click View Source. When you are done viewing, click the Close button.

Saving Pictures or Text from a Web Page

If you find information on a web page that you want to save for future reference or share with others, you can copy and paste it to another document or save it on your computer. When you copy information from a web page, make sure you're not violating any copyright laws.

Save a Picture from a Web Page

1. Open the web page with the picture you want to save.

2. Control-click the picture, and then click **Save Image As**.

 TIMESAVER *Control-click the picture, and then click Save Image to "Downloads" to quickly save an image to the Downloads folder.*

3. Type a name for the file.

4. Select the drive and folder in which you want to save the file.

5. Click **Save**.

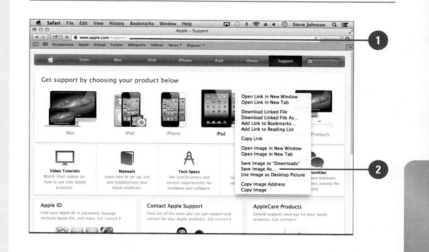

Copy Text from a Web Page

1. Open the web page with the text you want to copy.

2. Select the text you want to copy.

3. Control-click the selected text, and then click **Copy**.

4. Switch to where you want to paste the text.

5. Click the **Edit** menu, and then click **Paste**.

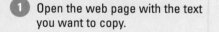

Did You Know?

You can copy a picture to the clipboard. Control-click the picture, and then click Copy Image.

Downloading Files Safely from the Web

There are thousands of sites on the Internet offering all sorts of files you can download to your computer, from trailers to the latest game demos. You can download files from any web site by finding the file you want, and then clicking the download link. Safari automatically downloads the file to the location specified in the General pane of Safari preferences. When a file is downloading, the Downloads panel in Safari displays a progress and status information. You can stop downloading a file, view a downloaded file in the Finder, and clear the Downloads panel when it gets too full. You can show and hide the Downloads panel from the Safari toolbar or View menu.

Download a File from a Web Page

1. Open the web page that you want to download a file.

2. Click a download link, or Control-click the link pointing to the actual file, and then click:
 - **Download Linked File** to download the file to the Downloads folder.
 - **Download Linked File As** to specify a download location.

3. Click the **Show Downloads** button on the toolbar.
 - You can also click the **View** menu, and then click **Show Downloads**.

 TIMESAVER *Press Option+⌘+L to show and hide the Downloads panel.*

 The Downloads panel appears, displaying the estimated time to download the file, along with the estimated transfer time, and a list previous file downloads.

4. Click the **Show Downloads** button on the toolbar again to close the Downloads panel.
 - You can also click the **View** menu, and then click **Hide Downloads**.

Download in progress

List of downloaded files

Downloaded files in the Downloads folder

Work with Files in the Downloads Panel

1 Click the **View** menu, and then click **Show Downloads**.

◆ Downloaded files are stored by default in the Downloads folder. In Finder, click the **Go** menu, click **Home**, and then double-click the **Downloads** folder.

2 Perform any of the following operations.

◆ **Stop a downloading file.** Click the **Stop** icon to the right of the file name; to restart the download, click the icon again.

◆ **View a downloaded file.** Click the **Magnifying Glass** icon to the right of the file name.

◆ **Clear the Downloads window.** Click the **Clear** button. Clearing the window does not clear files that are being downloaded.

◆ **Remove a downloaded file.** Control-click the file name, and then click **Remove From List**.

3 Click the **View** menu, and then click **Hide Downloads**.

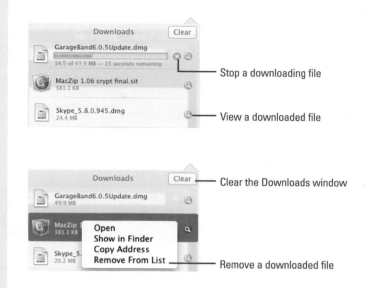

Stop a downloading file

View a downloaded file

Clear the Downloads window

Remove a downloaded file

See Also

See "Setting Safari Preferences" on page 260 for information on selecting the download file location and specifying when to remove downloaded items.

Did You Know?

You can access a site with lots of files to download. Try these sites to find plenty of files to download: *http://www.download.com* and *http://www.shareware.com*.

For Your Information

Downloading Disk Images and Installing Software

There are several different types of disk images. Safari works a little differently for each type. When you download a disk image, Safari decompresses the file and in some cases mounts a volume. OS X no longer automatically opens Disk Images (.dmg) and installer packages (.pkg) for security and safety purposes. If you download a disk image in the MacBinary, BinHex, or gzip file format, Safari simply decompresses the file.

Setting Safari Preferences

Safari preferences help you configure browser features and functionality in ten sections: General, Tabs, AutoFill, Passwords, Security, Privacy Notifications, Extensions, and Advanced. These preference areas allow you to turn features on and off as well as customize the way Safari works. In Extensions, you can install third-party functions, such as Twitter and Facebook, to Safari to show custom HTML content from the extension's toolbar. In Advanced, you can set miscellaneous options.

Set General Preferences

1. Click the **Safari** menu, and then click **Preferences**.

2. Click **General**.

3. Select or specify the various options you want to use:

 ◆ **Default Web Browser.** Select a default browser.

 ◆ **Default search engine.** Select a default search engine.

 ◆ **Safari opens with.** Select an option: A new window or All windows from last session (**New!**).

 ◆ **New Windows open with** or **New tabs open with.** Select an option: Home Page, Same Page, Empty Page, or Bookmarks.

 ◆ **Home page.** Specify a web address.

 ◆ **Remove history items.** Specify an interval to remove the history.

 ◆ **Save downloaded files to.** Select an option: Desktop or Choose Other (another location).

 ◆ **Remove download list items.** Select an option: Manually, When Safari Quits, or Upon Successful Download.

 ◆ **Top Sites show.** Select an option: 6, 12, or 24 Sites (**New!**).

 ◆ **Open "Safe" files after downloading.** Select to automatically activate safe downloaded files.

4. Click the **Close** button.

For Your Information

Selecting a Text Encoding

Text encoding determines how characters appear in a web page. When a web page doesn't specify text encoding, Safari uses the default text encoding specified in the Advanced pane of Safari preferences. Sometimes when the Safari default text encoding doesn't correspond with the desired web page text encoding, you can see garbled text. If the text in a web page is garbled, use the View menu to select a text encoding that corresponds to the language used in most of the web pages you visit. This may fix the problem.

Set Extensions Preferences

1. Click the **Safari** menu, and then click **Preferences**.

2. Click **Extensions**.

3. To enable or disable extensions, slide the switch to **On** or **Off**.

4. To get extensions, click **Get Extensions**, find the extension you want from the Apple web site, and then click **Install Now**.

5. To set options for an extension, select the extension, and then set the options you want..

6. To get automatic updates, click **Updates**, and then select the **Install Updates Automatically** check box.

7. Click the **Close** button.

Set Advanced Preferences

1. Click the **Safari** menu, and then click **Preferences**.

2. Click **Advanced**.

3. To set accessibility options, select the **Never user font sizes smaller than *x*** or **Press Tab to highlight each item on a webpage**.

4. Click the **Style sheet** pop-up to select a style sheet, which specifies a uniform format for the appearance of web pages.

5. Click the **Default Encoding** pop-up, and then select a character encoding set, which tells your browser how to interpret and display characters in a web page.

6. To change network proxy settings, click **Change Settings**.

7. Click the **Close** button.

Setting Security Preferences

When you browse the Internet, you can access and gather information from web sites, but web sites can also gather information about you and store documents as databases without your knowledge. Websites use JavaScript for buttons, forms, and other web content, use pop-up windows to display or gather information, and use plug-ins to display or play multimedia content. Most of the time these are used for normal website operation, however, sometimes they are used for harmful purposes. Safari's Security and Privacy pane options allow you to block or permit the use of these features; however, when you block them, you might not be able to access all web site features. You can also get a warning when you visit a fraudulent sites. If you have a lot of plug-ins installed for use with Safari and your system power seems to be draining, you can stop plug-ins (**New!**) in the Advanced pane.

Set Security Preferences

1. Click the **Safari** menu, and then click **Preferences**.

2. Click **Security**.

3. Select the **Warn when visiting a fraudulent website** check box to get a warning message.

4. To enable JavaScript, a programming language for displaying interaction, select the **Enable JavaScript** check box.

5. To allow plug-ins, select the **Allow Plug-ins** check box.

 ◆ To set option for individual plug-ins, click **Manage Website Settings (New!)**, select a plug-in, select an option (**Ask**, **Block**, **Allow**, **Allow always**, or **Plug-in is Unsafe**) to whether the plug-in can access your personal documents and data, and then click **Done**.

6. Click **Advanced**.

7. To stop plug-ins in order to save power, select the **Stop plug-ins to save power** check box (**New!**).

8. Click the **Close** button.

Installed plug-ins

Option on access to personal information

Set Privacy Preferences

1 Click the **Safari** menu, and then click **Preferences**.

2 Click **Privacy**.

3 Click **Remove All Website Data** to delete all cookies or click **Details** to remove individual ones.

4 Click the Accept Cookies option you want: **From third parties and advertisers**, **Always**, or **Never**.

5 Click an option to limit website access to location services.

- ◆ **Prompt for each website once each day.**
- ◆ **Prompt for each website one time only.**
- ◆ **Deny without prompting.**

6 Select or clear the **Ask websites not to track me** check box to allow or prevent websites from tracking your information.

This also occurs with Private Browsing.

7 Select or clear the **Do not preload Top Hit in the background** check box (**New!**) to allow or prevent it.

8 Select or clear the **Prevent search engine from providing suggestions** check box to allow or prevent it.

9 Click the **Close** button.

Did You Know?

You can show developer related commands in the menu bar. Click the Safari menu, click Preferences, click Advanced, select the Show Develop menu in menu bar check box, and then click the Close button.

Click the Details button to display dialog, where you can remove individual or all cookies on your computer.

Blocking Pop-Up Windows

When you open or close a web page, some pages display pop-up windows to advertise products and services or request login and other information. Pop-up windows can be extremely annoying. Most of the time you end up closing them. To avoid the continual borage of pop-up windows, you can block them in Safari. When you set Safari to block pop-up windows, the program only stops pop-up windows that appear when you open or close a page, but not when you click a link.

Block Pop-Up Windows

1 Click the **Safari** menu, and then click **Preferences**.

2 Click **Security**.

3 Select the **Block pop-up windows** check box.

> **TIMESAVER** *Click the Safari menu, and then click Block Pop-up Windows to display a check mark on the menu.*

4 Click **Block** to confirm the option selection to block pop-up windows.

5 Click the **Close** button.

Did You Know?

You can check security when browsing secure web sites. When you enter sensitive information on the web, you can make sure it's secure. To check security, look for the lock icon in the upper-right corner of the Safari window, or make sure the web sites address begins with "https," not "http."

For Your Information

When Web Pages Don't Work

If you are getting error messages or having problems displaying all or part of a web page, your security settings may be the cause of the problems. To potentially correct the problems, click the Safari menu, click Preferences, click Security, select the check boxes to use plug-ins, Java, and JavaScript, clear the Block Pop-Up Windows check box, and then click the Close button. A **Plug-in** is a software module developed by a third-party for use with Safari to provide additional functionality outside of HTML. Safari works with common plug-ins including Java, QuickTime and Shockwave Flash. To view which plug-ins recognized by Safari are installed on your computer, click the Help menu, and then click Installed Plug-Ins.

Changing Web Notifications

When you open a web page, some pages ask you for permission to set up an alert in the Notification Center. You can allow or deny their request. As you do this, Safari creates and manages a list of these websites in Notifications preferences. In Notification preferences for Safari, you can view the websites you have allowed or denied permission to post Notification Center alerts, and remove the ones you not longer want in the list. If you remove a website from the list and then revisit it later, the site will ask you for permission again.

Change Web Notifications

1 Click the **Safari** menu, and then click **Preferences**.

2 Click **Notifications**.

3 To change a website's notification permissions, select **Allow** or **Deny** next to the website address.

4 To remove all website notifications, select the site in the list, and then click **Remove**.

5 To remove a website notification, click **Remove All**.

6 To view and change how the Notification Center shows website alerts in Notification preferences, click **Notification Preferences**.

7 Click the **Close** button.

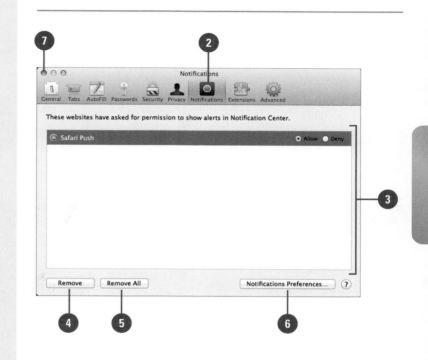

See Also

See "Setting Notification Preferences" on page 390 for more information on setting options for the Notification Center.

Selecting a Default Browser and Search

OS X comes with Safari as the default web browser and Google as the default search engine. If you prefer to use another browser as your default, you can remove Safari from your computer, install another browser, such as Microsoft Internet Explorer, Google Chrome, or Mozilla Firefox, and set it as your default web browser program. When you click links in other applications, such as Mail messages, or double-click a web Internet Location file icon, your default browser launches and opens the web page in a new window or tab in the current window. If you prefer to use another search engine as your default, you can change it to another one, such as Bing or Yahoo!.

Select a Default Browser and Search

1. Click the **Safari** menu, and then click **Preferences**.

2. Click **General**.

3. Click the **Default Web Browser** pop-up, and then select a web browser.

4. Click the **Default Search Engine** pop-up, and then select a search engine.

5. Click the **Close** button.

See Also

See "Downloading Files Safely from the Web" on page 258 for information on adding or removing applications.

For Your Information

Reset Safari Settings

If you use a shared or public computer, you might want to reset Safari to prevent other people from seeing what you have been doing. When you reset Safari, the web browser program clears the history list, Google search entries, and the Downloads window; removes all cookies saved by Safari and other related applications, such as any saved AutoFill data, such as user names and passwords; and empties the cache. To reset Safari, click the Safari menu, and then click Reset Safari.

Exchanging E-Mail Messages

Introduction

If you're like many people today who are using the Internet to communicate with friends and business associates, you probably have piles of information (names, e-mail addresses, phone numbers, etc) that you need often. Unless this information is in one convenient place, and can be accessed immediately, the information becomes ineffective and you become unproductive. Apple's Mail application solves these problems by integrating management and organization tools into one simple system. OS X includes Mail 7.0 or later, a powerful application for managing **electronic mail** (known as e-mail), and contact information like names, and e-mail addresses.

Using Mail with an Internet connection allows you to accomplish several tasks:

- ◆ Create and send e-mail messages
- ◆ Manage multiple e-mail accounts with different Internet service providers
- ◆ Use the Contacts to store and retrieve e-mail addresses
- ◆ Create a VIP list of contacts
- ◆ Add stationery to your e-mail messages
- ◆ Add a personal signature to your e-mail messages
- ◆ Attach a file to an e-mail message
- ◆ Organize e-mail messages by conversation
- ◆ Block junk e-mail messages
- ◆ Print e-mail messages

What You'll Do

Set Up Accounts in One Place

Start Mail

Set Up and Manage Accounts

View the Mail Window

Compose and Send an E-Mail

Address an E-Mail

Add Stationery to E-Mail

Format Message Text

Add an E-Mail Signature

Create Notes

Receive and Read E-Mail

Respond to E-Mail

Send and Retrieve a File

Manage and Delete E-Mail

Save E-Mail

Search E-Mail for Text

Block and Bounce E-Mail

Divert Incoming E-Mail to Mailboxes

Create a Smart Mailbox

Create a VIP List

Setting Up Accounts in One Place

In System Preferences, you can use the Internet Accounts pane (**New!**) to set up your accounts to use with Mail, Messages, Contacts, Calender, Reminders, Safari, and other apps on your Mac. It's a one stop shop for all your accounts. You can setup accounts for iCloud, Microsoft Exchange, Google, Twitter, Facebook, Linkedin (**New!**), Yahoo, AOL, Vimeo, Flickr, and more, which enables sharing in many apps. For example, when you setup a Twitter or Linkedin account, you can use Shared Links in Safari (**New!**). In most cases, all you need is your e-mail address and password. If you need to specify more account detail, you need to go into the related app, such as Mail, where you can set account options in Mail Preferences. After you setup an account, you can enable and disable the available features you want to use. If you no longer need an account, you can quickly delete it.

Set Internet Accounts Preferences

1 Click the **System Preferences** icon in the Dock.

2 Click the **Internet Accounts** icon.

3 To add an account, click **Add Account**, and then continue as follows:

◆ Click the type of account you want: iCloud, Microsoft Exchange, Google, Twitter, Facebook, Linkedin (**New!**), Yahoo, AOL, Vimeo, Flickr, or Add Other Account.

If you click **Add Other Account**, you can create an account for specific types, including Mac Mail, Messages, CalDAV, CardDAV, LDAP, and OS X server.

◆ Enter your name, user ID, password, and then click **Next**, **Set Up**, or **Sign In**.

4 To enable or disable feature options, click the account, and then select or clear the check boxes for the individual features, such as Mail, Messages, Contacts, Calendar, Reminders, and Safari.

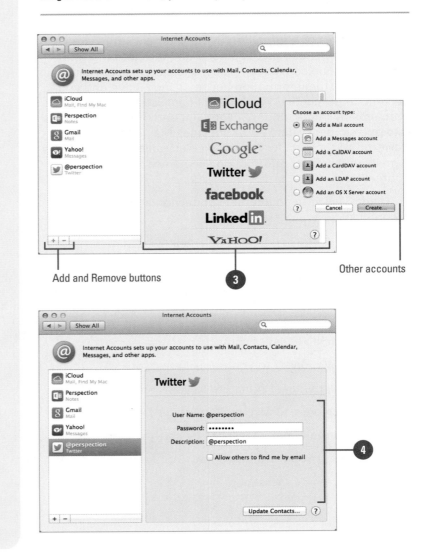

Add and Remove buttons

Other accounts

Starting Mail

Whether you want to exchange e-mail with colleagues and friends or join news feeds to access ideas and information, Mail provides you with all the tools you need. When you install OS X, an icon for Mail appears in the Dock. The first time you start Mail, you need to set up an e-mail account by simply entering your e-mail address and password and letting Mail do the rest. If you are switching from another e-mail application to Mail, you can import your mailboxes and e-mail messages into Mail by answering a few questions. You can set Mail as your default e-mail application so that whenever you click an e-mail link on a Web page or select the mail command in your Web browser, Mail opens. If you have unread messages after you set up your mail accounts, a red circle with the number of unread messages appears on the Mail icon in the Dock.

Start Mail

1. Click the **Mail** icon in the Dock.

 If you have a iCloud account, Mail automatically creates an e-mail account using your existing information.

2. When you start Mail for the first time, the application asks you:

 ◆ If you don't have an e-mail account, follow the one step instruction, enter your e-mail address and password.

 ◆ If prompted and you want to import mailboxes from another e-mail client. If so, click **Yes**, and then follow the on-screen instructions (see details on the next page). Otherwise, click **No**.

Open Mail icon indicates number of new mail messages

Did You Know?

You can set options to start Mail from your Web browser. Click the Mail menu, click Preferences, click General, click the Default Email Reader pop-up, click Mail (7.0), and then click the Close button.

For Your Information

Importing Mailboxes and E-Mail

If you are switching from another e-mail application to Mail, you can import your mailboxes and e-mail messages into Mail by answering a few questions. To start, click the File menu, and then click Import Mailboxes. In the dialog, click an option to select the importing application (use Other for Windows or UNIX), and then click Continue. Follow the on-screen instructions; the steps to import mailboxes and e-mail vary between applications. **Import from Apple Mail**. Mailboxes are located in Library/Mail/Mailboxes in your home folder. **Import from Windows or UNIX**. Use Standard mbox, except for Eudora or Netscape, which use their own. Microsoft Outlook, and Outlook Express for the PC are not supported. Some options require that you have the importing application, such as Entourage, open. The imported mail appears in the new Import mailbox.

Setting Up an Account

Before you can set up an e-mail account, you need your name, e-mail address, and password. For some accounts, you also need e-mail server type, and the names of your incoming and outgoing e-mail servers from your ISP or network administrator. You can use Add Account to help you set up an e-mail account by answering a series of questions, which is available in the Accounts pane in Mail preferences. Mail allows you to send and retrieve e-mail from different types of e-mail servers (including iCloud, Microsoft Exchange, Google, Yahoo, AOL, and an option for others), which are the locations where e-mail is stored before you access it. iCloud, Google, Yahoo, and AOL use an IMAP mail server type, while Microsoft Exchange use a POP or IMAP mail server type. Accounts allow you to have all your messages (in Mail), meetings (in Calendar), and contacts (in Contacts) in one place. You can set up Mail to receive e-mail from multiple accounts where each one can have multiple e-mail addresses.

Set Up an E-Mail Account by Answering Questions

1. Click the **Mail** menu, and then click **Preferences**.

2. Click **Accounts**.

3. Click the **Add** (+) button.

4. Click the type of account (**New!**) you want, and then click **Continue**.

 ◆ **Account Types.** iCloud, Exchange, Google, Yahoo, AOL, or Add Other Account.

5. Type the information requested (ask your ISP as needed), and then click **Continue**.

 ◆ **Full Name.** The name used in outgoing e-mail.

 ◆ **E-mail Address.** The From address in outgoing e-mail. You can type multiple addresses, each separated by a comma.

 ◆ **Password.** The method that provides secure access to the mail server. If you prefer to type a password every time you check mail, leave this empty.

6 Type the information requested (ask your ISP as needed), and then click **Continue** as prompted

The information varies depending on your account type. Some of the commonly requested information includes:

◆ **Other Account Types**. POP, IMAP, Exchange 2007 or 2010, or Exchange IMAP.

◆ **User Name and Password**. The name and password that identifies you to the mail server.

◆ **Description**. The account name (appears in mailbox list).

◆ **Incoming Mail Server**. The POP or IMAP name.

◆ **Incoming Mail Security**. Select the Use Secure Sockets Layer (SSL) check box, and then select an authentication option.

◆ **Outgoing Mail Server**. The SMTP name.

7 Click **Create** or **Setup**, and then click **Done** upon completion as prompted.

Review the account information in the Accounts pane in Mail preferences.

Did You Know?

You can create a new mail account using a mail script. Click the Scripts (S) menu, point to Mail Scripts, and then click Create New Mail Account. You can also start the script from the AppleScript Editor (in the Utilities folder). Click an account type, and then click OK. Type the information requested (ask your ISP as needed), and then click OK, or click Yes or No to the question.

Exchange

Name: Steve Johnson
Email Address: stevej@perspection.com
Password: •••••

4

Cancel Go Back Continue

Exchange

Account Settings

Account type: Exchange
Description: Work
User Name: stevej
Password: •••••
Server Address: mail.perspection.com

5

Cancel Go Back Continue

For Your Information

How Do I Select an E-Mail Server?

Mail supports three types of incoming e-mail servers: **POP** (Post Office Protocol), **IMAP** (Internet Message Access Protocol), and **Exchange** (Microsoft Exchange 2010 or later). A **protocol** is a set of rules that control the transmission of content, format, sequencing, and error management for information over the Internet or network much like rules of the road govern the way you drive. POP servers allow you to access e-mail messages from a single Inbox folder (requires you to log in and download messages), while IMAP servers allow you to access e-mail messages from multiple folder locations or different computers (messages stay on server). An example of an incoming e-mail server is *mail.server.com*. When you use POP or IMAP e-mail servers, you also need to provide an outgoing e-mail server. **SMTP** (Simple Mail Transfer Protocol) is used to send messages between e-mail servers. An example is *smtp.server.com*.

Managing Accounts

You can set up Mail to receive e-mail from multiple e-mail accounts and from different computers. As you work with multiple accounts, you can use the Accounts pane in Mail preferences to change the order, rename, or delete accounts. Account order indicates the mailbox list order and helps determine which account (if not specified) Mail uses to send an e-mail message. If an account changes, or you no longer need it, you can rename or delete it. If you're using an IMAP account, such iCloud, mail stays on the mail server so you can access it from any computer. If you're using a POP account, mail downloads to your computer unless you select an Accounts pane option to keep a copy on the mail server. If a POP or IMAP mail server requires a TLS certificate for security purposes (**New!**), you can select one under Account Information.

Manage E-Mail Accounts

1. Click the **Mail** menu, and then click **Preferences**.

2. Click **Accounts**.

3. Select the account you want to manage.

4. To turn this account on or off, select or clear the **Enable this account** check box.

5. To rename an e-mail account, click the **Account Information** tab, and then change the Description name.

6. To mail server options, click the **Account Information** tab, and then make the changes you want.

7. To delete an e-mail account, click the account name, click the **Delete** button (-), and then click **OK**.

8. Click the **Close** button, and then click **Save**.

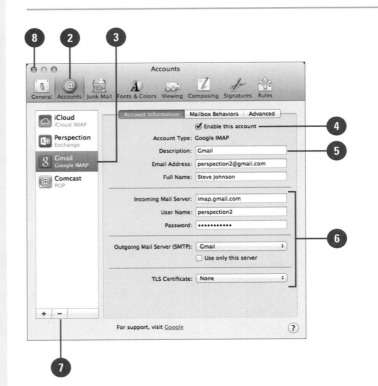

Did You Know?

You can view a list of all account and preference information. Click the Scripts menu, point to Mail Scripts, and then click Display All Accounts And Preferences. An e-mail appears with the information.

Set Advanced Account Options

1. Click the **Mail** menu, and then click **Preferences**.

2. Click **Accounts**.

3. Click the **Advanced** tab.

4. Select from the following options:

 ◆ **Include when automatically checking for new mail**. Check or clear to check or exclude this account from automatic mail checking.

 ◆ **Keep copies of messages for offline viewing (IMAP only)**. Click the pop-up to download e-mail to your computer for offline viewing.

 ◆ **Remove copy from server after retrieving a message (POP only)**. Check to check e-mail from different computers, and then specify a removal duration.

 ◆ **Prompt me to skip messages Over __ KB (POP only)**. Check to skip retrieval of large e-mail.

 ◆ **Use SSL**. If your mail provider supports Secure Sockets Layer (SSL), check for increased security.

 ◆ **Authentication**. Click the pop-up to specify a security access method. Typically, Password.

5. Click the **Close** button, and then click **Save**.

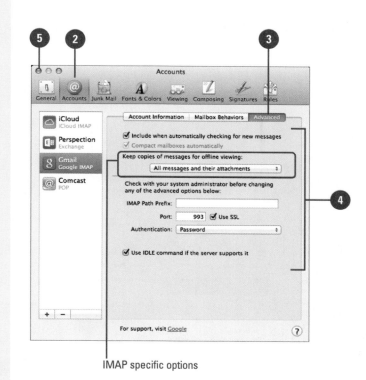

IMAP specific options

POP specific options

Did You Know?

You can access Internet Account from Mail. Click the Mail menu, and then click Accounts (**New!**) to open the Internet Accounts pane in System Preferences.

Viewing the Mail Window

Favorites bar
The Favorites bar contains buttons to your mail folders.

Mail toolbar
The Mail toolbar contains buttons for the most commonly used commands you need to work with mail messages.

Full Screen
Provides ability to work as a full-screen application.

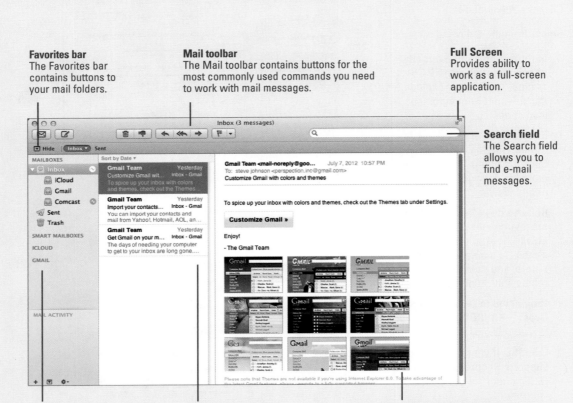

Search field
The Search field allows you to find e-mail messages.

Mailbox list
The Mailbox list contains all the folders in which Mail stores e-mail messages.

Message list
The Message list displays e-mail messages.

Mail Viewer window
The Mail Viewer window displays the contents of the current message selected in the Message list.

Composing and Sending an E-Mail

E-mail is becoming the primary form of written communication for many people. E-mail messages follow a standard memo format, with fields for the sender, recipient, date, and subject of the message. To send an e-mail message, you need to type the recipients e-mail address, type a subject, then type the message itself. You can send the same message to more than one individual, to a contact group, or to a combination of individuals and groups. If you type multiple addresses, you must separate the addresses with a comma (,). If you have multiple accounts, you can select which account you want to use to send the e-mail message.

Compose and Send an E-Mail

1. Click the **New Message** button on the Mail toolbar.

2. Type the e-mail addresses, names of each recipient, or groups for the To and Cc (carbon copy) fields.
 - ◆ **Use Contacts.** Click the **Add Contact** button (**New!**) in the To or Cc field, and then select a e-mail from a contact.

3. Type a subject that indicates the purpose of the message.

4. Select a From e-mail address and outgoing server.

5. To add custom mail options, click the **Customize** button, and then click an option.
 - ◆ **Bcc Address Field.** An address not included in recipients' list.
 - ◆ **Reply-To Address Field.** An alternate address for replies.
 - ◆ **Priority.** Add mail priority.
 - ◆ **Customize.** Use to select from multiple accounts.

6. Type the content of your message.

7. If a red dotted line appears under a word, Control-click the word, and then click the correct spelling.

8. Click the **Send** button on the toolbar.

 Messages are sent out, and then copies appear in the Sent mailbox.

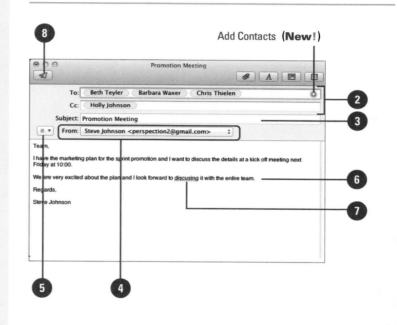

Add Contacts (**New!**)

For Your Information

Checking the Spelling and Grammar in E-Mail

Before you send an e-mail message, you should spell check the text and grammar to make sure your content is accurate. To start the spell check, click the Edit menu, point to Spelling and Grammar, and then click Show Spelling and Grammar. To have Mail spell check all of your e-mail messages as you type, click While Typing on the Check Spelling submenu (on the Spelling and Grammar submenu) to enable or disable the option. If a word appears with a dotted red line under it, you can Control-click the word, and then click the correct spelling, or other options, such as Ignore or Learn. To include grammar checking, click Check Grammar with Spelling on the Spelling and Grammar submenu.

Addressing an E-Mail

Mail gives you several ways to address an e-mail. You can type the address manually by entering it in the To or Cc field, or you can select (using the Add Contacts button (**New!**)) or drag an address from your Contacts. When you begin to type an e-mail address, Mail looks up the name and address in your Contacts, followed by your Previous Recipients list. If Mail finds a match, it automatically completes the recipients name. If you type multiple addresses, you must separate the addresses with a comma (,). You can make addressing easier to view by using Smart Addresses, which displays the recipient name only without the e-mail address for those in your Contacts and Previous Recipients list. You can display the Previous Recipients list to remove addresses you misspelled or don't need, or add addresses to your Contacts.

Select Names Using Address Complete

1. In the New Message window, type the first few letters of a name, address, or group.

 ◆ **Use Contacts.** Click the **Add Contact** button (**New!**) in the To or Cc field, and then select a e-mail from a contact.

 Mail suggests possible matches.

2. Click the name you want to enter.

Did You Know?

You can use Smart Addresses to show names. Smart Addresses are names and addresses in your address book, Previous Recipients list. Any names not found in your Contacts or Previous Recipients list still appear in full. To enable it, click the Mail menu, click Preferences, click Viewing, select the Use Smart Addresses check box, and then click OK.

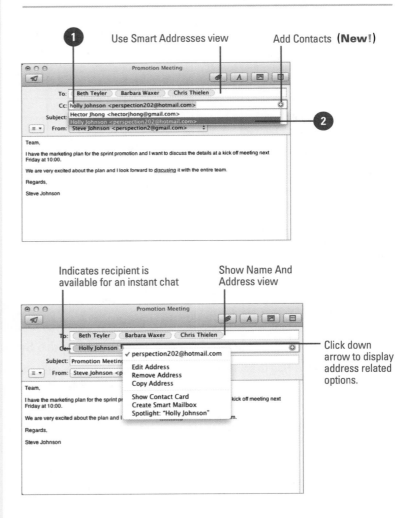

Use Smart Addresses view Add Contacts (**New!**)

Indicates recipient is available for an instant chat

Show Name And Address view

Click down arrow to display address related options.

Work with the Previous Recipients List

1 Click the **Window** menu, and then click **Previous Recipients**.

2 Select an address.

3 To remove the address, click **Remove From List**.

4 To add the address to Contacts, click the **Add To Contacts**.

5 Click the **Close** button.

Did You Know?

You can set addressing preferences. Click the Mail menu, click Preferences, click the Composing button, select or clear the following check boxes: Automatically Complete Addresses, When Sending To A Group, Show All Member Address, and Mark Addresses Not In This Domain, and then type a domain name such as *apple.com* to mark it as safe when using LDAP.

You can change the use of a mailbox for an IMAP account. Select a mailbox, click the Mailbox menu, point to Use This Mailbox For, and then click Drafts, Sent, Trash, or Junk.

See Also

See "Creating a Contacts List" on page 146 for information on creating a group of recipients.

Adding Stationery to E-Mail

Instead of using a standard white background for your e-mail, you can spruce it up with some stationery. If you want to send an e-mail message for a special occasion, such as a birthday, thank you, get well, or just for fun, you can quickly create the look you want by applying stationery templates with professionally designed layouts, fonts, and colors. If you want to use your own photos, you can use the Photo Browser in Mail to find photos in your iPhoto library or Photo Booth, and insert them into your e-mail messages.

Add Stationery and Photos

1. Open the message you want to apply a stationery.

2. Click the **Stationery** button on the toolbar to show it (toggle button).

3. Click a category.

4. Click the thumbnail of the template you want. To change the background for some templates, click the thumbnail again.

5. To add images, use any of the following methods:

 ◆ **Photo Browser.** Click the Photo Browser button, select/drag the images to the e-mail.

 ◆ **Finder.** Drag an image file from the desktop or Finder window.

6. To remove a template, click the **Stationery** category, and then click **Original**.

7. To add a template to your favorites list, drag it to the Favorites category. To remove it, click the **Delete** (x) button in Favorites.

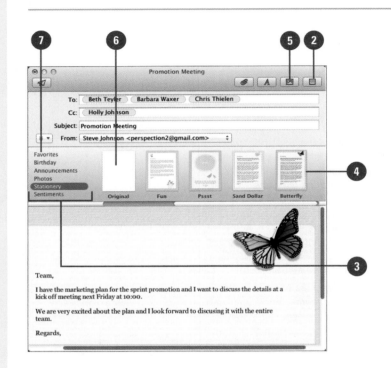

Did You Know?

You can have message text read aloud. Select the text you want to have read, click the Edit menu, point to Speech, and then click Start Speaking or Stop Speaking.

For Your Information

Using Data Detectors to Manage Information

Mail tries to recognize different types of data, such as an address or a date, so you can effectively manage and use it. When you place your pointer over data in messages, such as an e-mail address, street address, or date and time, you can use the data to create a new contact in your Contacts, map street directions on the web, or create an event in Calendar. In OS X, data detectors can identify flight numbers, which takes you to the Dashboard Flight Tracker widget.

Formatting Message Text

You can specify a file format for message text. The Plain Text format is one that all e-mail programs recognize, but it doesn't support text formatting. The Rich Text format allows text formatting, but it's not always supported. However, most programs that don't recognize Rich Text, convert the message to plain text. When you use Rich Text, you can use formatting tools, such as bold, italicize, underline, numbered and bulleted lists, indentations, and color text and backgrounds, on the Format bar, Format menu and in the Fonts and Color dialogs to help draw the reader's attention to key words and emphasize the meaning of your message.

Format the Message Text

1. Open the message you want to format.

2. Click the **Format** menu, and then click **Make Rich Text**, if available.

3. Select the text you want to format.

4. Click the **Format Bar** button on the toolbar to show it.

5. Use the Format bar to change any of the following:

 ◆ **Font and Size.** To use the dialog settings (type, size, style, and effects), click the **Font** button, and then click **Show Fonts**.

 ◆ **Color.** To use the dialog color wheel to select a color, click the **Color** button, and then click **Show Colors**.

 ◆ **Bold, Italic, and Underline.**

 ◆ **Alignment.**

 ◆ **Lists and Indention.**

Did You Know?

You can set font preferences. Click the Mail menu, click Preferences, click Fonts & Colors, select default fonts for the message list, message text (Rich Text), and plain text, and then click the Close button.

Adding an E-Mail Signature

If you type the same information at the end of each e-mail message, such as Best Regards and your name, then you can automate that task by creating a signature. You can add one signature to all messages or create several and select one when you compose a message. You can customize your signature with a variety of formatting styles, such as font type, size, and color, and you can even include a picture or attach your virtual business card, known as a **vCard**, from your Contacts.

Create a Signature

1. Click the **Mail** menu, click **Preferences**, and then click **Signatures**.

2. Select an account or **All Signatures**.

3. Click the **Add** (+) button.

4. Type a title for the signature.

5. Type/modify the signature text.

6. For a Rich Text signature, use the **Format** menu to change the text font, color, style, or alignment.

7. If you want, drag a picture or vCard, and then click **OK**.

8. Click the **Choose Signature** pop-up, and then select a signature, **None**, or an option.

9. Select or clear the **Place signature above quoted text** check box to place the signature above or below the quoted text.

10. To remove a signature, select it, and then click the **Remove** (-) button.

11. Click the **Close** button.

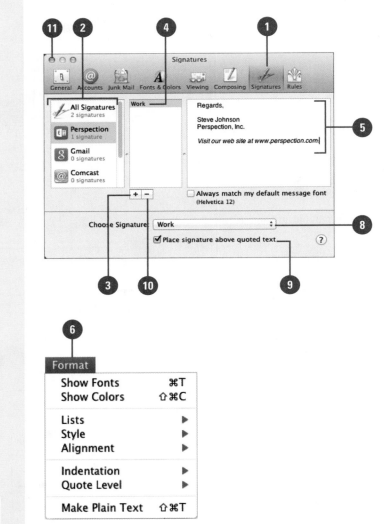

Did You Know?

You can add your signature to e-mail quickly. In an e-mail message, click where you want the signature, click the Signature pop-up, and then click a signature.

Customizing the Mail Window

The Mail window is broken down into 4 main areas: toolbar and favorites bar, sidebar, message list, and message preview. The Mail window provides flexibility and ease of use. The Favorites bar gives you easy access to mail folders in a horizontal layout and options to hide/show the sidebar. The message list displays a compact preview of each message, which includes the first two lines of the e-mail, along with contact photos. These options are all customizable in Mail Viewing preferences; you can even display the classic view (the default from Mail 4.0). When you point to the header in a message, convenient inline controls appear for ease of use. You can display the Mail window in full-screen view, which give you more screen area to read, respond, and manage to your e-mail messages.

Customize the Mail window

◆ **Show/Hide Toolbar.** Click the **View** menu, and then click **Show Toolbar** or **Hide Toolbar**.

◆ **Show/Hide Favorites Bar.** Click the **View** menu, and then click **Show Favorites Bar** or **Hide Favorites Bar**.

◆ **Show/Hide Sidebar.** Click the **Show Sidebar** or **Hide Sidebar** button on the Favorites bar.

◆ **Add/Remove from Favorites Bar.** Drag the item on or off the Favorites bar.

◆ **Sort Messages.** Click the **Sort by** button in the Message list, and then select a sort by option.

◆ **View Top Message.** Click the Sort bar at the top of the Message list to go instantly to the top of the list.

◆ **Viewing Preferences.** Click the **Mail** menu, click **Preferences**, click **Viewing**. Select options to use classic layout, show to/cc or contact photos in the message list.

◆ **Full Screen.** Click the **Full Screen** button in the title bar. To return, point to the top of the screen to display the menu bar, and then click the **Full Screen** button.

Favorites bar Sort by Toolbar Full Screen button

Sidebar Message list Inline controls

Message list options in Mail preferences

Receiving and Reading E-Mail

You can receive e-mail anytime—even when your computer is turned off. You can retrieve your e-mail manually or set Mail to do so automatically by setting options in Mail preferences. When you start Mail, it checks for new e-mail. It continues to check periodically, based on preferences, while it's open. New messages appear in the Inbox along with any messages you haven't stored elsewhere or deleted. It can also send a notification alert. A blue dot appears next to unread messages. The Message list displays the subject line and other information, such as date received, senders name, attachments, and priority flags, which you can customize to display the information you need.

Check for New E-Mail

1. Click the **Mail** menu, and then click **Preferences**.

2. Click **General**.

3. Click the **Check for new messages** pop-up, and then select a duration.

4. Click the **New messages sound** pop-up, and then select a sound.

5. Click the **Dock unread count** pop-up, and then select the mailboxes included in the unread mail count on the Mail icon in the Dock.

6. Click the **New message notifications** pop-up, and then select the mailboxes that you want to receive a notification alert.

7. Click **Accounts**.

8. Select an account, and then click the **Advanced** tab.

9. Select the **Include when automatically checking for new messages** check box.

10. Click the **Close** button.

11. To check for mail manually, click the **Get Mail** button on the Mail toolbar, or click the **Mailbox** menu, point to **Get New Mail**, and then click **In All Accounts** or an account name.

Open and Read an E-Mail

1. Click the **Inbox** icon in the Mailbox list or on the Favorites bar to view new messages.

2. Click an e-mail message to read it in the Mail Viewer window.

3. Double-click an e-mail message to open it in its own window.

Did You Know?

You can add a sender to Contacts.
Select the message in the Message list, click the Message menu, and then click Add Sender To Contacts.

Change the Message List View

1. Click the **View** menu, and then point to **Columns**.

2. Select a column to display:

 ◆ **Attachments.** Displays a paper clip for attachments.

 ◆ **Buddy Availability.** Displays buddy status information.

 ◆ **Date Received.** Displays date received.

 ◆ **Date Sent.** Displays date sent.

 ◆ **Flags.** Displays a priority flag.

 ◆ **From.** Displays sender name.

 ◆ **Mailbox.** Displays name/account.

 ◆ **Number.** Displays sequential numbers next to the messages.

 ◆ **Size.** Displays size of a message or mailbox.

 ◆ **To.** Displays recipient name.

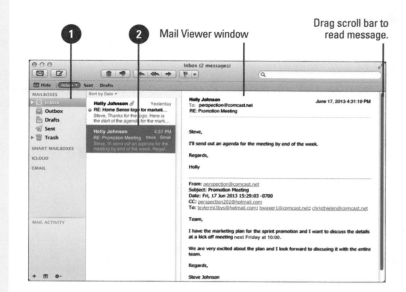

Mail Viewer window

Drag scroll bar to read message.

Status (always available)

Buddy Availability

Drag a column header to change positions.

Attachments

Classic layout; available in Mail preferences

Responding to E-Mail

You can respond to a message in three ways: reply to it, which creates a new message addressed to the sender(s) and other recipients; forward it, which creates a new message you can send to someone else; or redirect it, which creates a new message from the original sender you can send to someone else (useful when you receive a message by mistake). When you reply or forward a message, the original message appears in the message response. You can reply to the sender only, or to all the people who received the original message.

Reply to an E-Mail

1. Select the e-mail message you want to reply to.

2. If you want, select a portion of the text to include as quoted text.

3. Click the **Reply** button to respond to the sender only, or click the **Reply All** button to respond to the sender and all recipients listed in the e-mail.

4. Add or delete names from the To or the Cc field.

5. Type your message.

6. Click the **Send** button on the Message toolbar.

 A curved arrow appears in the Status column next to messages you reply to.

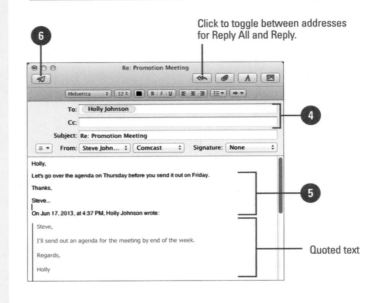

Click to toggle between addresses for Reply All and Reply.

Quoted text

Did You Know?

You can reply with an instant message. If you're logged into Messages, Mail displays a green dot indicator next to messages from buddies who are online, or a yellow dot indicator when the person is idle. Click the Mail menu, click Preferences, click the Viewing button, select the Show Online Buddy Status check box, and then click the Close button. Select a message in the Message list, click the Message menu, and then click Reply With Messages.

For Your Information

Quoting Text in E-Mail

When you reply to an e-mail message, you can include all or part of the original message, known as **quoted text**. The original message appears with a single quote bar to the left of the text. If the original message contained quoted text, you see an additional quote bar. To use quoted text, click the Mail menu, click Preferences, click the Composing button, select the Quote The Text Of The Original Message check box, and then click the Include Selected Text If Any, Otherwise Include All option. To change the color of quoted text, click Fonts & Colors, select the Color Quoted Text check box, and then select colors from the pop-up for Levels One, Two, and Three. When you're done, click the Close button. You can use the Quote Level submenu on the Format menu to change the number of quote bars.

Redirect an E-Mail

1. Select the e-mail message you want to redirect.

2. Click the **Message** menu, and then click **Redirect**.

3. Type or select names in the To or the Cc field.

4. Click the **Send** button on the Message toolbar.

 A segment arrow appears in the Status column next to messages you redirect.

Message text redirected without a quote bar.

Forward an E-Mail

1. Select the message(s) or open a message you want to forward.

2. Click the **Forward** button on the toolbar.

3. Type or select names in the To or the Cc field.

4. Type your message.

5. Click the **Send** button on the Message toolbar.

Quoted text

Did You Know?

Attachments aren't sent on replies.
When you reply to a message that has an attachment, the attachment isn't returned to the original sender. You can forward the message to the original sender if you need to send the attachment back.

Sending and Retrieving a File

You can easily share a file, such as a picture, document, vCard (virtual business card from your Contacts), sound, or movie by attaching it to an e-mail message. Some ISPs have trouble sending attachments greater than 5 megabytes MB, so it's a good idea to check with your ISP for limits on file size. Upon receiving the e-mail, the recipient can view it with Quick Look, open the file in the application that created it, or save it on a disk for use in other applications from the Mail Viewer window. The Message list displays the number and size of the attachments. If you send an e-mail to a Windows user, the attachment is automatically compressed in a standard zipped (gzip) format so it can be read.

Send a File with an E-Mail

1. Compose a new message or reply to an existing message.

2. Click the **Attach** button on the Message toolbar.

3. Select the drive and folder that contains the file, and then select it.

4. Select or clear the **Send Windows-Friendly Attachments** check box.

5. Click **Choose File**.

6. For images, click the **Image Size** pop-up, and then select a size. The message size appears on the Status bar.

7. Click the **Send** button on the Message toolbar.

Did You Know?

You should compress large files before you send them. Select the file or files you want to compress in the Finder, click the File menu, and then click Compress. Rename the compressed file with a *.zip* extension as necessary.

You can send a web link in an e-mail message. Type or paste the full URL, including "http://" in the body of the message. Your recipients can click the link to go directly to the web page.

Attached file

View or Open a File in an E-Mail

1. Select the message with the attached file.

2. Click **Quick Look** in the message header.

 ◆ You can also click the **File** menu, and then click **Quick Look Attachments**, or Control-click the attached file, click **Open Attachment**, or point to **Open With**, and then select a program.

Did You Know?

You can remove attachments from an e-mail. Select the e-mail, click the Message menu, and then click Remove Attachments.

Save Files in an E-Mail

1. Select the message with the attached file.

2. Use one of the following methods:

 ◆ **Save All.** Click the **File** menu, and then click **Save Attachments**, or click **Save** in the message header.

 ◆ **Save Individual.** Click and hold **Save** in the message header, and then click file name. You can also Control+ click the attached file, and then click **Save to Downloads Folder** (by passes Steps 3 and 4).

3. Click in the Tags box, select or enter one or more tags (**New!**).

4. Select the drive and folder where you want to save the files.

5. Click **Save**.

Attachment icon

Quick Look
in Preview

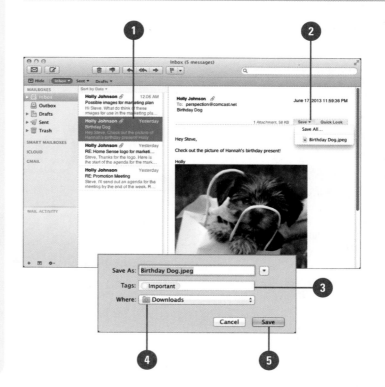

Managing E-Mail

A common problem with using e-mail is an overcrowded Inbox. To keep your Inbox organized, you should move messages you want to save to other mailboxes and subfolders (a mailbox inside another mailbox), delete messages you no longer want, and create new mailboxes as you need them. A mailbox can store messages on your computer, within a specific account, or within an existing mailbox. When a mailbox contains both messages and other mailboxes, the mailbox icon appears in blue. Mail automatically groups related messages together, known as a conversation, with each message streamlined and numbered, so you can identify and read messages in sequence. Since the messages are grouped, it's easy to find, reply, or even delete. Mail also hides quoted text to reduce repeated information for easy reading.

Create a New Mailbox

1. To create a subfolder in a mailbox, select the existing mailbox.

2. Click the **Add** (+) button at the bottom of the Mailbox list, and then click **New Mailbox**.

3. Click the **Location** pop-up, and then select **On My Mac** (local computer) or an IMAP account (online mail server).

4. Type a name for the new mailbox.

5. Click **OK**.

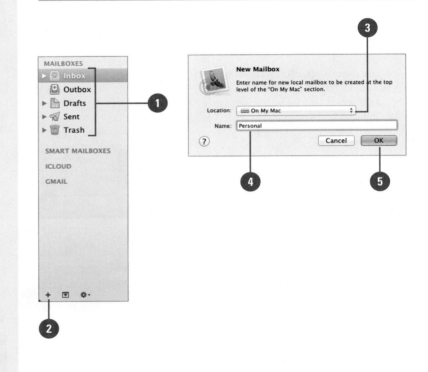

Did You Know?

You can show and hide the Mailbox list. Click the View menu, and then click Show/Hide Mailbox List.

You can move items in the Mailbox list. Drag the sidebar item to a new location in the Mailbox list.

You can delete a mailbox. Control+ click it, click Delete Mailbox, and then click Delete.

You can rename a mailbox. Control+ click the mailbox, click Rename Mailbox, change it, and then press Return.

For Your Information

Learning About the Standard Mailboxes

Mail comes with several standard mailboxes: Inbox, Drafts, Sent, and Trash. **Inbox** stores messages you have received from others; the Drafts mailbox stores messages you have written and saved, but not sent; and the Sent mailbox stores copies of messages you have sent. The Trash mailbox stores all your deleted messages.

Organize E-Mail in Mailboxes

1. Select the e-mail message you want to move. If necessary, press and hold down ⌘, and click to select multiple e-mail messages.

2. Drag the e-mail message(s) to the new folder.

Did You Know?

You can sort messages quickly.
To sort messages by from, to, subject, date, flag, or other method, click the Sort by in the Message list, and then click an item.

Organize E-Mail by Conversation

1. Open the mailbox with the e-mail you want to view as threads.

2. Click the **View** menu, and then click **Organize By Conversation** to display a check mark.

 ◆ To expand or collapse all conversations, click the **View** menu, and then click **Expand All Conversations** or **Collapse All Conversations**.

3. To show or hide the related messages in a conversation, click the message, and then click **Related Messages** button on the Mail toolbar.

4. To show or hide the names in a related message, click the message number arrow.

5. To ungroup, click the **View** menu, and then click **Organize By Conversation**.

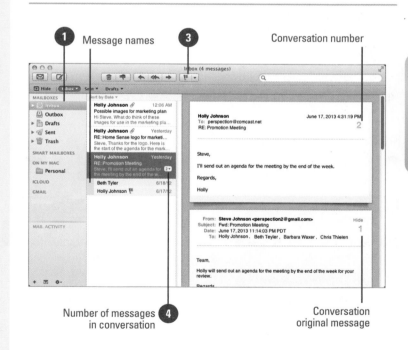

Message names

Conversation number

Number of messages in conversation

Conversation original message

Deleting E-Mail

Deleting unwanted messages makes it easier to see the new messages you receive and to keep track of messages to which you have already responded. When you delete an e-mail message, Mail simply moves it into the Trash mailbox. If you want to recover a deleted message, you just have to retrieve it from the Trash mailbox. To get rid of a message permanently, you need to open the Trash mailbox, select the message, and then click Delete. Mail automatically places e-mail messages in the Sent mailbox every time you send them. You'll want to periodically open the Sent mailbox and delete messages so your mail account doesn't get too large. You can also set account options to help you delete messages.

Delete Unwanted E-Mail

1. Click a mailbox icon in the Mailbox list with the e-mail you want to delete.

2. Click the unwanted e-mail.

3. Click the **Delete** button on the Mail toolbar.

4. To erase messages in the Trash mailbox, click the **Mailbox** menu, point to **Erase Deleted Items**, click **In All Accounts** or a specific account, and then click **Erase**.

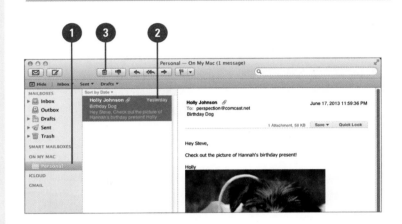

Recover E-Mail from the Trash

1. Click the Trash mailbox in the Mailbox list.

2. Select the e-mail message you want to retrieve.

3. Drag the e-mail message to another folder.

Did You Know?

You can resend a message. Select the message in the Sent mailbox, click the Message menu, click Send Again, add or change recipients, and then click the Send button.

Change E-Mail Delete Options

1 Click the **Mail** menu, and then click **Preferences**.

2 Click **Accounts**.

3 Select an account.

4 Click the **Mailbox Behaviors** tab.

5 Select any of the following:

◆ **Move deleted messages to the trash mailbox**. Check to move deleted messages to the Trash.

◆ **Store deleted messages on the server**. Check to keep deleted messages on the mail server for an IMAP account.

◆ **Permanently erase deleted messages when**. Click the pop-up, and then select based on the duration you want.

6 Click the **Close** button, and then click **Save**.

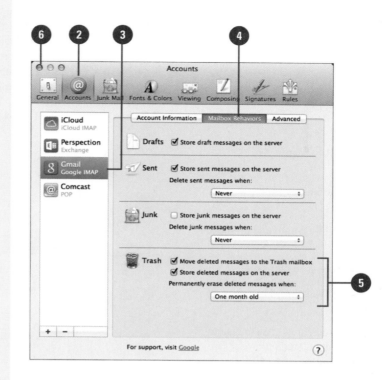

Did You Know?

You can save sent messages on the mail server. Click the Mail menu, click Preferences, click Accounts, click the Mailbox Behaviors tab, select the Store Sent Messages On The Server check box, and then click the Close button.

You can print e-mail messages. Select the message(s) you want to print, click the File menu, click Print, and then click Print. If you select multiple messages, the e-mails are combined into a single document in the order you selected them in the Message list.

For Your Information

Backing Up E-Mail

The information in your e-mail messages is important, so making a backup, or **archive**, of a mailbox is a good way to protect it. In Mail, select the mailboxes you want to back up, click one or more messages to archive, click the Message menu, and then click Archive. Mail creates an archive mailbox for each account whose message you archive. The archived messages remain in the Archive mailbox until you delete or move them. Mail backs up the mailboxes as .mbox packages.

Another method is to drag a mailbox from an IMAP account to On My Mac to copy it on your computer. Likewise, you can drag a mailbox from On My Mac to an IMAP account to copy it to your mail server online. To create a copy of a mailbox, drag the mailbox from the Mailbox list to your desktop.

Saving E-Mail

If you have not finished composing a message, you can save it in the Drafts mailbox and work on it later. If you quit Mail with an open message, Mail automatically saves it as a draft. If you want to use the text from a message in a word processing application, such as TextEdit, you can save a message as a separate file in the Rich Text or Plain Text format or export it as a PDF file (**New!**). You can also save messages in the Raw Message Source (mbox) format, which is a standard mail message format; you can import mbox into other mail applications, including Mail.

Save a Draft E-Mail

① Open a new or a reply to an existing e-mail message, and then type a message.

② Click the **File** menu, and then click **Save**.

③ Close the e-mail message.

④ Click the **Drafts** mailbox in the Mailbox list.

⑤ Double-click the e-mail message to view and change it.

⑥ Click the **Send** button.

Save or Export E-Mail as a File

① Open or create the message you want to save or export.

② Click the **File** menu, and then click **Save As** or **Export as PDF** (**New!**).

③ Type a name for the file.

④ Click in the Tags box, select or enter one or more tags (**New!**).

⑤ Select the hard drive and folder where you want to save the file.

⑥ For a save, click the **Format** pop-up, and then select a format.

⑦ Click **Save**.

Searching E-Mail for Text

If you're looking for an e-mail message with specific text, you can use the Mail Search field to search for text in a message, in all messages in a mailbox, in all messages for a specific account, or in all mailboxes. In the Search field, you can search for people, text in the subject and message, or attachments using it's filename or it's content. Mail finds messages containing the same beginning letters as you type with the most relevant match, yet it also makes search suggestions, such as people or subjects, in the Search field menu based on the content. To refine your search, use the words "and," "or," "not," and parentheses in the Search field. If you frequently search for the same text, you can create a Smart Mailbox to make it quick and easy to find in the future. In addition to the search field, you can also use Spotlight to find e-mails or text within a message using inline find to highlight all occurrences.

Search E-Mail for Text

1. To search in selected mailboxes, select the mailboxes or accounts.

2. Click in the Search field, and then type the text you want to find. As you type, Mail starts the search and displays the results.

 To narrow the search, select an option or suggestions on the Search field menu.

3. Click **All** or a specific mailbox on the Search bar to narrow the results.

4. To save the search as a Smart Mailbox, click the **Save** button on the Search bar, enter a name, and then click **OK**.

5. To search for text in a message, select the message, click the **Edit** menu, point to **Find**, and then click **Find**. Type the text you want to find to highlight in line. Click **Done** to cancel the search.

 TIMESAVER Press ⌘+F to find or replace text in an open e-mail.

6. To broaden the search, click the **Spotlight** icon on the menu bar, type the text you want, and then click the search result you want on the menu.

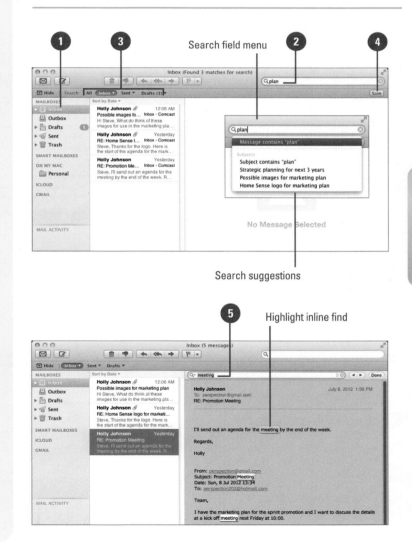

Search field menu

Search suggestions

Highlight inline find

Blocking and Flagging E-Mail

You can have Mail handle junk e-mail for you. You can specify what should be considered junk e-mail and how Mail should handle that e-mail. You can ensure that e-mail which might seem to be junk e-mail, but is actually from a person or site that you are interested in, gets to you. You can mark messages as junk mail to help train Mail (set rules) to more effectively distinguish between junk and non junk. If you receive an e-mail that you want to follow up on later, you can color-code, or flag, it for future reference. It's quick and easy. Simply select the one or more message you want to mark, click the Flag button on the Mail tool-bar, and then select a flag. Mail creates folders for your flagged messages for easy access. You can rename the color-code flags—which you use for searching—as well as clear flags from messages.

Change Junk E-Mail Options

1. Click the **Mail** menu, and then click **Preferences**.

2. Click **Junk Mail**.

3. Select the **Enable junk mail filtering** check box.

4. Click the option to leave it in my Inbox and change the text color or move it to the Junk mailbox.

5. Select the check boxes to exempt e-mail from junk filtering:
 - **Sender of message is in my Contacts**
 - **Sender of message is in my previous recipients**
 - **Message is addressed using my full name**
 - **Filter junk mail before applying my rules**

6. Click **Advanced**.

 The default junk mail rule appears, which you can customize.

7. Use the pop-ups, fields, and buttons to specify the criteria for the junk rule to apply to messages.

8. Click **OK**.

9. Click the **Close** button.

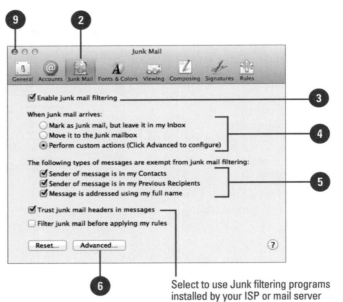

Select to use Junk filtering programs installed by your ISP or mail server along with Mail.

Mark E-Mail as Junk or Not Junk

① Select the e-mail you want to mark as junk or not as junk.

② Click the **Junk** button or **Not Junk** button on the Mail toolbar.

The button toggles between Junk and Not Junk.

③ To erase messages in the Junk mailbox, click the **Mailbox** menu, click **Erase Junk Mail**, and then click **Erase**.

Did You Know?

You can reset junk mail rules to the default. Click the Mail menu, click Preferences, click Junk Mail, click Reset, click Reset, and then click the Close button.

Flag an E-Mail

① Select the e-mail message you want to flag.

② Click the **Flag** button arrow on the Mail toolbar, and then select a flag.

③ To view flagged messages, show **Reminders** in the Sidebar, and then click **Flagged**.

④ To rename a flag, double-click a flag in the Sidebar (under Reminders), type a new name, and then press Return.

⑤ To clear a flag from a message, select the message, click the **Flag** button arrow, and then click **Clear Flag**.

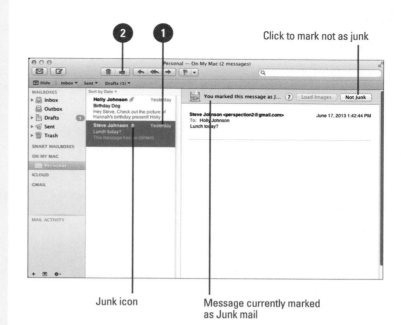

Click to mark not as junk

Junk icon Message currently marked as Junk mail

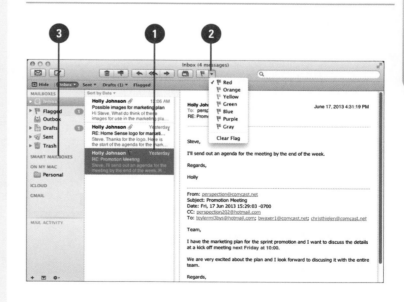

Diverting Incoming E-Mail to Mailboxes

Mail can direct incoming messages that meet criteria to other mailboxes in the Mailbox list rather than to your Inbox. You can set message rules to store any messages you receive from a friend in a different folder so they won't clutter your Inbox. When you are ready to read the messages, you simply open the mailbox and access the messages just as you would messages in the Inbox. You can also set rules to automatically reply to incoming messages, which is useful when you are *out of the office*, or forward incoming messages with additional message text. You can also color-code the messages that you send to or receive from particular people for quick and easy recognition.

Set Rules for Incoming E-Mail

1. Click the **Mail** menu, and then click **Preferences**.

2. Click **Rules**.

3. Click **Add Rule**.

4. Type a name for this rule.

5. Click the pop-up, and then click **Any** or **All** to set initial criteria.

6. Use the pop-ups and fields, to specify the criteria for the rule to apply to a message.

7. Click the **Add** (+) button or **Remove** (-) button to add or remove criteria.

8. Under the Perform The Following Actions area, use the pop-ups and fields to specify the actions you want to be taken if the criteria is met.

9. Click the **Add** button (+) or **Subtract** button (-) to add or remove actions.

10. Click **OK**, and then click **Apply** or **Don't Apply**.

11. To edit, duplicate, or remove a rule, select a rule, and then click **Edit**, **Duplicate**, or **Remove**.

12. Click the **Close** button.

Select to activate or clear to deactivate.

Creating a Smart Mailbox

A Smart Mailbox displays e-mail messages or to-do items based on a search criteria in an easy to use folder in the Mailboxes list. The message or to-do items are not moved to the Smart Mailboxes. Each time you select a Smart Mailbox, Mail performs a search to create an up-to-date list of results. A Smart Mailbox is like a Smart Folder for Mail. You can create a Smart Mailbox for RSS articles, specific content, or from a specific sender.

Create a New Smart Mailbox

1. To create a subfolder in a mailbox, select the existing mailbox.

2. Click the **Add** (+) button at the bottom of the Mailbox list, and then click **New Smart Mailbox**.

3. Type a name for the new mailbox.

4. Specify the criteria you want for the Smart Mailbox:

 ◆ **Contents.** Select **messages** or **to-do's**.

 ◆ **That Match.** Select **any** or **all**.

 ◆ **Conditions.** Use the pop-ups to specify the criteria you want for the Smart Mailbox.

 ◆ **Add or Remove Conditions.** Click the **Add** (+) or **Remove** (-) buttons. You can add as many as you want.

5. Select or clear the **Include messages from trash** or **Include messages from sent** check boxes.

6. Click **OK**.

7. To edit a Smart Mailbox, select the mailbox, click the **Mailbox** menu, and then click **Edit Smart Mailbox**.

8. To delete a Smart Mailbox, select the mailbox, click the **Mailbox** menu, click **Delete Mailbox**, and then click **Delete** to confirm.

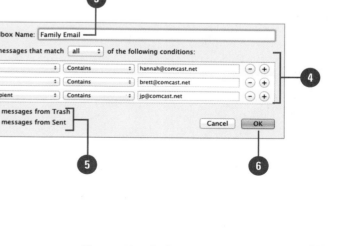

Creating a VIP List

VIPs are Very Important People. With Mail, you can specify the people who are most important to you by making them VIPs. It's simple to make someone a VIP. Just click the star next to a name at the top of a message. Any current e-mail message from the VIP are marked as VIP. When you receive an e-mail message from a VIP, it gets placed in the VIPs Smart Mailbox. To view all the e-mail messages, you can click VIPs in the Sidebar or Favorites bar.

Create a VIP List

1. Click the **Inbox** icon in the Mailbox list or on the Favorites bar to view new messages.

2. Click an e-mail message for the person you want to make a VIP.

3. Point to the name at the top of the message to display a Star icon.

4. Click the **Star** icon.

 ◆ You can also click the Contact name in the message, and then click **Add to VIPs**.

 The messages are tagged to appear in the VIPs smart mailbox.

5. To view the VIP messages, click the **VIPs** icon in the Mailbox list or on the Favorites bar.

6. To remove a person from the VIP list, click the **Star** icon again to remove it.

Sending Instant Messages

Introduction

OS X makes communicating with other computers over the Internet easier than ever with Messages 8.0. You can talk to others over the Internet (like you do on a telephone), use full screen video to see and be seen by others while you converse, share programs and files, and collaborate on documents. You can use Messages to exchange instant messages with a designated list of buddies over the Internet. An **instant message** is an online typewritten conversation in real-time between two or more buddies. Unlike an email message, instant messages require both parties to be online, and the communication is instantaneous.

Messages makes setup effortless. The first time you launch Messages, a setup screen appears to walk you step-by-step through the process. During the setup process, you need to create or provide a screen name, which is your instant messaging address. If you already have an Apple ID, iMessage, Google, AOL Instant Messenger (AIM), Yahoo!, or Jabber account, you can use it with Messages. iMessage is the default account type that is used by iOS devices. Otherwise, you can setup an Apple ID to get a screen name. To use the AV (Audio Video) features of Messages, you need to have a microphone (for audio only) or FireWire compatible video camera (for audio and video) installed on your computer and a fast Internet connection. Messages automatically identifies other local users who are logged in, and lets you send messages or files to each other.

In addition to using Messages over the Internet, you can also use it on your local network—known as **bonjour messaging**—at the office, school, or home. If you want to communicate with users on an iPad, iPhone, iPod Touch with iOS 5 or later), or another Mac, you can use FaceTime to make video calls.

What You'll Do

Start Messages

View Messages

Create a Messages Account

Chat on a Local Network

Change My Status

Use the Messages Status Menu

Add a Buddy

Change a Buddy Picture

Create and Manage Buddy Groups

Send and Receive Messages

Send a File During an Message

Work with Messages

Have a Audio and Video Chat

Enhance a Video Chat

Change Chat Message Options

Change the Chat Message Appearance

Get Chat Message Alerts

Block a Buddy

Get Started with FaceTime

Make a Video Call with FaceTime

Starting Messages

The Messages app allows you to exchange instant messages with a designated list of buddies over the Internet. An **instant message** is an online typewritten conversation in real time between two or more buddies. Instant messages require both parties to be online, and the communication is instantaneous. With iMessage, you can start a conversation on your Mac and then pick it up on your iPhone, iPad, or iPod touch with iOS 5 or later. When you sign in and enable an account, you're ready to go and can leave it alone. However, if you no longer want to receive messages, you can log out or disable account.

Start Messages and Log Out and In

1 Click the **Messages** icon in the Dock.

◆ Click the **Launchpad** icon in the Dock, and then click the **Messages** icon.

The Messages window opens.

2 If prompted, enter your Apple ID and password for iMessage, click **Sign In**, select other e-mail accounts, and then click **Done**.

Messages automatically signs in the accounts that are enabled in Accounts preferences.

3 To sign out, click the **Messages** menu, and then click **Log Out**.

TIMESAVER *Press ⌘+L to log in and out*

4 To log in, click the **Messages** menu, and then click **Log In**.

Did You Know?

You can stop signing in automatically. Click the Messages menu, click Preferences, click Accounts, select an account, clear the Enable This Account check box, and then click the Close button.

Click to add accounts Messages status menu

4 1 Messages window

Viewing Messages

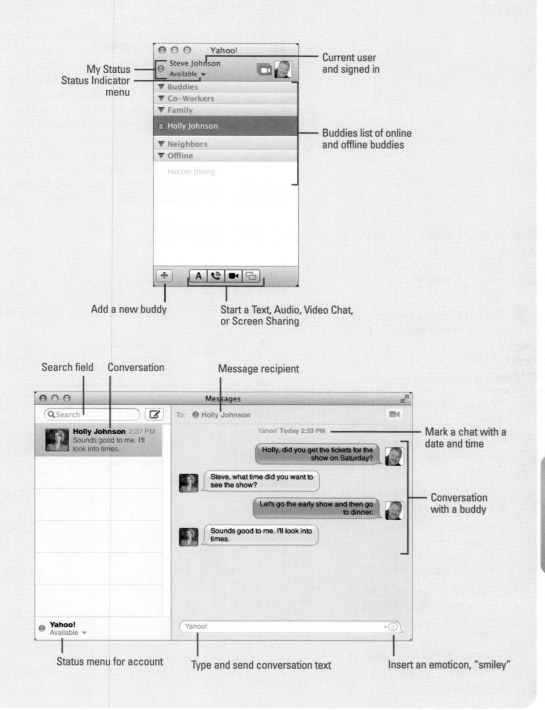

My Status — Status Indicator menu

Current user and signed in

Buddies list of online and offline buddies

Add a new buddy

Start a Text, Audio, Video Chat, or Screen Sharing

Search field Conversation Message recipient

Mark a chat with a date and time

Conversation with a buddy

Status menu for account Type and send conversation text Insert an emoticon, "smiley"

Creating a Messages Account

In order to use Messages you need to sign in and enable an account. To complete the process, you need to provide or create a screen name (your instant messaging address) to send and receive instant messages. If you already have an Apple ID using a me.com or Mac.com address, you can use it to register (sign in) for the iMessage account on the Mac, just like the one on your iOS device. If you have another type of instant messaging account, such as Google, Yahoo!, AOL Instant Messenger (AIM), Google Talk, or Jabber, you can use it too. If you added an account in Internet Account in System Preferences, you don't have to do it here, however some can only be done in Messages. An iMessage account uses your Apple ID email address, while other accounts, such as an AIM account uses a screen name, such as perspection. If you don't have an Apple ID, you can sign up for an account at *www.apple.com*. If you have multiple accounts, you can switch between them or use them separately. If you are using Messages over a local network for Bonjour messaging, you don't need a screen name.

Sign In and Enable an iMessage Account

1. Click the **Messages** icon in the Dock.

2. Click the **Messages** menu, and then click **Preferences**.

3. Click **Accounts**.

4. Click the **iMessage** account.

5. If needed, type your Apple ID and password, and then click **Sign In**.

6. Select any of the following options:

 ◆ **Enable this account.** Select to enable this account.

 ◆ **Address.** Select (**New!**), clear (**New!**), or add email addresses where you can be reached for messages.

 ◆ **Send read receipts.** Select to allow others to be notified when you have read their message.

 ◆ **Start new conversation from.** Select an address (**New!**).

7. Click **Close** button.

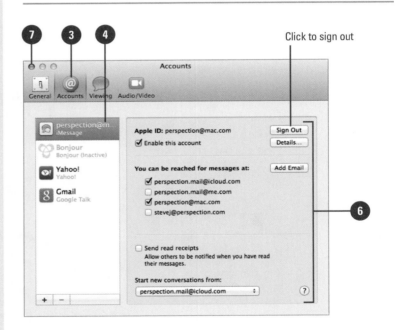

Create and Enable Other Accounts

1 Click the **Messages** menu, and then click **Preferences**.

2 Click **Accounts**.

IMPORTANT *If multiple people use a computer with separate accounts, they use their own screen names.*

3 To create another account, click the **Add** (+) button, select an account type (**New!**) (**Google**, **Yahoo!**, **AOL**, or **Other message accounts**), and then click **Continue**.

◆ **Google**, **Yahoo!**, or **AOL.** Enter a name, e-mail address, and password, and then click **Set Up** (**New!**).

◆ **Other message accounts.** Select an account type (AIM, Google Talk, Jabber, or Yahoo!) enter username and password, and then click **Create**.

TIMESAVER *Click the Message menu, and then click Add Account (**New!**) to create one.*

Your password is added to your keychain.

4 Click the **Account Information** tab.

5 Select the **Enable this account** check box to enable and display this account or clear it to not use it.

6 Some accounts, such as Gmail and Google Talk, also provide other options. Click the available tabs, such as Chat Settings and Server Setting, to set additional options.

7 Click the **Close** button.

Select an account type

For Your Information

Installing and Selecting AV Hardware

Before you can start or join a video chat, you need to connect and install a microphone, a FireWire based video camera, such as iSight by Apple, built-in USB, and a broadband Internet connection (384 Kbps or faster), such as cable or DSL, to your Macintosh computer. If you have a Digital Video (DV) camcorder with a FireWire cable, you can also use it with Messages. Once you attach and install (if necessary) your audio and video equipment, you can set options in the Video pane of Messages Preferences. If you are using a camera with a built-in microphone, Messages automatically uses the camera microphone unless you change it to another one you have attached to your computer.

Chatting on a Local Network

If you don't have an instant message account or server, you can still use Messages to chat with others on your local network. Instead of communicating with a central Internet server, each computer communicates directly with each other over network cables. Messages also works with a wireless connection using AirPort over a local network or the Internet. Bonjour allows you to chat with people on your local network or wireless local community. You can't add a Bonjour user to your Buddies list. The user names are based on the log-in settings on each person's computer and are not AIM screen names. Unlike regular instant message, when you type a Bonjour instant message, each character you type is sent immediately unless you turn off the default setting in the Accounts pane of Messages Preferences.

Turn On Bonjour Instant Messaging

1. Click the **Messages** menu, and then click **Preferences**.

2. Click **Accounts**.

3. Click **Bonjour**.

4. Select the **Enable Bonjour instant messaging** check box.

5. Select any of the following Bonjour options:

 ◆ **Publish my email and instant message address.** Select to make your email and instant message address available on the network.

 ◆ **Block others from seeing my status as Idle.** Select to have your status show as Available even when you're away from your computer.

6. Click the **Close** button.

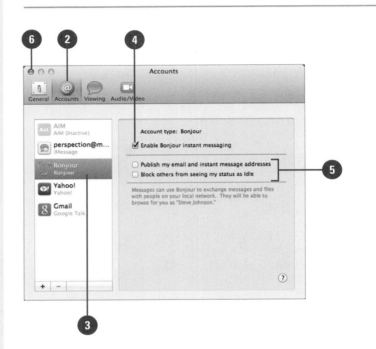

For Your Information

Having Problems Seeing Bonjour Users

If you're having problems seeing Bonjour users in the Bonjour window, your network connections might be contributing to the problem. If you have firewall protect turned on, you might be unable to receive messages from other users. To use Bonjour, you may need to allow activity on port 5298. If you connect to the Internet using PPP or PPPoE, you won't be able to see other users. Check with your network administrator for information related to your network setup.

Start Bonjour Messaging

1. Click the **Window** menu, and then click **Bonjour List**.

 The Bonjour window opens, showing Messages local network users who are available for chatting.

2. Double-click the user to whom you want to send an instant message.

3. Type your message in the box at the bottom of the window.

4. Press Return, and then wait for a reply.

5. When you're done, click the **Close** (x) button to end the session.

Did You Know?

You can share your screen with a buddy If you and your buddies are using OS X, you can use Messages with any of the support account types to share your screens as if you were sitting in front of it. When you share your screen, your buddy has the same control over your computer as you do. During the screen sharing session, Messages starts an audio chat so you can talk about what your doing. To share your screen, select your buddy, click the Buddies menu, and then click Share My Screen or Ask To Share. You can switch between the two open desktops and copy files between your computers. When you're done, press Control+Esc to end the screen sharing session.

Conversation

Bonjour account

Changing My Status

When you sign in/enable accounts with Messages, the program notifies buddies currently online from your Buddies list that you are available to chat (green status). While you're signed in, you might need to leave your computer for a meeting or lunch. Instead of signing out, you can change your online status (red) to let your buddies know that you're busy, away from your desk, on the phone, or out to lunch. When you're away, your buddies see that you're idle, and any message you receive is waiting for you. If you don't want your buddies to see or send messages to you, you can go offline. If you don't see the status message you want, you can quickly customize one to suit your own needs. If you are using multiple Accounts at the same time, you can have different status for each one or the same status for all accounts.

Change My Status

1. Click the Status Indicator.

2. Click a status type.

 ◆ **Status (Green).** Online available.

 ◆ **iTunes.** Online listening to a song.

 ◆ **Status (Red).** Online not available.

 ◆ **Offline.** Offline not available.

 ◆ **Use Same Status for All Accounts.** Check to set same status for all accounts.

Create a Custom Status Message

1. Click the Status Indicator, and then click **Custom Available** or **Custom Away**.

2. Type a custom message, and then press Return.

Did You Know?

You can change items from the Status Indicator menu. Click the Status Indicator menu, click Edit Status Menu, click the Add (+) or Remove (-) buttons, double-click items to edit, or drag items to order, and then click OK.

Using the Messages Status Menu

The Messages Status menu appears as a chat balloon icon on the menu bar. When the ballon icon is empty, you're online; when there is a line in the middle, you're away or offline. If you turn on the Messages Status menu, you can still receive instant messages, view online buddies, and change your status when you quit the Messages program. You can turn the Status menu on in the General pane of Messages Preferences, where you set other status options when you switch users or your computer is inactive. When the Status menu is turned off and you quit Messages, you're logged out of AIM and Bonjour messaging.

Turn On the Messages Status Menu and Other Options

1. Click the **Messages** menu, and then click **Preferences**.

2. Click **General**.

3. Select the **Show status in menu bar** check box.

4. Specify the following status options:

 ◆ **When I quit Messages, set my status to Offline**.

 ◆ **Set my status to Away after the computer is inactive**.

 ◆ **Auto-reply with my Away message**.

 ◆ **When I return** or **When switching users**.

5. Click the **Close** button.

Use the Messages Status Menu

1. Click the **Messages Status** menu, and then select an available option:

 ◆ **A status.** Click Offline, Invisible, Available, or Away; you can also select custom available or away messages.

 If you don't want to be seen offline, you can go invisible.

 ◆ **A buddy.** Click the name of an online buddy.

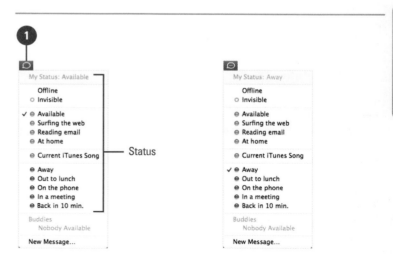

Adding a Buddy

Before you can send instant messages to other people, they need to be in your Buddies list. Your Buddies list shows you a unified list—no matter what the chat service—of who's currently online and offline, their audio and video capabilities, and if they are available for chatting. You can add a person who has a screen name from one or more chat accounts to your Buddies list. You can add as many buddies as you like to your Buddies list. You can add them from your Contacts or type new ones. When you add a new person to your Buddies list, a new card is added to your Contacts. Your Buddies list is stored on an instant message server, so you can log in to your account from any computer and see if your buddies are online.

Add a Buddy

1. If necessary, click the **Window** menu, and then click **Buddies** to display the Buddies window.

2. Click the **Add** (+) button, and then click **Add Buddy**.

 ◆ You can also click the **Buddies** menu, and then click **Add Buddy**.

3. Select an account (**New!**), enter an account name, select a group, type the email address or screen name for the person, or click the **Expand/ Collapse** button, and then select from Contacts.

 TIMESAVER *If your buddy uses more than one screen name, you can type more than one by separating each with a comma.*

4. Click **Add**.

Expand/ collapse button

Contacts

Did You Know?

You can quickly delete a buddy from your Buddies list. Click a buddy in the Buddy list, press Delete, and then click Remove. You can also click the Buddies menu, and then click Remove Buddy.

You can view and edit information about a buddy. Select a buddy in the Buddies list, click the Buddies menu, and then click Show Info.

Changing a Buddy Picture

You can change the picture that appears next to your name in the Buddies and in message windows, along with the ones that appear next to your buddies. The picture is known as the Buddy icon. The Buddy icon you select appears in the Buddies of those in which you have a chat. To change your Buddy icon, drag an image file—64 x 64 pixels is recommended—to your name in the Buddies. In addition to an image file, you can also use an animated picture, also known as a GIF or animated GIF, as a buddy picture, which you can also create using Photo Booth or iPhoto.

Change a Buddy Picture

1. If necessary, click the **Window** menu, and then click **Buddies** to display the Buddies window.

2. Select the buddy you want to change.

3. Click the **Buddies** menu, and then click **Show Info**.

4. Click the **Address Card** tab.

5. Clear the **Always use this picture** check box.

6. Drag the image or animated GIF you want to the picture box.

 ◆ **Enable Buddy Picture Animation.** Click the **Messages** menu, click **Preferences**, click **General**, select the **Animate buddy pictures** check box, and then click the **Close** button.

7. Select the **Always use this Picture** check box.

8. Click the **Close** button.

Did You Know?

You can change your picture. Click the Messages menu, click Change My Picture, click Defaults, Recents, Camera, or Other, select or take the picture you want, and then click Done.

For Your Information

Creating an Animated GIF in Photo Booth

If you don't have an animated GIF, you can create one using Photo Booth. Open Photo Booth from the Applications folder, and then click the button for four-up picture format. If you want to add effects, click the Effects button and then select a video effect. Click the Camera button to take a series of four pictures, select the animation, and then export it as a file or set it as a buddy picture. To export it, click the File menu, click Export, specify a name and folder, and then click Save.

Creating and Managing Buddy Groups

As your Buddies list grows, you may want to organize your buddies into groups. Messages makes it easy to create your own groups and use the one predefined group called Buddies that comes with Messages. Once you have organized your groups, you can simply drag buddies from one group to another. You can use the triangles next to the group name to hide and display buddies in a group. If a group changes, you can rename it, if a group is not where you want it, you can drag to move or merge it, or if you no longer need a group, you can remove it. You can also quickly search for buddies using the Search field.

Turn On or Off the Use of Groups and Offline Groups

1. Click the **View** menu.

2. Click **Use Groups** or **Use Offline Group**.

 TIMESAVER *Press Shift+⌘+H.*

3. To turn off the use of Groups or Offline Groups, click the **View** menu, and then click **Use Groups** or **Use Offline Group** again.

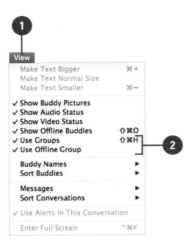

Create a Buddy Group

1. If necessary, click the **Window** menu, and then click **Buddies** to display the Buddies window.

2. Click the **Add** (+) button, and then click **Add Group**.

3. Type a name for the group.

4. Click **Add**.

Manage Buddies and Groups

1 If necessary, click the **Window** menu, and then click **Buddies** to display the Buddies window.

2 Select from the following options:

◆ **Search for buddies.** Press +F, enter a name or part of a name. As you type, Messages filters your buddies list. Select a buddy from the results. Click **Done** to exit it.

◆ **Display all group members.** Click the **View** menu, and then click **Use Groups** or **Use Offline Groups**.

◆ **Display group members.** Click the arrow next to the group name.

◆ **Move a buddy into a group.** Drag the buddy to a group.

◆ **Copy a buddy into a group.** Press and hold down the Option key while you drag the buddy to each group.

◆ **Move a group.** Drag the buddy group to a new position.

◆ **Merge groups.** Drag the buddy group onto another one.

◆ **Delete a group.** Click the **Add** (+) button, click **Edit Group**, select the group, click the **Delete** (-) button, and then click **OK**.

You can't delete a group with buddies in multiple groups, but you can delete a group with the only one buddy in it. You can't delete the last group in the list; you need to always have at least one.

◆ **Rename a group.** Click the **Add** (+) button, click **Edit Group**, select the group, click the group again, type a new name, and then click **OK**.

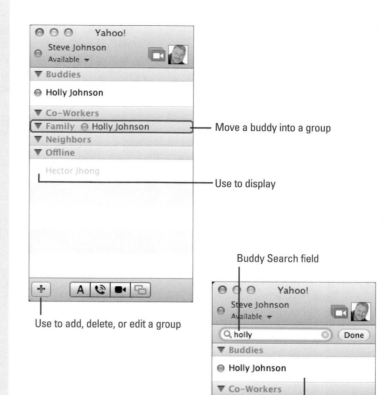

Move a buddy into a group

Use to display

Use to add, delete, or edit a group

Buddy Search field

Search results

<div style="border:1px solid #000; padding:8px;">

For Your Information

Changing Buddies View

If you are having trouble viewing the buddies you want, you can use the View menu to change the buddies view. There are buddy commands to Show Buddy Pictures and Show Offline Buddies, which shows your entire buddies list, including buddies not currently available. You can also use the submenu Buddy Names to display full names, short name or handles, and the submenu Sort Buddies to sort buddies by availability, first name, or last name. If you want to show all your offline buddies as a group, select Use Offline Group. If you're not sure whether buddies have cameras or microphones, select the Show Audio Status or Show Video Status.

</div>

Sending and Receiving Messages

An instant message is an online typewritten conversation in real-time between two or more buddies. As you type an instant message, you can format your messages by using fonts and color and by inserting graphical symbols called **emoticons**, or "smileys," such as a happy face, which help convey your emotions. You can have instant message conversations with several different buddies at once. When you send a instant message to a group, all participants receive the message and all responses are visible to everyone involved. If a buddy has multiple accounts, you can select the one you want to use to send to and from. With iMessage, you can start a conversation on your Mac and then pick it up on your iPhone, iPad, or iPod touch with iOS 5 or later.

Send and Receive Instant Messages

1. To start a chat, use any of the following:

 ◆ In the Messages window, click the **New Message** button, type a buddy name, phone number, or email address, and then press Return.

 As you type the recipient, autocomplete names tries to enter the rest.

 ◆ In the Buddies list, select one or more names in the Buddies list, and then click the **Start A Text Chat** button.

 TIMESAVER *Double-click a person in your Buddies list to start a chat session.*

2. If the buddy has multiple accounts, click the **Account** menu, and then select an account. Additional options are available.

3. Type your message in the box. To start a new line, press Shift+Return.

4. Press Return, and then wait.

 Ellipses appear when an response is coming.

5. To close a conversation, point to the Conversation (displays a Close button), click the **Close** button.

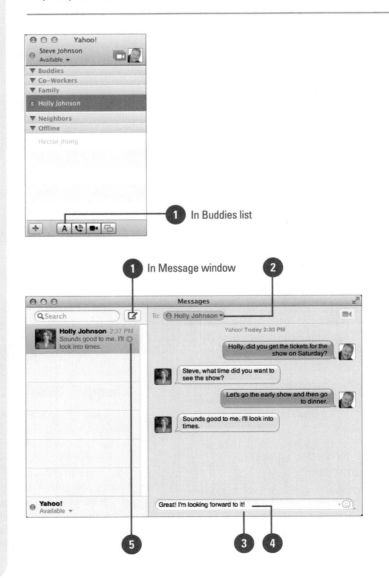

① In Buddies list

① In Message window ②

⑤ ③ ④

Format Message Text

1 Type and then select the text you want to format.

2 Click the **Format** menu, and then click the **Show Fonts**.

3 Specify the font, font style, size, color, and effect you want, and then preview the result in the sample box.

4 Click the **Close** button, and then send the formatted message.

Insert Emoticons

1 In the Messages window, Type your text, and then click the icon you want to insert into the conversation..

2 Click the **Emoticons** button.

TIMESAVER *Type a smiley using the keyboard, such as ":-)" and Messages inserts a corresponding graphic. Point to a smiley to view its type.*

3 Press Return.

<table>
<tr><td>

Did You Know?

You can save conversation history. Click the Messages menu, click Preferences, click Messages, select the Save History When Conversations Are Closed check box, and then click the Close button.

You can auto-reply when you're away. Click the Messages menu, click Preferences, click Messages, select the Auto-reply With My Away Message check box, and then click the Close button.

</td></tr>
</table>

For Your Information

Adding Date and Time Stamps

During a long chat, you can insert your date and time stamp to mark a transcript. In a chat, click the Edit menu, and then click Mark Transcript. To clear a chat, click the Edit menu, and then click Clear Transcript. This is helpful when you save a transcript for review later.

Sending a File During a Message

While you are conversing in Messages, you can send a buddy a file or hyperlink. You can send many different types of files, including pictures, documents, and music. When you send a file, a request to transfer the file is sent to your buddy, which allows you to send large files up to 100 MB. You are notified when your buddy accepts or declines your request. Before you receive files over the Internet, make sure you have virus protection software to protect your computer. You can also send a hyperlink that points to a web site. When your buddy receives a message with a link, the person can click it to open the web address in their web browser.

Send a File or Hyperlink

1. Start a chat with the buddy to whom you want to send the file or hyperlink.

2. Type your message in the box at the bottom of the window.

3. Use the following to send a file or hyperlink:

 ◆ **Send a File.** Click the **Buddies** menu, click **Send File**, navigate to and select the file you want to send (for best results, use JPEG or GIF), and then click **Send**. A icon appears to indicate the picture.

 TIMESAVER *Drag the picture file to the area where you type your message.*

 ◆ **Send a Hyperlink.** Click the **Edit** menu, click **Add Link**, type title for the link, type a web address, and then click **OK**.

4. Type any additional text if you want, and then press Return.

 If it's a file, wait for the recipient to accept or decline the file (check File Transfer status); or if it's a hyperlink, the link appears in the Messages window.

5. To open a file or hyperlink, click the file (to preview in Quick Look) or link in the Messages window.

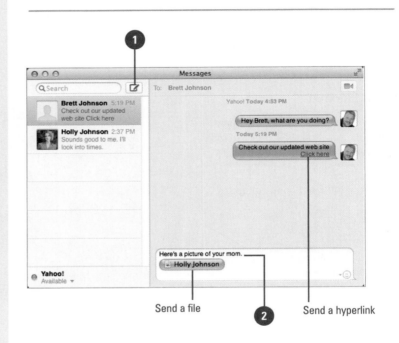

Send a file Send a hyperlink

For Your Information

Checking File Transfer Status

You can send or receive files from your buddies. File transfers with Messages don't have a size limit, so you can send large files. However, large files can take a while. To help you manage the file transfers, you can use the File Transfers manager in Messages. The File Transfers manager displays a list of transferred files and status for any current file transfers, just like the Downloads manager. To show the File Transfer window, click the Window menu, and then click File Transfers. Your buddy can accept or reject the file. You can send only one file at a time. If you want to send multiple files, compress them together into a single file.

Working with Messages

As you continue to create conversations in Messages, the number of conversations can clutter the Messages window. If you no longer want to keep a conversation, you can quickly close it. Instead of closing a conversation, you can clear the transcript to start al over again. If the chat is taking up to much room, you can change the display view to make it more compact. If you need to find specific text in a conversation, you can use the Search field to help you locate it. If you want to view multiple conversation at the same time, you can open a conversation in a separate window. If you want to share a message, you can forward it.

Work with Instant Messages and Conversations

◆ **Start a New Message and Conversation.** Click the **New Message** button.

◆ **Forward a Message** Control-click the message, and then click **Forward**.

◆ **Close a Conversation.** Point to a conversation, and then click the **Close** (x) button or click the **File** menu, click **Close Conversation**, and then click **Delete**.

◆ **Search a Conversat** the Search field, text you want to

As you type conv matching criteria cancel the search (x) button in the Se

◆ **Open a Conversatio Separate Window.** Control-click the conversation, and then click **Open Chat in Separate Window**.

◆ **Clear a Conversation Transcript.** Control-click within the chat window, click **Clear Chat Transcript**, and then click **Clear**.

◆ **Change the Message Display.** Click the **View** menu, point to **Messages**, and then select an option, such as Show as Balloons or Show as Compact, and Show Names and Pictures.

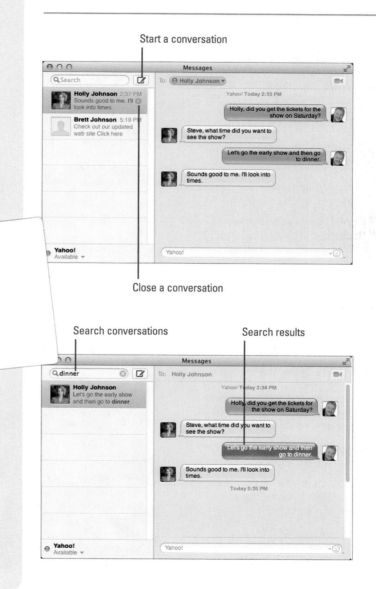

Start a conversation

Close a conversation

Search conversations

Search results

Having an Audio and Video Chat

With Messages, you can talk to others (up to three at a time with the same account type) over the Internet as you do on a phone, and you can use video to see others and let others see you as you converse. Once you set up your computer hardware and software, you're ready to communicate over the Internet. You have two communication choices: audio only, or audio and video. With audio only, you speak into a microphone and hear the other person's response over your speakers. With audio and video, you send video to others so they receive live images as well as sound. If the buddies you call don't have a video camera, they'll see you, but you won't see them. If you start a video chat with someone using an iMessage account, FaceTime opens; if it's with another type of account, a video chat window appears.

Have an Audio or Video Chat

1. If necessary, click the **Window** menu, and then click **Buddies**.

2. To start a chat, select a name in the Buddies list, and then click the **Start A Video Chat** button or **Start An Audio Chat** button.

 If you're using iMessage, see page 323 for details about FaceTime.

 To respond to an audio or video chat invitation, click the invitation window, and then click **Accept**.

 To decline or block a chat invitation, click **Decline** or **Block**.

3. Start talking.

4. Use video controls on the Video menu or use the following:

 ◆ **Size Video Window.** Click the double arrow button to switch between normal and full-screen modes or drag the bottom right corner of the video window.

 ◆ **Invite.** Click the **Invite** button to invite another person to chat.

 ◆ **Pause Video.** Option+click the **Microphone** button. Click the button again to start it.

 ◆ **Mute Audio.** Click the **Microphone** button.

5. When you're done, click the **Close** button to end the session.

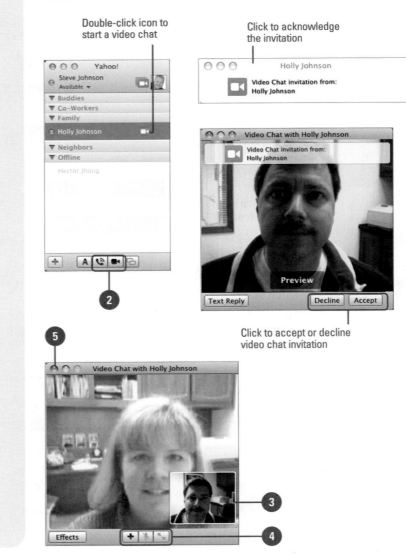

Double-click icon to start a video chat

Click to acknowledge the invitation

Click to accept or decline video chat invitation

Change Video Bandwidth Speed and Preferences

1 Click the **Messages** menu, and then click **Preferences**.

2 Click **Audio/Video**.

3 If available, click the **Camera** pop-up, and then select an installed camera.

4 Click the **Microphone** and **Sound output** pop-ups, and then select an installed microphone and speakers.

5 Click the **Bandwidth Limit** pop-up, and then select a video speed option for your computer's performance and quality.

6 Click the **Close** button.

Did You Know?

You can monitor a video chat. Click the Video menu, and then click Connection Doctor. The frame rate shows the number of frames the video plays per second (fps). The Bit Rate setting show the average number of bits that one second of video data consumes in kilobits per second (kbps). The call duration shows how long the chats lasts.

You can take a picture of your video chat. ⌘+click the video Messages window and drag the image (a JPEG file) out of the window to a buddy icon in your Buddies list or a location on your hard disk. You can also press ⌘+C to copy a picture of your chat and then press ⌘+V to paste it in another document.

Enhancing a Video Chat

As you hold a video conversation in Messages, you can enhance your experience by adding video effects or backdrops to the video window. The video effects are provided by Photo Booth and the backdrops are professionally designed by Apple. You can use the ones provided, download new ones, or create your own.

Enhance an Audio or Video Chat

1 Start a video chat with one or more buddies.

2 Click **Effects**.

3 To view the video effects and backdrops, click the left and right arrow buttons.

4 Click the video effect thumbnail you want to use.

◆ **Photo Booth Effects.** Unique video effects, such as X-Ray, Thermal Camera, and Pop Art.

◆ **Backdrops.** Backgrounds you can be in front of.

5 To add your own backdrop, drag it from the desktop or Finder window to a blank backdrop placeholder (User Backdrop 1, etc.) in the Video Effects window.

6 To remove the video effect, click the **Original** thumbnail.

7 When you're done, click the **Close** button to close the Video Effects window.

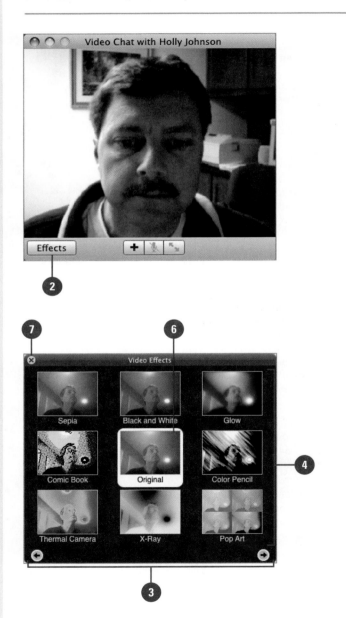

Changing Chat Message Options

You can set message preferences in the Viewing and General panes of Messages Preferences to make it easier to manage and work with messages and conversations. You can set options to save your conversation instead of deleting them when you close them, create a keyboard shortcut to bring Messages to the front, watch for your name in incoming messages, and automatically reply when you're away. When you select the option to save conversation history, it allows you to start a conversation on your Mac using an iMessage account and then pick it up on your iPhone, iPad, or iPod touch with iOS 5 or later.

Change Chat Message Options

1. Click the **Messages** menu, and then click **Preferences**.

2. Click **Viewing**.

3. Select or clear any of the following options:

 ◆ **Use a keyboard shortcut to bring Messages to the front.** Select to create a keyboard shortcut to bring Messages to the front.

 ◆ **Notify me when my name is mentioned in incoming messages.** Select to have Messages highlight your name with it's mentioned.

4. Click **General**.

5. Select or clear any of the following options:

 ◆ **Save history when conversations are closed.** Select to save your conversations when you close them. If you clear the check box, closing a conversation deletes it.

 ◆ **Auto-reply with my Away message.** Select to have Messages replay to messages for you when you're away from you computer. The reply includes your status.

6. Click the **Close** button.

Changing the Chat Message Appearance

Messages makes it easy to customize the appearance of a chat to suit your own style and preference. You can modify the appearance of the balloons, or change a font and font color in a chat for yourself and your sender. The changes you make affect the format of your messages on your screen as well as messages on your buddies screen. You can set your preferences in the Viewing pane of Messages Preferences.

Change the Appearance of Chat Messages

1. Click the **Messages** menu, and then click **Preferences**.

2. Click **Viewing**.

3. Select or specify the various options you want to use:

 ◆ **My background color.** Click the pop-up, and then select a balloon color.

 ◆ **My font color.** Click the pop-up, and then select a font color.

 ◆ **My font.** Click the pop-up, and then select a font.

 ◆ **Sender's background color.** Click the pop-up, and then select a balloon color.

 ◆ **Sender's font color.** Click the pop-up, and then select a font color.

 ◆ **Sender's font.** Click the pop-up, and then select a font.

4. Click the **Close** button.

Getting Chat Message Alerts

When certain events, such as when messages arrive or when you're not sure who sent messages, Messages can notify you with a sound or an alert. You can set alert options that apply to every buddy in the General pane of Messages Preferences. If you want to specify additional notifications for messages, you can set options in the Notifications pane in System Preferences.

Set Up Chat Message Alerts

1. Click the **Messages** menu, and then click **Preferences**.

2. Click **General**.

3. Select or clear the **Play Sound** check box.

 If you select it, click the **Message received sound** pop-up, select an occurrence, and then select or clear the Repeat check box if you want the alert to occur every time.

4. Select or clear the **Notify me about messages from unknown contacts** check box.

5. Click the **Close** button.

Did You Know?

You can specify where to save received files in chats. Click the Messages menu, click Preferences, click General, click the Save Received Files To pop-up, select a location, and then click the Close button.

You can specify the use of an AppleScript handler. Click the Messages menu, click Preferences, click General, click the AppleScript Handler pop-up, select None or a script, and then click the Close button.

General

General Accounts Viewing Audio/Video

Default IM application: Messages

Application: ☐ Save history when conversations are closed
 ☐ Notify me about messages from unknown contacts
 ☑ Play sound effects

Message received sound: Received Message

Buddy list: ☑ Show all my accounts in one list
 ☐ Animate buddy pictures

Account status: ☑ Show status in menu bar
 ☐ Use shapes to indicate status
 ☑ When I quit Messages, set my status to Offline
 ☐ Auto-reply with my Away message
 ☑ Set my status to Away after the computer is inactive

When I return: Ask what to do

When switching users: Set my status to Offline

Save received files to: Downloads

AppleScript handler: None

Blocking a Buddy

If you no longer want to receive instant messages from a specific buddy, you can block the buddy from sending you instant messages with an AIM account. When you block a buddy, you appear to be offline to the person, who doesn't know blocking is turned on. Blocking a buddy moves them from your Allow list to your Block list in the Privacy pane of Messages Preferences.

Block or Unblock a Buddy

1. Click the **Messages** menu, and then click **Preferences**.

 TIMESAVER *Select the buddy in the Buddy list, click the Buddies menu, click Block buddy name, and then click Block.*

2. Click **Accounts**, and then select the AIM account.

3. Click the **Privacy** tab.

4. Click a privacy option:

 ◆ **Allow anyone**. Click to unblock everyone.

 ◆ **Allow people in my Buddy List**. Click to unblock buddies in my Buddy List.

 ◆ **Allow specific people**. Click the option, and then click Edit List to select buddies.

 ◆ **Block everyone**. Click to block everyone.

 ◆ **Block specific people**. Click the option, and then click Edit List to add and remove buddies.

5. Select or clear the **Block others from seeing that I am idle** check box.

6. Click the **Close** button.

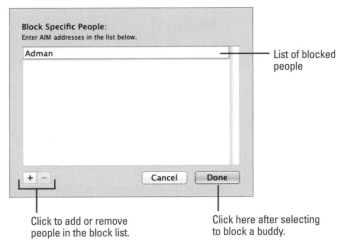

List of blocked people

Click to add or remove people in the block list.

Click here after selecting to block a buddy.

Did You Know?

You can search for a buddy in Spotlight. Select the buddy in the Buddies list, click the Buddies menu, and then click Search in Spotlight.

Getting Started with FaceTime

FaceTime for Mac allows you make video calls to iPad 2, iPhone 4, iPod Touch (4th generation with iOS 4.1 or later), or another Mac. You can hear a voice and see a face without distracting window frame and controls in 720p HD clarity along with support for a widescreen 16:9 aspect ratio. All you need to get started is an Ethernet or Wi-Fi connection to the Internet, a camera and microphone, and an Apple ID and email address, which you'll need to verify before first use. Just find the person you want to call in your contracts list or Contacts.

Get Started with FaceTime

① Click the **FaceTime** icon in the Dock.

② Enter your Apple ID and password, and then click **Sign In** or click **Create New Account** and follow the on-screen instructions.

 ◆ On first use, enter the email address you want to use, and then click **Next**. Check your email for a verification. It needs to be verified before you can use it with FaceTime.

③ Click the **FaceTime** menu, and then click **Preferences**.

④ Specify the FaceTime preference options you want:

 ◆ Turn On/Off FaceTime. Turns on or off FaceTime.

 ◆ Sign Out. Blocks all incoming calls. Click **Accounts**, and then click **Sign Out**.

 ◆ Location. Changes phone locations. Click **Accounts**, and then click **Change Location**.

 ◆ Email Address. Click to change or remove an email address.

 ◆ Add Another Email. Click to add another email account to FaceTime.

⑤ Click **Done**.

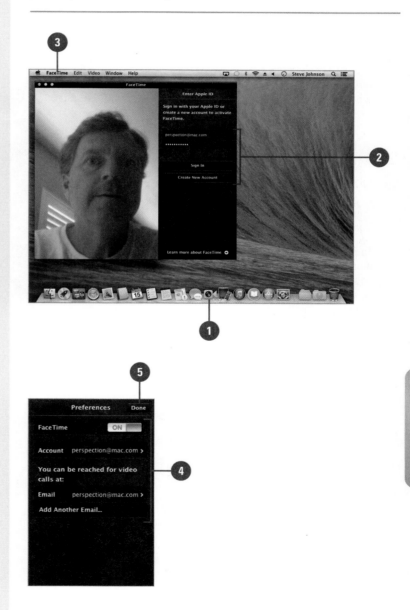

Making a Video Call with FaceTime

With FaceTime for Mac, video calls automatically adjust from landscape to portrait and back depending on the orientation or camera in use—front or rear—of the mobile device you're calling. However, if you prefer one over the other, you can set it in preferences. When you call an iPhone, you use a phone number. When you call an iPad, iPod touch or Mac, you use an email address. When someone tries to reach you, the call rings through on every Mac or mobile device—iPad, iPhone, or iPod touch—you own even if FaceTime isn't running, unless you turn off FaceTime in preferences.

Video Calling with FaceTime

1. Click the **FaceTime** icon in the Dock and then sign in.

 ◆ To quickly return or re-initiate a call, Control-click the **FaceTime** icon in the Dock, select a call from the Recent Calls list, and then click **FaceTime**.

2. Select a contact from **All Contacts** or a group (click **Contacts**, and then click **Groups**). You can use the Search field to find a contact.

3. To place a call, click a phone number (iPhone) or click an email address (iPad, iPod touch, or Mac). To end a call, click **End** or **Cancel**, or exit FaceTime.

4. To exit FaceTime (and still receive calls), click the **FaceTime** menu, and then click **Quit FaceTime**.

5. To receive a video call, click **Accept** in the call window. To block a call, click **Decline**.

6. To change orientation, click the **Video** menu, and then click **Use Portrait** or **Use Landscape**.

7. To turn FaceTime off (don't receive calls) or on, click the **FaceTime** menu, and then click **Turn FaceTime Off** or **Turn FaceTime On**.

 ◆ To pause a video call, click the **FaceTime** menu, and then click **Hide FaceTime**. To resume, click the **FaceTime** icon in Dock.

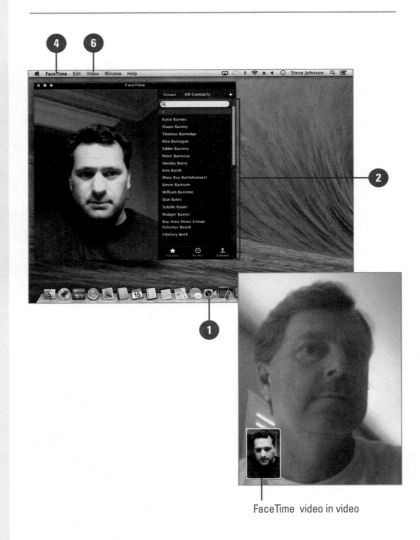

FaceTime video in video

Working with Music and Media

Introduction

Macs were born for multimedia, and even after more than 25 years, they're still considered a front runner when it comes to images, movies, and music. OS X is bundled with several old friends, iTunes, and DVD and QuickTime Players, as well as some newer ones, Photo Booth.

iTunes 11.1 is a software jukebox that comes with OS X, yet it's also available on Microsoft Windows, so you can share music between Macintosh and Windows. iTunes allows you to sort through and organize your digital music collection, convert CD's into the digital format, and even burn your favorite music onto a CD. If that's not enough, iTunes come complete with a built-in link to the iTunes Store. So if you have an Internet connection, you're one click away from a music store that contains the latest songs, as well as billions (yes, I said billions) of songs from the past. And for those of you that like to listen to the radio while you work, iTunes comes equipped with its own iTunes and Internet Radio.

If you have an built-in or external camera attached to your computer, you can use Photo Booth to capture photos just like you were sitting in a photo booth at a carnival. You can capture individual photos or create a short movie and add a backdrop or visual effects.

If your Mac includes an Apple Remote, you can use it to control iTunes, where you can access and play music and playlists, iPhoto slide shows, and videos and DVDs on your Mac or Apple TV. You can also use the Apple Remote to deliver Keynote presentations and play music with the iPod Hi-Fi and some third-party docks. The Apple Remote uses an infrared (IR) reception and works up to 30 feet within an unobstructed line of sight. If you have an iPhone, iPad, or iPod touch, you can use the free Remote app to use it as a remote control.

What You'll Do

Start and Set Up iTunes

View the iTunes Window

Set up iTunes to Automatically Play CDs

Get Music and Media from CDs, Hard Drives, and the iTunes Store

Create and Use Playlists

Add Media to a Playlist

Work with Media

Share Media at Home

Listen to iTunes or Internet Radio

Subscribe and Play Podcasts

Use iPod, iPhone, or iPad with iTunes

Export to MP3 Players

Set iTunes Preferences

Stream a Mac to Apple TV

Capture Photos in Photo Booth

Record Movies in Photo Booth

Add Photo Booth Effects

Play and Browse DVD Movies

Customize the DVD Player

Play and Create QuickTime Movies

Explore iMovie, iDVD, and iPhoto

Starting and Setting Up iTunes

You can conveniently start iTunes from the Dock. Simply, click the iTunes icon in the Dock to start iTunes. You'll need to create or use an existing Apple ID, which is an email address and password you use to login for just about everything you do with Apple, including the iTunes Store, iCloud, and App Store. The iTunes Store helps you discover new music, movies, and other media from your iTunes library. When you sign in to the iTunes Store, you authorize your computer to play purchases, which helps protect the copyrights of the purchased items. When you download a media item, Apple lets you copy and play that item on up to five authorized machines (Mac or Windows). An iPod, iPhone, iPad, or Apple TV don't count as a computer. If you want to use a sixth computer, you need to deauthorize one and then authorize the other.

Start and Set Up iTunes

1. Click the **iTunes** icon in the Dock.

 ◆ You can also click the **Launchpad** icon in the Dock, and then click the **iTunes** icon.

2. If you started iTunes for the first time, read and follow the welcome screens to use iTunes.

3. To use the iTunes Store, click the **Store** menu, click **Sign In** or **Create Account**, and then follow the account review or setup process as requested.

4. To authorize or deauthorize a computer, click the **Store** menu, and then click **Authorize** or **Deauthorize**.

 ◆ To deauthorize a computer to play items from the Audible web site, click the **Store** menu, and then click **Deauthorize Audible Account**.

 ◆ To deauthorize a computer you no longer own, you can deauthorize all your computers at once (only once a year). Click the **Store** menu, and then click **View Account**, In the dialog, sign in, click **View Account**, and then click **Deauthorize All**.

Welcome to the iTunes Store

Viewing the iTunes Window

When you open iTunes, you're working in an organized window (**New!**) that gives you access to your music, movie and other media, creates new playlists, view and change to the Up Next list (**New!**), adds existing music CD's to your iTunes music library, and syncs mobile devices with your media. In addition to your own media, you can also listen to iTunes Radio and podcasts, or purchase music, movies, books, TV shows, apps, and other media through the iTunes Store. The iTunes window allows you to show and hide elements, such as the Sidebar, Status bar, and Column Browser (three column view), to make it easier to navigate around iTunes. There is also a MiniPlayer (**New!**) you can switch to and from in order to play music while you do other things. You can also search (**New!**) for media and modify the Up Next list.

Change the iTunes Window

1. Click the **iTunes** icon in the Dock.

2. To show and hide window elements, click the **View** menu, and then click any of the following:

 ◆ **Sidebar.** Click **Show Sidebar** or **Hide Sidebar**.

 ◆ **Status Bar.** Click **Show Status Bar** or **Hide Status Bar**.

 ◆ **Column Browser.** Point to **Column Browser**, and then click **Show Column Browser** or **Hide Column Browser**.

3. To use full screen, click the **Full Screen** button. To exit, point to the top of the screen to show the menu bar, and then click the **Full Screen** button or press Esc.

4. To switch to the MiniPlayer (**New!**), click the **Switch to MiniPlayer** button.

 ◆ **Controls.** Point to the MiniPlayer to display play options and use all of them.

 ◆ **Up Next List.** (**New!**) Click the **Up Next** button to display, add, and remove songs from the play list. Click the **Show History** button to view all played songs, or the **Clear** button to erase it.

 ◆ **Return to iTunes Window.** Click the **Switch from MiniPlayer** button to return.

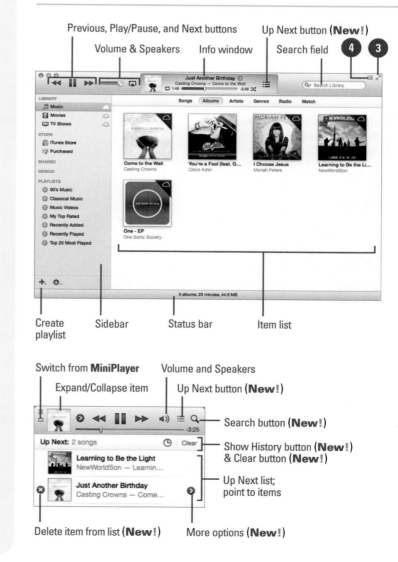

Previous, Play/Pause, and Next buttons · Up Next button (**New!**)

Volume & Speakers · Info window · Search field · 4 · 3

Create playlist · Sidebar · Status bar · Item list

Switch from **MiniPlayer** · Volume and Speakers

Expand/Collapse item · Up Next button (**New!**)

Search button (**New!**)

Show History button (**New!**) & Clear button (**New!**)

Up Next list; point to items

Delete item from list (**New!**) · More options (**New!**)

Setting Up iTunes to Automatically Play CDs

When you open the iTunes app for the first time you'll be asked a few preference questions. For example, you are asked if you want iTunes to be the app your Mac uses for playing music files from the Internet, whether you want iTunes to ask permission every time it connects to the Internet, and whether you want the program to scan your home folder for all of your music. If you select not to have iTunes automatically scan your home drive for music files, you can always drag a folder into the iTunes window. It will automatically scan the folder for any music files, and then place them within the active Playlist.

Set Up iTunes to Automatically Play CDs

1. Click the **System Preferences** icon in the Dock, and then click the **CDs & DVDs** icon.

2. Click the **When you insert a music CD** pop-up, and then select **Open iTunes**.

3. Click the **Close** button to close the System Preferences window.

Set Up iTunes to Play or Import CDs

1. In iTunes, click the **iTunes** menu, and then click **Preferences**.

2. Click **General**.

3. Select from the following options:

 ◆ **When you insert a CD.** Click the pop-up, and then select an option: **Show CD, Play CD, Ask to Import CD, Import CD,** or **Import CD and Eject**.

 ◆ **Import Setting.** Click to specify the encoding and audio quality settings, and then click **OK**.

4. Click **OK**.

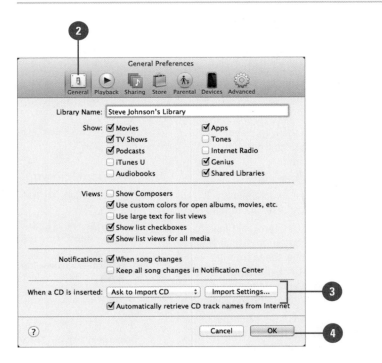

Getting and Playing Music

If you have music on CD, DVD, or hard drive, you can quickly import it into iTunes. If you have System Preferences for CDs & DVDs set to automatically open CDs in iTunes, all you need to do is insert the CD and iTunes does the rest. The music on your CD is copied to your computer in your iTunes music library. Importing music can also be accomplished using iTunes menus, or it can be as simple as a drag and drop. After you add music to your iTunes Library, you can view and work with the music displayed in a songs, albums, artists, or genres list. When you want to play a song, you can use the playback controls in the upper-left corner of the iTunes window or on the Controls menu to play it now or select an option to add it to the Up Next list (**New!**).

Get Music from a CD or Hard Drive and Play it in iTunes

1. Get the music using the following:
 - **CD.** Insert the CD into your drive, and then click **Yes** to import the music into iTunes.
 - **Drive.** Click the **File** menu, and then click **Add To Library**. Locate and select the music files, and then click **Open**.

2. Select **Music** from the Library pop-up on the toolbar or in the Sidebar.

3. Select a view category (**Songs**, **Albums**, **Artists**, or **Genres**) on the toolbar or in the Sidebar.

4. Select the album to expand it and track(s) you want to play.
 - If the album artwork is not there, click the **File** menu, point to **Library**, and then click **Get Album Artwork**.

5. To play next or add to the Up Next list, click the **More Options** button (**New!**), and then click **Play Next** or **Add to Up Next**.

6. To play the music, use the playback controls on the title bar or on the **Controls** menu.
 - **Play.** Press Space bar
 - **Stop.** Press ⌘+. (period)
 - **Volume Up or Down.** ⌘+Up Arrow or ⌘+Down Arrow.

Song importing from a CD

Getting Media from the iTunes Store

The iTunes Store is a dream come true for all of us that love music, movies, and other media. All you have to do to get started is click iTunes Store, sign in with an Apple ID and password and that's it. You're ready to start hunting for the music, movies, TV shows, apps from the App Store, books, podcasts and iTunes U you love. All the popular and new releases appear at the top for easy access (**New!**). As you browse, the iTunes Store keeps track of your history (**New!**), so you can quickly access it later. After you purchase and download a media item, you can play it in iTunes. In addition, Apple lets you copy and play that item on another computer or device using your Apple ID, which authorizes its use. If you have an iCloud account, you can set iCloud options in iTunes to automatically push your purchases of music and apps from the iTunes Store to your Apple devices, including iPhone, iPad, iPod touch, and Mac, as well as Windows computers.

Use the iTunes Store

1. Click the **iTunes** icon in the Dock.

2. Click **iTunes Store** on the toolbar or Sidebar.

3. If you're not signed in to the iTunes Store, click **Sign In**, enter your Apple ID and password, and then click **Sign In**.

4. To view media, click a category button (**Music**, **Movies**, **TV Shows**, **App Store**, **Books**, **Podcasts**, or **iTunes U**) on the toolbar. Click a button arrow to narrow down a category.

 ◆ To navigate back and forth, click the **Back**, **Next**, or **Home** buttons on the toolbar.

5. Use the Search field and type a title, artist, or keyword to search, and then press Return.

6. Click on any of the various links to access that particular title; click a media item to open it, if needed.

 ◆ The new releases appear in the cover view at the top (**New!**).

 ◆ See Wish List or Radio Songs. Click the **History** button (**New!**), click **Wish List** or **Radio**, and then click an item.

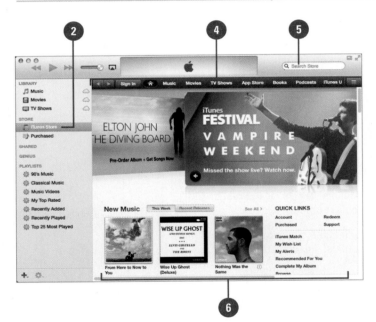

History button (**New!**)

Browse your wish list, iTunes radio, and previews

7. To preview an item, double-click the item or point to it, and then click the **Play** button; availability varies depending on the media item, such as Get Sample.

 ◆ **See Previews again.** click the **History** button (**New!**), click **Previews**, and then click an item.

8. Click the **Buy**, **Rent**, **Free**, or **Subscribe** button for the type of item you want; the button name varies depending on the item.

 IMPORTANT *If you haven't set up your payment options (credit cards), OS X prompts you to do so at this time.*

 The media item is downloaded to your iTunes library. While downloading, you can click the **Downloads** button on the toolbar to display progress or pause, resume, or stop the process.

9. To view purchased material, click **Purchases** on the Library pop-up on the toolbar or in the Sidebar.

10. Quit iTunes.

Did You Know?

You can view different aspects of iTunes. Equalizer displays a dialog where you can adjust sound levels. Click the Window menu, and then click Equalizer. Visualizer displays a colorful light show. Click the View menu, and then click Show Visualizer. Click the View menu, point to Visualizer, and then select an option.

You can use AirPlay with iTunes. When you play movie or TV shows with iTunes using AirPlay mirroring with Apple TV, it automatically switches to full-screen viewing.

Click for more information Downloads button

For Your Information

Using iTunes with iCloud

iCloud stores music, photos, apps, books, contacts, email, calendars, and more and wirelessly pushes them to your iOS devices and Mac or Windows computers. When you make new purchases of music and apps from the iTunes Store, iCloud can automatically push them to your iCloud enabled devices. To use iTunes with iCloud, you need to set automatic downloads for music and apps. Open iTunes and then open Preferences. In iTunes Preferences, click the Store tab, and then select the Music, Apps, and Always Check For Available Downloads check boxes, and then click the Close button. If you have previous purchases, you can manually download them to iCloud too. To manually download previous iTunes Store purchases, click Purchased in the Sidebar, and then click the iCloud Download icon for individual purchases or click the iCloud Download All icon. You can use the Show/Hide Music in the Cloud command (**New!**) on the View menu to show or hide music from iCloud. If you want the bene-fits of iTunes with iCloud for music you haven't purchased from the iTunes Store, including music from CDs, you can subscribe to **iTunes Match** for a yearly fee; it's built into iTunes and the Music app on your iOS devices. Click Match on the toolbar in the Music Library or click Turn On iTunes Match on the Store menu, and then follow the on-screen instructions. See Chapter 13, "Sharing Information in the Cloud" on pages 355-368 for more information on iCloud.

Creating and Using Playlists

The iTunes app lets you add media from several different sources. Instead of having one long list of songs in the Library, you can organize them into playlists. A **playlist** is a folder that holds and organizes your media in the order in which you want to play it. For example, you could have a Playlist for all your Country & Western songs, one for your Rock & Roll; even one for audio books. iTunes comes with a set of playlists, or you can create your own. Playlists come in two flavors—Playlists and Smart Playlists. Playlists let you play the songs in the list again, play the songs in random order, or stop when the last song plays. Smart Playlists rebuild themselves according to the criteria you setup. For example, you might create a Smart Playlist that only plays the songs in the library you rate a 4-star or only Christmas songs.

Create and Play a Playlist

1. Click the **iTunes** icon in the Dock.

2. Select **Music** from the Library pop-up on the toolbar or in the Sidebar.

3. Click **Playlists** on the toolbar.

4. Click the **Add** (+) button in the Sidebar, click **New Playlist**, type a name, and then press Return.

5. Drag songs to the Playlist pane; if prompted, click **Add to Playlist**. In the pane, you can drag songs to change the order.

6. Click **Done**.

7. To play a playlist, click the playlist in the Sidebar, and then click the **Play** or **Shuffle** button.

8. Quit iTunes.

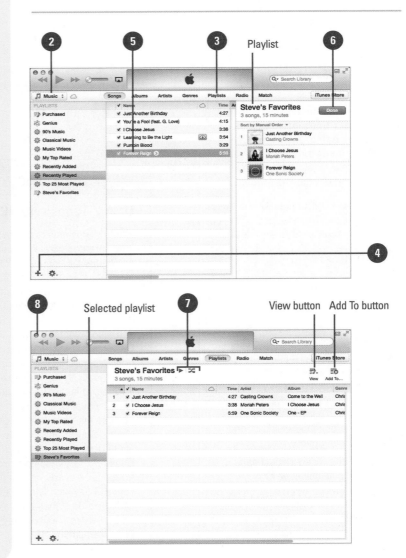

Did You Know?

You can edit a playlists. Click the File menu, point to Library, and then click Import Playlist. Only songs and videos in your iTunes are included.

You can import your playlists. Click the File menu, point to Library, and then click Import Playlist. Only songs and videos in your iTunes are included.

Add a Smart Playlist to iTunes

1. Click the **iTunes** icon in the Dock.

2. Click the **Library** pop-up, click **Music**, and then click **Playlists** on the toolbar.

3. Click the **Add** (+) button in the Sidebar, click **New Smart Playlist**.

4. Click the **Criteria** pop-up, and then select the main selection criteria.

5. Click the **Operator** pop-up, and then choose a selection method.

6. Type a word or phrase to search.

7. Click the **Add Criteria** (+) button to add an additional search option.

8. Select the **Limit To** check box and pop-up to limit the number of songs, time played, or max size.

9. Click the **Selected By** pop-up, and then select how to select songs.

10. Select the **Match only checked items** check box to limit selection to songs that are checked.

11. Select the **Live updating** check box to update the Smart Playlist as you add or subtract songs.

12. Click **OK**.

13. Name your Smart Playlist.

14. Quit iTunes.

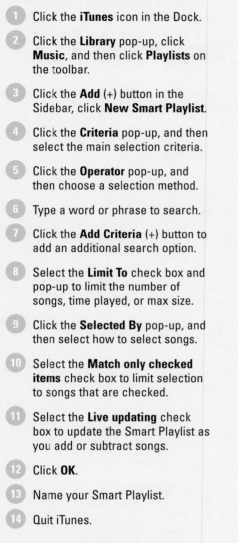

Did You Know?

You can rename a playlist. Select the playlist in the Sidebar, click the playlist name, type a new name in the edit box, and then press Return.

You can delete a playlist. Select the playlist in the Sidebar, click the Edit menu, and then click Delete.

For Your Information

Understanding Copyright Laws

When you create Playlists you're working smart. Most iTunes users have hundreds, if not thousands of songs on their hard drives, and Playlists and Smart Playlists are the only way to help organize all those songs. A word of caution, make sure they are your songs. Piracy is a big problem in the music industry today, and it's not just what you take off the Internet. The iTunes app gives you the ability to create music tracks from most music CDs. That does not mean you can borrow all of your friend's music CDs and transfer them to your computer. Enjoy your music, but know the laws involving piracy, and copyright violation. Use your browser to search for the latest information about copyright laws in the U.S.

Setting Notification Options in iTunes

In addition to the notification settings you can set for iTunes in the Notification pane of System Preferences, you can select notification in iTunes Preferences. In the General pane of iTunes Preferences, you can select options to send notification when a song changes (**New!**) or keep all song changes in Notification Center (**New!**).

Adding Media to a Playlist

Whenever you add media to the iTunes app, it stores the media in a library, and then creates a link to the selected playlist. As a matter of fact, playlists simply create links to the media in the iTunes library. If you delete a playlist or a media within a playlist, it does not remove the song from the iTunes library, only the link created in the playlist is removed. If you want help from iTunes, you can create a Genius playlist, which sends music information about your libraries to iTunes Store, and creates a personalized playlist for you. If you want to create a custom CD from a playlist, you can burn it to a CD directly from iTunes.

Add Media to or Edit a Playlist

1. Click the **iTunes** icon in the Dock.

2. To add media to a playlist, use any of the following options:

 - **Add from iTunes.** Drag media from an iTunes library to a playlist. As you start to drag, the Playlist pane appears (**New!**).

 - **Add from Finder.** Drag media files or folder from an open Finder folder to the Sidebar in the iTunes window.

 - **Create Genius Playlist.** Click the **Store** menu, and then click **Turn On Genius**. Follow the online steps to sign in and turn it on. Point to a song, click the **More Options** button, and then click **Start Genius**. Click **Genius** in the Sidebar to view the Genius playlist. When you're done, click the **Store** menu, and then click **Turn Off Genius**.

3. To edit a playlist, click **Playlists** on the toolbar in the Music Library, select the playlist in the Sidebar, click the **Actions** button, and then click **Edit Playlist**. When you're finished, click **Done**.

 - **Delete.** Select the songs to remove, press Delete, and then click **Remove** to confirm.

 - **Reorder.** Drag to move songs up or down the playlist.

4. Quit iTunes.

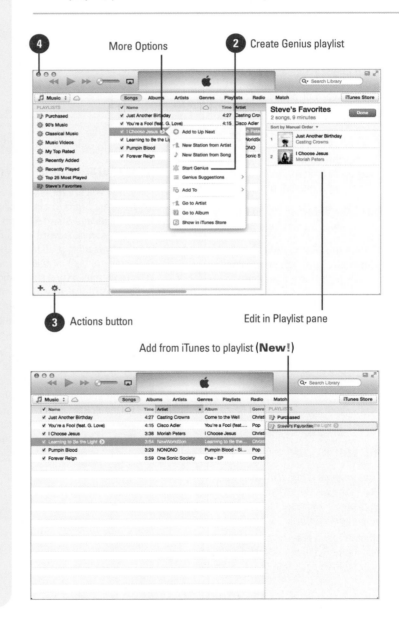

More Options

Create Genius playlist

Actions button

Edit in Playlist pane

Add from iTunes to playlist (**New!**)

Burn a Playlist to CD

① Click the **iTunes** icon in the Dock.

② Create and select the Playlist you want to burn onto the CD.

 iTunes uses the name of the Playlist as the name of the CD.

③ Insert a blank CD into your drive, and then click **Ignore**, if prompted.

 IMPORTANT *You must have a writable CD or DVD drive.*

④ Click the **Library** pop-up, click **Music**, and then click **Playlists** on the toolbar.

⑤ Click the **Actions** button in the Sidebar, click **Burn Playlist to Disc**.

⑥ Select a preferred speed, and disc format option, and then click **Burn**.

⑦ Quit iTunes.

Did You Know?

You can export your playlists. Select the Playlist, click the File menu, point to Library, and then click Export Library. To save all your Playlists, click the File menu, point to Library, and then click Export Playlist.

You can back up your iTunes library to a CD or DVD. Click the File menu, point to Library, click Back Up To Disc, select the options you want, insert a blank writable CD or DVD, and then click Back Up.

You can access the names of your songs on the Internet. Insert a music CD or DVD, click the iTunes menu, click Preferences, click General, select the Automatically Retrieve CD Track Names From Internet check box, and then click the Close button. This changes Track1, etc. with song names.

Work with Media

Whenever you point to a media item, a More Options button (greater than sign) appears with additional options, such as Play Next (**New!**), Add to Up Next (**New!**), New Station from Artist or Song, Start Genius, Genius Suggestions (**New!**), and Add To (playlists). When you start a playlist, it gets added to the Up Next list (**New!**), which you can add to or change at any time. If an iCloud icon appears associated with a song, it's downloaded from iCloud (**New!**). If the iCloud Download icon appears (with a down arrow), you can click it to manually download it. You can use Show/Hide Music in the Cloud (**New!**) on the View menu to show or hide music from iCloud.

Work with Media in iTunes

① Click the **iTunes** icon in the Dock.

② Select a library from the pop-up on the toolbar or in the Sidebar.

③ Select a view category on the toolbar or in the Sidebar.

④ Point to the media item, click the **More Options** button, and then click the option you want.

 ◆ **Play Next or Add to Up Next.** Adds to the top or bottom of the Up Next list (**New!**).

 ◆ **New Station from Artist or Song**. Creates an iTunes radio station (**New!**).

 ◆ **Start Genius or Genius Suggestions**. Creates a Genius playlist (**New!**).

 ◆ **Add To**. Adds to a playlist.

 ◆ **Go to Artist or Album or Show in iTunes Store**. Goes to item.

⑤ To work with the Up Next list, point to Info window, if needed, and click the **Up Next** button (**New!**).

 ◆ Reorder. Drag in list.

 ◆ Delete. Point to an item, and then click **Delete** button (x).

 ◆ Clear. Click **Clear** to remove all.

 ◆ History. Click the **History** button to show/hide history. Point to an item, and then click the **Add** (+) button to add it to the list.

⑥ Quit iTunes.

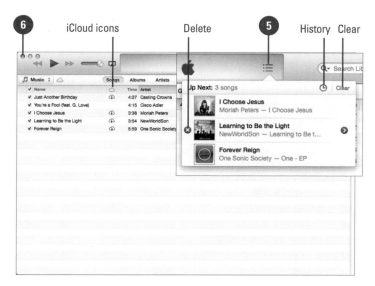

iCloud icons Delete History Clear

Sharing Media at Home

With Home Sharing, you can share music, movie, and other media among the other computers in your home. All you need to do is use the same Apple ID on up to five computers to create a Home Sharing network. This allows you to import media items from the other authorized computers. You can also stream media content using Apple TV (with Home Sharing enabled) to your home theater system from any of the iTunes libraries on your Home Sharing network.

Share Media in iTunes at Home

1 Click the **iTunes** icon in the Dock.

2 To turn on Home Sharing, click the **File** menu, point to **Home Sharing**, and then click **Turn On Home Sharing**. Type your Apple ID and password, and then click **Turn On Home Sharing**.

3 Select the shared library from the pop-up on the toolbar or in the Sidebar to load it.

◆ To open a specific library (Music, Movie, etc.), select the library from the Library pop-up.

4 Select a view category on the toolbar or in the Sidebar.

5 Click the **Show** pop-up, and then select **Items not in my library**.

6 To play a media item, select it, and then click the **Play/Pause** button.

7 To import (copy) media items to your computer, select them, and then click **Import**.

◆ **Automatic Import.** Click **Settings**, select the types you want, and then click **OK**.

8 To turn off Home Sharing, click the **File** menu, point to **Home Sharing**, and then click **Turn Off Home Sharing**.

9 Quit iTunes.

Selected media on shared iTunes

For Your Information

Using the Remote App to Control iTunes

If you have an iPhone, iPad, or iPod touch, you can use the Remote app (available for free from the App Store) to control your iTunes library from a distance, as long as the devices are on the same wireless network. All you need to do is pair the app to the iTunes library. In the Remote app (2.0 or later) and Home Sharing is turned on, you can pair to any iTunes library on the Home Sharing network as well as Apple TV. In the Devices pane in iTunes Preferences, you can unpair all remotes.

Listening to iTunes Radio

Listening to your own collection of music is great. However, sometimes you may want to branch out and listen to something different. That's where iTunes radio comes in. Maybe you want to try Top 40 pop, rock, hip hop, country, classical, or jazz music. Whatever direction your tastes run, you are probably able to find it on iTunes radio (**New!**), which plays music collections from the iTunes Store. iTunes makes the process of selecting, customizing, and listening to iTunes radio as easy as traditional radio. If you like a song as it plays, you can buy it on the spot.

Listen to iTunes Radio

1. Click the **iTunes** icon in the Dock.

2. Select **Music** from the Library pop-up on the toolbar or in the Sidebar.

3. Click **Radio** (**New!**) on the toolbar.

4. To play or pause a station, point to it and then click the **Play/Pause** button.

5. To add a station, click the **Add** (+) button, and then select a station or use the Search field to find one.

 ◆ **Add Station from Library.** Point to a song or album, click the **More Options** button, and then click **New Station from Song** or **New Station from Artist**.

6. Click a station (off the Play/Pause button) to expand it.

7. Drag the slider to adjust the type of songs you want to hear.

8. To play more or never play songs like this, click the **Add an artist or song** button, and then select an artist or song.

9. To custom the station as songs play, click the **Favorites** button, and then click **Play More Like This**, **Never Play This Song**, or **Add to iTunes Wish List**.

10. To collapse the station, click the **Delete** button (x).

11. Quit iTunes.

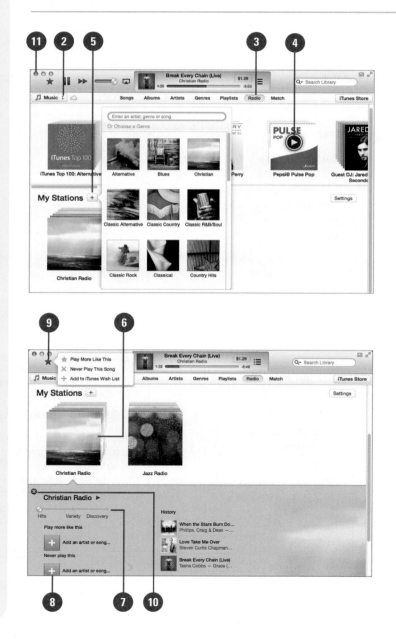

Listening to Internet Radio

Listening to music is great, so is curling up with a cup of hot chocolate and your favorite audio book. However, sometimes you would just like to listen to a radio station. Maybe NPR (National Public Radio) is your thing, or possibly you're looking for a radio station that just plays classical or jazz music. Whatever direction your tastes run, you are probably able to find it on the Internet radio, and iTunes makes the process of selecting and listening to a radio station as easy as turning on a traditional radio.

Listen to Internet Radio

1. Click the **iTunes** icon in the Dock.

2. Select **Music** from the Library pop-up on the toolbar or in the Sidebar.

3. Click **Internet** (New!) on the toolbar.

 ◆ If Internet is not on the toolbar, click the **iTunes** menu, click **Preferences**, click **General**, select the **Internet Radio** check box, and then click the **Close** button.

4. Click the expand button (triangle) to open the group.

5. Double-click on a station to begin the broadcast.

6. Use the **Play/Pause** button to turn the selected station on or off.

7. Use the **Previous** and **Next** buttons to move up and down through the radio station list.

8. Quit iTunes.

Did You Know?

You can add radio stations to the iTunes radio list. Click the Advanced menu, and then click Open Stream. Type in the station's web address, and then click OK.

Subscribing and Playing Podcasts

Podcasts are radio and TV shows you can download from the Internet to your iTunes library. The iTunes Store provides free podcasts you can download at any time. If you like a podcast, you can subscribe to it and have it automatically downloaded as it becomes available. If you have an iPod, iPhone, or iPad, you can add podcasts to your player and play them on the go when you're not connected to the Internet.

Subscribe and Play Podcasts

1. Click the **iTunes** icon in the Dock.

2. Click **iTunes Store** on the toolbar or Sidebar, and then click **Podcasts** on the toolbar or Sidebar.

3. Search for the podcast you want.

4. To subscribe to a podcast (only need to do once), display the podcast you want, click **Subscribe**, and then click **Subscribe** again if prompted.

 The podcast is downloaded to your iTunes library. While downloading, you can click **Downloads** on the toolbar to view the process.

5. Click **Library** on the toolbar to return to the iTunes Library.

6. Select **Podcasts** from the Library pop-up on the toolbar or in the Sidebar.

7. Click **Unplayed**, **Podcasts**, or **List** to display the podcasts you want.

 ◆ In List view, click the triangle to expand/collapse the listing.

8. Click **Get All** to download all the podcasts or click **Get** to download an individual podcast.

9. To play a podcast, double-click the podcast. Point to the player to display playback controls and **Close** button to exit.

10. To unsubscribe, select the podcast, and then click **Unsubscribe**.

11. Quit iTunes.

Click the adjust download settings

Using iPod, iPhone, or iPad with iTunes

With the popularity of iPod, iPhone, and iPad devices, the need to synchronize your media over multiple devices is more important than ever. When you plug your iPod, iPhone, or iPad cable into your computer, it automatically opens the iTunes app and synchronizes music, playlists, movies, TV shows, podcasts, books, photos, and apps from App Store, to your device based on the sync options. You can access the sync options by selecting the device in iTunes on the toolbar or Sidebar. You can also manually synchronize content as well as make individual changes, such as deleting media you no longer want or dragging media to a device. You can prevent automatic syncing in the Devices pane in Tunes Preferences. If you want to automatically download new purchases made on other devices and enable its use with iCloud, select options in the Store pane in iTunes Preferences.

Use iPod, iPhone, or iPad with iTunes

1. Plug your iPod, iPhone, or iPad device into your computer. This also recharges the device.

2. Click the device name on the toolbar or in the Sidebar.

3. Click the category tabs and then set sync item options you want.

4. Click **Sync** or **Apply**.

 ◆ For a manual sync, use the Summary tab. You can also manually backup your device.

 ◆ You can also click the **File** menu, and point to **Devices** to sync, transfer, and backup.

5. To view the media on the device, click **On This** *device*.

6. To remove media, select an item, and then press Delete.

7. To add media to the device, click the **Add To** button, drag a media item or Playlist to the device in the Source pane.

8. Click **Done** to return to the iTunes Library.

9. Click the **Eject** button to eject and remove the device.

10. Quit iTunes.

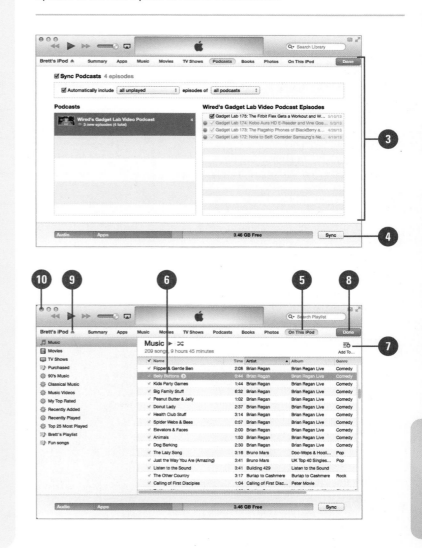

Exporting to MP3 Players

Digital music players, more commonly known as MP3 players, hold music files using the MP3 digital format. MP3 players can be thought of as a hard drive that holds music files, and then plays them back to you through a set of speakers or a headset. Many smartphones and tablets include an MP3 player. Check the mobile device to see if it includes an MP3 player. When you get an MP3 player, it typically comes with software designed to move music files from your computer to the drive located on the MP3 player. Some MP3 players, when connected to your computer, appear as an external removable drive. If so, you can copy your songs from iTunes to your MP3 device to export them. iTunes copies and organizes your media in folders on your Mac based on settings in the Advanced pane in iTunes Preferences.

Export to MP3 Players

1. Open iTunes Preferences, and then click **Advanced**.

2. Identify the iTunes Media folder location, and then select the following check boxes:
 - **Keep iTunes Media folder organized.**
 - **Copy files to iTunes Media folder when adding to library.**

3. Click **OK**.

4. In the Finder, navigate to the iTunes music folder; see Step 2.

5. Select a folder or a list of iTunes files that you want to move.

6. Drag the music files to the hard drive icon of your MP3 music player.

 IMPORTANT *Not all MP3 music players allow you to drag music files between your hard drive and the player icon. When this occurs you'll have to use the transfer software that came bundled with the player. Simply load the software and follow the onscreen instructions.*

7. Click the **Eject** button in the Sidebar (Finder) or control-click the MP3 player desktop icon, and then click **Eject**.

Setting iTunes Preferences

Like any app, iTunes gives you a Preferences panel that helps you adjust the software to fit your specific needs. The iTunes Preferences give you precise control over how the program operates on your computer.

To set your preferences, or to review the defaults that have been set in iTunes, simply click the iTunes icon in the Dock. Click the iTunes menu, and then click Preferences. There you'll find almost every conceivable setting that is used in iTunes. For a summary view, we've shown you commonly used screens and what is contained on that Preference screen. After making any changes to the screens, simply click OK to change the setting or click Cancel to undo your change.

General: Controls text within the iTunes window (**New!**).

Advanced: Gives you options to store and organize iTunes files on the Mac (**New!**).

Sharing: Lets you share your music files with other users.

Store: Controls automatic downloads on devices (**New!**), including iPod, iPhone, and iPad.

Select options to enable syncing with iCloud

Streaming a Mac to Apple TV

Apple TV is a device that allows you to turns what's on your Mac into a widescreen experience on your HDTV. For example, you can stream video optimized for HD (High Definition) up to 1080p with stereo audio to your HDTV. AirPlay mirroring allows you to wirelessly stream exactly what's on your Mac screen to everyone viewing your HDTV and speakers using security encryption. AirPlay mirroring scales the content on your Mac to fit on your HDTV. When you play movie or TV shows with iTunes, it switches to full-screen viewing. In addition to Macs, you can also use AirPlay mirroring with your other iOS devices, such as iPhone or iPad. If you have Apple TV connected to your TV and to the same network as your computer, your Mac will automatically detect the device. In the Display pane of System Preferences, you can turn on Apple TV and arrange it as mirror displays (same displays) or as a separate extended display (**New!**) with its own menu bar (**New!**). You can select an option to show an AirPlay menu for easy access to mirroring options.

Stream a Mac to Apple TV

1. Click **System Preferences** icon in the Dock, and then click the **Displays** icon.

2. Click the **Display** tab.

3. Select from the following options:

 ◆ **AirPlay mirroring.** Click the pop-up , and then select **Apple TV** or AirPlay device (auto detected when it's on the same network as the computer).

 ◆ **Show mirroring options in the menu bar when available.** Select to display the AirPlay icon on the Apple menu bar.

4. To arrange separate displays, click the **Arrangement** tab (**New!**), deselect the **Mirror Displays** check box (**New!**), and then drag a display or menu bar (**New!**).

5. Click the **Close** button.

> ## Did You Know?
>
> *You can use audio with AirPlay.* In the Sound pane of System Preferences, you use AirPlay to play audio only through Apple TV.

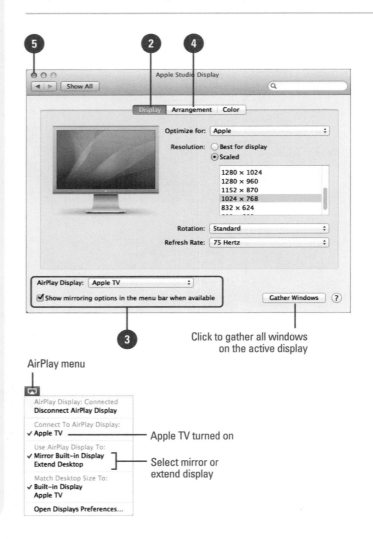

Click to gather all windows on the active display

AirPlay menu

Apple TV turned on

Select mirror or extend display

Capturing Photos in Photo Booth

If you have an iSight or other camera attached to your computer, you can use Photo Booth to capture photos just like you were sitting in a photo booth at a carnival. If you have a high-resolution FaceTime camera, Photo Booth can take high-resolution photos. You can capture individual photos or create a short movie. Photo Booth provides a full-screen view with a theater look. Photo Booth saves your photos as JPEG files and movies in a folder called Photo Booth, located in the Pictures folder. When you're done capturing photos, you can use them as a user account, Messages buddy, iPhoto, or Twitter profile picture and present them in a slide show or print them in a proof sheet. In addition, you can send photos and movies using AirDrop, Mail, Messages, Facebook, Twitter, Flickr, and Vimeo.

Capture Photos in Photo Booth

1. Attach an Apple iSight or other video camera to your computer.

2. Click the **Photo Booth** icon in the Dock.

3. Click the **Take a still picture** button.

4. When you're ready to take a still picture, click the **Shutter** button.

 After a 3-second countdown, the screen flashes and Photo Booth takes a photo. The picture appears as a thumbnail in the bottom pane.

5. To preview a photo, select the thumbnail in the bottom pane.

6. To permanently delete a photo, select the thumbnail, and then click the **Delete** button in the bottom left corner of the thumbnail.

7. Click the **Shutter** button again to go back to live images.

8. To e-mail a photo, add to iPhoto, or use a photo in a user account, buddy, or Twitter picture, use the **Share** button.

9. To present a slide show, click the **View** menu, click **Start Slideshow**, and then use the toolbar to navigate through the slide show.

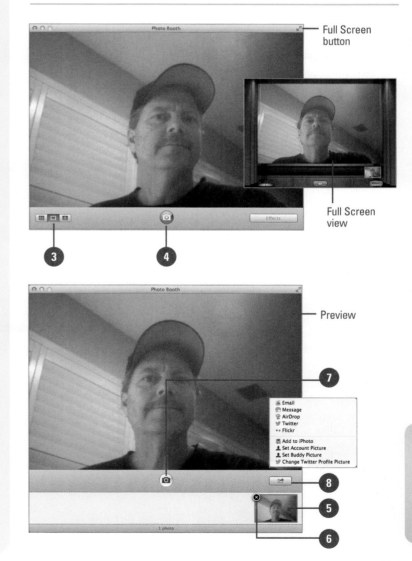

Full Screen button

Full Screen view

Preview

Recording Movies in Photo Booth

In addition to capturing individual still photos, you can also record a movie in Photo Booth. You can create two types of movies, either a movie clip or a 4-up movie. A movie clip is a continuous recording of frames, while a 4-up movie is four snapshots taken very quickly to simulate a movie. The 4-up movies are saved as four JPEG files, while movie clips are saved as QuickTime MOV files. However, you can export the movie clip or 4-up movie as an animated GIF, which you can also use as a Messages buddy icon. If the movie is too long, you can pick the start and end frames to trim the edges. With the Share button, you can send movies using AirDrop, Mail, Messages, Facebook, and Vimeo.

Record Videos in Photo Booth

1. Attach an Apple iSight or other video camera to your computer.

2. Click the **Photo Booth** icon in the Dock.

3. Click the **Take four quick pictures** or **Take a movie clip** button.

4. When you're ready, click the **Shutter** or **Record** button.

 For a 4-up movie, a 3-second countdown and a flash occurs for each photo. For a movie clip, the recording starts after a 3-second countdown.

5. When you're done recording a movie clip, click the **Stop** button.

6. To preview a movie, select the thumbnail, point to the bottom of the live image to display and then use the slider and **Pause/Play** button to view a movie clip.

7. To trim a movie, select the thumbnail, point to the bottom of the live image to display, click **Trim**, drag end points, and then click **Close** or **Accept**.

8. To permanently delete a movie, select the thumbnail, and then click the **Delete** button in the left corner of the thumbnail.

9. Click the **Shutter** button again to go back to live images.

Play/Pause button

Drag end point to trim movie Close and Accept buttons

Adding Photo Booth Effects

Photo Booth includes backdrops and visual effects you can add to visuals to have some fun and create more interesting photo effect. A backdrop is a background that appears behind the camera image. You can use one of the backdrops provided by Photo Booth, such as New York, Paris, or Yosemite, to make it seem like you're in an another place, or add and use one of your own. In addition to backdrops, Photo Booth also includes a set of visual effects, such as Comic Book, Sepia, X-Ray, and Light Tunnel, that you can use to create a fun and unique effect.

Add Photo Booth Effects

1 Attach an Apple iSight or other video camera to your computer.

2 Click the **Photo Booth** icon in the Dock.

3 Click the **Effects** button.

4 Click the Left and Right Arrows or swipe your trackpad or Magic Mouse to display more effects.

5 Select the backdrop or visual effect you want to use.

6 Point to the bottom of the live images. If a slide appears, drag it to adjust the visual effect level.

7 To remove an effect, select the **Normal** effect in the middle.

8 To add your own backdrop, drag it to a "Drag Backdrop Here" place holder.

9 When you're ready, select a picture button, and then click the **Shutter** button.

Did You Know?

You can export a movie as an animated GIF. Select a 4-up movie or movie clip in the bottom pane, click the File menu, click Export, type a name, specify a location, and then click Save.

Backdrops

Visual effects

Swipe to display more effects

Playing and Browsing DVD Movies

Okay, it's time to break out the popcorn and soda, because the DVD player in OS X is here. Using the DVD player, you can access a movie chapter by chapter, freeze the action, move forward and backward through the movie, and even play a movie in slow motion frame-by-frame. You can even watch your video in full screen mode while you work on another display. In addition, the DVD Player offers closed captioning. All that translates into a great viewing experience—sounds like a winner to me. If you have an Apple Remote, you don't even need to get up to control the DVD player.

Play and Browse DVD Movies with the DVD Player

1 Insert a DVD into the DVD drive of your computer to start the movie.

◆ You can also click the **Launchpad** icon in the Dock, and then click the **DVD Player** icon to start it.

2 Select from the following DVD Player options:

◆ Click the **Left**, **Right**, **Up**, **Down**, or **Return** buttons to navigate.

◆ Click the **Previous** or **Next Chapter** buttons to move between movie chapters.

◆ Click the **Play/Pause** or the **Stop** button to play/pause or stop the movie.

◆ Click the **Eject** button to stop the movie and eject the DVD.

◆ Click the **Title** or **Menu** buttons to view the movie title or menu.

◆ Drag the volume control to raise or lower the volume.

◆ Open the Options panel, and then select between Slow Motion, Step Frame, Return, Sub Title, Audio, or Angle.

3 At the top of the window, click the Video menu, and then select between the various viewing options.

4 To exit the movie without using the controller, press ⌘+Q.

Movie Player

Slow Motion
Step Frame
Navigate
Volume Control
Sub Title
Options panel
Audio
Previous; Hold to Fast Rewind
Stop
Return
Angle
Play & Pause
Next; Hold to Fast Forward

Customizing the DVD Player

In addition to the main DVD player controls, you can also customize your playback experience. With the new full-screen interface and Image Bar, you can quickly access playback controls, subtitles, and audio tracks, change the screen view and scale, and browse DVD content. You can also create video snippets from any DVD and set bookmarks, also known as key points, you can view again later.

Customize the DVD Player

1. Insert a DVD into the DVD drive of your computer to start the movie.

2. Select from the following Movie Player options:

 ◆ **Show/Hide Full Screen.** Press ⌘+F.

 ◆ **Image Bar.** Point to the bottom of the screen in Full Screen.

 ◆ **Create Video Clip.** Position the video, click the **Controls** menu, click **New Video Clip**, set the start and end frame, and then click **Save**.

 ◆ **Bookmark.** Position the video, click the **Controls** menu, click **New Bookmark**, enter a name, and then click **Add**.

 ◆ **View Bookmarks, Video Clips, and Chapters.** Click the **Window** menu, and then click **Bookmarks**, **Video Clips**, or **Chapters**.

 ◆ **Video Zoom or Color.** Click the **Window** menu, and then click **Video Zoom** or **Video Color**, select the **On** check box, and then adjust the levels.

 ◆ **Keyboard Shortcuts. Play**: Space bar, **Stop**: ⌘+. (period), **screen size**: ⌘+0 thru ⌘+3, **Switch to Finder**: Option+⌘+F.

3. To exit the movie without using the controller, press ⌘+Q.

Full Screen

Image bar Movie controls

Playing QuickTime Movies

QuickTime Player supports H.264 video decoding capabilities using the GPU (Graphics Processing Unit). QuickTime works with the MPEG4 format and other common formats, giving you access to movie clips. In addition, QuickTime delivers several performance enhancements, including ColorSync management, live resize, zero-configuration streaming at the best connection speed, surround sound in up to 24 channels, full screen playback, additional keyboard shortcuts to mirror Final Cut Pro, improved A/V controls, and closed captioning with up-to-date standards, and timecode or frame count display instead of movie time. QuickTime Player plays movies in a redesigned window with fade away playback controls and full-screen option. If you open a movie and it's upside down or sideways, you can rotate it. If your movie contains chapter markers, QuickTime Player displays them in frame-based thumbnail images.

Play QuickTime Movies

1. Click the **Launchpad** icon in the Dock, and then click the **QuickTime Player** icon.

2. Click the **File** menu, and then click **Open** to load individual QuickTime (or other formatted) movies or click **Open URL** to load URLs.

 ◆ To open a recent movie, click the **File**, point to **Open Recent**, and then select a movie.

3. To rotate a movie, click the **Edit** menu, and then click **Rotate Left**, **Rotate Right**, **Flip Horizontal**, or **Flip Vertical**.

4. Point to the movie to display movie controls (if necessary), drag the slider, and then click the movie controls to **Play/ Pause** and **Rewind** or **Forward** the movie.

 TIMESAVER *Press the Spacebar to play/pause a movie.*

5. To adjust the volume, drag the Volume slider.

6. Click the **View** menu, and then select from the available viewing options.

7. Quit QuickTime Player.

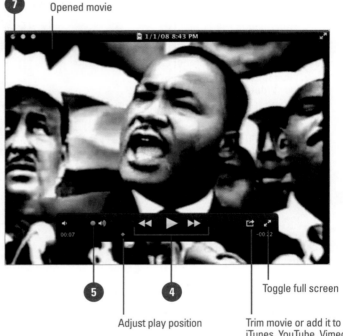

Opened movie

Toggle full screen

Adjust play position

Trim movie or add it to iTunes, YouTube, Vimeo, Flickr, Facebook, or Mail

Customize QuickTime Playback

① In the QuickTime Player, select from the following options:

◆ **Show/Hide Full Screen.** Press ⌘+F or click the **Full Screen** button . Point to top of screen to display it in full screen.

◆ **Change Screen View.** Press ⌘+1 for Actual Size; press ⌘+3 for Fit to Screen; press ⌘+4 for Fill Screen; press ⌘+5 for Panoramic; press ⌘++ or ⌘+- for Increase Size or Decrease Size.

◆ **Show/Hide Chapters.** Click the **View** menu, and then click **Show Chapters**.

◆ **Closed Captioning.** Click the **View** menu, and then click **Show Closed Captioning**.

◆ **Show Movie Inspector.** Click the **Window** menu, and then click **Show Movie Inspector** to display movie information, and then click the **Close** button.

◆ **Show Export Progress.** Click the **Window** menu, and then click **Show Export Progress** to display progress information, and then click the **Close** button.

Point to top of screen to show menu bar Full Screen button

Full Screen view Movie controls

Show Movie Inspector

Did You Know?

You can listen to a movie in a different language. Click the View menu, point to Languages, and then select a language. If the languages are grayed out, the movie doesn't support it.

You can show movie subtitles while a movie plays. Click the View menu, point to Subtitles, and then select a language. If the languages are grayed out, the movie doesn't have subtitles.

Creating QuickTime Movies

QuickTime 10.x provides powerful commands to record live video and audio directly from an iSight camera, FireWire camcorder, or microphone or capture all or part of your desktop screen with mouse clicks to disk. After you create or open a QuickTime movie, you can trim it shorter, or remove unwanted content, such as silence, or merge clips together. QuickTime allows you to share your media using Messages or Mail, and publish your media to YouTube, Vimeo, Flickr, and Facebook. You can also use the Export and Export To commands to export your media in formats compatible with the Web, iMovie, and iTunes for use on an iPod touch, iPhone, iPad, Apple TV, or Mac & PC.

Create Movies, Audio, or Screens

1. Click the **Applications** folder in the Dock, and then click the **QuickTime Player** icon.

2. Click the **File** menu, and then click **New Movie Recording**, **New Audio Recording**, or **New Screen Recording**.

3. Click the **Down** arrow to select commands to adjust recording devices, quality, destination, and options, such as Show Mouse Clicks in Recording.

4. Click the **Record** button.

 ◆ For a Screen Recording, click to record full screen or drag to select a screen area, and then click **Start Recording**.

5. When you're done, click the **Stop** button.

 The media is automatically saved in the Movies folder.

6. To export the movie in another format, click the **File** menu, click **Export**, type a name, select a format and destination, and then click **Export**.

7. To export the movie to the web, click the **File** menu, click **Export for Web**, type a name, select a destination and export format, and then click **Export**.

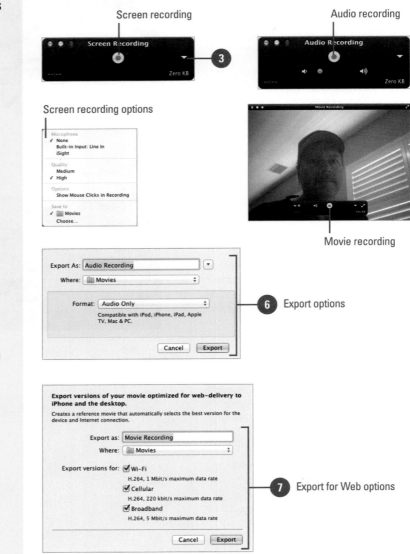

Screen recording

Audio recording

Screen recording options

Movie recording

Export options

Export for Web options

Edit QuickTime Movies

1. In the QuickTime Player, click the **File** menu, and then click **Open File**, select the movie you want to edit, and then click **Open**.

2. To merge multiple movies, drag one movie from the original window to another movie window.

 Quicktime automatically scales or crops them as needed.

3. Click the **Edit** menu, click **Trim**, and then use any of the following:

 ◆ Drag play head as needed, and then drag the start and end of the trimming bar (yellow handles) to select the part of the movie you want to keep.

 ◆ Click the **Edit** menu, and then click **Select All Excluding Silence** to exclude the silent part of the movie.

4. Click **Trim**.

Red vertical line play head

Share QuickTime Movies

1. In the QuickTime Player, click the **File** menu, and then click **Open File**, select the movie you want to edit, and then click **Open**.

2. Click the **File** menu, point to **Export To**, and then select an option:

 ◆ **iTunes.** Compatible with iPod, iPhone, and Apple TV.

 ◆ **IMovie** or **Web.** Compatible with the format.

3. Click the **File** menu, point to **Share**, and then select an option:

 ◆ **YouTube, Vimeo, Flickr,** or **Facebook.** Uploads to your service account after sign in.

 ◆ **Mail** or **Messages.** Creates a movie attachment after selecting a movie size.

iTunes options

YouTube options

Exploring iMovie, iDVD, and iPhoto

The **iPhoto** app lets you organize your images into user-defined folders, edit them, and even distribute them to your friends, by placing them on a CD or DVD, or directly over the Internet. iPhoto is part of the iLife suite of apps, which is sold separately from OS X.

When you open the iPhoto app, you're treated to the ultimate in organization and simplicity. For example, you own a digital camera, and you want to move the images from the camera to your computer. Most digital cameras come with their own proprietary programs that let you hook your camera up (USB or FireWire port), and then organize and manage your files. Fortunately, iPhoto does away with camera-specific programs. When you plug your camera in, iPhoto recognizes the device and lets you move the image files from the camera to iPhoto.

The **iMovie** app lets you create high-quality, professional movies. Using footage from your digital camcorder (MiniDV or Digital 8 format), you can edit and combine different movie files, create transitions between scenes, even capture live video, and then add an audio track (voice or music). iMovie is part of the iLife suite of app, which is sold separately from OS X.

The iMovie app is simple to operate, yet powerful when it comes to creating professional movies, using footage from your digital movie camera, or any other digital multimedia files; including image stills and audio files.

The iMovie window is your working studio. Inside this one window, you have the ability to draw together all of the elements of your movie, and then arrange them by adding titles and transitions; you can even use special effects. For example, you could create a movie of a family members birthday, using a dozen movie clips, plus background music and narration. You can also add still images, create seamless fades between photos, and movies. It's all here inside the iMovie window.

The **iDVD** app comes bundled on all Macintosh computers that have a DVD burner. Using iDVD, you can create slideshows of pictures, or become a director and create your own DVD movies, using a digital camcorder. You even have iMovie to help you edit your home movies. iDVD is part of the iLife suite of app, which is sold separately from OS X.

If you've ever wanted to test your skills at movie production, then the iDVD app is just what you've been waiting for all these years. There are all kinds of layout apps, such as apps for laying material out on paper (Adobe InDesign and Quark Xpress), and there are programs that layout web pages (Adobe Dreamweaver). With that in mind, think of iDVD as a layout app for the creation of your Oscar-winning production. This gives you the ability to generate slideshows, videos, or a combination of both, along with menus, buttons (just like any other DVD), and then burn it onto a blank DVD that can be viewed by anyone that owns a DVD player.

The iDVD app is powerful, but just like any other layout program, it requires material to use for the layout. For example, when you open iDVD, you need access to video files, audio files, and graphics. The iDVD app doesn't create the materials that make up the DVD; it only organizes them. And, not all DVD players are created equal. Some DVD disks do not work in all the players on the market; especially older DVD players. For information on compatibility issues between DVD writers and DVD players, point your browser to: *http://www.dvdrhelp.com*.

Sharing Information in the Cloud

Introduction

When Apple first introduced OS X, they touted it as a digital hub. The concept of a digital hub involves placing the information you use on a daily basis into the system one time. Then the hub would keep the data up-to-date and in sync with any other places and devices the same data is stored. The folks at Apple achieved the dream of creating a true, easy-to-use digital hub with iCloud.

iCloud is Apple's cloud service, which stores your music, photos, apps, calendars, and documents and wirelessly pushes them to all your devices, such as iPhone, iPad, iPod touch, and other Macs or Windows PCs. iCloud integrates with your apps, so everything happens automatically. iCloud requires no syncing or management. iCloud is free for iOS5 or later and OS X 10.8 or later users.

When you sign up for a free account, you get 5 GB of storage, which is plenty of space, considering that music, apps, books, and photos in Photo Stream don't count against your free storage. When you update your iPad, iPhone, or iPod touch to iOS6 or later, content from apps—such as Mail, Contacts, Calendar, Reminders, Notes, Safari, Keychain, Photos (Photo Stream), Automator, Preview, AppleScript Editor, TextEdit, iTunes, and iBooks—become integrated with iCloud. Files are redundantly stored on multiple devices across multiple storage facilities—powered by Heroku and Amazon's Simple Storage Service—preventing data corruption and loss.

What You'll Do

Join the iCloud Community

Set iCloud Preferences

Use Back to My Mac

Find Your Mac

Use iCloud on the Web

Use iCloud on the Mac

Use iCloud Enabled Apps

Manage iCloud Files on the Mac

Joining the iCloud Community

iCloud is a cloud service that stores your content—music, photos, apps, contacts, calendars, e-mail, documents and more—and wirelessly pushes it to all your devices, such as your iPad, iPhone, iPod touch, Mac, and PC. iCloud integrates with your devices and computers and requires no syncing or management, but you may need to update software and set preferences to use icloud services. You can sign in and setup your iCloud account by using iCloud Preferences or the web at *www.apple.com/icloud*. You'll need to create or use an existing Apple ID, which is an email address and password you use to login for just about everything you do with Apple, including the iCloud, iTunes Store, and App Store, and setup Keychain options (**New!**). You'll also need to set automatic download options in iTunes and iPhoto or Aperture to complete the setup process.

Get Prepared for iCloud

◆ **Mac.** Update to latest version of OS X 10.8 or later and iTunes 11 or later. Click the **Apple** menu, click **Software Update**, and then update or install from the App Store.

 ◆ **Photo Stream.** iPhoto 11 (v9.4 or later) or Aperture 3.4 or later.

 ◆ **iWork.** iWork 09: Pages 4.3 or later, Number 2.3 or later and Keynote 5.3.

◆ **iPhone, iPad, and iPod touch.** Update to iOS 6 or later on your device and iWork 1.7 or later. Tap **Settings**, **General**, and then **Software Update**.

◆ **Windows PC.** Update to Windows 7 or later, Microsoft Outlook 2007 or 2010, iCloud Control Panel 2.1.2 or later, and iTunes 11 or later.

 ◆ **Download the iCloud Control Panel.** It works like the Mac. Available at *www.apple.com/icloud/setup/pc.html*.

 ◆ **Download iTunes 11 or later.** Available at *www.apple.com*.

◆ **Browser.** Safari 6 (Mac) or Safari 5.1.7 (Win) or later, Firefox 16 or later, Chrome 23 or later, or Internet Explorer 9 (Win) or later.

◆ **Apple TV.** Apple TV version 5.1 or later.

Update OS X

Installing iPhoto for use with iCloud

Set Up iCloud on Your Mac or Windows PC

1 Open System Preferences (Mac) or Control Panel (Win), and then click the **iCloud** icon.

If iCloud Preferences appear, you're signed in; skip to Step 6.

2 If you want to get more information about iCloud, click **Learn more about iCloud** to open your browser.

3 If you don't already have an Apple ID, click **Create an Apple ID**, and follow the on-screen instructions.

4 Enter your Apple ID and password, and then click **Sign in**.

5 Select the check boxes to enable the services you want, and then click **Next**. If prompted, set up iCloud Keychain (**New!**), and allow Find My Mac to use your location.

6 In iCloud preferences, select check boxes with the services you want and deselect the ones you don't.

7 Click the **Close** button.

8 To set automatic downloads for music and apps, open iTunes and then open Preferences:

◆ In Preferences, click the **Store** tab, and then select the **Music**, **Apps**, and **Always check for available downloads** check boxes. Select other Cloud and Sync check boxes (**New!**).

9 To enable Photo Stream and set automatic options, open iPhoto 11 (v9.4 or later) or Aperture 3.4 or later, and then open Preferences:

◆ In Preferences, click the **iCloud** tab, select the **My Photo Stream** check box, and then select the **Automatic Import**, **Automatic Upload**, and **Photo Sharing** check boxes as desired.

For Your Information

Setting Up iCloud on Your iOS Device

To sync content on your iOS device, such as an iPhone, iPad, or iPod touch, you need to set up iCloud on the device too. For iCloud, tap Settings, tap iCloud, sign in, and turn sync options on or off. You can also tap Storage & Backup to manage storage and turn on iCloud Backup. For iTunes, tap Settings, and tap Store to turn on Automatic Downloads for music, apps, and books. To download previous purchases, tap Purchases in iTunes, and then tap individual iCloud Download icons or the Download All icon.

Setting iCloud Preferences

iCloud stores music, photos, apps, documents, contacts, email, calendars, and more and wirelessly pushes them to your iOS devices and computers. For example, when you snap a photo on your iPhone, it's automatically sent to your computers and iPad. In addition, iCloud can also automatically backup up your iOS devices, find your Apple device, find your friends (iOS5 device or later), and connect remotely to your Mac. In iCloud Preferences, you can turn iCloud services on and off. These services including Mail, Contacts, Calendars, Reminders, Notes, Safari, Keychain (**New!**), Photos, Documents & Data, Back to My Mac, and Find My Mac. When you turn off some services or sign out to iCloud, you may be prompted to remove information from your device, however any information in iCloud will remain intact. In iCloud Preferences, you can also view account information, buy more storage (5 GB comes free with an iCloud account), and manage the way information, documents, and data are backed up, stored, and removed to free up space. Also, your purchased music, apps, books, and TV shows as well as your Photos, don't count against the 5 GB of free storage.

Turn iCloud Services On or Off

1 Open System Preferences (Mac) or Control Panel (Win), and then click the **iCloud** icon.

 ◆ **Mac.** Click the **System Preferences** icon on the Dock, and then click the **iCloud** icon.

 ◆ **Window.** Click the **Start** button, click **Control Panel**, click **Network and Internet**, and then click **iCloud**.

2 Click to select (turn on) or deselect (turn off) the check boxes beside each service. Click **Options** next to services for more settings (**New!**).

3 To turn off iCloud completely, click **Sign Out**, and then if prompted, click the options you want to delete or keep data.

 ◆ You also need to turn off automatic download options under Store in iTunes Preferences or iOS Settings.

4 To view account information, click **Manage**, and then click **View Account**.

5 Click the **Close** button.

Manage iCloud Storage

1 Open System Preferences (Mac) or Control Panel (Win), and then click the **iCloud** icon.

2 Click **Manage**.

3 Select the tab with the service or iCloud enabled app—such as Pages, Mail, Spotlight, and Backups—you want to view and manage.

◆ When you click the **Mail** tab, a message appears providing direction to free up storage used by Mail; you can erase messages in Junk and Trash folders in Mail.

4 Select the item you want to delete.

5 Click **Delete** or **Delete All**, and then click **Delete** to confirm it.

IMPORTANT *You cannot undo this action after the confirmation.*

When you delete an item, iCloud may turn off the related syncing service.

6 To purchase more storage, click **Buy More Storage**, and then follow the on-screen instructions.

7 Click **Done**.

8 Click the **Close** button.

Current storage usage

Did You Know?

You can turn off iCloud completely on your iOS device. Tap Setting, iCloud, and then Delete Account. If you delete your account, iCloud will no longer back up your iOS data. You can still back up your device in iTunes.

For Your Information

Freeing Up Space in iCloud Storage

You can free up additional iCloud storage space by deleting email messages from your iCloud email account. You can do this from your desktop email app, such as OS X Mail or Microsoft Outlook, iOS device, or the *icloud.com* website. Simply, open the mail program or system, erase the email messages, and then permanently empty or delete them. For example, to permanently delete messages in Mail, click the Mailbox menu, point to Erase Deleted Items, and then select your iCloud account. You can also free up space by deleting Junk mail.

Backing Up Your iOS Device

You can use the storage space in iCloud to back up your iOS devices. When you enable the the iCloud Backup option in Settings, iCloud automatically backs up your iOS device daily over Wi-Fi when it's connected to a power source and the device is screen locked. To enable iCloud backups on an iOS device, tap Settings, iCloud, Storage & Backup and then turn on iCloud Backup. To set backup options, tap Manage Storage. To start a backup manually, tap Back Up Now. iCloud backs up your purchased music and TV shows, apps, books, device settings, app documents and data, Home screen and app organization, messages (Messages, SMS, and MMS), and ringtones.

Sharing with Back to My Mac

If you have an iCloud account, you can use Back to My Mac to access your other Mac computers from any Internet connection. You can use Back to My Mac to share files and use Screen Sharing to control the remote computer provided that File Sharing and Screen Sharing options are turned on and access privileges set in the Sharing pane in System Preferences. Back to My Mac also requires a network router that supports NAT Port Mapping Protocol (NAT-PMP) or Universal Plug and Play (UPnP) in order to share services. If connection problems occur, check your router. You can use Airport Utility to check an Airport router. Its firmware may need to be updated or an option set.

Use Back to My Mac

1. On each computer or iOS device you want to use, open iCloud Preferences, sign in to iCloud with your Apple ID and password.

2. Select the **Back to My Mac** check box to enable the service.

3. If prompted, click **More**, and then click **Open Sharing** to turn on.

 - **File Sharing.** See pages 422-423 for details and instructions.

 - **Screen Sharing.** See pages 438-439 for details and instructions.

4. Click the **Close** button.

5. To display shared computers in the Sidebar of a Finder window, click the **Finder** menu, click **Preferences**, click **Sidebar**, select the **Back to My Mac** check box, and then click the **Close** button.

6. To connect to shared computers, open a Finder window, and then click the shared computer in the Shared section of the Sidebar.

 - **File Sharing.** Click **Connect As**, enter name, password, and then click **Connect**. Work with files, and then click **Disconnect**.

 - **Screen Sharing.** Click **Screen Share**. The shared computer screen appears. See page 439 for details. When you're done, Quit Screen Sharing.

Shared computer Files on shared computer

Finding Your Mac

You can use the Find My Mac (Mac) or Find My iPhone (iOS5 or later) service in iCloud to locate your Mac computer or iOS device, such as an iPhone or iPad, on a Google map. You can locate a device from a computer's web browser or from an iOS device using the Find My iPhone app, which is available for free from the App Store. Before you can find a Mac or iOS device, you need to enable the service in iCloud Preferences (Mac) or Settings (iOS). The Find My Mac or iPhone service displays a map or indicates the device is not available. Either way, you can choose to play a sound to the device. If you lose your device, you can also remotely lock or even erase it clean (wipe) with a passcode to protect your contents.

Find Your Mac or iOS Device

1 To find a Mac or iOS device, you need to enable the **Find My Mac** service in iCloud Preferences (Mac) or **Find My iPhone** service in Settings (iOS5 or later).

2 Open the Find My iPhone app, and then sign in to iCloud with your Apple ID and password as needed.

◆ **iOS Device.** Open the **Find My iPhone** app.

◆ **Web Browser.** Go to *www.icloud.com*, and then click the **Find My iPhone** icon.

3 Click the device pop-up, and then select the device you want to display on a Google map.

4 To access other options, click the green dot to display location information, click the **i** or **>** icon.

5 Select any of the following:

◆ **Play Sound.** Click **Play Sound** to play a sound on the device, and then click **OK**.

◆ **Lock.** Locks the device with its password. Click **Lock**, and then click **Lock**.

◆ **Lost Mode.** Sends a phone number to the device.

◆ **Erase.** Click **Erase** *device*, and then click **Erase**. An erase cannot be canceled.

6 Close your browser or app.

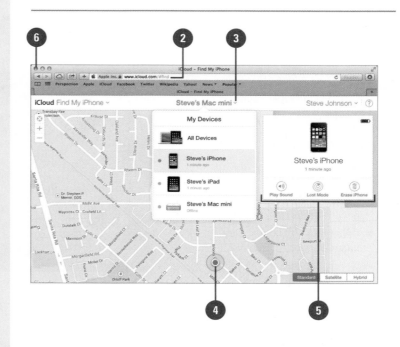

For Your Information

Finding Friends on Your iOS Device

Just like the Find My iPhone app on your iOS device can help you find its location on a map, you can also download and install the free Find My Friends app on your iOS device to locate your friends and family.

Using iCloud on the Web

In addition to using iCloud on your Mac, PC, or iOS device, you can also use it in a web browser at *www.icloud.com*. At the site, you can access and manage mail, contacts, calendars, and documents—Keynote presentations, Pages word processing documents, and Numbers spreadsheets—from iWork. The changes you make in the iCloud web site are synced with all your devices that are signed in, enabled and connected to iCloud. Each application corresponds with the same one in iCloud Preferences, except iWork, which corresponds to Documents & Data. In addition, you can find your Mac and iOS devices on a Google map, play sounds to find a device, lock a device, or erase it.

Use iCloud on the Web

1. Open your web browser, go to *www.icloud.com,* and then sign in to iCloud with your Apple ID and password as needed.

 The iCloud home page appears with apps you can use online.

2. Click the app icon with the content you want to manage:

 ◆ **Mail.** Provides a web-based version of Mail.

 ◆ **Contacts.** Provides a web-based version of Contacts.

 ◆ **Calendars.** Provides a web-based version of Calendar.

 ◆ **Notes.** Provides a web-based version of Notes (**New!**).

 ◆ **Reminders.** Provides a web-based version of Reminders (**New!**).

 ◆ **Find My iPhone.** Find Mac and iOS devices on a Google map.

 ◆ **Keynote, Pages, and Numbers.** Provides a web-based version of the iWork apps (**New!**). You can edit, delete, duplicate, download (as Pages, PDF, or Word), and upload documents.

3. Use app specific options to display and edit content directly in iCloud.

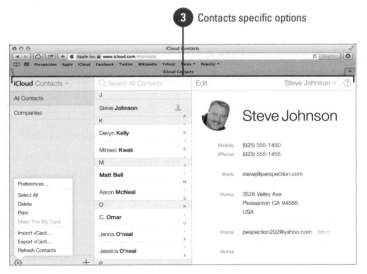

3 Contacts specific options

4 To perform tasks, select an item, click the **Show Actions** menu, and then select the option you want.

5 To exit the app, and return to the iCloud home page, click the **iCloud Home** button.

6 To change language or time zone account settings, click your Apple ID account name, click **Account Settings**, and then make the changes you want. When you're done, click **Done**.

◆ **Language.** Click **Language**, and then select the one you want.

◆ **Time Zone.** Click **Time Zone**, and then select the zone you want on the map..

7 To log out, click your Apple ID account name, and then click **Sign Out**.

8 Close your browser.

See Also

See "Finding Your Mac" on page 361 for information on using Find My iPhone. It works just like the Mac.

5 3 Pages specific options 4

8 6 7

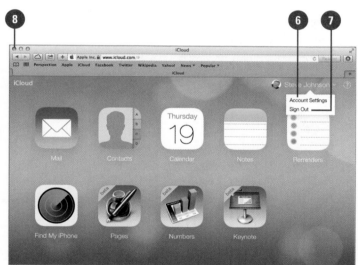

Using iCloud on the Mac

After you enable an iCloud service on a device, iCloud automatically goes to work pushing information from device to device as it changes. You can specify what type of information is stored in iCloud by setting iCloud, iTunes, and Photo Stream (in iPhoto or Aperture) preferences. You can store mail and settings from Mail, contacts from Contacts, calendars and reminders from Calendar, bookmarks and tabs from Safari, photos for the last 30 days using Photo Stream from iPhoto or Aperture, and Documents & Data from iCloud supported apps, such as Preview, Text Edit, Automator, AppleScript Editor, Keynote, Pages, and Numbers in iWork. When you make purchases of music, apps, and books in iTunes, iCloud automatically pushes them to your devices. If you have previous purchases, you can manually download them. When you take or import photos, iCloud automatically uses Photo Stream to bring them into iPhoto or Aperture and then push them to your devices.

Use iCloud on the Mac

1. On each computer or iOS device you want to use, sign in to iCloud with your Apple ID and password.

 - **Mac.** Click the **System Preferences** icon on the Dock, and then click the **iCloud** icon.

2. Select check boxes with the services you want to enable and deselect the ones you don't.

3. Click the **Close** button.

4. To manually download previous iTunes Store purchases, open **iTunes**, click the **Store** menu, and then click **Check for Available Downloads**. In a library (typically in List view), click the iCloud **Download** icon for individual purchases or click the iCloud **Download All** icon.

5. To manually add photos to iCloud using Photo Stream, open iPhoto or Aperture, select a library in the Source list, and then drag the photos you want to iPhoto in the Source list.

 - To view photos in iCloud, click **iCloud** in the Source list.

Purchased items

Added to iCloud in iPhoto

Use iCloud with Apps on the Mac

◆ **iCloud Document Library.** In iCloud apps, like TextEdit, you can open iCloud documents using the iCloud Document Library.

 To enable the use of the library, select the **Document & Data** check box in iCloud Preferences.

 ◆ **Open iCloud Documents.** In TextEdit, click the **File** menu, click **Open**, click **iCloud**, select a document, and then click **Open**.

 ◆ **Create Document Folders.** In the iCloud Document Library, drag one document icon onto another to create a folder with both items.

 ◆ **Sort Documents.** In the iCloud Document Library, click the **List View** icon, click a Label column, and then click to toggle the arrow.

 ◆ **Share Documents.** In the iCloud Document Library, select the documents, click the **Share** button, and then select a service.

◆ **Auto Save.** When an app automatically saves a document, it is instantly moved to iCloud.

 If the document is untitled, it's saved to iCloud.

See Also

See "Managing iCloud Files on the Mac" on page 368 for information on accessing and managing iCloud files on the Mac.

Click to display iCloud documents iCloud Documents Library

Click to create a new iCloud document Click to open documents

Icon view List view

Using iCloud Enabled Apps

After you enable an iCloud service in iCloud Preferences on your Mac, OS X enables iCloud options in some of its apps. For example, when you enable the Safari check box, an iCloud button is added to the Address bar in Safari, where you can access browsing tabs from another iCloud synced device. When you enable the Documents & Data check box, the Open dialog in apps like Text Edit and Preview changes to the iCloud Document Library dialog, where you can create and open iCloud documents. You can also use the Move To command on the File menu or Document title menu to send a local document to iCloud.

Use iCloud Tab in Safari

1 Click the **System Preferences** icon in the Dock, click the **iCloud** icon, select the **Safari** check box, and then click the **Close** button.

2 Click the **Safari** icon in the Dock.

3 Click the **Show iCloud Tabs** button on the toolbar.

A list of tabs from another iCloud device.

4 Click the tab you want to use.

5 Close your browser.

Did You Know?

You can share Automator and AppleScript Editor files on iCloud. In addition to TextEdit and Preview, you can also share documents and data from Automator and AppleScript Editor files. In iCloud Preferences, click Options next to Documents & Data, select Automator and/or AppleScript Editor check boxes, click Done, and then click the Close button.

See Also

See "Using iCloud on the Web" on page 362 for more information on using iCloud from your web browser.

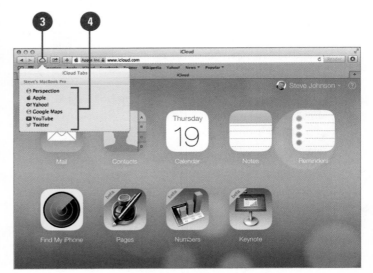

Create or Open iCloud Documents

1. Click the **System Preferences** icon in the Dock, click the **iCloud** icon, select the **Documents & Data** check box, and then click the **Close** button.

 ◆ To turn individual apps on or off, click **Options** (New!), select or clear the check boxes, and then click **Done**.

2. Click the **Launchpad** icon in the Dock, and then click the **TextEdit** or **Preview** icon.

3. Click **iCloud** on the title bar of the iCloud dialog.

 ◆ To open a document on your Mac, click **On My Mac** on the title bar.

4. Click the document you want to open, and then click **Open**.

 ◆ **Create New iCloud Document.** Click **New Document**.

 ◆ **Open iCloud Document.** Select a document. icon, and then click **Open**.

 TIMESAVER *You can click the File menu, point to Open Recent, and then select an iCloud document.*

5. Add text and pictures to create or edit the document in TextEdit.

6. Click the **File** menu, and then click **Save**. For a new document, enter a name.

Did You Know?

You can move a document to iCloud. Open a local document, click the File menu, click Move To, select iCloud, and then click Move.

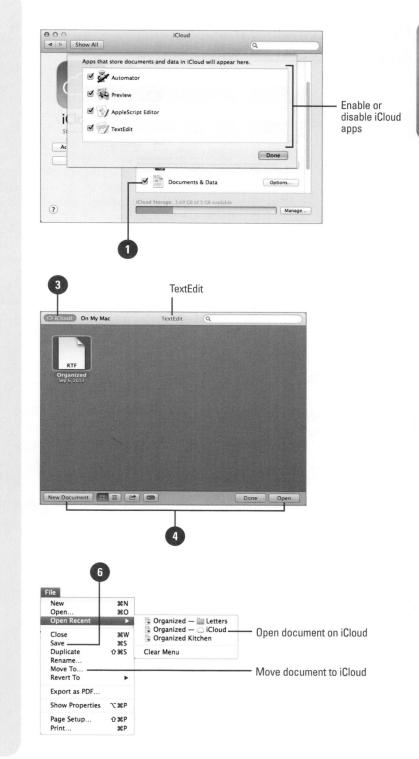

Enable or disable iCloud apps

TextEdit

Open document on iCloud

Move document to iCloud

Managing iCloud Files on the Mac

iCloud is an app centered approach to working on the cloud instead of a file management one. If you want to work with an iCloud document, you need to open it using the iCloud supported app, such as Preview, Text Edit, Automator, AppleScript Editor, Keynote, Pages, and Numbers in iWork. This provides a convenient way to open and update documents on the cloud, however it is limiting when you want to delete the file or open it in another app. OS X manages all files in iCloud through a single synchronized folder, which is called Mobile Documents and is located in the user library folder. You can access the files from subfolders within the Mobile Documents folder where you can delete, copy, or move them. If you have other document types, such as Word document, that you want to edit/convert in Text Edit or Pages, you can drag them into the Documents folder for Text Edit or Pages, where they will be synced to iCloud.

Work with iCloud Files on the Mac in the Finder

1. In the Finder, hold down the Option key, click the **Go** menu, and then click **Library**.

2. Double-click the **Mobile Documents** folder.

 Folders are each iCloud program appear.

 IMPORTANT *The folder names are for internal use. Don't change them, it will create problems.*

3. Double-click the folder associated with the iCloud program, and then double-click a subfolder, such as Documents.

 The iCloud files for the program appear in the folder.

4. Manage the files in the folder just like any other set of files in Finder.

 ◆ Delete. Drag the file(s) to the Trash, and then click **Delete**.

 ◆ Move or Copy. Drag (move) or Option-drag (copy) the file(s) to the Desktop or another folder.

 You can also move or copy files to the Documents folders in the Mobile Documents folder, which are synced to iCloud.

Drag to the Trash to delete

Tracking and Managing Information

Introduction

Computers can indeed be a blessing and a curse. On the one hand they give you instant access to mountains of information; on the other hand you're the one who has to organize and keep track of all that data. There are a lot of programs out there that claim to help you stay organized, using everything from day-planner software to relational databases. There's only one problem, you have to actually use those programs. That typically means learning new third party software, loading all your data and schedules, and then trying to keep it current, even if you move it to a different computer. This paragraph defined the problem; the next provides the solution.

When Apple introduced OS X, they touted it as a digital hub. The concept of a digital hub involves placing your daily schedules and contact data into the system one time. Then the hub would keep the data up-to-date and in sync with any other places and devices the same data is stored. With the release of OS X, and applications like Calendar, Reminders, and Notes, the folks at Apple achieved the dream of creating a true, easy-to-use iCloud that can keep your information up-to-date on all your devices. When the latest version of OS X was released, along with improved versions of its iCloud syncing and management system, I was finally able to get control of the mountains of information that make up my daily life.

What You'll Do

View the Calendar Window

Change Calendar Views

Create and Work with Calendars

Add and Edit Calendar Events

Invite Attendees to Calendar Events

Print Calendars

Publish and Subscribe to a Calendar

Share a Calendar with iCloud

Create Reminder Lists

Work with Reminder Lists

Add Notifications to Reminders

Enable Accounts for Reminders and Notes

Create and Manage Notes

Set Notification Preferences

Use the Notification Center

Post to Social Media

Viewing the Calendar Window

Calendar is a scheduling and time-management app. There are other programs out there that schedule and manage your time; however, Calendar's native architecture (built by Apple), its stability, and ability to transfer and sync information easily across multiple applications, makes it an easy choice for the busy executive, the harried designer/animator, or anyone who owns a Mac, and wants to keep track of what they're doing. Calendar assists you by helping you automate repetitive events such as: Yoga every Friday at 8pm, the kids soccer practice, or that quarterly conference call with management. In addition, Calendar notifies you of an event by using an alarm sound, pop-up note, or even e-mail. Calendar uses a streamlined new look user interface and full screen view with more room

to make it easier to use. To access Calendar, click the Calendar icon in the Dock or open Launchpad, and then click the Calendar icon.

Adding Calendar Accounts

If you use Facebook (**New!**), Yahoo!, Google, or Gmail calendars, Calendar can automatically set them up and display their calendars and events, including Facebook (**New!**). Click the Calendar menu, click Preferences, click Accounts, click the Add (+) button, enter your account e-mail address, and then click Create. Calendar account assistance looks for any calendar accounts associated with the e-mail address. You can also add a calendar account for Exchange 2007 or later and CalDAV, however, you need to provide account details.

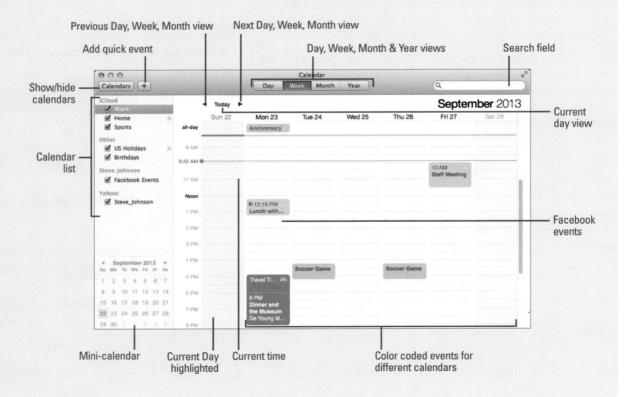

Changing Calendar Views

Calendar provides different views for you to look at your calendar. You can view events by Day, Week, Month, and Year. The Day view provides a running list of your events on one side and a detailed schedule on the other, so you have everything you need at a glance. Day view also includes a mini month so you can quickly switch between days. In addition to the traditional Week and Month views, you can also view 12 months at a time with Year view. In Year view, Calendar displays a map using colors to represent availability for each day. If you need more room on the screen to view your calendar, you can switch to full screen view. You can also continuously scroll smoothly through weeks and months (**New!**) and stop when you want.

Change Calendar Views

1. Click the **Calendar** icon in the Dock.

2. To view the Calendar window in full screen view, click the **Full Screen** button.

 ◆ **Exit Full Screen**. Point to the top of the screen to display the menu bar, and then click the **Full Screen** button.

3. Click a view button on the toolbar.

 ◆ **Day**. Displays a list of events and schedule for the day.

 ◆ **Week**. Displays a weekly schedule for each day of the week.

 ◆ **Month**. Displays a monthly schedule for each day of the month and highlights the current week (**New!**).

 ◆ **Year**. Displays a yearly view of availability for each day of the year.

4. To display the current day, click **Today**.

 ◆ You can also click the Left and Right Arrow buttons to switch between days.

5. To view a specific date, click the arrows in the mini-calendar, and then click a date.

Day view

Month view

Current week (**New!**) Continuous scrolling (**New!**)

Creating and Working with Calendars

With Calendar, you can keep track of all your activities, either work or personal. You can create separate calendars for different people, such as your family, or a team, or different types of activities. Separating your calendars makes it easy to focus on the information for a specific activity and share only that calendar with the people you want. Withe the Calendar list in the Sidebar, you can select, move, rename, or delete calendars to suite your needs. If you need to find an event, you can use the Search field, which make suggestions and allows you to combine searches to help you find what you need. In addition, you can instruct Calendar when to delete old events and even turn off alarms and time zone support.

Create and Manage Calendars

1. Click the **Calendar** icon in the Dock.

2. To add a calendar, click the **File** menu, point to **New Calendar**, select where you want to add the calendar, type a name for the calendar on the Calendar list, and then press Return.

3. To show and hide the Calendar list in the Sidebar, click the **Calendars** button.

4. Select from the following options to manage calendars:

 ◆ **Rename.** Click the calendar name , click it again, type a new name, and then press Return.

 ◆ **Delete.** Control-click the calendar in the Calendar list, and then click **Delete**.

 ◆ **Move.** Drag to a another position in the Calendar list.

5. To search for events, enter search text in the Search field, and then view the suggestions.

 When you select a suggestion, Calendar creates a token displaying a list of events that match the criteria. You can combine multiple tokens to refine a search. Click the **Close** button to cancel the search.

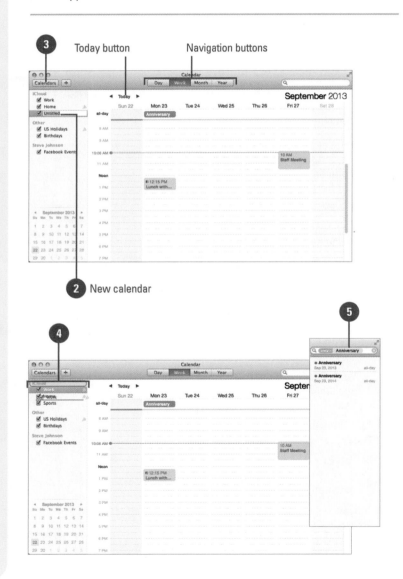

Today button Navigation buttons

2 New calendar

Change Calendar Properties

1. Click the **Calendars** button to display the Calendars list.

2. Control-click the calendar, and then click **Get Info**.

3. Select from the following options:

 ◆ **Name and Description.** Use the pop-ups to specify defaults.

 ◆ **Color.** Use the pop-up to select a default calendar.

 ◆ **Ignore alerts.** Select to ignore any alerts.

4. Click **OK**.

Change Calendar Preferences

1. Click the **Calendar** menu, and then click **Preferences**.

2. Click **General**.

3. Select from the following Calendar preferences:

 ◆ **Day and Week Defaults.** Use the pop-ups to specify defaults.

 ◆ **Default Calendar.** Use the pop-up to select a default calendar.

 ◆ **Show Time and Birthdays Calendar.** Select to show time in month view and the birthdays calendar. Birthdays automatically come in Calendar from Contacts, including those from Facebook (**New!**).

4. Click **Alerts**, and then specify alert options (**New!**) for events and birthdays, and notification alerts for shared calendar and invitation messages.

5. Click **Advanced**, and then select to options you want to enable.

6. Click the **Close** button.

Adding and Editing Calendar Events

When you first create your Calendar calendar, it represents where you are with your schedule at that moment in time. Unfortunately, things change and they can change often. Therefore, Calendar gives you the ability to add new events or modify existing events directly in the Calendar window. You can also use Quick Add to enter an event using a regular language phrase like "Soccer Game at 4:00 Tuesday." Calendar makes calendar modifications easy, and once complete, they can be transferred to other applications and devices. If you need detailed information for multiple events, you don't have to edit each one, you can use the Inspector window to display you what you need by simply clicking it.

Add or Edit Calendar Events

1. Click the **Calendar** icon in the Dock.

2. To quickly add an event, click and hold the **Quick Add** button, select a calendar, type event information (a regular language phrase with name, time, and location), press Return, specify event details, and then click off the event.

 ◆ **Quick Add.** Click to add an event to the default calendar.

3. Click the **Calendars** button, and then click the calendar you want to add an event.

4. Click a view button to find the date to add.

5. Drag a time interval on the day you want to add an event.

6. Type a title for the event.

7. Specify any other information you want for the event.

8. Click off the event to exit.

9. To adjust the time or day in the Day or Week view, use the following options:

 ◆ **Adjust Event Time.** Drag the top or bottom edge of the event.

 ◆ **Move Event Day.** Drag the title to a new location.

For Your Information

Working with Attachments for an Event

If you have an attachment you want to include with an event, you can quickly attach it by dragging it to the event in the Calendar window just like a drop box. When you send e-mail invitations to your attendees, the attachments go along with it. While you edit an event, you can also preview an attachment. Simply select it in the Edit dialog, and then press the Spacebar. Click the Close button to exit it. To delete an attachment, select it, and then press Delete.

Show or Edit Calendar Events Details

1 Click the **Calendar** icon in the Dock.

2 To show event details, click the **Edit** menu, click **Show Inspector**, and then click an event.

3 Double-click the event you want to edit; click sections in the event to expand or collapse options.

4 Add the following event options:

- ◆ **Calendar.** Click to select the calendar this event is linked.
- ◆ **Location.** Enter a location for the event. Select a suggested location, which displays a map and weather forecast (**New!**).
- ◆ **All-day.** Check for all day event.
- ◆ **From/To.** Enter a From/To date.
- ◆ **Repeat.** Sets event to repeat.
- ◆ **Travel Time.** Select a travel time to the event or one provided based on your location (**New!**).
- ◆ **Alert.** Lets you be notified before the event.
- ◆ **Add Invitees.** Adds attendees to the event list.
- ◆ **Add Attachments.** Adds file attachments to the event.
- ◆ **Add URL.** Adds a URL address to the event.
- ◆ **Add Note.** Adds any notes.

5 Click off the event to exit.

Did You Know?

You can quickly delete an Calendar event. In Calendar, select the event you want to delete, and then press Delete.

Click to expand

Click to collapse

4

5

Location map and weather forecast

2 Inspector window

Shows in Calendar

Inviting Attendees to Calendar Events

After you schedule an event, such as a meeting, you can invite others to attend it. Every event includes options to invite attendees to it. You can enter an e-mail address or use Contacts to specify the attendees you want to invite with an e-mail. After you select your attendees, you can specify invitee options—such as optional, invite again, send email or remove invitee—and check the time availability for each to make sure everyone can make it by using the Availability panel. The Availability panel makes it easy to find free availability times for all those involved in the event. You can reply to an event invitation in Calendar using the Notification Center or one in Mail with a response.

Invite Attendees to Events

1. Click the **Calendar** icon in the Dock.

2. Double-click the event you want to invite attendees.

3. Click **Add Invitees**.

4. Enter e-mail addresses or a name from your Contacts (add a comma between items).

 ◆ **Address Panel.** You can also click the **Window** menu, and then click **Address Panel** to add invitees.

 ◆ **Invitee Options.** Point to a contact, click the down arrow, and then select an option, such as **Optional**, **Remove Invitee**, **Invite Again**, or **Send Email**.

5. Click to expand the pane, and then specify the meeting time and any other options you want.

6. Click the **Window** menu, click **Availability**, and then review the availability times for the meeting.

 ◆ Use the view buttons to show and adjust times.

 ◆ Click **Next Available Time** to search for open times.

 ◆ Drag the meeting as desired.

7. Click **Done**.

8. Click **Send** or click **Revert** to cancel.

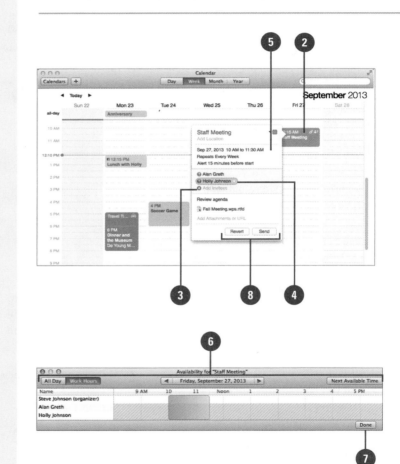

Printing Calendars

Just like you can print documents and photographs, you can also print any of your calendars and reminders. Calendar gives you the flexibility to specify the calendars you want to print and the related details you want to include, such as all-day events, mini-months (next and previous calendar months in the upper right corner of the page), and calendar keys (a print legend).

Print Calendars

1. Click the **Calendar** icon in the Dock.

2. Click the **File** menu, and then click **Print**.

3. Click the **View** pop-up, and then select the print layout you want.

4. Use the **Starts** and **Ends** pop-up to specify the date range you want.

5. Select the check boxes next to the calendars you want to print.

 If you select a calendar group, all the calendars are included.

6. Specify any other print options you want.

 ◆ **All-Day Events.** Includes all day events.

 ◆ **Mini-Months.** Includes the next and previous months.

 ◆ **Calendar Keys.** Includes a calendar legend.

 ◆ **Black and White.** Prints in black and white.

7. Click the **Text size** pop-up, and then select a text size for event headings.

8. Click **Continue**.

9. Select a printer and any print presets, and then click **Print**.

Publishing and Subscribing to a Calendar

You can create a calendar that lists all of your appointments with detailed information and a reminder list that helps you keep track of everything. But what good is that information, if you're out of town, and you forgot to bring your Mac? By publishing your Calendar calendar with the ICS format, you wouldn't have a problem. If you have a CalDAV workplace calendar server, publishing your calendar gives you access to that information anywhere there's a computer and an Internet connection. With CalDAV, you can also check the availability of people and resources. In addition, if someone else has published a calendar, you can gain access to it by subscribing. Not only does this give you access to your calendar, but any one that requires your scheduling information. A published calendar appears with a broadcast icon next to it in the Calendar list, which you can click to view information and options.

Publish a Calendar

1. Click the **Calendar** icon in the Dock.

2. Click the **Calendars** button, and then select a CalDAV calendar to publish.

3. Click the **Edit** menu, and then click **Publish**.

4. Type a name for the calendar.

5. Specify a URL, Login, and Password for the server location.

6. Select the publishing options you want: **Publish changes automatically, Publish titles and notes, Publish To Do items, Publish alarms,** and **Publish attachments**.

7. Click **Publish**.

8. Write down the URL as it appears. This is very important if you want to view your calendar or allow someone else to subscribe to it.

9. Click **Visit Page, Send Mail** or **OK** in the confirmation message.

 A broadcast icon appears next to the calendar in the calendar list.

10. To unpublish a calendar, select it, click the **Edit** menu, click **Stop Publishing**.

Broadcast icon

For Your Information

Backing Up or Importing Calendars

If you already have an electronic calendar, you can import it into Calendar. To import all your calendars, click the File menu, point to Import, click Import, select the backup file, and then click Import. It's important to save a backup of your calendar for safe keeping. To backup all your calendars, click the File menu, point to Export, click Calendar Archive, type a name, select a location, and then click Save.

Subscribe to a Calendar

1. Click the **Calendar** icon in the Dock.

2. Click the **File** menu, and then click **New Calendar Subscription**.

3. Type the URL full path name to the calendar with an ICS extension. You need to get the exact URL from the person who published it; click the **Calendars** button, select the calendar, click the **Edit** menu, and then click **Get Info**.

 TIMESAVER *Click the Broadcast icon for the calendar.*

4. Click **Subscribe**.

5. Select from the following options:

 ◆ **Name and Description**. Type a name and description for the calendar subscription.

 ◆ **Remove Alarms or Attachments**. Check to remove any of the items.

 ◆ **Auto-refresh**. Select to update the calendar, and then select how often the update occurs.

6. Click **OK**.

7. To unsubscribe to a calendar, click the **Calendars** button, Control-click the calendar in the Calendar list, and then click **Delete**.

Did You Know?

You can export or import events. To export as a .ICS file, click the File menu, point to Export, click Export, type a name, specify a location, and then click Export. To import a .ICS file, click the File menu, click Import, select an import option, click Import, select the file, and then click Import.

Broadcast icon

For Your Information

Adding and Showing Birthdays in Calendar

In order to show birthdays in Calendar, you first need to add them in Contacts. In Contacts, select the contact, click the Add (+) button, click Birthday, enter a date, and then click Done. Facebook contact birthdays are added automatically to Contacts when you have a Facebook account setup in Internet Accounts. In Calendar, click the Calendar menu, click Preferences, click General, select the Show Birthdays calendar check box, and then click the Close button.

Sharing an iCloud Calendar

If you have an iCloud account, you can share calendars with others who also have an iCloud account using Calendar, the Calendar app available on iPhone, iPad, and iPod touch, and Microsoft Outlook. You can share an iCloud calendar privately by invitation only or publicly to the masses. A privately shared calendar gives users Read only or Read & Write privileges, while a publicly shared calendar is Read only. Read-only privileges allow users to view information, while Read & Write allow users to create, edit, and delete items. If multiple items are changed at the same time, the changes saved first are kept. Anyone with the calendars web address can subscribe to it.

Share an iCloud Calendar

1. Click the **Calendar** icon in the Dock.

2. Click the **Calendars** button, and then select an iCloud calendar to share.

3. Click the **Edit** menu, and then click **Share Calendar**.

4. To make the calendar public for anyone to subscribe to as a read-only version, select the **Public Calendar** check box.

5. To invite specific people to share a calendar, enter e-mail addresses or a name from your Contacts (add a comma between items).

 ◆ **Privileges.** Point to a contact, click the down arrow, and then click **View & Edit** or **View Only**.

6. To share the calendar with an email link, or with Messages or Facebook, click the **Share** button, and then select an option.

7. When you're ready to share an iCloud calendar, click **Done**.

 A broadcast icon appears next to the calendar in the calendar list.

8. To stop sharing a calendar, select it, click the **Edit** menu, and then click **Stop Sharing**.

 Calendar participants are notified the calendar is no longer shared.

Invitations sent for private calendar use

Set privileges

Send invite again

Website address for public read-only access

Use a Shared Calendar

1 Start from the following options:

◆ **Everyone.** In Calendar, click the **Calendar** menu, and then click **Subscribe**, enter the calendars URL address, and then click **Subscribe**.

◆ **Only the people you invite.** In the invitation email, click **Join Calendar**. Sign in to the iCloud web site with your Apple ID and password.

2 Click the shared iCloud calendar to view it and then make any changes you want to the contents.

Broadcast icon indicates a shared iCloud calendar.

3 To log out, click your Apple ID account name, click **Sign Out**, and then close your browser.

Shared iCloud calendar

Change Calendar Account Preferences

1 Click the **Calendar** menu, and then click **Preferences**.

2 Click **Account**.

3 Select the account you want to change.

4 Select account options:

◆ **Enable this account.** Use to enable or disable this account.

◆ **Refresh Calendars.** Use to select a sync interval. Push syncs when items change.

5 To edit account information using Internet Accounts preferences, click **Edit Account**.

6 To add or remove an account, use the **Add** (+) or **Remove** (-) buttons.

7 Click the **Close** button.

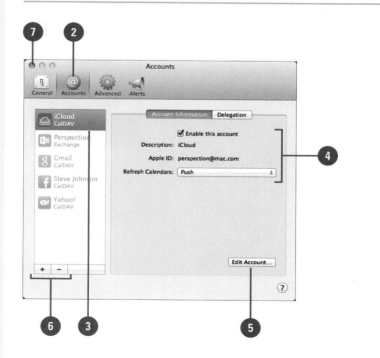

Creating Reminder Lists

We all have things to do (my wife calls this a honey do list). And most of the time I need to write them down, so I can keep track of them and not forget to do it. With the Reminders app, you can create one or more list of different reminders using one or more accounts, such as iCloud, CalDAV, Microsoft Exchange, Google Calendar, Yahoo! Calendar, or On My Mac. For example, you can have a Personal list of things you need to repair at home, or you can have a Work list of things you need to complete at the office. For each reminder on a list, you can specify how and when you want a reminder alert. This is an easier solution than your wife tapping you on the shoulder, and asking you if you remembered to fix the screen on the back porch door.

Use the Reminders Window

1 Click the **Reminders** icon in the Dock.

2 Use any of the following to work with the Reminders window:

- ◆ Sidebar. Click the **Sidebar** button to show or hide the Sidebar.

 When the Sidebar is hidden, you can click the dots to switch between lists.

- ◆ Calendar. Click the **Calendar** button to show or hide the Calendar.

- ◆ Search Field. Type text to find lists and reminders.

- ◆ Add List. Click the **Add List** button to create a new blank list.

- ◆ Add Reminder. Click the **Add Reminder** button, and then type to create a new blank list.

- ◆ Edit Reminder. Point to a reminder, and then click the **Edit Reminder List** button to set due date related information.

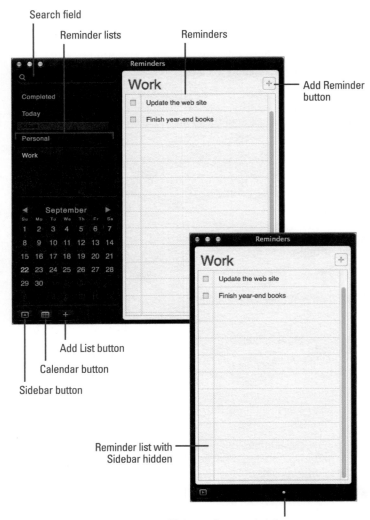

Search field

Reminder lists

Reminders

Add Reminder button

Add List button

Calendar button

Sidebar button

Reminder list with Sidebar hidden

Click or swipe to switch lists

Create a Reminder List

1. Click the **Reminders** icon in the Dock.

2. Click the **Sidebar** button to display the Sidebar.

3. If you have more than one account, select an account.

4. To create a new list, click the **Add List** (+) button, type a list name, and then press Return.

 ◆ You can also click the **File** menu, and then click **New List**.

5. Select the List in the Sidebar to which you want to add a reminder.

6. To create a new reminder, click to place the insertion point in a reminder line, and then type the reminder text.

 A cleared check box appears to the left of the reminder, which you can select to mark it as complete.

 ◆ You can also click the **Add Reminder** (+) button or click the **File** menu, and then click **New Reminder**.

7. To add another reminder, press Return, and then type the reminder text.

Did You Know?

You can use gestures to view reminder lists. In Reminders, position the pointer over your reminders (not the Sidebar), and then swipe left or right on the trackpad or mouse to quickly move between reminder lists.

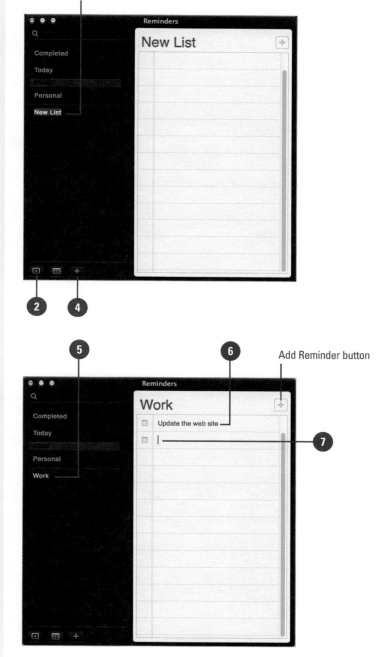

New list in the Sidebar

Add Reminder button

Working with Reminder Lists

After you create a reminder list or two, it's important to understand how to work with them in order to get the most out of it. You can work with individual lists and reminders or select multiple ones. You can view one or more lists at the same time, view lists as separate windows, which you can use on your desktop, or view reminders by date using the Calendar or by completion. If you no longer need a list or reminder, you can delete it at any time.

Work with Reminder Lists

1 Click the **Reminders** icon in the Dock.

2 Click the **Sidebar** button to display the Sidebar.

3 If you have more than one account, select an account.

4 Use any of the following to work with reminder lists:

◆ **View Single List.** Click the list in the Sidebar. If the Sidebar is hidden, you can click the dots.

◆ **View Multiple Lists.** Shift-click to select multiple lists in the Sidebar.

◆ **View Lists by Date.** Click the **Calendar** button to display it, and then click a date.

◆ **View Lists in a Separate window.** Double-click the reminder list in the Sidebar.

◆ **Delete List.** Select the reminder list in the Sidebar, click the **Edit** menu, click **Delete**, and then click **Delete** to confirm.

◆ **Reorder Lists.** Drag one or more reminders up or down in the list. To select multiple reminders, hold down the ⌘ key. You can't drag a list to a different account.

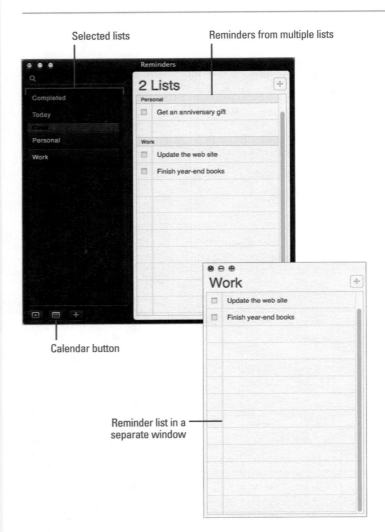

Selected lists

Reminders from multiple lists

Calendar button

Reminder list in a separate window

Work with Reminders

1. Click the **Reminders** icon in the Dock.

2. Click the **Sidebar** button to display the Sidebar.

3. If you have more than one account, select an account.

4. Select the List in the Sidebar to which you want to work.

 ◆ **View Reminders by Date.** Click the **Calendar** button to display it, and then click a date.

5. Use any of the following to work with reminders:

 ◆ **Select Reminders.** Click to the right of reminder name to select it. To select multiple reminders, hold down the ⌘ key.

 ◆ **Edit Reminders.** Click to place the insertion point, and then edit the text.

 ◆ **Reorder Reminders.** Drag one or more reminders up or down in the list.

 ◆ **Move Reminders.** Drag a reminder from one list to another in the Sidebar.

 ◆ **Delete Reminder.** Select the reminder tex,t and then press Delete.

 ◆ **Mark Reminders as Complete.** Select a reminder's check box. The item gets moved the the Completed list.

 ◆ **Mark Reminders as Incomplete.** Click the Completed list in the Sidebar, clear a reminder's check box. The item gets moved back to its original list.

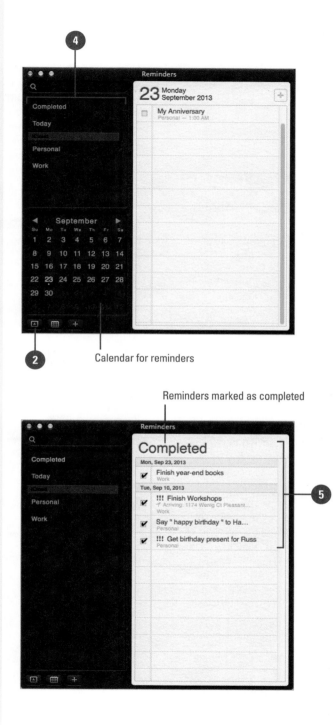

Calendar for reminders

Reminders marked as completed

Adding Notifications to Reminders

With Reminders, you can manage your reminders by due dates and with notifications. When a deadline for a reminder approaches or is due based on a specified date, you'll receive a notification. If you want to view any up coming notifications, you can display them in the Notifications Center. If you're on the go, you can add a location to a reminder on your Mac and receive a notification on your iPad, iPhone, iPod touch or other Mac when you depart from or arrive at the specified location. iCloud keeps your reminders and lists up to date on all your Mac and iOS devices.

Add Notifications to a Reminder

1. Click the **Reminders** icon in the Dock.

2. Click the **Sidebar** button to display the Sidebar.

3. If you have more than one account, select an account.

4. Select the List in the Sidebar to which you want to work.

5. Double-click the reminder you want to change.

 ◆ You can also point to the reminder and then click the **Information** (i) button.

6. Use any of the following to work with reminders:

 ◆ **On a Day.** Select to specify a date for a reminder alert.

 ◆ **At a Location.** Select to get an alert when leaving or arriving at a location on the specified date. The location is monitored by Location Services, which you can view in the Privacy pane of Security & Privacy preferences.

 ◆ **Repeat and End.** Specify a repeat option and end date.

 ◆ **Priority.** Specify a Low, Medium or High priority.

 ◆ **Note.** Enter a text note about the reminder.

7. Click **Done**.

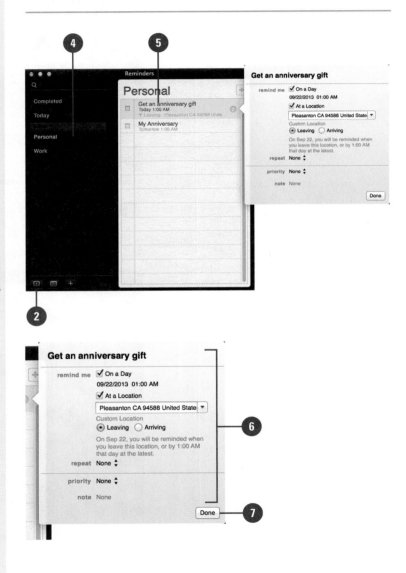

Using Accounts for Reminders and Notes

With the Reminders or Notes apps, you can use one or more accounts, such as iCloud, CalDAV, Microsoft Exchange, Google Calendar, Yahoo! Calendar, or your Mac. You can enable the use of Reminders and Notes by using the Internet Accounts pane in System Preferences, which you can quickly access from the apps themselves. You can set up iCloud on your Mac, iPhone, iPad, and iPod touch to have your reminders wherever you go. Any changes you have on one iOS5 or later device are made on all devices so you always have your most up-to-date reminders. You can use the iCloud Calendar at *www.icloud.com* to view the lists.

Enable Multiple Accounts

1. Click the **Reminders** or **Notes** icon in the Dock.

2. Click the **Reminders** or **Notes** menu, and then click **Accounts**.

 ◆ You can also click the **Internet Accounts** icon in System Preferences.

3. Click the account you want to use.

4. To enable or disable an account for reminders, select or clear the **Reminders** and **Notes** check boxes.

5. Click the **Close** button.

Did You Know?

You can automate reminders. With AppleScript, you can use scripts to add, change, or read reminders. With Automator, you can link several actions into a workflow.

Creating and Managing Notes

Notes is a full screen app that allows you can create notes (like the sticky note pads) and organize them into folders. With Notes, you always have a note pad handy for jotting down things you want to remember or to keep photos, files, or URL links handy when you need them. If you have a microphone, you can use dictation to enter your notes. Notes works with different accounts, such as iCloud, Gmail, Google, or On My Mac. Each account stores notes in a Notes folder. If you're on the go, you can use iCloud to keep all your notes up to date on all your Mac and iOS devices.

Use the Notes Window

1 Click the **Notes** icon in the Dock.

2 Use any of the following to work with the Notes window:

- ◆ **Folders List.** Click the **Show Folders** or **Hide Folders** button to show or hide the folder list of accounts.

- ◆ **Calendar.** Click the **Calendar** button to show or hide the Calendar.

- ◆ **Create a Note.** Click the **Add Note** (+) button to create a blank new note.

- ◆ **Search Field.** Type text to find note text.

- ◆ **View a Note.** Click a folder, and then click the note in the Notes list.

- ◆ **View a Note in a Separate Window.** Double-click the note in the Notes list. To keep the note in front of all windows, click the **Window** menu, and then click **Float On Top**.

- ◆ **View in Full Screen.** Click the **Full Screen** button. To exit, press Esc.

- ◆ **Delete.** Select a note in the Notes list, click the **Edit** menu, and then click **Delete**.

- ◆ **Share.** Click the **Share** button to share notes using Mail or Messages.

Click to display all notes in all accounts

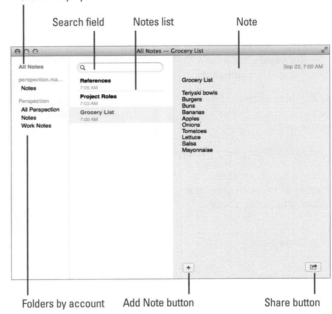

Search field Notes list Note

Folders by account Add Note button Share button

Create a Note

1. Click the **Notes** icon in the Dock.

2. Click the **View** menu, and then click **Show Folder List** to display the folder list of accounts.

3. If you have more than one account, select a folder for the account or click **All Notes**.

 ◆ To create a new folder, click the **File** menu, click **New Folder**, edit the name, and then press Return.

 ◆ You can drag to move a folder or Control-click a folder to rename or delete it.

4. To create a new note, click the **Add Note** (+) button.

 ◆ You can also click the **File** menu, and then click **New Note**.

5. Type the note text, and then press Return as desired. The initial text appears as the title of the note.

 ◆ To use dictation, click the **Edit** menu, and then click **Start Dictation**.

6. To format text in a note, select it, click the **Format** menu, and then use commands on the Font, Text, Lists, and Indentation submenus.

7. To add an image, file, or URL link, select and drag it from a window or desktop to the note.

 You can't add attachments to an Exchange account.

8. To share a note, select it, click the **Share** button, and then click email **This Note** or **Messages**.

9. To move a note into another folder, drag it from the Notes list to a folder in the Folder list.

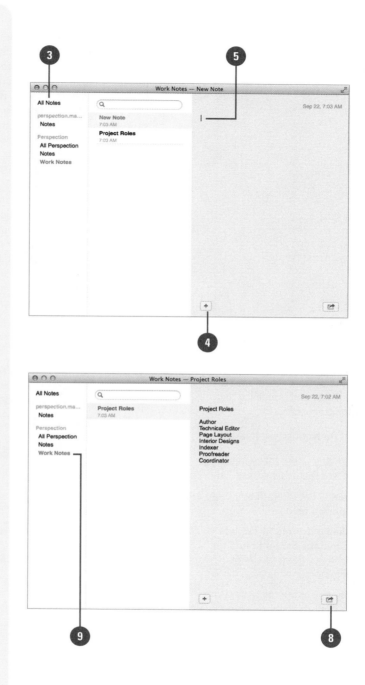

Setting Notification Preferences

While you work in an app or if you step away from your Mac, you can get notifications (**New!**) to let you know what's happening in other places. In Notifications Preferences, you can specify notification options for many apps, including Safari, Calendar, Reminders, Notes, Mail, FaceTime, Messages, iTunes (**New!**), iCloud Photos (**New!**), Maps (**New!**), Twitter, Linkedin, Facebook, and Game Center. If you want to send Messages, Twitter posts, Linkedin posts, or Facebook posts from the Notification Center, you can enable the Share Button. Apps appear in the Notification Center list unless you drag them to the Not in Notification Center list at the bottom of the pane. If you don't want to be disturbed with notifications, you can specify options (**New!**) when you don't want to be disturbed and whether you want to allow FaceTime calls. After you set up Notification preferences, you can respond to banner or alert notifications, some with previews (**New!**), as they appear in the upper-right hand corner of the screen or open the Notification Center to view your notices. In addition to these preferences, you can also select notification options in the General pane of iTunes Preferences to send a notification when a song changes (**New!**) or keep all song changes in Notification Center (**New!**).

Set Do Not Disturb Notifications Preferences

1 Click the **System Preferences** icon in the Dock, and then click the **Notifications** icon.

2 Select **Do Not Disturb** (**New!**).

3 Specify any of the following Turn on Do Not Disturb options:

◆ **From.** Select to turn on during a specify a time.

◆ **When mirroring to TVs and projectors.** Select to turn on when mirroring to TVs or projectors.

4 Specify any of the following When Do No Disturb is turned on options:

◆ **Allow FaceTime calls from.** Select to allow FaceTime calls from Every.

◆ **Allow repeated calls.** Select to show a badge in Notification Center.

5 Click the **Close** button.

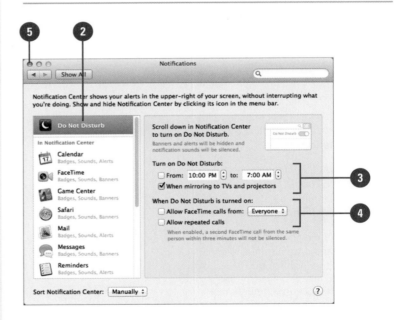

Set App Notifications Preferences

1 Click the **System Preferences** icon in the Dock, and then click the **Notifications** icon.

2 To show or hide notifications for individual apps, drag the app to or from In Notification Center or Not In Notification Center list.

3 Select the app, and then specify any of the following options:

◆ **Reminder alert style.** Click an alert style: **None**, **Banners**, or **Alerts**.

Banners appears and go away automatically, while alerts stay until you dismiss them.

◆ **Show notifications on lock screen.** Select to show notifications when the lock screen (**New!**) appears.

◆ **Show in Notification Center.** Select to show a specified recent number of items.

◆ **Show message preview.** Select always or when unlocked (**New!**) to show a preview for apps like Mail and Messages.

◆ **Badge app icon.** Select to show a badge in Notification Center.

◆ **Play sound when receiving notifications.** Select to play a when you receive a notification.

◆ **Options.** Click to set additional option, if available. For example, you can set added notifications with Twitter.

4 Click **Sort Notifications Center** pop-up, and then click **Manually** or **By time**.

5 Click the **Close** button.

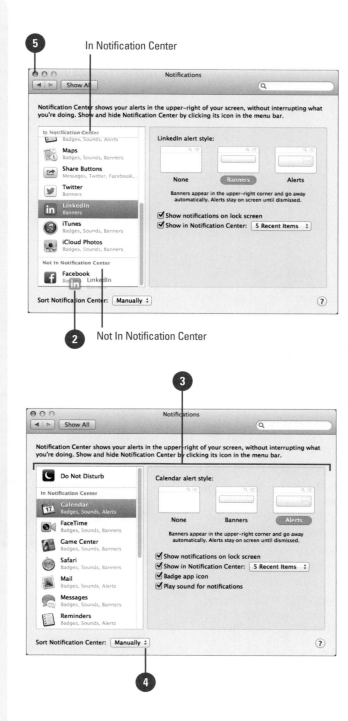

In Notification Center

Not In Notification Center

Using the Notification Center

The Notification Center is a central place where you can get notices and respond to them from different apps—such as Safari, Calendar, Reminders, Notes, Mail, FaceTime, Messages, iTunes (**New!**), iCloud Photos (**New!**), Maps (**New!**), Twitter, Linkedin, Facebook, and Game Center—even if you're working in an app or away from your Mac. With Apple's Push Notifications (APNs) (**New!**), you can receive notices from websites, such as breaking news or sports scores, even if Safari is not open. You can respond to notifications as they appear in the upper-right hand corner of the desktop or lock screen (**New!**) while you're away as a text banner or alert—some with previews (**New!**)—along with optional sound or a numbered badge on the app icon, or open the Notification Center to view your notices. You can quickly access the Notification Center whenever you need it by clicking the Notification Center icon on the menu bar or a swipe on the trackpad. If you don't want to be disturbed by notifications, you can turn them off (**New!**).

Get Notifications

1. If a notification alert appears, view a preview (if available), and then click an option button to respond.

 Click **Close** to close the alert with no response or click **Snooze** to have the alert repeat later. Other responses may appear depending on the app.

 If a banner appears, you can click it to go directly to the banner or wait 5 second to let it disappear into the Notification Center.

2. Click the **Notification Center** icon in the menu bar or swipe left from the right edge of your trackpad with two fingers or Magic Mouse.

 The Notification Center opens as a column from the left side of the screen.

3. To show the Do Not Disturb option, scroll down the Notification Center. Drag the slider to turn on or off.

4. To open an app, click the notification associated with the app.

5. To remove notifications for an app, click the **Close** (x) button

Notification preview from Facebook

Click to open Notification preferences

Request and Receive Push Notifications from a Website

① Open Safari.

② Navigate a website with Apple's Push Notifications (APNs) (**New!**).

③ Click the button or link to request the push notification service (**New!**) from the website.

④ Click **Allow**.

⑤ Quit Safari.

⑥ Click the **System Preferences** icon in the Dock, and then click the **Notifications** icon.

⑦ Select the Push Button for the website.

⑧ Specify any of the following options; settings may vary:

◆ **Show or Hide in Notification Center.** Drag the app to or from the In Notification Center or Not in Notification Center list.

◆ **Reminder alert style.** Click an alert style: **None**, **Banners**, or **Alerts**.

Banners appears and go away automatically, while alerts stay until you dismiss them.

◆ **Show notifications on lock screen.** Select to show notifications when the lock screen (**New!**) appears.

◆ **Show in Notification Center.** Select to show a specified recent number of items.

⑨ Click the **Close** button.

⑩ Wait for the notifications from the website to appear as banners or alerts and in the Notification Center.

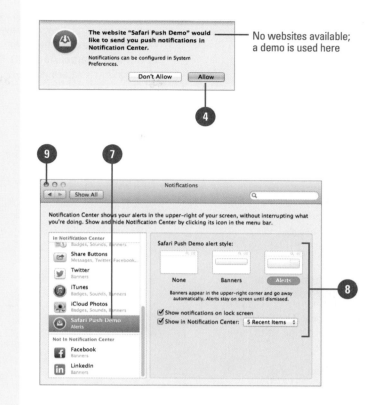

No websites available; a demo is used here

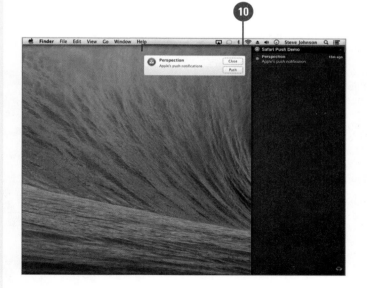

Posting to Social Media

With the Notification Center, you can quickly send posts to social media, such as Twitter, Linkedin (**New!**), and Facebook (**New!**), as well as Messages (**New!**) whenever you want. When you enable social media account in Internet Accounts Preferences and the Share Button in Notifications Preferences, you can send posts directly from the Notification Center.

Set Notification Options

① Click the **System Preferences** icon in the Dock, and then click the **Notifications** icon.

② Drag the Share Button and Twitter icons into the In Notification Center list, if needed.

③ Select **Share Button**.

④ Select the **Show share button in Notification Center** check box.

⑤ Select **Twitter, Linkedin, or Facebook**, and then select the options you want.

⑥ Click the **Close** button.

Post to Social Media

① Click the **Notification Center** icon in the menu bar.

② Click icon for the social media you want to use.

③ Enter your post text.

④ To add a location to a Twitter tweet or Facebook post, click **Add Location**.

⑤ Click **Send** or **Post**.

Setting Up Accounts and Maintaining Security

Introduction

OS X was designed from the ground up for sharing, and it really doesn't matter what you want to share. For example, you might want to set up a simple home-based network to share files between family members, or even hook your Mac into a major network using a combination of Windows, Unix, and Mac machines. In Chapter 16, "Managing Files Using a Network," you'll learn how to set up a functional network using a variety of methods; however in this chapter you'll learn how to create user accounts, manage those accounts, and even protect your information from being accessed by unauthorized individuals, using the File Vault application. In addition, OS X lets multiple users log in and switch between accounts with the click of a button.

Correctly setting up user accounts is important to the security of your computer, so each account is assigned its own name, and individual password. Take care when setting up accounts that you don't give the user more privileges (access) than needed to perform their job. Also, when setting up accounts and passwords, make sure to be accurate in your typing of passwords. Passwords are case-sensitive, and if forgotten, data can be lost forever. When setting up accounts, you can have shared files that can be available for all users on your computer or network.

Remembering your passwords can be a real pain. With iCloud Keychain, you don't have to. iCloud Keychain stores your website user names and passwords on your Mac and updates them to your approved iCloud devices using AES 256-bit encryption. iCloud Keychain also works with credit card information, so checking out after a purchase is a snap.

What You'll Do

Understand User Accounts

Activate the Login Window

Add a User Account

Delete a User Account

Set File Access Permissions

Set Account Access Privileges

Set Account Parental Controls

Specify Log In and Start Up Items

Set Fast User Switching

Set Security Preferences

Set Privacy Preferences

Protect Your Computer with FileVault

Restore Password Access

Add Keychains and Passwords

Work with Keychains and Passwords

Modify Keychains and Passwords

Set Up for iCloud Keychain

Use AutoFill with iCloud Keychain

Understanding User Accounts

OS X was designed for multi-users, and Mavericks has continued that tradition with the inclusion of tighter file security and keychains. Think of a user account as a file drawer within a large file cabinet, where each drawer is a separate user. A specific user owns each file drawer, and they have access to that drawer through a unique key. Users can do anything they please within their own drawer; including throwing away or adding files, but they can't access the other drawers. A user account holds all of the user's folders, files, applications, desktop, and preference settings; anything they decide to add or subtract from their account.

The Administrator holds all the keys to all the accounts; they're the ones that set up the user accounts and decide who can do what. If you're the owner of the computer, you're the Administrator. Each user is assigned privileges that define where they can go, and what they can access.

User accounts are stored in the Users folder on your Mac's main hard drive. The Users folder contains individual user account folders, and a Shared folder. Each user account is assigned a Home folder. The **Home folder** is where all your account stuff is stored. That means all of your files, anything that you've created within your personal account—including system and app preferences—are stored in this folder. When users sign on to their accounts, they have the ability to add or delete files to their Home folder; however, they cannot access the Home folder of any other user, and they cannot add folders or delete files from any place else but their own Home folder. This gives you a tremendous degree of control over users, and prevents them from accidentally (or purposely) deleting or reading sensitive data. For exam-

ple, users cannot create folders on the main hard drive, nor can they delete apps from the Applications folder. The other areas of the computer are effectively locked out.

What if you want to give a file to another co-worker, but you can't drop it into their folder, and the co-worker can't access your Home folder. That's where the Mac comes to the rescue with shared folders.

When you open your Home folder you'll see a folder named Public. The Public folder contains a nested folder named Drop Box. The **Drop Box folder** is a place where anyone can drop items for you to use. As another user, I can place things into your Drop Box, and you can place things in my Drop Box, but I can't see what's in your Drop Box, nor can I change any items. In other words, files check in but they don't check out.

Finally, there is a **Shared folder**, located in the Users folder. The Shared folder is the only folder (other than your own Home folder) where you have full access to the files it contains.

Users folder Individual users Shared folder

Home folder for stevejohnson Public folder

Activating the Login Window

When you turn on your Mac for the first time, it's set up for instant access. You were asked during the initial setup to name your computer and assign a password. By default, the password protection system is not activated, so the next time you start up your Mac, you are granted access without having to select your account and type in your password. Before setting up User Accounts, it's a good idea to first activate password login, and then set up any additional accounts. When active, the login window appears every time you start up your computer and contains a list of all those with valid user accounts.

Activate the Login Window

1 Click the **System Preferences** icon in the Dock, and then click the **Users & Groups** icon.

2 If the screen is locked, click the **Lock** icon, type your password, and then click **Unlock**.

3 Click **Login Options**.

4 Click the **Automatic login** pop-up, and then select **Disabled** or a user.

When you select a user, your computer automatically starts with this user account.

5 Click the **List of users** or **Name and password** options.

6 Select or clear the following settings to show options in the Login window:

◆ **Show the Restart, Sleep, and Shut Down buttons.**

◆ **Show Input Menu in login window.**

◆ **Show password hints.**

7 Select or clear the **Use VoiceOver at login window** check box.

8 Select the **Show fast user switching menu as** check box if there is more than one user, and then use the pop-up to select a view.

9 Click the **Close** button.

Adding a User Account

Setting up user accounts involves careful consideration as to who is this person, and what they'll be able to access and do on the computer. You can create different types of accounts: Administrator, Standard, Managed with Parental Controls, Sharing Only, and Group. Each account provides different privileges. An Administrator account has full access to all accounts and applications, and all file or application changes on the hard drive, while a Standard account only allows access to their own personal Home folder and applications on the hard drive. They don't have access to any other account, nor are they able to modify or delete any files or applications on the hard drive.

Add a User Account

1. Click the **System Preferences** icon in the Dock, and then click the **Users & Groups** icon.

2. Click the **Add** (+) button.

3. Click the **New Account** pop-up, and then select an account type.

 ◆ **Administrator**. Creates an account with full privileges.

 ◆ **Standard**. Creates an account with standard user privileges.

 ◆ **Managed with Parental Controls**. Creates an account with parental controls.

 ◆ **Sharing Only**. Creates an account to share files.

 ◆ **Group**. Creates an account that assigns the same privileges to a group of members.

4. Change the Account name as desired (used by the server).

 IMPORTANT *The Account name cannot contain any spaces and is case sensitive.*

5. Type and verify the password.

6. Type a password hint (optional).

7. Click **Create Account**.

8. Click the picture icon, and then select a picture, take a picture, or drag a picture file from a window.

9. Click the **Close** button.

Chapter 15

Deleting a User Account

Things change quickly in the computer world; an account for an employee that was valid a week ago is now invalid due to the employee quitting. Deleting user accounts is easy, and if planned correctly does not mean that the user's data and files are deleted. You can specify to hold all of the deleted account information in a temporary holding area; where it can be accessed for as long as necessary.

Delete a User Account

1. Click the **System Preferences** icon in the Dock, and then click the **Users & Groups** icon.

2. Select an account from the available users.

3. Click the **Delete** (-) button.

4. Select from the following options:

 ◆ **Save the home folder in a disk image**. Click to save the home if you want the user back later.

 ◆ **Do not change the home folder**. Click to deactivate the account and keep the home folder.

 ◆ **Delete the home folder**. Permanently delete the home folder.

5. Click **OK**.

6. Type your password, and then click **OK** to delete the account.

7. Click the **Close** button.

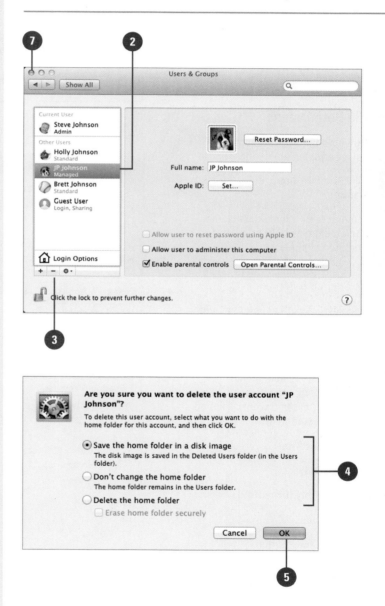

Setting File Access Permissions

As the Administrator, you have one additional area where you can control what users have access to is the File Info. The **File Info** window lets you, as the Administrator, decide who has access to which files and folders on your computer. For example, you could create a folder on the hard drive and give every user account access, or you could select one file within that folder and restrict access. In fact, you can give users the ability to read a file, but not modify, or let them read and modify the file. Since handling individual files would be a bit time consuming (computers typically hold thousands of files), your Mac helps out by assuming users do not have access to the hard drive's files and folders (it's up to you to give them access), and you can apply general access settings to all the files and folders nested within a folder (this saves you time).

Set File Permissions

1. Open the hard drive and then select a folder, application, or file.

2. Click the **File** menu, and then click **Get Info**.

3. If the screen is locked, click the **Lock** icon, type your password, and then click **OK**.

4. Click the expand button (triangle) for Sharing & Permissions.

5. If locked, click the **Lock** icon, enter password, and then click **OK** to unlock it.

6. Click the **Privilege** pop-ups to the right of system, admin, and everyone, and then select what type of access you want assigned to the selected item.

 ◆ **Read & Write**

 ◆ **Read Only**

 ◆ **Write Only (Drop Box)**

 ◆ **No Access**

7. Click the **Close** button.

Setting Account Access Privileges

Once you have set up a user account, it's up to you to decide exactly what that particular user can and cannot have access to. For example, you might create a user account for a graphic designer and give them access to all the design applications such as Adobe Photoshop and Illustrator; however, you don't want them messing around with the accounting programs, so you deny access to those specific applications. Once the access privileges are set for an account, they can be changed at a later date, but the Administrator is the only person authorized to change them.

Set Account Access Privileges

 Click the **System Preferences** icon in the Dock, and then click the **Parental Controls** icon.

 Select the account you want to modify.

 Click **Enable Parental Controls**, if necessary.

 Click the **Apps** tab.

 Select the **Only allow selected applications** check box, and then select the check boxes for the application you want this user to access.

 Select or clear the **Prevent the Dock from being modified** check box to enable or not.

 Click the **Others** tab.

 Select to restrict the user's ability to perform certain functions:

- **Disable built-in camera. (New!)**
- **Disable Dictation.**
- **Hide profanity in Dictionary.**
- **Limit printer administration.**
- **Disable changing the password.**
- **Limit CD and DVD burning.**

 Click the **Close** button.

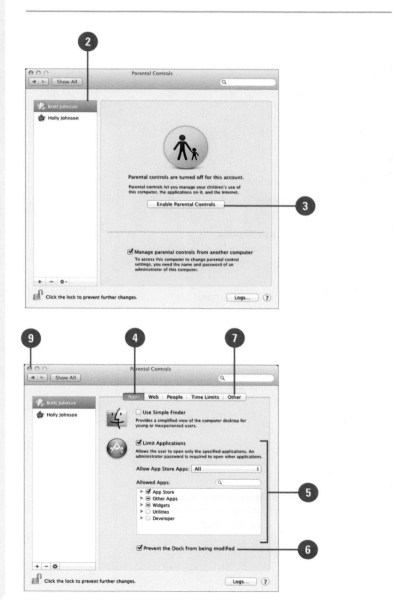

Setting Account Parental Controls

After you have set up a user account as the Administrator, you can enable and set parental controls. Parental Controls help you manage how your children use the computer. Parental Controls allows you to set limits on your children's web access, Mail, Messages, and Game Center usage, the amount of time spent logged on the computer, and which games and programs they can use. You can set different settings for each user account on your computer, so you can adjust the level you want for each child. You can also review activity reports on a periodic basis to see what your children are doing on the computer.

Set Account Content Controls

1. Click the **System Preferences** icon in the Dock, and then click the **Parental Controls** icon.

2. Select the account you want to modify, and then click **Enable Parental Controls**, if necessary.

3. Click the **Web** tab.

4. Select one of the options:

 ◆ **Allow unrestricted access to websites.**

 ◆ **Try to limit access to adult websites automatically.** Click **Customize** to specify sites.

 ◆ **Allow access to only these websites.** Click the **Add** (+) and **Remove** (-) buttons to add and delete items from the allowable web site list.

5. Click the **Other** tab.

6. Select or clear the **Hide profanity in Dictionary** check box.

7. Click the **Close** button.

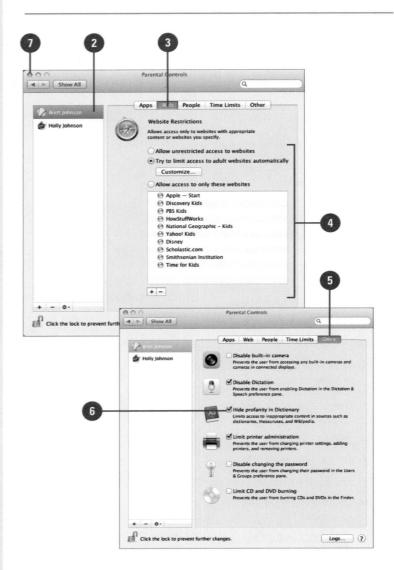

Did You Know?

You can view user account log activity. In Parental Controls Preferences, click the Apps tab, click Logs, use the pop-ups to show activity and group the results, select a log collection and log, and then click Open.

Set Mail, Messages and Game Center Controls

1 Click the **System Preferences** icon in the Dock, and then click the **Parental Controls** icon.

2 Select the account you want to modify, and then click **Enable Parental Controls**, if necessary.

3 Click the **People** tab.

4 Select or clear the **Allow joining Game Center multiplayer games** and **Allow adding Game Center friends** check boxes.

5 Select or clear the **Limit Mail** and **Limit Messages** check boxes. If you want get permission, select the **Send permission requests to** check box, and then type an e-mail address.

6 Click the **Add** (+) and **Remove** (-) buttons to add and delete addresses from the allowable list.

7 Click the **Close** button.

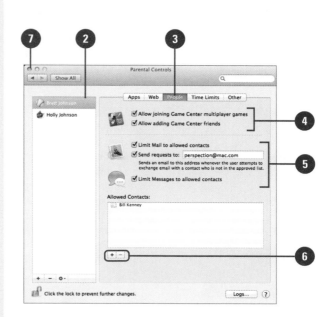

Set Time Limits

1 Click the **System Preferences** icon in the Dock, and then click the **Parental Controls** icon.

2 Select the account you want to modify, and then click **Enable Parental Controls**, if necessary.

3 Click the **Time Limits** tab.

4 Specify options for the following time limits:

- ◆ **Weekday time limits.**
- ◆ **Weekend time limits.**
- ◆ **Bedtime.**

5 Click the **Close** button.

Specifying Log In and Start Up Items

When you first turn on your computer, it begins by access the operating system and performing a standard start up. A normal start up involves performing a system check, and then if login is activated, opening the login window and requiring you to select your account and type in your password. At that point, OS X opens your desktop and it's off to work. However, there is a way that you can alter the start up procedure, by specifying Start Up, and/or Log In items. **Start Up items** are applications or scripts that you decide to launch every time your computer is turned on. **Log In items** are specified by individual users, and launch whenever their account is accessed. For example, you might have a Start Up item (a script) that accesses the company network. In addition, you have a Log In item (a file) that launches your personal day planner, when you log in. The network script launches each time the computer is turned on, but the day planner only launches when you log in to your account. The individuals who own accounts on your computer set up log in items. In fact, log in items are one of the few things the Administrator cannot do—the user must set them up.

Work with Log In Items

1. Click the **System Preferences** icon in the Dock, and then click the **Users & Groups** icon.

2. Select your account (Administrator only).

3. Click the **Login Items** tab.

4. Click the **Add** (+) button to locate a particular application or file you want opened every time you log in.

5. If necessary, click the **Remove** (-) button to remove an item from the startup list.

6. Select the **Hide** check box to open the application or file but hide it until you're ready to work.

7. Click the **Close** button.

> **TIMESAVER** *To see a list of all hidden applications or files, press* ⌘+Tab. *You'll see a list of all open applications. Continue to press A, and then press Tab to move through and select any hidden application.*

Adds or Deletes an account.

Work with Start Up Items

1. Open the System folder.
 - ◆ Click the **Go** menu, click **Computer**, and then open your hard drive.
2. Open the Library folder and then open Startup Items folder.
3. Add items to the folder by dragging and dropping.
4. Remove items by dragging them out of the folder.

Did You Know?

If you don't want to drop an application into the Startup Items folder, create an alias of the application (or file), and place the alias into the folder. That way, you still have access to the original item, and if you no longer want the item in the Startup Items folder, all you have to do is move it to the trash.

You can create Startup commands. Since Start Up items load every time your computer is running; it's a great way to perform routine maintenance and security. For example, you can create a script that instructs the system to perform hard drive diagnostics every seven days. Since the items are placed within the Startup Items folder, it doesn't matter who logs into the computer; the functions load and perform as instructed.

See Also

See "Creating Aliases" on page 90 for information on how to create and use an alias.

Setting Fast User Switching

One of the advantages to having multiple users and owning OS X, is the ability to quickly switch between users. For example, one of your users wants to quickly check her e-mail. Before Leopard, you would have to close out all your files, log out, and then let her log in, but not any more. OS X allows more than one user access to your computer, and lets you switch back and forth on the fly without closing anything. Think of a large box, and each side of the box represents a user account, along with their personalized desktop, specific folders and applications. To access a new account you simply rotate the box to display another face. That's exactly how it looks when you switch users using Fast User Switching. As you watch, the screen rotates to another face on the box displaying another user, and your account is still active. When she's finished checking her e-mail, all you have to do is switch back. It's that simple, and on systems with multiple users, this one feature can save you a lot of wasted time.

Enable Fast User Switching

1. Click the **System Preferences** icon in the Dock, and then click the **Users & Groups** icon.

2. If the screen is locked, click the **Lock** icon, type your password, and then click **Unlock**.

3. Click the **Login Options** button.

4. Select the **Show fast user switching menu as** check box.

5. Click the pop-up, and then select a user view option: **Full Name**, **Short Name**, or **Icon**.

6. Click the **Close** button.

See Also

See "Switching Users" on page 24 for information on switching between different users.

Setting Security Preferences

The General tab in the Security & Privacy pane of System Preferences allows you to set options that prevent others from using your computer, such as changing your password, requiring a password or showing a message to wake your computer from sleep or screen saver, disabling automatic login all together, and allowing applications downloaded from Mac App Store, identified developers, or anywhere. There are also advanced options that allow you to automatically update the safe downloads list and log you out if you're inactive for a certain amount of time. By monitoring app downloads, you can help secure your computer from malicious software, known as **malware**, by preventing the distribution and installation of harmful software, such as viruses, worms, or trojan horses, that tries to damage your computer, collect confidential information, or send spam email.

Set Security Options

1. Click the **System Preferences** icon in the Dock, and then click the **Security & Privacy** icon.

2. Click the **General** tab.

3. Specify the settings for any of the following:

 ◆ **Change Password.** Click to change the login password for the current user.

 ◆ **Require password after sleep or screen save begin.** Select to require a password after a specified idle interval.

 ◆ **Show a message when the screen is locked.** Select to enter a message for those who login to your computer.

 ◆ **Disable automatic login.** Select to require a password to login to your computer.

 ◆ **Allow applications downloaded from: Mac App Store, Mac App Store and identified developers**, or **Anywhere**.

4. To specify additional security settings, click **Advanced**, select or clear options, and then click **OK**.

5. Click the **Close** button.

Advanced options

Setting Privacy Preferences

The Privacy tab in the Security & Privacy pane or System Preferences provides a central location for enabling and disabling location services and Apple's diagnostic and usage data collection. You can view which apps have requested access to your location information or contacts from local Wi-Fi networks. When an app requests your location or contacts, an app appears in the Privacy tab, where you can enable or disable individual apps. Apple uses the diagnostic and usage data to help improve its products and user support, while still maintaining your privacy.

Set Privacy Options

1. Click the **System Preferences** icon in the Dock, and then click the **Security & Privacy** icon.

2. Click the **Privacy** tab.

3. Click the **Location Services** category.

4. Select or clear the **Enable Location Services** check box to allow or prevent apps and web sites to use your computer's current location to provide information and services.

5. If you select the Enable Location Services check box, select or clear check boxes for apps to allow or prevent access to your current location.

6. Click an app category.

7. Select or clear check boxes for apps to allow or prevent access to the app.

8. Click the **Diagnostics & Usage** category.

9. Select or clear the **Send diagnostic & usage data to Apple** check box to allow or prevent Apple from gathering customer improvement information.

10. Click the **Close** button.

Protecting Your Computer with FileVault

FileVault 2 gives you security over your sensitive files and applications. FileVault 2 gives you the ability to encrypt all the files on a hard disk—including external USB and FireWire drives—using password encryption (your log in password). It's so strong, that if you forget your password and don't know the password, no one is able to open the files—they are lost forever. It's theorized that breaking the FileVault 2 encryption with XTS-AES 128 data security would take a password-guessing program over 100 trillion years to figure it out. Therefore, if you decide to use FileVault, please don't forget your password, known as a recovery key. To help you keep it safe, you can send it to Apple, where you can call them with security information to get it. After you set FileVault, the security encryption and decryption happens on the fly, so you don't have to worry about doing anything; simply use your files normally. If someone else tries to access them, FileVault keeps them out.

Protect Your Computer with FileVault

1. Click the **System Preferences** icon in the Dock, and then click the **Security & Privacy** icon.

 IMPORTANT *Encrypting the entire contents of your hard drive requires the System Administrator.*

2. Click the **FileVault** tab.

3. Click **Turn On FileVault** (all other users must be logged off).

4. If necessary, click **Enable User**, and enter the password for each user, and then click **Continue**.

5. Write down the recovery key and place it in a safe place, and then click **Continue**.

6. Select an option to store or not store the key with Apple, and then click **Continue**.

7. Click **Restart** to begin the encryption process.

 You can check the progress of the encryption in the FileVault tab in Security & Privacy preferences.

Restoring Password Access

System Administrators are the ones that control the computer; they're the ones that set up other user accounts, and they are the ones, that tell you what you can and cannot access on that particular computer. The System Administrator knows all... sees all. However, what if the System Administrator forgets their password? Well first of all, don't tell anyone and don't worry, because you have two possible ways to get back to work. If you forget your login password with FileVault disabled, you can use an Apple ID associated with your account to reset your login password. You can set the Apple ID association in Users & Groups preferences. If you forget your login password with FileVault enabled, you can use the recovery key produced when you turned it on. In the login screen, click the account, click the Question Mark (?) in the password field, and then click the Arrow (FileVault off) or Reset it using your Recovery Key link (FileVault on). If you know the administrator password and want to change account passwords, you can use the Password tab in Users & Groups preferences to make the change.

Set and Restore a Password Using your Apple ID

1. Click the **System Preferences** icon in the Dock, and then click the **Users & Groups** icon.

2. Select the administrator account.

3. Click the **Password** tab.

4. Click **Set**.

5. Enter your Apple ID and password, and then click **OK**.

 ◆ If you don't have an Apple ID, you can click **Create Apple ID** to get one.

6. Click the **Close** button.

7. In the login window, click the account, click the Question Mark (?) in the password field, and click the following:

 ◆ **FileVault off.** Click **Reset it using your Apple ID**, enter an Apple ID and password, and then click **Reset Password**.

 ◆ **FileVault on.** Click **Reset it using your Recovery Key**, and then enter your recover key.

Reset Password for Specific Users

① Click the **System Preferences** icon in the Dock, and then click the **Users & Groups** icon.

② Select the administrator account or any other account.

③ Click the **Password** tab.

④ Click **Change Password**.

⑤ Enter your old and new password, password hint, and then click **Change Password**.

⑥ Click the **Close** button.

Did You Know?

You can allow a user to act like an administrator. Click the System Preferences icon in the Dock, click the Users & Groups icon, click the lock icon, enter name and password, click Unlock, select the user, click the Password tab, select the Allow User To Administer This Computer check box, and then click the Close button.

You can reset your administrator or a user password with the Reset Password utility. Restart your computer, hold down ⌘+R during start up to open installer utilities. Click the Utilities menu, and then click Terminal. Type resetpassword, and then press Return. In the Reset Password utility program, select the volume containing the user account, select the user account (System Administrator (root) or a specific user), enter a new password as requested, enter a password hint, click Save, and then click OK. Quit Reset Password, Terminal, and OS X Utilities.

For Your Information

Resetting the Master Password

Your operating system has an Administrator password, and a Master password. If you know the master password, you have no problems whatsoever. However, if you set up a master password, turned on FileVault, and then forgot your Master password... well, not even OS X can help you out of that situation, you're data is lost forever. It is therefore recommended that you create a Master password, and use FileVault to secure your sensitive documents. To reset the Master password, click the System Preferences icon in the Dock, click the Users & Groups icon, select the administrator account, click the Actions button, click Change Master Password, enter a password (current, new, and verify) and a hint, and then click OK. You use the Master password in the login window. In the login window, click the administrator account, click the Question Mark (?) in the password field, click Reset it using your Master Password, and then enter your password.

Adding Keychains and Passwords

Every time you type your login password, you're typing in the master key, and Keychain responds by filling in all the passwords blanks from that point forward. Although Keychain runs in the background, and is therefore invisible to most Mac users, you have the ability to add additional keychains to the current set. To do this you'll need detailed information on the keychain that you want to add, and an application to perform the addition. Apple's Keychain Access program allows you to add addition keychains to the existing set. For example, you might want a keychain to manage your computer (default keychain), and another keychain to manage and secure your business documents. Since the keychain application allows you to modify existing elements within a keychain, you could easily wind up locking yourself out of devices or web sites. Caution is advised when using Keychain Access.

Add a Keychain and Password

1. Click the **Launchpad** icon, click the **Other** folder, and then click the **Keychain Access** icon.

2. Click the **File** menu, and then click **New Keychain**.

3. Type a keychain access name, and then select a save location.

4. Click **Create**.

5. Type a password for the keychain, verify it, and then click **OK**.

6. Click the **File** menu, and then click **New Password Item**.

7. Type the keychain name or URL for easy reference, an account name, and password.

 NOTE *Keychain passwords are case sensitive. Click the Show Typing check box to make sure your password is accurate.*

8. Click **Add**, type a password, and then click **OK**.

 IMPORTANT *Keychains store all of their information as encrypted data, and the password is part of the cipher that restores the information. If you forget your password, there is nothing you can do to restore the information.*

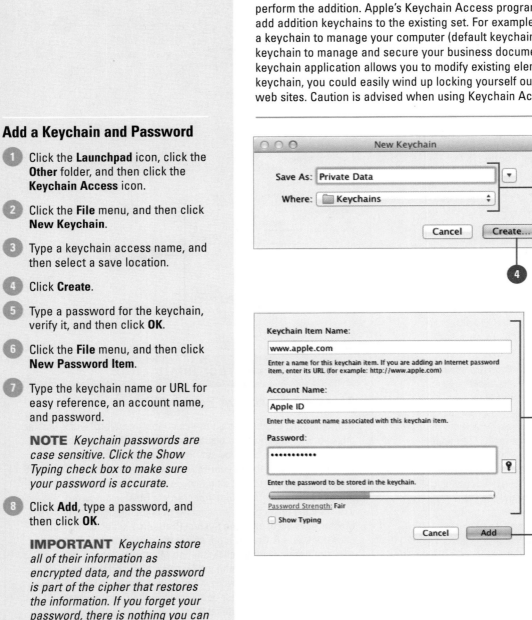

Working with Keychains and Passwords

You typically don't have to worry about Keychains, except when there is a problem. That's when you need Keychain Access. When you open Keychain Access, you'll probably already have a list of keychains. With keychains in view, you can unlock and lock access to them, delete them, and add secure notes. Keychains are organized by type: login, iCloud (**New!**), System, and System Roots (internal use) and each type contains categories: Passwords, Secure Notes, My Certificates, Keys, and Certificates (external ones). If you receive a digital certificate from the Internet, you can add it to your keychain for easier access next time. A digital certificate validates users and web sites on the Internet for credibility.

Work with Keychains

- **Show/Hide Keychains.** Click the **View** menu, and then click **Show Keychains** or **Hide Keychains**.

- **Unlock Keychain Access.** Select the keychain (such as login or System), click the **Lock** icon, type your password, and then click **OK**.

- **Lock Keychain Access.** Select the keychain (such as login or System), and then click the **Lock** icon.

 To change the password for Keychain access, click the **Edit** menu, and then click **Change Password for Keychain** *name*.

- **Delete Keychain Access.** Select the keychain (such as login or System), click the **File** menu, click **Delete Keychain** *name*, and then click **Delete References & Files** or **Delete References.**

- **Add a Secure Note.** Click the **File** menu, click **New Secure Note Item**, type a keychain name, type the note, and then click **Add**.

- **Change Default Keychain.** Select a new keychain, click the **File** menu, and then click **Make Keychain** *name* **Default**.

- **Remove a Keychain.** Select a keychain, press Delete, and then click **Delete**.

- **Add a Certificate to a Keychain.** Drag the certificate file onto the Keychain Access icon or double-click the certificate file, select a keychain, and then click **OK**.

Lock or unlock selected keychain Keychains types

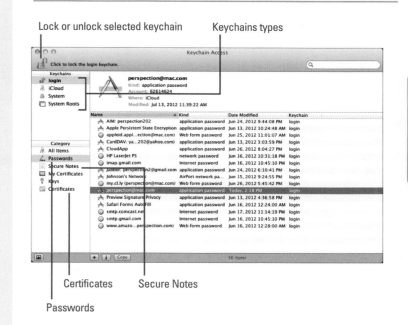

Passwords Certificates Secure Notes

Modifying Keychains and Passwords

Keychain Access gives you the ability to modify the elements within a keychain. For example, you could add an additional level of password protection, or insert a secure note. It would even be possible to delete or change the parameters of an existing element within the keychain. Since your Mac manages the keychain quite well in the background, it just depends on how much control you wish to exert over the Keychain already setup by your computer.

Modify Keychains

1. Click the **Launchpad** icon, click the **Other** folder, and then click the **Keychain Access** icon.

2. Click the **View** menu, click **Show Keychains**, and then select the keychain you want to manage.

3. Double-click a keychain password from the list.

4. Click the **Attributes** tab.

5. Select from the following options:

 ◆ **Name**. Type a new name for the keychain item.

 ◆ **Kind**. Type a new kind such as an Internet Connect.

 ◆ **Account**. Type a new account name for the keychain item.

 ◆ **Where**. Type a new location for the keychain item.

 ◆ **Comments**. Type any comments into the comments field.

6. Select or clear the **Show password** check box to show the password for this keychain item.

7. Click **Save Changes**.

8 Click the **Access Control** tab.

9 Select from the following options:

- **Allow all applications To access this item**. When selected, this item is not restricted.

- **Confirm before allowing access**. When selected, users have to click through to get to the item.

- **Ask for keychain password**. Select or clear the check box to require users to type the keychain password.

IMPORTANT *When you click the check box to show the keychain items password, you'll first be prompted for the keychain's master password.*

10 To add specific applications, click **Add** (+) button, and then select the applications.

11 To remove specific applications, click the application, and then click the **Remove** (-) button.

12 Click **Save Changes** to record your changes to the active keychain.

Setting Up for iCloud Keychain

iCloud Keychain (**New!**) stores your website user names and passwords on your Mac and updates them to your approved iCloud devices using AES 256-bit encryption. iCloud Keychain also works with credit card information, so checking out after a purchase is a breeze. All you need to enter is your card's security code. Before you can use iCloud Keychain to remember your website user names and passwords and credit cards, you need to setup AutoFill information first. AutoFill is a service that helps you complete online forms, credit card information (**New!**), and log in to web sites with a user name and password from Passwords preferences and information from your Contacts. You use the AutoFill pane of the Safari preferences to select, modify, or delete which information AutoFill uses to complete a form, log in, or credit card. If you want to securely update your iCloud devices with the same information, you need to enable Keychains in iCloud Preferences.

Enable iCloud Keychains for Use on iCloud Devices

1. Click the **System Preferences** icon on the Dock, and then click the **iCloud** icon.

2. Select the **Keychain** check box to turn on iCloud Keychain.

3. Click the **Close** button.

See Also

See "Filling Out Forms on the Web" on page 250 for more information on using AutoFill on websites using Safari.

Credit Cards for AutoFill

1 Open Safari.

2 Click the **Safari** menu, click **Preferences**, and then click **AutoFill**.

3 Select the **Credit Card** check box.

4 Click **Edit**.

5 To add a credit card, click **Add**, enter the descriptive title, card number, expiration date, and cardholder; press Tab to move between fields.

6 To remove a credit card, select it, and then click **Remove**.

7 Click **Done**.

8 Click the **Close** button, and then quit Safari.

Passwords for AutoFill

1 Open Safari.

2 Click the **Safari** menu, click **Preferences**, and then click **Passwords**.

3 Select the **AutoFill user names and passwords** check box.

4 To show passwords, select the **Show passwords for selected websites** check box, enter your Apple ID password, click **OK**, and then select a website.

5 Select or clear the **Allow AutoFill even for websites that request passwords not be saved** check box.

6 To remove a password, select it, and then click **Remove**.

7 Click the **Close** button, and then quit Safari.

Using AutoFill with iCloud Keychain

Remembering your passwords can be a real pain. With iCloud Keychain, you don't have to. iCloud Keychain (**New!**) stores your website user names and passwords only on your Mac and updates them using iCloud to your approved devices using using AES 256-bit encryption, so they are safe and sound. When you need them, iCloud Keychain automatically fills them in for you. You don't have to remember it or type it in. When you need to come up with a new password for a website, Password Generator suggests a unique, hard-to-guest password. If you use the suggestion, iCloud Keychain saves it. If you add your own password, Safari asks you to save it in iCloud Keychain. iCloud Keychain also works with credit card information, so checking out after a purchase is a snap. All you need to enter is your card's security code.

AutoFill Passwords or Credit Cards

1 Open Safari.

2 Navigate to website with places to enter a password or credit card.

3 When you click in a field with a password, AutoFill automatically filled in. If a password is not available, Password Generator provides a secure suggested password.

If you select the suggestion, it inserts the password and adds it to Passwords preferences in Safari and to iCloud in Keychains.

If you don't use the suggested password and type your own, an alert appears asking you want to add the password to keychain. Click **Update Password** or **Not Now**.

4 When you click in a field for a credit card, AutoFill provides a list of credit cards (provided in AutoFill Preferences). Click the credit card you want, and then enter the card's security code as needed.

5 When you're done, quit Safari.

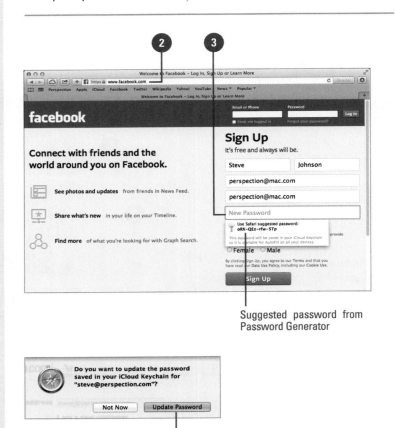

Suggested password from Password Generator

Add or updates password in Keychain

Managing Files Using a Network

Introduction

Networks are interesting systems. Not too many years ago, a network was defined as two or more computers, connected together by physical cables or telephone lines. They were slow, and they went down (crashed) as much as they were up. The word, network, could bring fear to the hearts of even the stoutest computer system managers. Today, networks are rock solid and reliable. The web can be defined as one huge network of interconnected computers around the world.

Networks connect more than computers; they work with tablets, cell phones, televisions, and even wristwatches. And no longer do networks require physical cables. If your computer is equipped with a wireless port, you can connect to the Internet and surf the web or even check your e-mail, from most major airports and hotel lobbies, without plugging your computer into anything.

In addition, the speed of today's networks allows us to move massive amounts of information, and even conduct real-time video-conferences. Mac computers were born to network, even when networking was a difficult proposition, the minds at Apple were working hard to make it fast, easy, and secure; and with the release of OS X, the ability to set up a local network, or one that stretches around the world, is becoming easier and easier.

Using built-in systems, you can even configure a wireless network—using Wi-Fi or Bluetooth (wireless technologies). You can share files and information with other computers with ease and even set up protection (firewalls) to guard against unauthorized access or potential viruses. It's all made possible with a Mac, and the OS X operating system.

What You'll Do

Use Network Sharing Services

Set Up File Sharing

Share an Internet Connection

Configure an Internet Firewall

Set Up a Local Area Network

Set Up a Network Connection

Set Up for Different Network Connections

Set Up a Bluetooth Wireless Network

Move Items with Bluetooth

Set Bluetooth Preferences

Browse the Network with the Finder

Connect to Another Computer

Share Files Wirelessly with AirDrop

Control a Computer with Screen Sharing

Set Up Mac and Windows to Share Files

Connect from a Windows Computer

Connect to a Network Over the Internet

Explore Additional Utility Applications

Using Network Sharing Services

Sharing Services are a collection of options that allow you to define what your computer shares with other computers over a network. For example, if you want to share the printers on your computer with anyone else on the network, you would select the Printer Sharing service, or if you want to share files with other computers, you would select the File Sharing service. When you share files on a network, you need to tell other users your computer's Internet Protocol (IP) address or name. If your computer goes to sleep, you can continue to share its files with other computers and devices. If you're on a local network, you can use the .local hostname as an alternative to a network address. You can find and change your computer name in Sharing Preferences. To prevent accidental changes to your settings, click the Lock button, located in the bottom-left corner of the Sharing window. The next time you try to make changes, you'll be prompted for your Administrator's password.

Use Network Sharing Services

1. Click the **System Preferences** icon in the Dock, and then click the **Sharing** icon.

 Your computer's name appears at the top of the Sharing pane. The network location for this computer appears below the name.

2. To change your computer's name, modify the text in the Computer Name field.

3. Select or clear the check box next to any of the following network services to activate or disable it:

 ◆ **DVD or CD Sharing**. Select to allow users access the DVD or CD disc drive on your computer (Available only if you have a DVD or CD disc drive installed on your computer).

 ◆ **Screen Sharing**. Select to allow other users to access and control your computer.

 ◆ **File Sharing**. Select to allow other users to access this computer's Public folders.

 ◆ **Printer Sharing**. Select to allow other users to share this computer's printers.

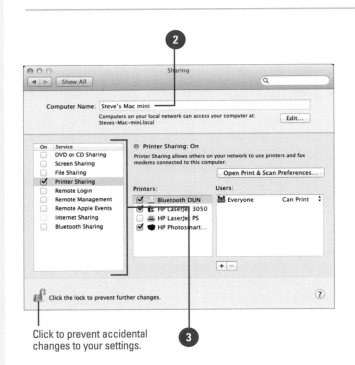

Click to prevent accidental changes to your settings.

- **Remote Login**. Select to allow others to login to this computer.

- **Remote Management**. Select to allow users access to this computer through the Apple Remote Desktop application.

- **Remote Apple Events**. Select to allow users to send Apple Events to this computer (optional password protection).

- **Internet Sharing**. Select to allow users access to the Internet through your connection.

- **Bluetooth Sharing**. Select to allow users access to connected Bluetooth wireless devices.

4 Select or specify the options you want for the selected network service; options vary depending on the service.

5 Click the **Close** button.

Did You Know?

You can change your computer's local name. Click the Edit button to change the name of your local computer. The local computer name is the name that displays with all the other computer names in a network listing.

For Your Information

Using Remote Disc

If you don't have an internal or external DVD or CD disc drive—such as Apple USB SuperDrive or MacBook Air SuperDrive—on your Mac, such as a MacBook Air, you can use a DVD or CD shared from another computer's disc drive on the network. On the Mac with the disc drive, open the Sharing pane in System Preferences, select the DVD or CD Sharing check box, select or clear the Ask Me Before Allowing Others To Use My DVD Drive check box, and then click the Close button. Insert the disc that you want to share in the DVD or CD disc drive. On the Mac without a disc drive, open a Finder window and then select Remote Disc under Devices in the Sidebar. Double-click the computer's icon and click Connect. If prompted, click Ask to use. On the computer sharing its disc drive, click Accept.

In addition to sharing the disc drive on a Mac, you can also share a disc drive from a Windows PC on a network. On the Windows PC, download and install the DVD or CD Sharing Update 1.0 for Windows from the Apple website. In the Control Panel, click Hardware and Sound, click DVD or CD Sharing Options, and then select the options you want to enable it.

Setting Up File Sharing

Whenever you set up a network, regardless of the type, you'll have to configure your computer to communicate with the network. Mac computers are big on security, and they won't let your computer talk to any other computer unless you give the other computers permission. Permission involves setting up file sharing options, and then creating accounts with specific user names, passwords, and permissions.

Set Up File Sharing and Permissions

1. Click the **System Preferences** icon in the Dock, and then click the **Sharing** icon.

2. Select the **File Sharing** check box.

3. Select the shared folder you want to set permissions.

 ◆ To add a shared folder to the list, click the **Add** (+) button, select the folder, and then click **Add**.

4. Select the user you want to change permissions.

 ◆ To add a user to the list, click the **Add** (+) button, select a user from your Contacts, and then click **Add**.

5. Use the pop-ups to the right of the user name to set any of the following permissions:

 ◆ **Read & Write.**

 ◆ **Read Only.**

 ◆ **Write Only (Drop Box).**

 ◆ **No Access.**

6. Click the **Close** button.

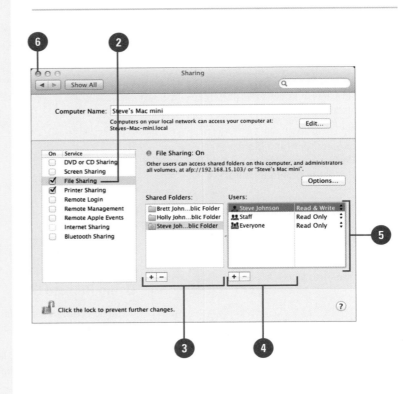

For Your Information

Creating Privileges for Users and Groups

You can decide who gets to go where and do what. There are four levels of access—Read & Write (allows user to access and change the file), Read Only (allows user to access the file, but not make changes), Write Only (Drop Box), and No Access. The levels are pretty self-explanatory; however, if you give someone Read & Write privileges, you're giving them full control over the file. For example, someone could open a text document and basically erase the contents of the letter or completely rewrite it.

Set Advanced File Sharing Options

① Click the **System Preferences** icon in the Dock, and then click the **Sharing** icon.

② Select the **File Sharing** service; the option doesn't have to be turned on (checked).

③ Click **Options**.

④ Select from the following options:

◆ **Share files and folders using SMB.** Select to share files with Microsoft Windows computers. Select the user accounts you want to use, and type a password upon request.

◆ **Share files and folders using AFP.** Select to share files with Mac computers using AFP (Apple Filing Protocol).

⑤ Click **Done**.

⑥ Click the **Close** button.

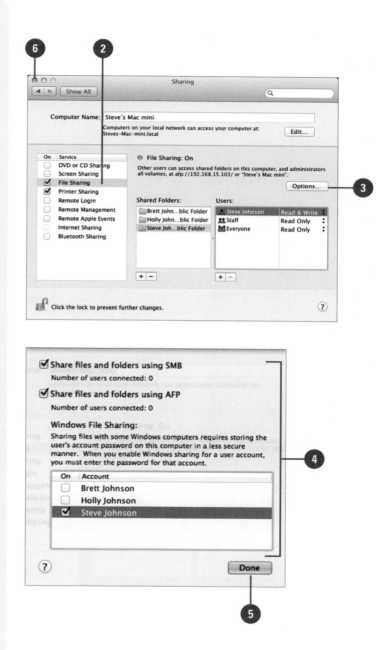

Sharing an Internet Connection

If you have an always-on Internet connection, such as a cable modem or DSL, you can share that connection with all the other people in your network in two ways: purchase a router and gate everyone into the connection, or use the built-in Internet Sharing (it's free). The one requirement is that Internet Sharing must be activated on the Mac that's connected to the Internet.

Share an Internet Connection

1. Click the **System Preferences** icon in the Dock, and then click the **Sharing** icon.

2. Select **Internet Sharing**.

3. Click the **Share Your Connection From** pop-up, and then select the method used for sharing.

4. Check Ports that other computers are using.

5. Select the **Internet Sharing** check box.

6. Click **Start**.

 IMPORTANT *If the Internet computer is shut down or in Sleep mode, the other network users won't be able to access the Internet.*

7. Click the **Close** button.

Configuring an Internet Firewall

If you're using a broadband Internet connection (always on), it's possible that a hacker could gain entrance to your system without your knowledge, and do some extensive damage or make off with your secret recipe for beef paprikash. Fortunately, OS X comes equipped with Firewall protection. A **Firewall** is a gatekeeper that in essence, stands guard over your computer; keeping it safe from all attackers. If vandals try to gain entrance to your computer, the Firewall attempts to shut them out. While no Firewall provides perfect protection from all Internet attacks, you can probably sleep soundly, knowing you have one of the most sophisticated protection systems on the market today.

Configure an Internet Firewall

1. Click the **System Preferences** icon in the Dock, and then click the **Security & Privacy** icon.

2. Click the **Firewall** tab.

3. Click **Turn On Firewall** to enable firewall settings or click **Turn Off Firewall** to disable it.

4. To set specific firewall settings, click **Firewall Options**, set the options you want, and then click **OK**.

 - ◆ **Block all incoming connections.** Select to block all incoming connections.

 - ◆ Click the **Add** (+) and **Remove** (-) button to modify the applications list of allowable incoming connections.

 - ◆ **Automatically allow signed software to receive incoming connections.** Select to allow an incoming connection for certified signed software.

 - ◆ **Enable stealth mode.** Select to provide no response from uninvited traffic.

5. Click the **Close** button.

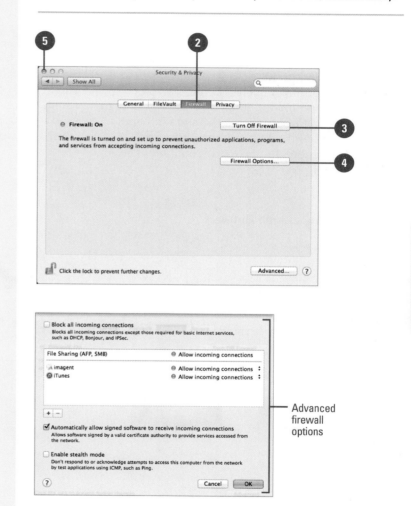

Advanced firewall options

Setting Up a Local Area Network

Almost any Mac computer comes out of the box network ready. Setting up a Local Area Network or LAN, is fairly straightforward. **Local Area Networks** are a group of local computers hooked together. For example, you could create a LAN for the computers in your office or create a LAN for your home computers. Mac even allows you to connect with Windows computers without having to purchase additional software. In fact, all of the software you'll need to create and maintain a LAN is built into Mac OS X. All you have to do is buy a couple of cables, connect two or more computers together, and you're ready to network. Let's complicate the situation and say that you're going to hook up more than two computers. In that case, you'll need an Ethernet cable for each computer and an Ethernet hub. A **hub** is a device that lets you connect multiple computers together. Every Mac sold comes with an Ethernet port. To set up a LAN, draw out the layout for the network to determine where the computers are and the distance between each unit. Purchase the cables (make sure they're long enough), and the Ethernet hub (you can purchase Ethernet supplies at almost any electronic store). Plug one end of the Ethernet cables into each of the computers, and the other end into the hub (make sure you plug the hub into an electrical outlet). Once the network is established, you'll need to set up the individual computers for file sharing and to recognize the LAN.

Local Area Network

Hub device

Setting Up a Network Connection

With OS X, you can connect to other computers, local and wide area networks and to the Internet. You can can connect to other computers or networks using an Ethernet, FireWire, or Wi-Fi connection. If you are connecting to the Internet, you can connect with a DSL or cable modem, a Wi-Fi wireless connection, or a telephone modem. After you set up the physical network hardware, you can use the Network pane in System Preferences to set up a network connection. To make the process easy, you can use the Network Setup Assistant to walk you through the steps. If you're having problems with a network, you can also use the Network Setup Assistant to help you fix the problem.

Set Up a Network

1. Click the **System Preferences** icon in the Dock, and then click the **Network** icon.

2. Click **Assist Me**.

3. Click **Assistant**.

 - **Diagnostics.** If you're having problems with a network connection, click **Diagnostics**, and the follow the instructions.

4. Type a location name, such as Home or Work, and then click **Continue**.

5. Click the option with the network connection you want to make.

6. Click **Continue**.

7. Enter network specific information for the selected network, and then click **Continue**; the requested information varies depending on the selected network.

8. Click **Done**.

Click for diagnostics

See Also

See "Setting Up an Ethernet Connection" on page 231 or "Setting Up a Wireless Connection" on page 232 for information on manually setting up networks.

Setting Up for Different Network Connections

If you connect to networks and the Internet in different ways, you can save network connects to suit your needs. For example, you connect to your network at home with a wireless Wi-Fi connection and your network at the office with an Ethernet connection. You can save different network configurations for different purposes, so you can optimize your network connections. When you have multiple network connections, OS X tries to connect in the order provided in Network Preferences. You can change the network connection order and save the network connection as a new location, so you only need to do this once. The default location, Automatic, provides setting for each of your computer's network services, including Ethernet, Wi-Fi, or a dial-up modem.

Set Up or Modify Different Networks Connections

1. Click the **System Preferences** icon in the Dock, and then click the **Network** icon.

2. Use the following methods to work with your connections:

 ◆ **Edit a Location.** Click the Location pop-up, and then select the location you want to modify.

 ◆ **Create a Location.** Click the **Location** pop-up, click **Edit Location**, click the **Add** (+) button, type a name, and then click **Done**.

 ◆ **Remove, Rename or Duplicate.** Use the Edit Location dialog to delete, rename or duplicate a network location.

3. To change the connection priority, click the **Actions** button, click **Set Service Order**, drag the network service icons to the positions you want, and then click **OK**.

4. To remove a network connection, click the **Remove** (-) button.

5. To revert your changes, click the **Revert**.

6. Click the **Close** button.

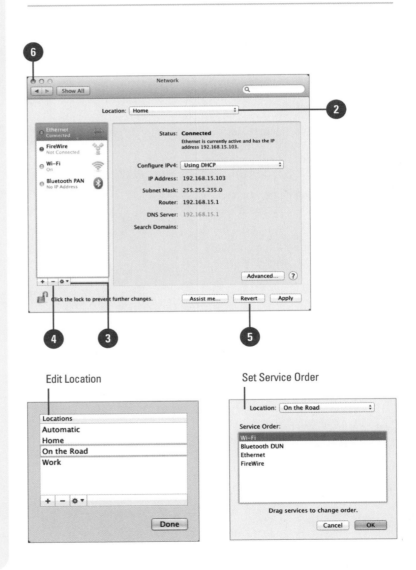

Edit Location

Set Service Order

Setting Up a Bluetooth Wireless Network

Mac computers have several methods for creating networks. There are standard networks using Ethernet cables, and hubs; there are wireless networks; and then there are Bluetooth networks, either personal area network (PAN) or dial-up network (DUN). **Bluetooth** technology is more than a network, it is a wireless technology that lets you transmit files and data to any other Bluetooth equipped device or over the Internet for communicating among devices, including cell phones and tablets. For example, you could use Bluetooth to sync to your Bluetooth mobile device, or even use your Contacts, and Bluetooth to automatically dial your Bluetooth cell phone. If you really want to throw away the cables, Apple makes a Bluetooth enabled keyboard and mouse. Bluetooth uses radio signals to communicate with any other Bluetooth device, up to a maximum range of thirty feet. Think of it this way, any Bluetooth device can communicate with any other Bluetooth device, if they are both turned on and within thirty feet of each other. And setup is a breeze with the Bluetooth Setup Assistant. You

Set Up a Bluetooth Wireless Network

1. Click the **System Preferences** icon in the Dock, and then click the **Networ**k icon.

2. Select Bluetooth in the list.

 ◆ If Bluetooth is not available, click the **Add** (+) button, select **Bluetooth DUN** or **Bluetooth PAN**, and then click **Create**.

3. Turn on the Bluetooth device and place it within 30 feet of your computer.

4. Click **Set Up Bluetooth Device**.

5. In the Bluetooth Setup Assistant, click **Continue**, and the step through the assistant specifying the device type and passkey to pair the device and the computer.

 The Bluetooth Preferences dialog appears.

6. To delete a pairing, select it, and then click the **Delete** (-) button.

7. Click the **Close** button.

Moving Items with Bluetooth

Once you've set up your Bluetooth devices, it's a simple matter to transfer files to the Bluetooth device. For example, you have a tablet device and you want to move a text file from your computer to the device. The process of moving a file from your computer to your Bluetooth device is the same; however, since each Bluetooth device is different, the process of moving a file from the device to your computer is different for each device. Consult your owner's manual for information on how to move information to your computer, from the Bluetooth device.

Move Items with Bluetooth

1. Turn on the device and place it within 30 feet of your computer.

2. Click the **Launchpad** icon in the Dock, click the **Other** folder, and then click the **Bluetooth File Exchange** icon.

3. Select the file you want to send.

4. Click **Send**.

5. Select the Bluetooth device from the available list.

6. Click **Send**.

7. Click the **Close** button.

Setting Bluetooth Preferences

After you set up a Bluetooth wireless network on your computer, you can use System Preferences to control how to send and receive files between your computer and other Bluetooth devices. You can use the Settings tab to make your Mac discoverable by other Bluetooth devices and specify whether you want to require a password. The File Exchange tab allows you to indicate what happens when someone sends you a document: accept it, refuse it, or ask what to do. Finally, the Devices tab lets you set up the use of other Bluetooth devices; use pairing to set passwords for security purposes.

Set Bluetooth Preferences

1. Click the **System Preferences** icon in the Dock, and then click the **Bluetooth** icon.

2. Select or clear the check boxes you want:

 ◆ **Bluetooth Power.**

 ◆ **Discoverable.**

3. To set the following advanced options, click **Advanced**, and the click **OK**.

 ◆ **Open Bluetooth Setup Assistant at startup if no keyboard is detected.**

 ◆ **Open Bluetooth Setup Assistant at startup if no mouse or trackpad is detected.**

 ◆ **Allow Bluetooth devices to wake this computer.**

 ◆ **Reject incoming audio requests.**

4. To use the Bluetooth Status menu, select the **Show Bluetooth Status in the menu bar** check box.

5. Click the **Close** button.

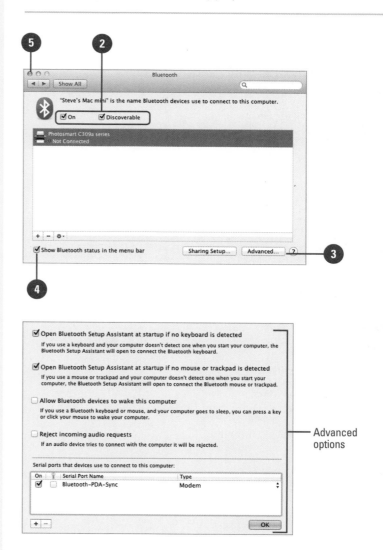

Advanced options

Browsing the Network with the Finder

The Finder serves as a focused network browser application. From the Go menu, you can access the Network window, which displays all the computers available on your network. If you're not sure what is available, this is the place to browse the network. You can also access a network from the Sidebar, which displays all shared computers. After you display a networked computer, you can use all the find tools available on your Mac to locate files. For example, you're looking for a file with a specific name. You've used the Finder application, and checked on your machine, but can't seem to find it. The other option is that it's on your co-workers computer. The good news is that with the Finder application, not only can you search your computer; you can search any other computer on the network.

Browse All Networks with the Finder

1. In Finder, click the **Go** menu, and then click **Network**.

2. Double-click a network computer to browse its contents.

Browse a Specific Network with the Finder

1. Open a Finder window.

2. Click the Shared triangle to display available networks, if necessary.

3. Select the network you want to view.

4. Double-click a folder to browse its contents.

Search for Files in a Network

1. Login to another computer on the network.

2. Open the Finder window.

3. Select the network in which you want to search in the Sidebar under Shared.

4. In the Search field, type the search criteria.

5. In the Search bar, select the network name.

Access Networks from the Finder Sidebar

1. Click the **Finder** menu, and then click **Preferences**.

2. Click **Sidebar**.

3. Select the check boxes under Shared that you want to display:

 ◆ **Back to My Mac**

 ◆ **Connected Servers**

 ◆ **Bonjour Computers**

4. Click the **Close** button.

Connecting to Another Computer

Once you've connected several computers together into a network, and configured your computer for file sharing, the next step is to begin communicating. In order to communicate with another computer, you'll need access to a user account. Typically a user account defines you with a specific name, password, and permissions. Once you log into the other computer, you'll be able to access the areas (permissions) granted to you by the Systems Administrator.

Connect to Another Computer

1. Turn on all the computers.

2. Click the **Go** menu, and then click **Connect To Server**.

3. Connect using one of the following methods:

 ◆ Click **Browse**, and then double-click on one of the available server icons.

 ◆ Type the computer's Server Address, and then click **Connect**.

 ◆ **Windows (SMB/CIFS).** Example: *smb://DNSname/sharename; smb://IPaddress/sharename*

 ◆ **Macintosh (AFP).** Example: *afp://ComputerName.CompanyName.com*

 ◆ **FTP.** Example: *ftp://user@DNSname; ftp://DNSname; ftp://user:password@DNSname*

 ◆ **NFS.** Example: *nfs://DNSname/pathname*

 ◆ Click the **Recent Servers** button, and then select a server address from the list of available options.

4. Type your Name and Password.

5. Click **Connect**.

Type Server Address Recent Servers

6 Select the area of the other computer you want to access.

7 Click **OK**.

IMPORTANT *The other computer now functions and acts as a hard drive on your computer.*

8 Click the network computer icon in the Sidebar to display its contents.

9 Work with your computer; drag files from your computer to the networked computer or vice versa.

Did You Know?

You can identify the IP (Internet Protocol) address of your computer. Click the Apple menu, and then click System Preferences. Click Network, and then select the network connection in the list. The current IP address is displayed next to the network connection when available.

Click to connect as a different user

Sharing Files or Folders with Others

OS X maintains a set of personal folders and options for everyone on your computer to make sure the contents remain private, unless you decide to share the contents with others. If you want the other users on your computer, or those connected to your computer over a network to have access to files, you can place those files in the Shared folder that each user can access. The Shared folder is located in the Users folder. It is set up with Read & Write permissions so that all users can open the files in this folder and copy files to the folder. If you want to share files with a specific user on your computer, you can use their Public folder. A Public folder is set up with Read Only permissions that allow others to see and copy its contents, but not change it. Each Public folder is located in the users' Home folder and also contains a Drop Box folder, which is set up with tighter permissions so other people can copy files to a Drop Box, but they cannot see its contents.

Share Files in the Shared Folder or a Public Folder

1. Open the drive or folder containing the files or folders you want to share.

2. Select the files or folders you want to share.

3. Click the **Edit** menu, and then click **Copy** or press ⌘+C to copy.

4. Click the **Go** menu, click **Computer**, and then double-click the **Hard Disk** icon for your computer.

5. Double-click the **Users** folder.

6. Open the folder you want to use to share files:

 ◆ **Shared folder**. Double-click the Shared folder.

 ◆ **Public folder**. Double-click the user name, and then double-click the Public folder.

7. Click the **Edit** menu, and then click **Paste** or press ⌘+V to paste.

8. To use the Drop Box folder in a Public folder, drag the files and folder onto the Drop Box folder.

Users folder Shared folder for the computer.

Public folder resides in each users folder.

Sharing Files Wirelessly with AirDrop

AirDrop allows you to quickly send files wirelessly to anyone around you. AirDrop doesn't require any setup, passwords, or preferences to change. It's as simple as dragging and dropping. AirDrop automatically for people nearby within about 30 feet of you who are using AirDrop. Simply, click the AirDrop icon in the Sidebar of a Finder window. AirDrop displays nearby users with their contact pictures and computer names in the AirDrop window. To share a file with someone, simply drag it to that person's picture in the AirDrop window. Once the person accepts the file, it's transferred directly to their Downloads folder. AirDrop creates a firewall between you and the person you are sharing a file with as a safety precaution to prevent anyone from accessing your computer. AirDrop uses TLS encryption for secure transfers. When you're done, simply close the Finder window or click outside AirDrop, which also makes your Mac no longer visible to others. AirDrop uses Wi-Fi to transfer files, so you need to make sure it's enabled in Network preferences.

Share Files with AirDrop

1. In a Finder window, click **AirDrop** in the Sidebar.

 The people nearby your computer appear in the AirDrop window.

2. Open another Finder window with the files you want to send.

3. Drag the file you want to send to the person's picture.

4. Click **Send**.

 ◆ On the other person's computer, click **Save and Open**, **Decline**, or **Save**. Upon acceptance, the file is downloaded to their the Downloads folder.

5. To cancel an incoming transfer, open the Downloads stack in the Dock, and then click the **Close** button (x) in the icon.

Did You Know?

You can use Spotlight with AirDrop.
From the Spotlight menu, you can drag items to AirDrop.

Drag file to contact icon in AirDrop

Controlling a Computer with Screen Sharing

You can share your computer with other users. In fact, you can let other users display your screen on their monitor in full screen view and control your computer as if they were sitting in front of it. If a friend needs assistance, you can use screen sharing to take control and provide online help. You can control a Mac with any user account without interrupting someone using another user account. You can use an Apple ID to access another computer with OS X; simply add their Apple ID to the list of authorized users and they can log in with their credentials. While you control another computer, you can observe only or have full access to everything on the machine and copy files between the computer by simply dragging. The Sharing toolbar is available with a variety of tools, such as screen resolution, Clipboard access and screen capture. Before you can use screen sharing, you need to enable the option in Sharing Preferences.

Set Permissions for Screen Sharing

1. Click the **System Preferences** icon in the Dock, and then click the **Sharing** icon.

2. Select the **Screen Sharing** check box.

 TROUBLE? *If Remote Management is already selected, you don't need to select Screen Sharing. Remote Management includes screen sharing.*

3. Select from the following screen sharing options:

 ◆ **All users**. Select to allow all users to access and control your computer.

 ◆ **Only these users**. Select to allow specific users access to access and control your computer. Click the **Add** (+) button and then select the users you want from your Contacts.

4. To set access options, click **Computer Settings**, select the check box settings you want for access permission, and then click **OK**.

5. Click the **Close** button.

Computer settings

Share Computer's Screen

1. Enable screen sharing on the computer you want to share in Sharing Preferences.

2. Click the Mac computer in the Sidebar under Shared.

3. Click **Share Screen**.

4. Select a sharing option, and specify your username and password as needed.

 ◆ **By asking for permission.** Asks permission from the current user to share their screen.

 ◆ **As a registered user.** Connects using a login name and password; if the remote computer is set to the *Only these users* option, the login name needs to be in the list.

 ◆ **Using an Apple ID.** Uses an authorized Apple ID in Users & Groups preferences to share their screen.

5. Click **Connect**.

 The screen for the other computer appears in the sharing viewer.

6. Use your Mac computer as if you were in front of it.

 ◆ **Show/Hide toolbar.** Click the **View** menu, and then click **Show Toolbar** or **Hide Toolbar**.

 ◆ **Switch between Control and Observe mode.** Click toggle button on toolbar.

 ◆ **Capture screen to file.** Click button on toolbar.

 ◆ **Preferences.** Click the **Screen Sharing** menu, and then click **Preferences**.

7. When you're done, click **Connection** menu, and then click **Close**.

Full Screen button

Shared screen Screen Sharing app icon

Setting Up Mac and Windows to Share Files

Before you can share files between Macintosh and Windows computers, you need to set up file sharing options. When you enable file sharing on a Mac computer to share files with Windows users, OS X uses the Samba server software to provide SMB/CIFS file services. Now Windows users can connect to a Mac computer using normal network services. After you share a folder on a Windows computer, you can share files with Mac users. You may need to disable the Internet Connection Firewall or make sure the TCP port 445 is open. To connect to the Windows computer, users need the network address, workgroup name, and the user name and password for the shared folder.

Set Up a Mac to Share Files with Windows

1. Click the **System Preferences** icon in the Dock, and then click the **Sharing** icon.

2. Select the **File Sharing** check box.

3. Click **Options**.

4. Select the **Share files and folders using SMB** check box.

5. Select the check boxes to enable a user account for sharing.

6. Type a password, and then click **OK**.

7. Click **Done**.

8. Provide the address of your computer displayed in the Sharing pane to Windows users you want to share your computer.

9. Click the **Close** button.

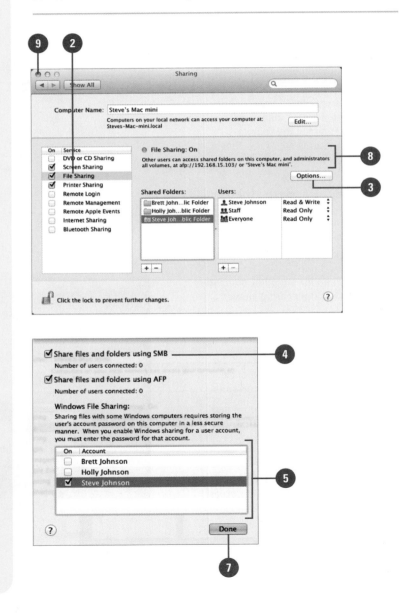

Connecting from a Windows Computer

After you enable File Sharing in the Sharing Services area of the System Preferences, Windows computers (versions 8, 7, Vista, or XP) can connect to your computer. Most networks consist of multiple types of computers and operating systems. For Windows, the Network window lets you view the entire network, including servers, domains, and workgroups. For a Windows computer on your immediate network, you can browse the network to access the Mac computer.

Connect from a Windows Computer on a Local Network

1. Display the Networks connected to your computer.

 ◆ **Windows 8.** Click the **Desktop** tile, click the **File Explorer** icon on the taskbar, and then click **Network** in the Navigation pane.

 ◆ **Windows 7.** Click the **Start** button, click **Computer**, and then click **Network** in the Navigation pane.

 ◆ **Windows Vista.** Click the **Start** button, and then click **Network**.

 ◆ **Windows XP.** Click the **Start** button, click **My Network Places**, click **View Workgroup Computers**, and then navigate to the Mac computer.

 TROUBLE? *For those using different versions of Windows, consult the online help system for specific instructions.*

2. Double-click the Mac Computer icon to display the shared files, folders, and devices on the computer. If necessary, type a user name and password for the Mac account.

3. Double-click a Mac drive or shared folder.

4. When you're done, click the **Close** button.

Windows 8

Login to the Mac

Connecting to a Network Over the Internet

You can create a VPN (Virtual Private Network) connection to securely connect your computer to a network over the Internet. The computer you want to connect to must support a VPN and Internet connection. Before you create a connection, you need to have the server or IP address of the VPN computer. The first time you setup a VPN, you need to select a VPN protocol, either L2TP Over IPSec or PPTP. Use L2TP (Layer Two Tunneling Protocol) over IPSec (Internet Protocol Security), where security is a concern between your computer and Windows XP, or use PPTP (Point-to-Point Tunneling Protocol) where security issues are not as much a problem, but where backward compatibility with older systems is a concern. You can use the Show VPN Status menu to easily connect and disconnect from the VPN, and show connection information. If you want to create a private connection within your physical network, you can create a VLAN (Virtual Local Area Network).

Create a VPN Connection

1. Click the **System Preferences** icon in the Dock, and then click the **Network** icon.

2. Click the **Add** (+) button.

3. Click the **Interface** pop-up, and then click **VPN**.

4. Click the **VPN Type** pop-up, and then click **L2TP Over IPSec** or **PPTP**.

5. Type a name for the connection.

6. Click **Create**.

7. Type the Server Address and Account Name.

8. Click **Authentication Settings** to specify a password or other credentials.

9. To display the modem menu for easy connection access, select the **Show VPN Status In Menu Bar** check box.

10. Click **Connect** to start a VPN connection.

11. When you're done, click the **Close** button, and then save the configuration, if necessary.

Create a VLAN Connection

1. Click the **System Preferences** icon in the Dock, and then click the **Network** icon.

2. Click the **Actions** button, and then click **Manage Virtual Interfaces**.

3. Click the **Add** (+) button, and then click **New VLAN**.

4. Type a name for the VLAN connection.

5. Click the **Interface** pop-up, and then click a network connection.

6. Click **Create**.

7. Click **Done**.

8. Specify any settings provided for the network, such as IP Address, Subnet Mask, and Router, and DNS Servers.

 ◆ If you want assistance, click **Assist Me**, and then follow the instructions.

9. When you're done, click the **Close** button, and then save the configuration, if necessary.

See Also

See "Setting Up an Ethernet Connection" on page 231 for information on setting up a LAN connection.

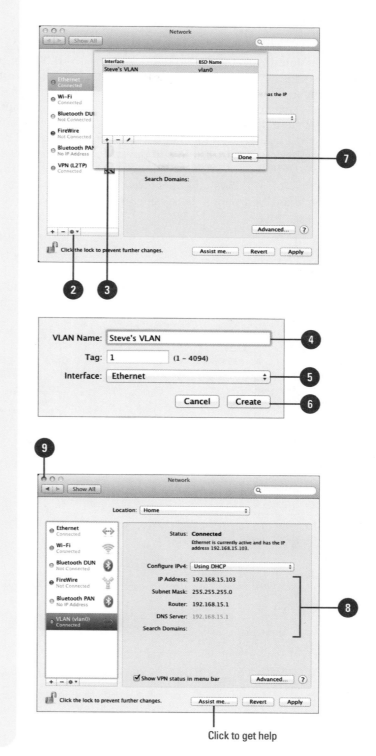

Click to get help

Exploring Additional Utility Applications

The Utilities folder, located within the Applications folder, is host to several dozen applications and utilities that help you manage the daily activities with running your Mac computer system, internet and wireless connections, and troubleshooting. It's possible that you might go your entire life and never access some of the more obscure utilities located in this folder; however you should explore the available options, because some of them are useful.

Network Utility

The Network Utility holds information on web sites, and offers the ability to perform standard Internet services such as: Info, NetStat,

Ping, Finger, and Whois. Info displays your IP (Internet Protocol) address and other network information. NetStat displays technical information about your network. Ping allows you to test an Internet connection. Finger allows you to find out about an e-mail address, while Whois allows you to find out about a domain. When you're experiencing problems with your service, it's possible that a service technician may ask you some of this information.

AirPort Utility

The AirPort Utility lets you monitor the connections within an existing AirPort/Wi-Fi network. In addition, you can use the utility to manually setup new connections.

Info

NetStat

Ping

Whois

Maintaining Your Computer

Introduction

Once you've bought your Mac computer, installed the operating system and all your apps, it's important to be able to keep all that software up-to-date; especially the operating system software. With the consistent updates that Apple is making to the operating system, OS X helps you keep all the software up-to-date with the click of a button.

In addition, loss of data can be a tragic occurrence, so OS X lets you archive or copy data from your computer to an external disk (just remember to keep your backups offsite). It also helps you monitor activities on your system, see who is currently using your computer, and how much processing power each program is using. This gives you the ability to fine-tune your system for maximum performance. If your system seems to be slowing down, or you're experiencing more crashes than usual (a rare occurrence on a Mac), you can use programs to optimize and repair day-to-day problems, and keep your system in tiptop shape.

Remember that maintaining your computer requires more on your part than the launching of a couple of programs. The Mac computer comes with several internal fans that help keep the inner workings cool; however, those fans also pull in dust. You should open your computer and vacuum out the interior about once a year, and dust the exterior surface about once a month. In addition, make sure the computer has enough room around it for air to circulate. Finally, make sure all the cables you have strung from the computer to all your peripherals are out of harms way, and in good condition. In past years, attempting to maintain your computer system was a challenge; however, today it's easy to keep things running smoothly.

Downloading and Updating Software

In addition to the software you install from the App Store, OS X comes with literally dozens of system software apps—everything from disk repair utilities to image-capture apps. As developers make enhancements and changes to your software, it's important to keep up with all the updates and fixes. If you install an app from the App Store, you can use the Updates section to install updates individually or all at once; you can even install updates later or send you a reminder (**New!**). The App Store can automatically download app updates for you, so they are ready to be installed. If you installed an app from a disc or separate installer program (downloaded from web), you can get updates by using an Updates command within the app (check the software for specifics), or by running a separate update program (downloaded from web).

Download and Update Software Apps

1. Click the **Apple** menu, and then click **Software Update**.

 ◆ **Notification.** If an Updates Available notification appears, click **Restart** or **Later** (**New!**). Point to Later to display an arrow for more options (*step 3*).

 The App Store opens, and then checks for any updates.

2. Click the **More** link to find out more about an update.

3. Click the **Update All** button to install all the updates or click individual **Update** buttons.

 ◆ **Options.** Click the **Update All** button arrow (**New!**), and then click **Install Now**, **Try in an Hour**, **Try Tonight**, or **Remind Me Tomorrow**.

4. If prompted, type your Administrator name and password, and then click **OK**.

5. If your computer needs to restart, click **Download & Restart** or **Not Now**.

 OS X begins installing the software. When it's done, the item doesn't appear in Updates.

6. If you want to pause an update, click the **Pause** button.

Installing update

For Your Information

Uninstalling Software Apps

When you purchase an app from the App Store, you can uninstall it from the Launchpad. Click the Launchpad icon in the Dock, hold down the app's icon until all the icons wiggle, and then click an app's Delete button (x). If an app doesn't have a Delete button, it can't be uninstalled, such as apps that come with OS X. For other apps, you can uninstall it by using an Uninstall program (if available from the developer) or dragging the app from the Applications folder to the Trash icon in the Dock, and then empty it.

Automating Software Updates

Trying to keep up with all your software updates in the App Store use to be a hassle, but not any more. Not only does OS X let you quickly download and install all your operating system software and app (**New!**) updates; it lets you automate the process. When you automate software updates, you can check for and download OS X and app updates in the background, so it doesn't interrupt your workflow. With the ability not only to update your software, but also to automate the entire process, there is no longer any excuse for not having up-to-date software. If you purchase apps on other Macs, you can have OS X automatically download them to your current Mac using your Apple ID and the App Store.

Automate Software Updates in the App Store

1. Click the **System Preferences** icon in the Dock, and then click the **App Store** icon (**New!**).

2. Select the **Automatically check for updates** check box.

 ◆ **Manual Update.** Clear the Automatically check for updates check box, and then manually check for updates in the App Store under Updates.

3. To download new updates, select the **Download newly available updates in the background** check box.

4. To install app updates, select the **Install app updates** check box (**New!**).

5. To install OS X updates, select the **Install system data files and security updates** check box.

6. Select or clear the **Automatically download apps purchased on other Macs** check box.

7. To display all the updates you've currently installed in the App Store, click the **Show Updates**.

8. Click the **Close** button.

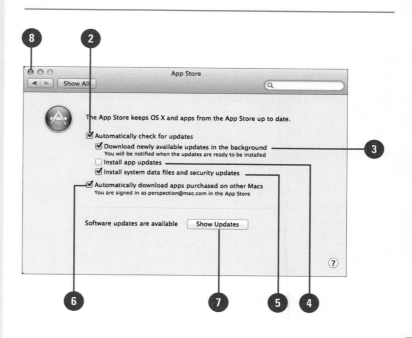

Opening Compressed Files

Not all compressed file formats are self-extracting. For those files you'll need a program capable of uncompressing (extracting) the files. Stuffit Expander is a universal utility that helps you open up all those pesky compressed files that other users and companies send you. The latest version, opens almost any compressed format including: .sit, .sea, .hqx, and, .bin. In addition, Stuffit can open files compressed using WinZip (Windows compression utility), and the UNIX formats: .tar, .gzip, and .bzip. For example, you receive a WinZip file from your parents showing pictures of their trip to Hawaii or you download the latest software patch for your word-processing program, and it came in the .hqz format. With Stuffit Expander, you're only seconds away from viewing those pictures and updating that word processor.

Open Compressed Files with Stuffit Expander

1 Open the **Applications** folder or the **Stuffit** folder to locate the Stuffit Expander.

2 Select a compressed file.

◆ You can also open the Stuffit Expander app, click the **File** menu, click **Expand**, select the compressed file, and then click **Open**.

3 Drag and drop the file over the **Stuffit Expander** icon.

4 Stuffit Expander uncompresses the file, and places it in the same location as the compressed file.

Did You Know?

The .dmg file format is self-extracting. A very popular format for OS X is the .dmg (disk image) format. When you double-click a .dmg file, it extracts the contents and creates a disk icon, which you can access and use just like any other Mac disk.

Mounted drive

Compressing and Uncompressing Files and Folders

You can compress files and folder in special files that compress the contents to decrease the size of the files they contain. Compressed folders are useful for reducing the file size of one or more large files, thus freeing disk space and reducing the time it takes to transfer files to another computer over the Internet or network. A compressed file is denoted by a ZIP icon. You can compress one or more files into a compressed file by using the Compress command on the File menu. When a file is compressed, a copy is used in the compression, and the original remains intact. You can uncompress, or extract, a file from the compressed folder by double-clicking the compressed file icon. The compressed files and folder are uncompressed into a folder called Archive.

Compress and Uncompress Files and Folders

1 Select a file, group of files, or a folder.

2 Click the **File** menu, and then click **Compress.**

Archive creates a zipped file with the same name as the original item.

3 To restore an archived zip, double-click its icon.

> **IMPORTANT** Remember that a back up of your data is your insurance of recovery after a disk crash or other catastrophic system failure. Always keep your backups offsite, or in a protected location, such as a fireproof safe. As tragic as a fire would be, the damage would be compounded if your backups were also destroyed.

See Also

See "Opening Compressed Files" on page 448 for information on opening compressed files with Stuffit Expander.

Uncompressed files · **3** · Compressed file

Using Application Services

Application Services are a OS X feature that lets you efficiently use content from one application to another application. Services are available on the Application menu in an application, such as TextEdit or Finder, based on the situation or in a shortcut (context) menu. For example, you could use the Services option to send selected text information in an e-mail, create a Twitter tweet, create an iTunes track, or make a sticky note in TextEdit. You can individually disable or enable each service in the Keyboard preferences. With Automator, you can now build your own services, making a repetitive task simple to use.

Use Application Services

1 Open an application.

2 Click the **Application** menu, and then point to **Services**.

3 Select from the available commands in the Services application you want.

Change Services Preferences

1 Click the **System Preferences** icon in the Dock, and then click the **Keyboard** icon.

2 Click the **Shortcuts** tab.

3 Click **Services** in the left column.

4 Select or clear the check boxes next to the services you do or don't want under the task type, such as Text, Internet, or Pictures.

5 Click the **Close** button.

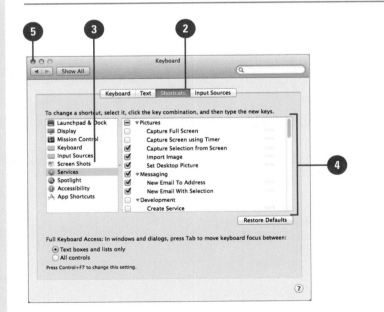

Understanding Disk File Systems

When you work on a computer, you're utilizing apps that are stored on the computer's hard drive. As you work, you're accessing and writing files back to the hard drive. For example, you open MS Word, create a document, and then save it using the name: MyLetter.doc.

OS X stores files and programs on your hard drive using a system of tracks and sectors; similar to a pie cut into equal triangular pieces. In addition, OS X divides the hard drive into logical file systems, which can help you organize your files and projects.

When you open your hard drive, you'll see that OS X has created several folders to organize your creative efforts. There's a folder for apps, and a folder for the System files—there's even a folder that contains all the users for the particular computer, and another for your documents.

Typically, when you load an app for the first time, you're asked to hold the app within the Applications folder. This gives OS X the ability to control the program, and even helps you when it comes time to check for updates. As you use your computer, you'll probably begin adding folders for your various projects. It's important that you create a disk file system that's well organized. Well organized file systems help you locate and retrieve files quicker and, if properly created, help you to move them from machine to machine. For example, you create a project folder for a major video project: everything that pertains to that project (video, audio, files, text, graphics), are all organized into folders within that one folder. When it come times to publish, move, or archive that information, all your files are conveniently organized in one location.

Tracks

Sectors

Organized contents with folders

File folder

Formatting and Copying a Disk

With the Disk Utility, you can format and erase a disk—securely or unsecurely—or make a disk copy. When you format and erase a disk, you're actually telling the Mac OS to delete the access information (pointers) to the files on the disk, but not the actual files themselves (unless you set a security option to securely and permanently overwrite them), and prepare it for use. The disk space is marked as free space, however the files remain on the disk until new data is written over them. As a result, the files can be recovered. When you copy a disk, you're creating a mirror copy of the original. This differs from dragging and dropping a file onto a disk icon, which places the new files in whatever space is available. When you use Disk Utility, it places the files in exactly the same tracks and sectors as the original.

Format and Erase a Disk

1. Click the **Launchpad** icon in the Dock, click the **Other** folder, and then click the **Disk Utility** icon.

2. Select the volume (disk) you want to format (not the startup drive).

3. Click the **Erase** tab.

4. Click the **Volume Format** pop-up, and then select the options:

 ◆ **Mac OS Extended (Journaled).** Uses the same HFS Plus filing system as Mac OS Extended, and keeps a journal of your activities. Journaling makes for shortened startup times, and helps in the event of a crash.

 ◆ **Mac OS Extended.** Formats the disk using HFS Plus filing system (helps to compress files and maximize file space).

 ◆ **UNIX File System.** Formats a disk for use on a UNIX system.

 ◆ **MS-DOS File System.** If available, formats a disk for use on a Windows (MS-DOS) system.

5. Type a Name for the disk.

6. To permanently erase, click **Security Options**, use the slider to choose how many times to write over the data, and then click **OK**.

7. Click **Erase**.

Warning message

Volume or disk statistics

Copy a Disk

1 Click the **Launchpad** icon in the Dock, click the **Other** folder, and then click the **Disk Utility** icon.

2 Click the **Restore** tab.

3 Drag a disk image into the Source input box (the disk to copy).

4 Drag a disk image from the Disk Volume column into the Destination input box (the disk to copy onto).

5 Click **Restore**.

6 Click the **Disk Utility** menu, and then click **Quit Disk Utility**.

Did You Know?

You can copy information from a disk over the Internet. Type the URL of the disk you want to restore from into the Source input box.

You can create a new disk image. Select a disk or folder icon in the Disk Volume column, and then click the New Image button.

You can write over disk space to permanently remove deleted files. In Disk Utility, select the disk or partition with the disk space you want to over write, click the Erase tab, click the Erase Free Space button, use the slider to specify how many times to write over the free space, and then click Erase Free Space. This command only erases files deleted by emptying the Trash; it doesn't erase any other files on your disk. If you see a message that indicates you're running out of disk space, you can ignore it. Note: the amount of free disk space won't change, because you are over writing already deleted files.

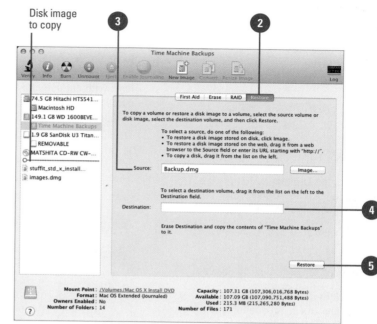

Disk image to copy

For Your Information

Freeing Up Disk Space

There are several ways to free up disk space on your hard drive. The most basic is to empty your Trash regularly. Besides the trash, you can also empty trash/delete in Mail, iPhoto, iMovie, and iTunes. If you keep a lot of old e-mail, you can archive it to another drive to back it up and save space. If you no longer use an app, you can copy it to an external drive or DVD, or remove it to the Trash; AppZapper is a good third-party utility to help with this. After you download and use a disk image (.dmg) file—typically stored in the Downloads folder—to expand an install app, you don't need it and can delete it to the Trash. To improve performance, web browsers store downloaded pages and files in a cache so they can be quickly re-used. You can clear the cache in the web browser to free up some space. If you don't use your system in other languages, you can remove all system and app localization files not used for your language; DeLocalizer and Monolingual are good third-party utilities for this. This does not remove the ability to read and type languages other than English. Other good free system maintenance utilities, like MainMenu and Onyx, can help clean up temporary files, system caches and logs.

Fixing Disk Problems

It's not unusual for a hard drive to experience problems. When problems occur on the main hard drive, it can produce lock ups and slower performance. Apple helps to solve this problem by letting you perform disk repairs to any drives with the exception of the start up drive. For example, you could use disk repair to fix problems on a damaged drive, or a secondary hard drive. Apple's Disk Utility locates and fixes problems with catalog and storage files. When information in these areas is damaged, it can cause trouble opening files and slowing down performance.

Fix Disk Problems

1. Click the **Launchpad** icon in the Dock, click the **Other** folder, and then click the **Disk Utility** icon.

2. Click the **First Aid** tab.

3. Select a non-startup volume (you cannot repair the startup drive).

4. Click **Repair Disk**. If Repair Disk Permission is not available, click **Verify Disk** first.

 IMPORTANT *You cannot repair the Startup volume. To perform a Repair Disk on the Startup volume, you'll have to reboot from a different disk.*

5. Repeat steps 3 and 4 until all your disks have been repaired.

 TIMESAVER *Apps such as Norton Utilities and Tech Tools can help to further enhance and optimize your hard drives, by performing a defrag, or by performing error checks to files not available with the Apple Disk Utility.*

6. Click the **Disk Utility** menu, and then click **Quit Disk Utility**.

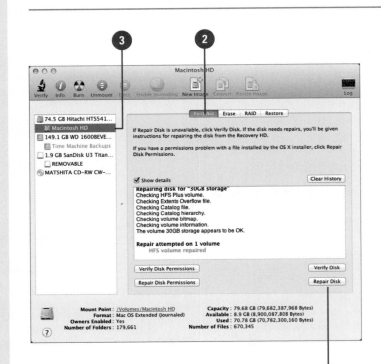

Fixing Disk Permission Problems

When OS X install system files onto your hard disk, it defines permission for each file for security purposes. Permission define whether an file can be read, written to, or executed. Permissions are initially set during installation, which includes a .bom (bill of materials) file that provides a list of all files and their permissions. If you or OS X has problems accessing one or more system files, you can use Repair Disk Permissions in the Disk Utility to correct file or folder permissions. Repair Disk Permissions uses the .bom file to verify and repair permission problems.

Fix Disk Permission Problems

1. Click the **Launchpad** icon in the Dock, click the **Other** folder, and then click the **Disk Utility** icon.

2. Click the **First Aid** tab.

3. Select the Startup volume from the available options.

4. Click **Repair Disk Permissions** (available only for volumes with Mac OS X installed). If Repair Disk Permission is not available, click **Verify Disk Permission** first.

 IMPORTANT *Disk Permissions are required by the operating system, and can become damaged. When they are damaged, normal operations become slower.*

5. Click the **Disk Utility** menu, and then click **Quit Disk Utility**.

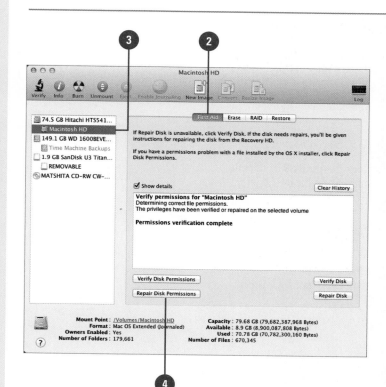

Erasing a CD or DVD Disc

If you want to reuse a CD-RW or DVD-RW disc, you need to erase it first, which you can do with Disk Utility. Before you start, there is one thing you need to know. You can't erase a standard CD or DVD that was a previously recorded CD-R or DVD-R disc. During the process, you have the option to select Quick Erase. When you select Quick Erase setting, the contents on the CD or DVD gets overwritten when new information is placed over it. If you don't select Quick Erase setting, the contents is overwritten with zeros to completely erase the CD or DVD, which takes longer to finish.

Erase a CD or DVD Disc

① Click the **Launchpad** icon in the Dock, click the **Other** folder, and then click the **Disk Utility** icon.

② Select the disc in the left column you want to erase.

③ Click the **Erase** tab.

④ Click the **Quickly** or **Completely** option.

⑤ Click **Erase**.

⑥ Click **Erase** to confirm you want to erase the CD.

⑦ Click the **Disk Utility** menu, and then click **Quit Disk Utility**.

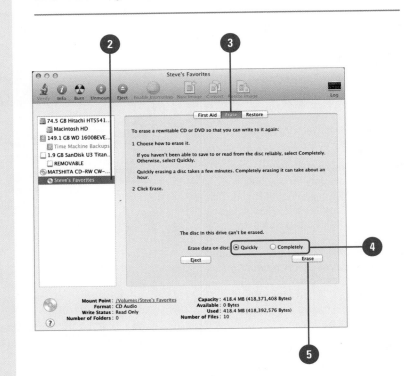

Migrating Information Between Macs

Instead of trying to re-create Mac settings manually from an old computer on a new Mac computer, you can use the Migration Assistant. With two connected computers, you can use the Migration Assistant to transfer important files and Mac settings from one computer to another. You can transfer information to a Mac from another Mac or PC on the same network, a backup disk, or another startup disk, or you can transfer information from a Mac to another Mac on the same network.The Migration Assistant can transfer user accounts, apps, network and computer settings, files, and volumes. For a PC, you can transfer documents, contacts, calendars, e-mail accounts, and photos. Before you can use the Migration Assistant, you need the administrator user name and password to gain access.

Use the Migration Assistant

1. Click the **Launchpad** icon in the Dock, click the **Other** folder, and then click the **Migration Assistant** icon.

2. Click **Continue**.

3. Enter the administrator name and password, and then click **OK**.

4. Select the migration method you want to use:

 ◆ **From another Mac, Time Machine backup, or startup disk.** Transfers information to this Mac from another Mac, Time Machine backup, or other startup disk.

 ◆ **From a Windows PC.** Transfers information to this Mac from a Windows PC.

 ◆ **To another mac.** Restores information tp another mac on the same network.

5. Click **Continue**.

6. Follow the on-screen instructions for your migration option, which includes selecting the information you want to transfer; steps vary depending on your method; click **Continue** as prompted.

7. When the process is complete, click **Quit**.

Monitoring System Activities

Mac OS X lets you view exactly how much processor power (CPU), memory, energy (**New!**), disk, and network usage the various files and apps you have open are using, by utilizing the Activity Monitor. The Activity Monitor is a highly accurate tool that gives you up-to-date information on the various operations currently being used on your computer. It gives you the ability to view the process on a live graph, and even to halt various processes. In addition, if you own a multi-processor Mac, you'll see a separate graph for each processor to let you know how well the operating system is dividing the load.

Monitor System Activities

1 Click the **Launchpad** icon in the Dock, click the **Other** folder, and then click the **Activity Monitor** icon.

2 Select from the following monitoring tabs:

- **CPU**. Select to view a graph of the process currently active.

- **Memory**. Select to view the current distribution of system memory.

- **Energy**. Select to view information on the current energy impact from app usage and which apps are asleep with App Nap (**New!**).

- **Disk**. Select to view disk usage on the selected disk (click the Disk pop-up to select a disk).

- **Network**. Select to view the current activity across the network.

3 To search for a specific process, enter a search string in the Filter field.

4 To view processes by different types, click the **View** menu, and then select a process option:

All Processes, My Processes, System Processes, Other user Processes, Active Processes, Inactive Processes, Windowed Processes, or Selected Processes.

2 CPU activities

3

Memory activities

5 Select a process you want to view from the selected monitoring tab.

6 To view more information about the selected process, click the **Inspect** button. When you're done, click the **Close** button.

7 To save the current process list, click the **File** menu, and then click **Save**.

8 To force a quit of the selected process, click the **Quit Process** button.

9 Click the **Close** button.

Did You Know?

Your Mac puts apps to sleep to battery life. App Nap (**New!**) looks at which apps are not doing anything in the background, or which have their windows out of view, and puts them to sleep, just like when you close the lid of your MacBook. When App Nap puts apps to sleep, it provides better performance for other running apps and saves batter life on laptops. When a sleeping app is activated or needed, it immediately wakes up and is ready to go. This is done all behind the scenes. You don't have to do anything.

Your Mac saves battery life with Timer Coalescing. Timer coalescing (**New!**) groups low-level operations together in the background, creating tiny periods of idle time that allow your CPU to enter a low-power state more often to save battery life on laptops. This is done all behind the scenes. You don't have to do anything.

Energy activities (**New!**)

App Nap (**New!**)

Disk activities

Network activities

Viewing System Messages with the Console

The Console utility is a viewer that displays all the text-based messages sent between the Mac operating system, and all open applications. While this utility may seem a bit much for the average Mac user, it's of great value to programmers, or would-be programmers, because it gives you information on how the operating system communicates with OS X applications.

View System Messages with the Console

1. Click the **Launchpad** icon in the Dock, click the **Other** folder, and then click the **Console** icon.

2. Click **Show Log Lists**, and then select from the available Console logs.

3. To erase the current log, click **Clear Display**.

4. To reload the active log, click **Reload**.

5. To add a day/date stamp to the log, click **Insert Marker**.

6. To look for a specific function, type a search value into the Filter field.

7. To add or subtract buttons from the Console toolbar, click the **View** menu, and then click **Customize Toolbar**. Drag the item to add or subtract.

8. To change the font used in displaying Console messages, click the **Font** menu, and then click **Show Fonts**.

9. If necessary, make any changes to the Font family and size.

10. Click the **Close** button.

11. Click **Done**.

Viewing System Information

The System Information gives you an exact record of what apps you have installed on your computer; along with information on the installed hardware, system extensions, and current network. It's a great place to go, if you're curious about what you've got. For example, the System Information not only gives you information on your installed apps, it also tells what version (including patches) you've got, and the last time you updated it. The System Information also gives you detailed information on your processor; its speed, and any external devices, such as your hard drives and scanners.

View System Information

1. Click the **Launchpad** icon in the Dock, click the **Other** folder, and then click the **System Information** icon.

2. Select an item from the Contents column.

3. View information on the selected item in the Info window.

4. Click the **View** menu, and then select from **Short Report**, **Standard Report** (default), or **Extended Report**.

5. Click the **File** menu, and then click **Save Print** or **Export** the current report.

6. Click the **Close** button.

Selected app

Did You Know?

You can use System Information to check if you have a CD or DVD recordable drive on your computer. Launch System Information from the Utilities folder, click the triangle to expand the Hardware category, click the ATA (internal), USB, FireWire, or SCSI category, and then look for CD-R, DVD-R, CD-RW, or DVD-RW. Any of these means you can burn a CD or DVD. If it says simply CD or DVD, then you can't.

Forcing a Restart

When OS X was first unveiled to the Apple community, many users sat back and waited to see how this new operating system would fit into the Mac world, and over the years, it has won over even its harshest critics. With its ability to process information ultra fast, and its UNIX base, it has become the system of choice for the discriminating Mac user. Apple OS X is the first "true" multi-processing operating system to appear in the Mac market. When you open a program, the UNIX-based operating system runs the app within a protected area of the CPU memory. When a second program is opened, it gets its own CPU working areas. What that means to you is that a program crash no longer means restarting your computer. All you have to do is force the program to quit. In the event of a system lockup, you can even instruct the operating system to force a restart.

Force a Restart

1. Click the **Apple** menu, and then click **Force Quit**.

2. Click **Finder**.

3. Click **Relaunch** to conduct a mini restart of the operating system.

 TIMESAVER *If your system is so locked up that you can't access the Force Quit command, just hold down the ⌘+Control+Power keys to force your computer to restart.*

4. Follow any onscreen instructions for restarting.

Did You Know?

When you perform a mini restart, you're just relaunching the Finder. Any other programs that were open remain open.

Managing Hardware

18

Introduction

Computer systems are composed of more than just a computer (that's why they're called systems). A computer houses a hard drive, and is connected to a keyboard, mouse, trackpad and video display. All of these hardware devices are required to operate your computer. For most users that's just the start, you'll probably have one or more printers, a scanner; maybe even a second monitor. Then of course, there are digital cameras, fax machines... you get the idea.

Computers are made up of a group of hardware devices, and like a conductor at a symphony, OS X helps you work with those devices, by making the installation, management, and removal easy. In addition, OS X can help you manage color between devices, help you install MIDI (audio) devices, and even make Internet communications easy. If the worst of the worst problems occur (a system crash), there are steps you can perform to bring your computer system back on line, and you don't even have to be a techie.

Installing Hardware Devices

Years ago, hardware installation required all kinds of techniques and special skills. A hardware device such as a printer, could take hours to set up. There were all kinds of cabling problems, and even after it was installed, there were numerous settings to complete before you could use the device. Today, many devices are plug-and-play. You can now go out to your local computer store, pick up a FireWire hard drive, plug it in to your computer, and immediately begin using it. The same is true for many other devices, such as card readers and digital cameras. Even if the device requires the installation of a driver (printers and scanners usually do), a double-click on the install application and answering a few simple questions is typically all that's needed.

Install Hardware Devices

1 Insert the install CD or DVD into your computer (assuming the device is not plug-and-play) or navigate to the installer on your computer or network.

2 Launch the installation application.

> **TROUBLE?** *Some installations require the device be plugged into your computer. Make sure the device is plugged in, and if necessary, powered on.*

3 Follow the instructions for installing the device (some devices may require a reboot of the system).

4 When the installation is finished, follow the on-screen instructions to end the process.

Did You Know?

You can run a hardware test. Disconnect all external devices except keyboard, mouse, display and speakers. Restart your computer and hold down D during startup. At the Apple Hardware Test chooser screen, select a language, press Return, and then follow the on-screen instructions, which varies depending on the hardware.

Removing Hardware Devices

When you remove a hardware device (unplug it), the software (drivers, etc.) that ran the device is still on your computer. It's important to remove any software that is no longer needed for two reasons: it takes up space on your hard drive, and it could cause problems in the future with the installation of other hardware devices. To remove the software, you can start the installer program or insert the installation CD or DVD and follow the onscreen instructions to uninstall it.

Remove Hardware Devices

1. Startup your computer.

2. Use the third-party software's installer CD/DVD or program to remove the installed software.

 IMPORTANT *If you do not have the original CD or DVD, check the manufacturer's web site. Most have an uninstall program that you can download for free.*

3. If you are uncertain about which software was installed last, perform the following steps:

 ◆ Open the Startup Items folder, located in the Library folder, and temporarily remove one or more items.

 ◆ Perform a restart and see if the problem goes away.

4. If the problem still exists, perform the additional steps:

 ◆ Open the Extensions folder or hardware device, such as Printers, folder located in the Library folder.

 ◆ View files by Date Modified.

 ◆ Temporarily move into a folder any relevant, recently modified, third-party .kext files, and then restart the computer.

 ◆ Add back the moved .kext files one at a time and restart, until the problem reoccurs.

5. Click the **Close** button.

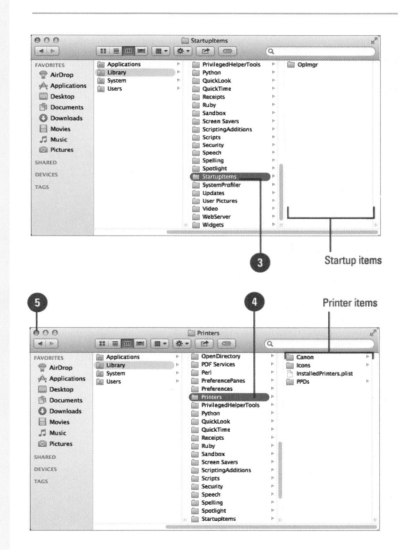

Startup items

Printer items

Viewing Hardware Settings

Most hardware devices have settings that control how the device operates. For example, all ink-jet printers have settings that control the type of paper used, how the inks are applied to the paper and, if your printer has more than a single paper tray, which tray is used for the current printing process. OS X uses the System Preferences panel to display all of the available hardware settings for the major components of the operating system. In addition, when you install specific hardware devices such as a third-party mouse or video-control board, you'll see an icon for controlling the device in the System Preferences.

View Hardware Settings

① Click **System Preferences** icon in the Dock.

The Hardware section holds the icons to the standard hardware devices for OS X.

② Click an icon to view or modify the hardware settings of the selected device.

③ When you're finished viewing or modifying the settings, select the following options:

◆ **About.** Provides information on the manufacturer of the device; including the hardware version and web site (if any).

◆ **Help.** Gives you access to the Help dialog for the selected device.

◆ **Revert.** Puts the settings back to their previous selections.

◆ **Apply Now.** Applies the changes to the settings.

◆ **Close.** Closes the pop-up.

Hardware section

Changing Keyboard Settings

Your keyboard is another one of those wonderful devices that help us communicate with a computer. Keyboards have what is called a **tactile feel** (the way the keys bounce back when they're pressed). Although you can't control the tactile feel of a keyboard, you can control how the keyboard's repeat functions work through System Preferences. Keyboard shortcuts allow you to quickly perform a task by pressing keys on your keyboard. You can change or disable many global keyboard shortcuts, the same shortcuts in all applications, to avoid conflicts or customize to suit your own work preferences.

Change Keyboard Settings

1 Click **System Preferences** icon in the Dock, and then click the **Keyboard** icon.

2 Click the **Keyboard** tab.

3 Drag the **Key Repeat Rate** slider to adjust the speed at which a repeating key is typed.

4 Drag the **Delay Until Repeat** slider to adjust the length of time you have to hold down a key before it begins repeating.

5 Click the **Close** button.

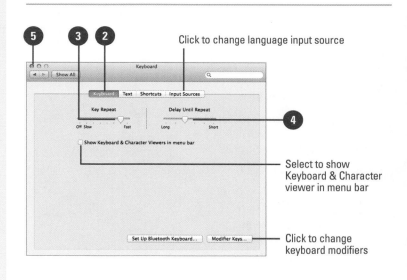

Click to change language input source

Select to show Keyboard & Character viewer in menu bar

Click to change keyboard modifiers

Customize Keyboard Shortcuts

1 Click **System Preferences** icon in the Dock, and then click the **Keyboard** icon.

2 Click the **Shortcuts** tab.

3 Click the category with the shortcuts you want to customize.

4 To disable a shortcut, clear the check box next to the description.

5 To change a key combination, click the characters, hold down the new shortcut key combination you want.

6 Click the **Close** button, and then restart any application that uses it.

Click to restore default OS X shortcuts

Changing Mouse Settings

When you use any computer, a mouse is an important part of the computing experience. Computers communicate with the user through a series of Graphical User Interfaces or a G.U.I. (pronounced Gooey). The user communicates with the computer through several devices, such as: a touch screen, a keyboard, a drawing tablet and a mouse. Using a mouse requires a bit of hand-to-eye coordination: You see something on the screen (a button perhaps), and you move the mouse pointer over the object and click. Apple understands the importance of the mouse, and gives you ways to control its movement and sensitivity through preferences located in System Preferences. If you have a Magic mouse, you can set options for gestures; see Trackpad preferences on the next page for similar option related information. If you have a Bluetooth wireless mouse, you can set it up a new device, check battery levels, and select other Bluetooth-related options.

Change Mouse Settings

1. Click **System Preferences** icon in the Dock, and then click the **Mouse** icon.

2. Drag to adjust the following options:

 ◆ **Tracking Speed.** Controls the speed of the mouse as you drag across your mouse pad.

 ◆ **Scrolling Speed.** Controls the scrolling speed of the mouse.

 ◆ **Double-Click Speed.** Controls the speed at which you must double-click your mouse.

3. To set Bluetooth wireless options, click **Set Up Bluetooth Mouse**, and then follow the on-screen instructions.

4. Click the **Close** button.

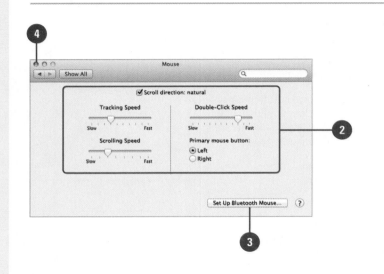

Changing Trackpad Settings

If you're using a Mac notebook with a Multi-Touch trackpad, you can use a variety of gestures to move around and get work done on your Mac. In Trackpad preferences in System preferences you can set options in three categories—Point & Click, Scroll & Zoom, and More Gestures—to enable the gestures that you want to use. You can set options to enable swipe between pages and full-screen apps, as well as access Mission Control, Notification Center (**New!**), App Expose, Launchpad, and the desktop.

Change Trackpad Settings

1. Click **System Preferences** icon in the Dock, and then click the **Trackpad** icon.

2. Click the following tabs to adjust trackpad options:

 ◆ **Point & Click.** Select options related to pointing and clicking.

 ◆ **Scroll & Zoom.** Select options related to scrolling and zooming.

 ◆ **More Gestures.** Select options related to launching and working with apps.

3. For individual options, click the Down arrow or drag a slider to select a specific setting.

4. To set Bluetooth wireless options, click **Set Up Bluetooth Mouse**, and then follow the on-screen instructions.

5. Click the **Close** button.

Did You Know?

You can set scroll direction preference. When you scroll or swipe, content moves in the same direction as your finger. If you want to restore the previous operating system scroll behavior, simple clear the Scroll with finger direction check box in Mouse or Trackpad preferences.

Point & Click options

More Gestures tab

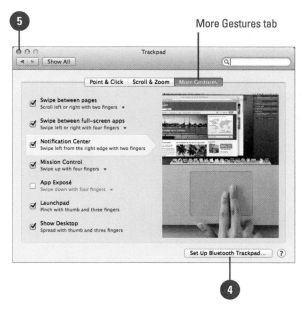

Changing Monitor Display Settings

A monitor displays all your programs and mouse movements. OS X gives you the ability to modify how your monitor displays the screen using options—such as resolution, rotation, refresh rate, and brightness—as well as extend the screen to multiple monitor in the Display pane in System Preferences. For multiple monitors, you can arrange them as mirror displays (a single display) or as a separate extended display (**New!**) with its own menu bar (**New!**). If you have Apple TV connected to your TV and network, you can use AirPlay Display to wirelessly stream—with security encryption—what's on your Mac or iOS device to your HDTV as a separate monitor (**New!**). For example, you can stream 720p video with stereo audio to your HDTV and still use your Mac.

Change Monitor Display Settings

1. Click **System Preferences** icon in the Dock, and then click the **Displays** icon.

2. Click the **Display** tab.

3. Select a resolution option:

 ◆ **Best for display.** Click the option to let OS X determine the best monitor resolution.

 ◆ **Scaled.** Click the option, and then select a display resolution from the options.

4. Select from the following options:

 ◆ **Rotation.** Click the pop-up to select a rotation screen option (for monitors).

 ◆ **Refresh Rate.** Click the pop-up to set a refresh rate (for monitors).

5. To detect additional displays attached to the computer, press Option, and then click **Detect Displays**.

 ◆ The Detect Displays button doesn't appear until you press the Option key.

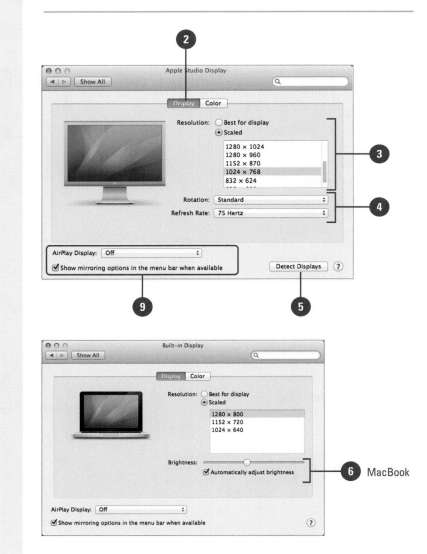

MacBook

6 Select from the following options, which vary depending on the display:

◆ **Brightness.** Changes the brightness of the monitor (a Mac laptop feature).

◆ **Automatically Adjust Brightness As Ambient Light Changes.** Automatically adjusts the brightness of the monitor to compensate for external lights (a Mac laptop feature).

7 Click the **Color** tab.

8 Select from the following color options:

◆ **Show Profiles For This Display Only.** Check to display profiles for the current monitor.

◆ **Open Profile.** Click to open a profile.

◆ **Delete Profile.** Click to delete a profile.

◆ **Calibrate.** Click to calibrate the color of the monitor.

9 To use AirPlay, select from the following options:

◆ **AirPlay Display.** Click the pop-up, and then select the AirPlay device, such as Apple TV, (automatically detected when it's on the same network as the computer). To turn it off, select Off from the pop-up.

◆ **Show mirroring options in the menu bar when available.** Select to display the AirPlay icon on the Apple menu bar.

10 Click the **Close** button.

Display Calibrator Assistant

For Your Information

Smoothing Fonts On-Screen

If the fonts on your screen look fuzzy, you can set a screen option to smooth the fonts appearance. Click the System Preferences icon in the Dock, click the General icon, select the Use LCD Font Smoothing When Available check box, and then click the Close button.

Using Multiple Monitor Displays

When you connect multiple monitors to a Mac—such as a larger monitor, projector, or Apply TV—to a MacBook Pro laptop, you can make full use of the screens. There's no longer a primary or secondary display (**New!**). Each display has its own menu bar (**New!**), and the Dock is available on whichever display you're working on (**New!**). You can have multiple app windows running on either display or run an app full screen on each one. Mission Control can give you a big picture view of the displays (**New!**) making it easy to drag app thumbnails between them to customize your view. You can even use AirPlay and Apple TV (**New!**) to turn your HDTV into a display. This is helpful when you want to show something on your TV and work on your Mac at the same time. You can arrange displays as a mirror (same displays) or as a separate extended display (**New!**) with its own menu bar (**New!**).

Setup Multiple Monitor Displays

1. To use an additional external monitor, connect it to your computer. To use Apple TV, continue to turn it on in Step 5.

2. Click **System Preferences** icon in the Dock, and then click the **Displays** icon.

3. Click the **Display** tab.

4. To detect displays attached to your computer, hold the Option key to display the button, and then click **Detect Displays**.

5. To use Apple TV with AirPlay, select from the following options:

 ◆ **AirPlay Display.** Click the pop-up, and then Apple TV or AirPlay device (same network).

 ◆ **Show mirroring options in the menu bar when available.** Select to display the AirPlay icon on the Apple menu bar.

6. To arrange separate displays, click the **Arrangement** tab (**New!**), deselect the **Mirror Displays** check box (**New!**), and then drag a display or menu bar (**New!**).

7. To gather all windows on the active display, click **Gather Windows**.

8. Click the **Close** button.

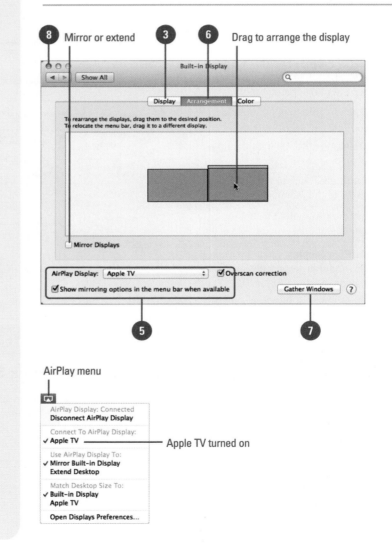

Use Multiple Monitor Displays

◆ **Set Displays to Separate Spaces.**
Click the **System Preferences** icon
in the Dock, click the **Mission
Control** icon, select the **Displays
have separate Spaces** check box
(**New!**), and then click the **Close**
button.

 IMPORTANT *You need to log
 out when you change the setting.*

◆ **View All Spaces in Mission
Control.** Click the Mission Control
icon, or press the Mission Control
key (F3) or Control+Up Arrow, or
swipe up using three or four
fingers.

 Separate Mission Controls appear
 on each display or the same
 Mission Control appears on both.

◆ **Switch Between Spaces.** Press
Control+Right Arrow or Control+
Left Arrow, or swipe left or right
using three or four fingers.

◆ **Activate a Display.** Move the
pointer to the display. Click the
menu bar to activate it (**New!**).

◆ **Move the Dock Between Displays.**
Point to the bottom of the
destination display until the dock
appears on the display (**New!**).

◆ **Mirror or Extend Display.** Click the
AirPlay menu, and then click
Mirror *display* or **Extend** *display*.

◆ **Match Desktop Size.** When you
mirror the display, you can specify
which display size you want to
use. Click the **AirPlay** menu, and
then select a display (**New!**).

◆ **Turn Apple TV On or Off.** Click the
AirPlay menu, and then click
Apple TV.

◆ **Gather Windows.** Open the
Display Preferences dialog on the
destination display, and then click
Gather Windows (**New!**).

Selected space Full screen app

Mission Control icon

Open windows in the selected space; drag a window to another space to move it.

AirPlay menu

Apple TV turned on

Select to mirror or extend the display

Select to optimize the screen size to a display

Select to open Display Preferences

Measuring Display Colors with the Digital Color Meter

Have you ever wondered what the exact color value of an item on your monitor would be if measured using RGB (red, green, and blue) values? Or how about the hexadecimal value of a color (useful if you design web pages)? Color is an important part of any designer's life, and the Digital Color meter lets you accurately sample colors from your monitor. Since the cursor determines the sampled color, you'll need to learn a few shortcut keys to lock the color information.

Measure Display Colors with the Digital Color Meter

1 Click the **Applications** folder in the Dock, click the **Other** folder, and then click the **Digital Color Meter** icon.

2 Click the **Color** pop-up, and then select a color space to measure.

3 Drag the **Aperture Size** slider left or right, to decrease or increase the area used for the taking of a screen shot.

4 Move the mouse over the monitor to measure the color directly underneath the cursor.

5 To lock the aperture's location horizontally, press ⌘+X. To unlock it, press ⌘+X again.

6 To lock the aperture's location vertically, press ⌘+Y. To unlock it, press ⌘+Y again.

7 To show/hide the mouse location in the preview, press ⌘+L.

Selecting Colors with the Color Picker

The world of color on a computer is a very subjective place to live. For example, you might be using a new Macintosh Studio Display, and someone else might be using a Sony LCD monitor. What this means to you is, a color displayed on your hardware device (monitor) might look slightly different on another computer using a different monitor. In addition, it's possible that two people, owning the same monitor, may have them adjusted differently. While creating consistent color output is a difficult thing, OS X gives you a stable color picking system, which helps to stabilize colors systems. The Macintosh Color Picker is accessed through an application, such as TextEdit, Microsoft Word or Adobe Photoshop, or any application that lets you select colors.

Select Colors with the Color Picker

1. Open an application, such as Microsoft Word or TextEdit.

2. Display the Colors window.

 ◆ In Microsoft Word, select a button, such as text color, and then click **More Colors**.

 ◆ In TextEdit, click the **Format** menu, point to **Font**, and then click **Show Colors**.

3. Click a palette, and then select a color from the available color profiles:

 ◆ **Color Wheel.** Drag the scroll bar vertically to adjust the brightness, and then click inside the ball, to select a color.

 ◆ **Color Slider.** Select a color mixing method from the pop-up, and then drag the sliders to select a color.

 ◆ **Color Palettes.** Select a pre-designed color palette from the pop-up, and then select the color from the available list.

 ◆ **Image Palettes.** Displays a spectrum of colors. Click in the spectrum to select a color.

 ◆ **Crayons.** Select a color from the available crayons.

4. Click the **Close** button.

1 TextEdit

2

4 Color Wheel 3 Color Palettes Crayons

Matching Colors to Devices with ColorSync

The ColorSync utility gives the designer the ability to match up colors between devices, and to check on and repair the device color profiles present on the computer. As you might have figured out by now, computer monitors are not the best at maintaining color accuracy; especially between monitor and print. The ColorSync utility strives to maintain a color standard between devices, by acting as a translator between different devices. The original scanned image, your monitor, and the output printing device are all examples of where color needs to be synced, and it is achieved though the ColorSync utility.

Match Colors to Devices with ColorSync

1. Click the **Applications** folder in the Dock, click the **Other** folder, and then click the **ColorSync Utility** icon.

2. Click **Profile First Aid**.

3. Click **Verify** (to view) or **Repair** (to fix) the color profiles installed on your computer.

4. Click **Profiles**.

5. View a gamut grid of the color profiles installed for your computer (click the user option to view color profiles created by you).

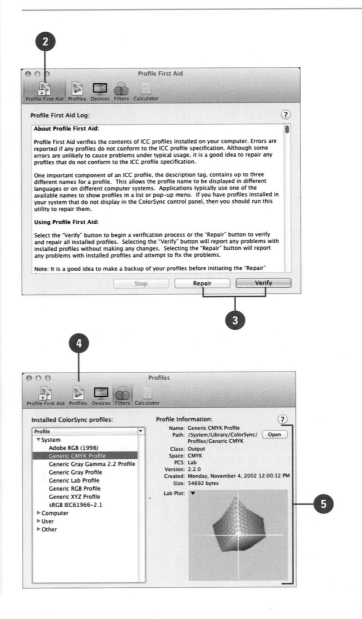

6️⃣ To select and assign color profiles to all installed devices, click **Devices**.

7️⃣ To view information on the currently installed filters, click **Filters**.

8️⃣ Click **Add** (+) or **Remove** (-) button to add a new filter, or delete the selected filter.

9️⃣ Click the **Down Arrow** icon, point to any of the following commands, and then select the option you want:

- ◆ **Duplicate Filter.**

- ◆ **Add Color Management Component.**

- ◆ **Add Image Effects Component.**

- ◆ **Add PDF Retouch Component.**

- ◆ **Add Domain Information.**

- ◆ **Add Comments.**

IMPORTANT *The ColorSync Utility gives you the ability to view and change the color profiles used by different devices. This is an area where you don't want to experiment. Have a good understanding of color theory, before attempting to change any of the ColorSync settings.*

🔟 Click the **Close** button.

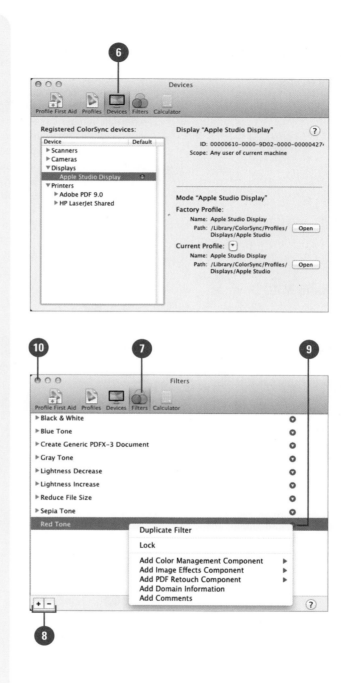

Configuring Audio MIDI Devices

Macintosh computers were born to work with music, and as the years advanced they got better and better. The Audio MIDI (Musical Instrument Digital Interface) Setup utility is designed to help you set up all your input and output sound equipment, such as AirPlay, microphones, speakers, and multichannel audio interfaces, either built-in or external. In most cases, the default settings work the best. However, if you do work a lot with audio, Apple has made the process of adding, monitoring, and adjusting external devices, such as electronic keyboards and speakers, a snap. If you have multiple audio devices, you can combine them together, known as aggregating devices, to add capacity. For example, if you have an two 6 channel audio devices, you can combine them to work as a single 12 channel audio device. If you have Apple TV connected to your TV and network, you can set adjust audio settings for AirPlay mirroring to wirelessly stream what's on your Mac, such as videos, to your HDTV.

Configure Audio MIDI Devices

1. Click the **Applications** folder in the Dock, click the **Other** folder, and then click the **Audio MIDI Setup** icon.

2. To create an aggregate device, click the **Add** (+) button.

 ◆ To remove an aggregate device, select it, and then click the **Remove** (-) button.

3. Select the audio device you want to configure.

4. To use the selected device for sound input or sound output, or to play system sounds, click the **Actions** button, and then select an option.

5. If you're using an audio device that sends its own timing messages, click the **Clock source** pop-up, and then select an option.

6. Click the **Input** or **Output** tab, if available.

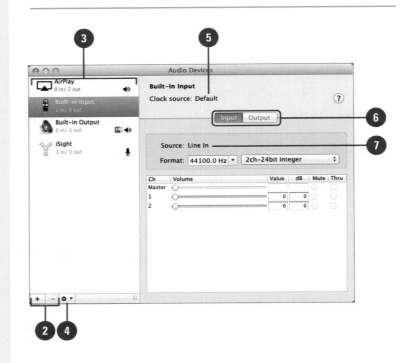

7. If you have multiple sources and prefer a different source option, click the **Source** pop-up, and then select an option.

The Mac automatically selects the appropriate source option for you.

8. Based on your audio device, click the **Sample Rate** and **Bit Depth** pop-ups (under Format), and then select an appropriate setting.

9. To set the volume for each channel, drag the **Volume** sliders.

10. To configure surround sound (multichannel) speakers, click **Configure Speakers**, select the options you want, click **Apply**, and then click **Done**.

 ◆ Select **Stereo** or **Multichannel** device type, and then select a surround sound version for multichannel.

 ◆ Select the device channel for each speaker.

 ◆ To test the speaker connection, click a speaker to play a sound.

11. Click the **Close** button.

Speaker configuration options

Preventing Hardware Problems

Whenever you add hardware devices to your computer, the possibility exists that a problem will occur. Problems can fall into several categories: The device doesn't work, the device doesn't work the way you expect, or the computer refuses to boot. Apple's built-in management systems make hardware problems a rare event. However, a few careful steps on your part can help to make problems almost non-existent.

Check for hardware device compatibility

Not all hardware devices are compatible with your particular version of Macintosh. For example, you could purchase a video driver board, which works fine on an older Mac model, but won't function on a newer Mac model.

Check for software compatibility

Many hardware devices require installation software to operate. Even though OS X has been in the market for a couple of years, there are still hardware devices with accompanying installation software that is not compatible with the OS X operating system. In addition, the operating system changed the rules on computer architecture; therefore, make sure the software is not just OS X compatible, but is also Mavericks compatible.

Check the Internet

Software changes (almost on a weekly basis), when you purchase a piece of hardware, that box may have been sitting on the shelf for months. Make sure you access the device's Internet site, and determine if you have the latest version of the software.

Plan for the future

If you haven't purchased an Intel-based Mac (yet), you probably will in the future. Be advised that some of your hardware devices may not work with the new architecture. When you purchase new hardware, check the manufacturer's web site, and see if they plan on supporting future Macintosh computers.

When the worst happens

Sometimes you install a hardware device, and your Macintosh refuses to start up. Many times it's because you just installed a new hardware device. Unfortunately, when you disconnect the device your Mac still won't start up. The reason is because the software that runs the device is still installed. When this happens you can attempt a fix by performing a "Safe" boot.

First, you'll need to power down your computer. After your computer has shut off, go ahead and press the power button. After you hear the startup tone, immediately press and hold the Shift key. You'll release the Shift key when you see the gray Apple and progress indicator (looks like a spinning gear).

The Safe Mode takes a while to boot (several minutes). That's because Safe Mode performs a system check before starting. Then, you'll use the hardware device's installation DVD to remove the installed hardware. After that is done, restart your computer the normal way (without holding the Shift key).

If removing the device software does not solve the problem, your glitch may be caused by something more serious. You can attempt a reinstall of the OS X operating system, but before doing that, go online and check out the Apple web site and search for help on your problem. When there is no solution but to start over, or get a new device, you'll need to remove the hardware device and the software that controls it.

Working with OS X Along with Windows

Introduction

If you have an Intel-based Mac computer, you can install and run Windows 7 or later on your computer. All you need is Boot Camp Assistant, and your Microsoft Windows installation disc or USB Flash drive that contains the ISO image.

The Boot Camp Assistant helps you set up a Windows partition on your computer's hard drive and then start the Windows operating system installation. After you complete the initial installation, you need to install Boot Camp drivers to complete the installation and start your Mac in either Windows or OS X. The Boot Camp drivers, available with the OS X installation, allow you to use your Apple keyboard to emulate a standard PC keyboard, an Apple Remote (if your computer is equipped with one) to control iTunes and Windows Media, Bluetooth wireless devices, an iSight camera, and Wi-Fi wireless network connectivity, and change brightness and contrast controls for built-in displays. After you finish the Windows installation and Boot Camp driver update, you can use Windows on your Mac.

If you already have Microsoft Windows XP (Service Pack 2 or later), Windows Vista, or Windows 7 on your Mac computer and upgrade to OS X, Boot Camp supports the existing installations.

If you no longer want to run Microsoft Windows on your Mac computer, you can remove it using Boot Camp Assistant. When you remove Windows, the Boot Camp Assistant removes the Windows software and restores your hard disk back to a single partition.

What You'll Do

Prepare a Mac for Windows

Install Windows on a Mac

Start Up with OS X or Windows

Use Windows on a Mac

Remove Windows

Preparing a Mac for Windows

Before you can install Microsoft Windows 7 or later on your Mac, you need to meet the minimum hardware requirement for your Mac, create a partition on your hard disk for the Windows software, and have a single-full Windows installation disc or ISO image on a USB flash drive. You can use the About This Mac command on the Apple menu to check your hardware configuration and Boot Camp Assistant to create a partition for the Windows and install support software. Before you install Windows on your Mac computer, it's critical to make a back up of the important files on your computer; better safe than sorry.

Prepare a Mac for Windows

① Before you can install and set up Windows on your Mac, your computer needs to meet the following minimum requirements:

◆ An Intel-based Mac computer.

◆ A USB keyboard and mouse, or a built-in keyboard and touch pad.

◆ OS X version 10.8 or later; the lastest version of the OS X is recommended.

◆ Internal disk with a single partition, formatted as a OS X Extended (Journaled) volume.

◆ A single full-install licensed 64-bit version of Windows 7 Home Premium, Professional, or Ultimate or Windows 8 or Windows 8 Pro (**New!**) on a disc or USB flash drive with 8 GB (**New!**) or more.

② Click the **Launchpad** icon in the Dock, click the **Other** folder, and then click the **Boot Camp Assistant** icon.

③ Read the Introduction screen, and then click **Print Installation & Setup Guide** to have this important document handy during your Windows installation, and then click **Continue**.

About This Mac computer information

Other folder ②

 To use a Windows installation disc, follow this method:

- Select the **Download the latest Windows support software from Apple** check box, and then click **Continue**.

- Select the **Burn a copy to CD or DVD** or **Save a copy to an external drive** option, and then click **Continue**.

- Follow on-screen instructions to burn a CD or DVD or save the support software, including a helper tool, to an external drive.

To use an ISO image on a USB flash drive, follow this method:

- Select the **Create a Windows 7 or later version install disk** check box, and then click **Continue**.

- Choose the ISO image, select a destination disk (USB drive), and then click **Continue**.

- Click **Continue** to confirm the drive will be erased.

NOTE *The USB flash drive includes the Windows support software.*

 When you're done, click **Quit**.

Go to the next page and follow the instructions to create a partition and start the Windows installation.

.

Options for USB flash drive

Installing Windows on a Mac

After you create a partition on your Mac computer for the Windows software, you can start the Microsoft Windows 7 or later installation on your Mac with a single-full Windows installation disc or ISO image on a USB flash drive. During the Windows installation, you need to reformat the new Windows partition, so you can boot (startup) from Windows. You can reformat the Windows partition with the NTFS format. NTFS provides reliability and security, which allows you to read and write file on the Windows partition from OS X. After you complete the Windows installation, you need to update Boot Camp drivers on your Mac computer, which are available from the Boot Camp Assistant, to install Mac-specific drivers for graphics, networking, audio, Wi-Fi wireless connectivity, Bluetooth, iSight camera, Apple keyboards, Apple Remote, and brightness control for built-in displays.

Install Windows on a Mac

1 Create a partition on your Mac computer for the Windows software; see "Preparing a Mac for Windows Software" on page 482 for specific details.

> **IMPORTANT** *To install Windows using Boot Camp, you must be logged in as an administrator.*

2 Click the **Launchpad** icon in the Dock, click the **Other** folder, and then click the **Boot Camp Assistant** icon, and then click **Continue**.

3 Click the **Install Windows 7 or later version** check box.

4 Click **Continue** to specify options to create a partition for Windows.

5 If your computer has more than one internal disk, select the disk you want to use, select the partition option you want, and then click **Continue**.

6 Use the default size (recommended), or specify the size you want. Either, drag the divider to set the size of the partition or click **Divide Equally**.

The partition must be at least 5 GB and leave at least 5 GB of free space on the OS X partition.

7 Insert your Windows 7 or later installation disc or the USB flash drive with the ISO image of Windows 7 or later.

IMPORTANT *Boot Camp Assistant doesn't support a new installation for Windows XP or Vista.*

8 Click **Install**, and then wait for the completion of the partition.

Your computer reboots and starts the Windows 7 or later installation.

9 Follow the Windows 7 or later installation instructions until you need to decide where to install Windows.

◆ **Format Partition NTFS.** Click **Disk 0 Partition 3 BOOTCAMP**, click **Drive options (advanced)**, click **Format**, and then click **OK**.

10 Finish the Windows installation, and then eject the Windows 7 or later installation disc.

11 When your computer reboots to Windows 7 or later, open the CD, DVD, or external drive with the Windows support files, double-click the **Setup.exe** icon to install Boot Camp and drivers.

12 Follow the on-screen instructions. Don't click Cancel in any of the dialog boxes; click **Next**, click **Install**, click **Finish**, and then click **Yes** to restart.

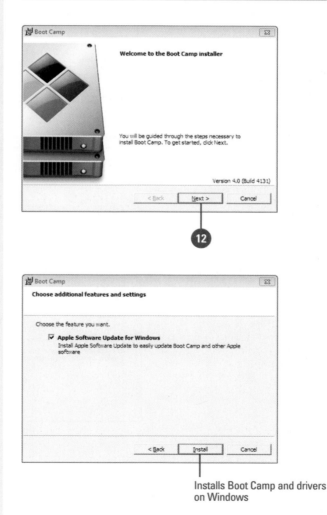

Installs Boot Camp and drivers on Windows

Starting Up with OS X or Windows

After you install Microsoft Windows and Boot Camp drivers, you can start up your Mac computer in either OS X or Windows. You can set the default operating system you want to use on a regular basis using Startup Disk preferences on the Mac or the Boot Camp Control Panel on Windows, and then use quick controls to directly restart your computer in the other operating system or select an operating system while starting your Mac computer.

Set the Startup Disk for Mac OS X or Windows

1. Start up using either of the following:

 ◆ **In the OS X.** Click the **Apple** menu, click **System Preferences**, and then click **Startup Disk**.

 ◆ **In Windows.** Click the **Boot Camp** icon in the notification area on the taskbar, and then click **Boot Camp Control Panel**. Click **Continue** to access the system utility.

2. Select the startup disk with the operating system you want to use by default.

3. To start up that operating system now, click **Restart**, and then click **Restart** again as needed.

4. Click the **Close** button (Mac) or **OK** (Win).

OS X

| 4 |

Startup Disk

Show All

Select the system you want to use to start up your computer

BOOTCAMP
Windows

Macintosh HD
OS X, 10.9

2

You have selected OS X, 10.9
on the disk "Macintosh HD."

Restart...

3

Click to restart this computer in target disk mode
After you restart this computer in target disk mode, you can connect it
to another computer using a Thunderbolt or FireWire cable and use it as
a hard disk.

Target Disk Mode...

Click the lock to prevent further changes.

Windows

Boot Camp Control Panel

Startup Disk | Remote | Keyboard | Power

Select the system you want to use to start up your computer

Macintosh HD
Mac OS X

BOOTCAMP
Windows

2

You have selected Windows
on the disk "BOOTCAMP."

Restart...

3

Click to restart this computer in Target Disk Mode.
After you restart this computer in Target Disk Mode, you can connect it
to another computer using a FireWire cable and use it as a hard disk.

Target Disk Mode...

OK | Cancel | Apply | Help

4

Start Up with OS X or Windows

◆ **Select an OS when you startup.** As your computer starts up, hold down the Option key until disk icons appear, select the startup disk with the operating system you want, and then click the arrow below the icon.

◆ **Restart to Mac from Windows.** In Windows, click the **Boot Camp** icon in the notification area, click **Restart in OS X**, and then click **OK**.

◆ **Restart to Windows from Mac.** In OS X, click the **Apple** menu, click **Restart**, click **Restart**, hold down the Option key until disk icons appear, select Windows, and then click the arrow below the icon.

Select an OS when you start up

Click to restart to Mac OS X from Windows Boot Camp icon

Click to confirm restart

Using Windows on a Mac

After you finish the Windows installation and Boot Camp driver update, you can use Windows on your Mac. The Boot Camp drivers allow you to use your Apple keyboard to emulate a standard PC keyboard, use function keys, eject discs using the Eject key on the keyboard, change the volume using the Volume Down or Up keys, right-click using an Apple Magic Mouse or trackpad, use an Apple Remote (if your computer is equipped with one) to control iTunes and Windows Media, use Bluetooth wireless devices, attach and use an iSight camera, and connect to a wireless network using Wi-Fi. In addition, you can work with files between your OS X and Windows disks. Due to HFS+ support, you can now access files (read-only) on your Mac from Windows for review or save with a different name to make changes.

Use Windows on a Mac

◆ **Disable remote control.** In Windows, click the **Boot Camp** icon in the notification area, click **Boot Camp Control Panel**, click the **Remote** tab, select the **Disable remote control infrared receiver** check box, and then click **OK**.

◆ **Pair or Unpair a remote control.** A Mac computer can only use one remote at a time. To use a remote, you need to pair it with the computer. Hold the remote close to the computer (3 to 4 inches) and point the remote at the front, press and hold down Menu and Next buttons on the remote for 5 seconds until a chain link symbol appears.

If you want to change remotes, you need to unpair the current one first. In Windows, click the **Boot Camp** icon in the notification area, click **Boot Camp Control Panel**, click the **Remote** tab, click **Unpair**, and then click **OK**.

◆ **Restart after a power failure.** In Windows, click the **Boot Camp** icon in the notification area, click **Boot Camp Control Panel**, click the **Power** tab, select the **Restart automatically after a power failure** check box, and then click **OK**.

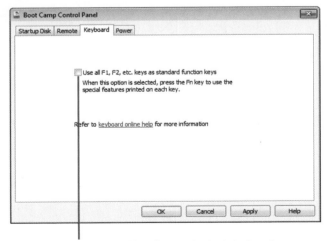

Remote control options

Use standard functions on the Apple keyboard

- **Use a Bluetooth Device.** In order to use a Bluetooth wireless device with Windows, you need to pair the device with your computer.

 In Windows, open the Bluetooth Devices control panel, click the **Devices** tab, click **Add**, and then follow the wizard instructions.

 Use the following numeric passkeys: Wireless Magic Mouse, enter four zeros: *0000*. Apple Wireless keyboard, enter six to sixteen digits.

- **Copy Files Between OS X and Windows.** Since you installed Windows 7 or later on a partition formatted with NTFS, you can open files on your Windows disk from OS X, or copy files from Windows to OS X. However, you cannot copy or save any files to the protected Windows disk.

 IMPORTANT *Windows files need extensions (for example, .doc) to identify the file type. Most programs come in both Mac and Windows versions, so there should be no problem there. If it's a Mac only file type, you may need to convert it for Windows use.*

- **Use the Apple Keyboard with Windows.** In Windows, click the **Boot Camp** icon in the notification area, click **Boot Camp Control Panel**, click the **Keyboard** tab, select the **Use all F1, F2, etc. keys as standard function keys** check box, and then click **OK**.

 Refer to the table for specific keyboard commands you can use on your Apple keyboard to emulate a standard PC keyboard.

 You can also use the Eject key and Volume Down and Up keys on the Apple keyboard to perform commands not available on the standard PC keyboard.

File on Mac disk Windows Disk Mac disk

Files on Windows disk

Apple Keyboard with Windows

PC Key Command	Apple External	Built-in Mac
Control+Alt+Delete	Control-Option-Delete	Control-Option-Delete
Alt	Option	Option
AltGr	Control-Option	Control-Option
Backspace	Delete	Delete
Delete	Delete	Fn-Delete
Enter	Return	Return
Enter (num keypad)	Enter	Enter
Insert	Help	Fn-Enter
Num lock	Clear	Fn-F6
Pause/Break	F16	Fn-Esc
Print Screen	F14	Fn-F11
Print active window	Option-F14	Option-Fn-F11
Scroll/Lock	F15	Fn-F12

Removing Windows

If you no longer want to run Microsoft Windows on your Mac computer, you can remove it using Boot Camp Assistant. When you remove Windows, the Boot Camp Assistant removes the Windows software and restores your hard disk back to a single partition. All the information on the Windows partition is erased, so it's critical to make a back up of the important files on your computer before you start the removal process.

Remove Windows from a Computer with a Single Internal Disk

① Start your Mac computer in OS X.

② Click the **Launchpad** icon in the Dock, click the **Other** folder, and then click the **Boot Camp Assistant** icon.

③ Click **Continue**.

④ Click the **Remove Windows 7 or later version** check box.

⑤ Click **Continue**.

⑥ Enter your name and password, and then click **OK**.

⑦ Click **Restore**.

⑧ When you're done, click **Quit**.

Did You Know?

You can use Disk Utility to remove Windows on a single-volume disk. Click the Launchpad icon in the Dock, click the Other folder, and then click the Disk Utility icon to erase the disk and reformat it as a OS X volume.

Remove Windows from a Computer with Multiple Internal Disks

1. Start your Mac computer in OS X.

2. Click the **Launchpad** icon in the Dock, click the **Other** folder, and then click the **Boot Camp Assistant** icon.

3. Click **Continue**.

4. Click the **Remove Windows 7 or later version** check box.

5. Click **Continue**.

6. Select the disk with the Windows software.

7. Click the **Restore to a single OS partition** option.

8. Click **Continue**.

9. Enter your name and password, and then click **OK**.

10. Click **Restore**.

11. When you're done, click **Quit**.

Backing Up Everything with Time Machine

Introduction

Backing up your files is an important part of protecting and maintaining your computer. If you accidentally deleted a file or lose files due to a computer problem, you can recover them with a backup.

Time Machine is an OS X application that allows you to back up everything on your computer on a regular basis without any additional work on your part after the initial set up. The first time you use Time Machine, it backs up everything on your computer, including system files, applications, accounts, preferences, music, photos, movies, and documents. As you work and make changes on your computer, Time Machine backs up only the things that have changed.

Time Machine works best when you dedicate and use the same disk for your backups. You can use an internal or external disk as the back up disk. You can keep your backups secure by backing up to an external USB or FireWire drive encrypted with FileVault 2. When you attach an external disk to your Mac computer, Time Machine asks if you want to use the device for backups and automatically sets everything up for you.

Backups are organized and stored by date. You can browse and recover individual files, folders, or your entire computer. You can also burn backup CDs and DVDs, copy files onto another disk, or use your iCloud account.

What You'll Do

Set Up Time Machine for Backups

Perform a Backup

Exclude Items from a Backup

Work with a Backup

Recover Backed Up Items

Recover an Entire Computer System

Create a Disk Image to Backup Files

Burn a CD or DVD from a Disk Image

Restore a Disk Image

Back Up Files onto a CD or DVD

Setting Up Time Machine for Backups

Time Machine works best when you dedicate and use the same disk for your backups. You can use an internal (except for your startup disk) or external disk (such as a FireWire or USB disk) with encryption using FileVault 2 as the back up disk. You can even use multiple disks. If you have partitioned a disk, you can use the partition as a back up disk too. The disk you use must be in the Mac OS Extended (Journaled) format, and must have Access Control Lists (ACLs) enabled. When you attach an external disk to your Mac computer, Time Machine asks if you want to use the device for backups and automatically sets everything up for you. The first time you start Time Machine, it backs up everything on your computer. You can also use Time Capsule (a wireless hard drive designed to work with Time Machine) with encryption to back up files about 50 percent faster. As you work and make changes on your computer, Time Machine backs up only the things that have changed.

Set Up Time Machine Preferences

1. Click **System Preferences** icon in the Dock, and then click the **Time Machine** icon.

2. To show a status menu, select the **Show Time Machine in menu bar** check box.

3. Slide the switch to **ON**.

4. Click **Select Disk**.

5. Click one of the available disks you can use for backups. If you have Time Capsule, select **Other Time Capsule**, and then click **Set Up** to open the AirPort Utility.

6. To encrypt the disk, select the **Encrypt backups** check box.

7. Click **Use Disk**. To use multiple disks, select another one, click **Use Disk**, and then click **Both**.

 ◆ If you encrypt, enter the password information, and then click **Encrypt Disk**.

8. If your disk needs to be erased, click **Erase** or **Choose Another Disk** to select another one.

9. Click the **Close** button.

Selected drive

Performing a Backup

Time Machine keeps track of everything on your Mac computer. The first time you start Time Machine, the program backs up everything on your computer. As you work and make changes on your computer, Time Machine backs up only the things that have changed. If you want to manually perform a backup, you can click the Time Machine Status menu or Control-click the Time Machine icon in the Dock to access the Back Up Now command.

Start a Manual Back Up

① Click the **Time Machine Status** menu, or Control-click the **Time Machine** icon in the Dock.

② Click **Back Up Now**.

Time Machine status information appears in the Time Machine Status menu.

③ To stop the backup, click the **Time Machine Status** menu or Control-click the **Time Machine** icon in the Dock, and then click **Stop Backing Up**.

◆ You can also click the **Stop** button (X) in the Time Machine preferences window.

Did You Know?

You can back up all the Macs in your wireless network. If you have a hard disk connected to your AirPort Extreme Base Station or Time Capsule, you can use Time Machine to back up all your Macs wirelessly. All you need to do is select your AirPort Disk or Time Capsule as the backup disk for each computer connected to the wireless network.

You can use Power Nap to perform a backup. With Power Nap enabled in the Energy Saver pane in System Preferences, you can perform Time Machine backups to Time Capsule.

① Time Machine Status menu

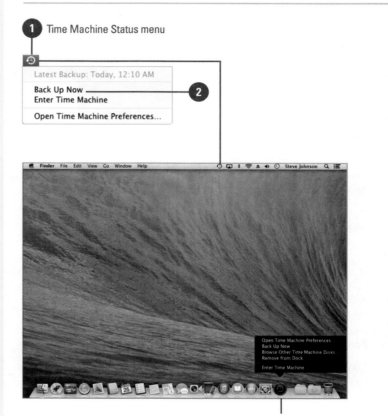

Control-click Time Machine icon

Current status of the back up

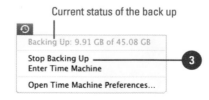

Excluding Items from a Backup

If you already have copies of files, such as third-party programs (Microsoft Office, Adobe Creative Suite, etc.), on CD, DVD, or in another location, you can exclude them from regular backups to save space on your backup disk. Time Machine assumes you want to back everything up unless you specifically add it to the nonbackup list, which you can modify using Time Machine preferences.

Exclude Items from a Backup

1. Click **System Preferences** icon in the Dock, and then click the **Time Machine** icon.

2. Click **Options**.

 A list appears with the available disks you can use for backups with Time Machine.

3. Click **Add** (+), and then select the items you don't want to be backed up, and then click **Exclude**.

 ◆ If you select the System folder, an alert appears, asking you for confirmation.

 The backup disk is automatically included in the list.

4. To remove an item from the list, select the items you want to be backed up, and then click **Remove** (-).

5. Select or clear the **Notify after old backups are deleted** check box.

6. Click **Done**.

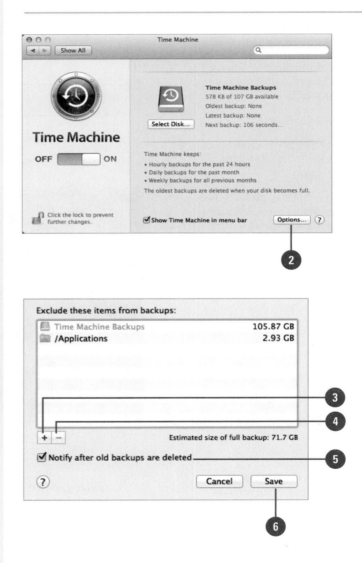

Working with a Backup

If a backup is interrupted for some reason, such as a network connection problem, detached external disk, or power outage, Time Machine tries to automatically resume the backup when the problem is corrected. If Time Machine doesn't automatically resume, you can manually restart it. If you want to pause a backup, you can also manually stop it by using the Time Machine Status menu or by using the Time Machine icon in the Dock. The Time Machine Status menu icon rotates as the takes place. If a problem occurs, the icons changes to an alert symbol. Also, the first item on the menu displays status information about the current or last back up.

Work with a Backup

◆ **Pause/stop a backup.** Click the **Time Machine Status** menu, and then click **Stop Backing Up**.

◆ **Resume/start a backup.** Click the **Time Machine Status** menu, and then click **Back Up Now**.

◆ **Run out of space.** As the backup disk fills up, Time Machine deletes older backups to make room for new ones. If you run out of space, you can attach a new backup disk to complete the process.

◆ **Local snapshots.** When you're away from your Time Capsule or backup drive, Time Machine keeps a spare "local snapshot" copy of the files you create, modify, or delete right on your portable Mac; not on desktops. If you accidentally delete a file while on the road, you can recover it from a local copy. To stop taking local snapshots, turn the Time Machine off in preferences.

◆ **Combined timeline.** When you connect your Mac to your Time Capsule or backup drive, Time Machine automatically displays everything you did while not connected with your existing backups, so it looks like you never left.

Time Machine Status menu

Latest Backup: Today, 12:10 AM

Back Up Now
Enter Time Machine

Open Time Machine Preferences...

Open Time Machine Preferences...
Back Up Now
Browse Other Time Machine Disks...
Remove from Dock
Enter Time Machine

Resume/ start a backup

Current status of the back up

Backing Up: 9.91 GB of 45.08 GB

Stop Backing Up
Enter Time Machine

Open Time Machine Preferences...

Pause/stop a backup

Icon changes to indicate a problem

Latest Backup: Failed...

Back Up Now
Enter Time Machine

Open Time Machine Preferences...

Click to find out the problem

Recovering Backed Up Items

If you've been using Time Machine to back up your computer, and you lose or accidentally delete a file or folder, you can use Time Machine or Time Machine along with Spotlight to recover it. You can even recover older versions of files that you have changed. Spotlight makes it easy to perform a search for the backup file or folder you want to recover, and Time Machine allows you to recover it. The recovered item is restored to its original location on your computer. Time Machine may ask if you want to overwrite one or more folders so it can restore an item to its original location. If you encrypted the backup disk with FileVault 2 in Time Machine, you need to provide the password to restore the data.

Recover Items Using Time Machine and Spotlight

1. Open a Finder window.

2. Type a search word or phrase in the Search box from the item you want to recover.

3. Click the **Launchpad** icon in the Dock, click the **Other** folder, and then click the **Time Machine** icon.

4. Use the arrows and the timeline to browse through the Time Machine backups. Your search is performed in every window.

5. Narrow down your search to find the item you want to restore, and then select it.

6. Click **Restore**.

 The window appears on the desktop along with a Copy dialog box.

7. Click **Keep Original** to keep the original file instead of the backup, **Keep Both** to keep the original and the backup, or **Replace** to replace the original with the backup.

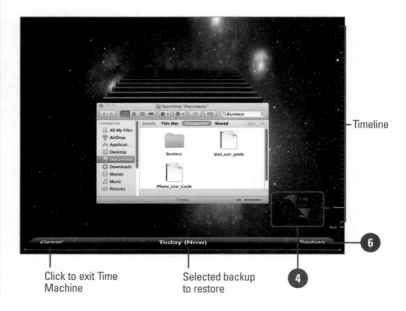

Timeline

Click to exit Time Machine

Selected backup to restore

Recover Items Using Time Machine

① Open the window or location (desktop or e-mail Inbox) where the recovered item will appear.

② Click the **Launchpad** icon in the Dock, click the **Other** folder, and then click the **Time Machine** icon.

③ Use the arrows and the timeline to browse through the Time Machine backups. Your search is performed in every window.

④ When you find the item you want to restore, select it.

⑤ Click **Restore**.

The window appears on the desktop along with a Copy dialog box.

⑥ Click **Keep Original** to keep the original file instead of the backup, **Keep Both** to keep the original and the backup, or **Replace** to replace the original with the backup.

Click to exit Time Machine

Selected backup

Recovering an Entire Computer System

If your entire computer system or startup disk becomes corrupt or damaged, you can recover it using Time Machine. If you're experiencing problems after you install a OS X software update, you can use Time Machine to revert back to a previous version of the Mac OS to fix the problem. Remember, any additional changes you've made to your computer after installing the OS X software update will be removed, so you need to make copies of those changes on another disk. To perform a recovery, you don't need a OS X Installation disc to start the process; all you need to do is hold down ⌘+R during a bootup to access OS X Recovery; it's always available. If you have a Time Machine backup disk locally attached to your computer, you can boot into OS X Recovery.

Recover an Entire System Using Time Machine

1. Connect your Time Machine backup disk to your computer, if necessary.

2. Click the **Apple** menu, click **Restart**, and then click **Restart**.

3. During bootup, hold down ⌘+R.

 The built-in OS X Utilities program starts.

4. In the installer, click **Restore From Time Machine Backup**.

5. Click **Continue**.

6. In the Restore Your System screen, click **Continue**.

7. Select the Time Machine backup volume you want to use.

8. Click **Continue**.

 - If network drive, click **Connect to Remote Disk**, enter name and password, and then click **Connect**.

9. Select the Time Machine backup you want to restore.

10. Click **Continue**.

11. Select the restore destination volume.

12. Click **Restore**.

Revert Back to a Previous Version of OS X

① Connect your Time Machine backup disk to your computer, if necessary.

② Click the **Apple** menu, click **Restart**, and then click **Restart**.

③ During bootup, hold down ⌘+R.

 The built-in OS X Utilities program starts.

④ In the installer, click **Restore From Time Machine Backup**.

⑤ Click **Continue**.

⑥ In the Restore Your System screen, click **Continue**.

⑦ Select the Time Machine backup volume you want to use.

⑧ Click **Continue**.

 ◆ If network drive, click **Connect to Remote Disk**, enter name and password, and then click **Connect**.

⑨ Select the most recent Time Machine backup to restore your computer to the state it was before you installed an update.

⑩ Click **Continue**.

⑪ Select the restore destination volume.

⑫ Click **Restore**.

Creating a Disk Image to Backup Files

If you can't fit all the files and folders you want to backup onto a single CD or DVD, you can use the Disk Utility to create a compressed disk image of the files and folders. A **disk image** is a file that contains other files and folders you can mount on your desktop like a hard disk or CD or DVD disc. You can create a disk image with an existing disk, volume, CD or DVD, or folder, or create a blank one, and then drag files to it. After you create a disk image (.dmg extension), you can burn it on a CD or DVD, copy it to another Mac or network, or e-mail it to another Mac user. Creating a disk image of your OS X installation disc is a useful way to make a backup copy of your OS X installation for added protection.

Create a Disk Image to Backup Files and Folders

1. Click the **Launchpad** icon in the Dock, click the **Other** folder, and then click the **Disk Utility** icon.

2. Click the **File** menu, point to **New**, and then click **Disk Image from Folder** or **Disk Image from** *disk name*.

3. If you want to create a disk image from a folder, select it.

4. Click **Image**.

5. Type the name you want for the disk image, and then specify the location where you want to save it.

6. Click the **Image Format** pop-up, and then click **compressed** to create a smaller disk image or **read-only** to create a faster disk to create and open.

7. To require a password to open the disk image, click the **Encryption** pop-up, and then select the option you want.

8. Click **Save** to create a .dmg file. If you required a password, enter it twice, and then click **OK**.

9. To check the image for a restore, select the disk image (.dmg), click the **Images** menu, and then click **Scan Image for Restore**.

Create a Blank Disk Image as a Backup

① Click the **Launchpad** icon in the Dock, click the **Other** folder, and then click the **Disk Utility** icon.

② Click the **File** menu, point to **New**, and then click **Blank Disk Image**.

③ Type a name for the disk image, select or specify tags (**New!**), and then specify the location where you want to save it.

④ Select from the following options:

- ◆ Enter a name or use the default.

- ◆ Click the **Size** pop-up, and then select the size you want.

- ◆ Select the **Format** pop-up, and then select **Mac OS Extended (Journaled)** for Mac computers or **MS-DOS (FAT)** for Windows or Mac computers.

- ◆ To require a password to open the disk image, click the **Encryption** pop-up, and then select the option you want.

- ◆ Click the **Partitions** pop-up, and then select the partition scheme that matches the type you want to create.

- ◆ Click the **Image Format** pop-up, and then click **read/write disk image**.

⑤ Click **Create**.

⑥ If you required a password, enter it twice, and then click **OK**.

The blank new disk image mounts on your desktop.

⑦ Drag the files and folders you want to include in the disk image onto the mounted disk on your desktop.

For Your Information

Recording or Duplicating a Data CD or DVD

You can use Disk Utility to quickly create a CD or DVD from data on your computer or make a copy of a CD or DVD that contains information. Once you create a disk image, you can make multiple copies from the same disk image. If you select the Leave Disc Appendable option during the process, you can create a **multisession CD** or **DVD**; you burn data on a CD-R or DVD-R now, and then add to it later until there is no more room, just like a CD-RW or DVD-RW. You can use the CD or DVD to transfer files from one computer to another, backup data for safekeeping, or restore the files on a disk.

Burning a CD or DVD from a Disk Image

After you create a disk image, you can burn it on a CD or DVD, which makes it easy to make a backup copy of important files, move files to another computer, or share files with other Mac users. This is also a useful way to make a backup of your OS X installation DVD from a disk image of the installation DVD disc. After you select the disk image you want to burn to a CD or DVD in Disk Utility, you can select the Burn options you want before the actual burn takes place.

Burn a CD or DVD from a Disk Image

1. Click the **Launchpad** icon in the Dock, click the **Other** folder, and then click the **Disk Utility** icon.

2. Click the **Burn** button on the toolbar.

3. Navigate to and select the disk image you want to burn.

4. Click **Burn**.

5. Click the **Down Arrow** button to show advanced burn options.

6. Select the Burn Options and After Burning settings you want.

7. Insert a writable CD or DVD disc into your read/writable drive.

8. Click **Burn**.

 A status bar appears, indicating the current progress of the burn.

9. Click **OK**.

Restoring a Disk Image

After you create a disk image, you can use Disk Utility to restore it to a disk. This is useful when you want to re-create all the contents of the disk image to a disk. Disk Utility allows you to select the source and destination for the restored files. You can even erase the destination before the restoration occurs. If you only want to restore only a few files, you can access the content of the mounted disk image on your desktop like any other hard disk and copy it to another location.

Restore a Disk Image to a Disk

1. Click the **Launchpad** icon in the Dock, click the **Other** folder, and then click the **Disk Utility** icon.

2. Select the disk in the list at the left.

3. Click the **Restore** tab.

4. Drag the disk image to the Source field or click **Image**, and then select the disk image.

5. Drag the destination disk you want to the Destination field.

6. Click **Restore**, and then click **Restore** again to confirm the restoration.

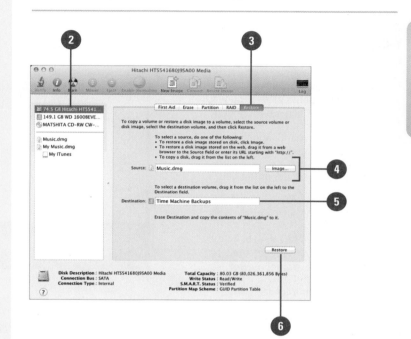

Did You Know?

You can get information about your disk. Click the Launchpad icon in the Dock, click the Utilities folder, click the Disk Utility icon, select the disk or volume in the list at the left, click the Info button. When you're done, click the Close button twice.

Backing Up Files onto a CD or DVD

If you can write (burn) files to a CD or DVD, you can create and use a burn folder to backup important files. Burn folders are useful for regularly backing up a set of files or for burning multiple copies of a folder. You can create a burn folder from the Finder. The files and folders you drag into the burn folder are ready to be written to a CD or DVD. The Finder creates aliases to the items in the burn folder. The original items are not moved. When you burn the files to a CD or DVD, the original files are burned to the disc.

Copy Files onto a CD or DVD from the Finder

1 Click the desktop background or open the window where you want to create and use a burn folder.

2 Click the **File** menu, and then click **New Burn Folder**.

3 Type a name for the burn folder.

4 Drag the items you want to burn to a disc into the burn folder.

The Finder creates aliases to the items in the burn folder. The original items are not moved.

5 Open the burn folder to burn a CD or DVD.

6 Click **Burn**.

TIMESAVER *If the burn folder is in the sidebar of the Finder window, click the burn icon next to the burn folder name.*

7 Insert a writable CD or DVD disc into your read/writable drive.

The original files and any folders are burned to the disc.

◆ If the Finder can't find an original file, it asks you to cancel the burn or continue without the file.

8 Type a name for the CD or DVD, and then select a burn speed.

9 Click **Burn**.

Automating Your Work

Introduction

Automator is a program that lets you automate the things you frequently like to do on your Mac. You don't need to be a programmer to create automations. With Automator, all you need to do is assemble a series of **actions** into a workflow to complete a task. Each action performs an individual step, such as opening a file, creating an event in Calendar, or importing photos in Image Capture. You can create your own actions or use one of the many pre-built ones available in Automator library.

When you start Automator, a dialog box appears asking you to choose from a group of templates, also known as starting points, that help you create the first part of your workflow. There are several templates you can use to help you get started: Workflow, Application, Service, Folder Action, Print Plugin, Calendar Alarm, and Image Capture Plugin. After you choose a template, you see an untitled workflow with a blank workflow action in the Workflow pane you can fill in. You create a workflow by dragging additional actions or variables into the Workflow pane, arranging them into the order you want from top to bottom, and specifying the settings you want for each action or variable.

When you have more than one action in a workflow, Automator frequently passes information from one action to another starting from the top. When you run a workflow, each action receives information from the previous action (input) and passes information to the following action (output). If an action needs to receive a certain type of information, it needs to be placed in the workflow following an action that outputs that type of information.

In addition to Automator, you can also use AppleScript, an English-like scripting language, to run prebuilt or custom-made scripts to automate actions performed by the computer. AppleScript lets you write your own mini applications to help with repetitious tasks.

What You'll Do

Introduce Automator

Get Started with Automator

Open an Existing Workflow

Work with an Example Workflow

Add Actions to a Workflow

Add Variables to an Action

Record an Action

Work with Workflows

Run and Stop a Workflow

Save a Workflow

Use a Workflow as a Plug-in

Understand AppleScript Basics

Use Ready-Made AppleScripts

Write and Record AppleScripts

Use AppleScript with Automator

Introducing Automator

Anyone can create a workflow in Automator. All it requires is the Automator application available in the Applications folder, and a little knowledge about the process.

When you start Automator, a dialog box appears asking you to choose from a group of templates that help you create the first part of your workflow. There are several templates you can use to help you get started: Workflow, Application, Service, Folder Action, Print Plugin, Calendar Alarm, and Image Capture Plugin. If you already have an existing workflow, you can open it from the dialog box.

After you choose a template, you see an untitled workflow with a blank workflow action (except for Custom) in the Workflow pane you can fill in. You create a workflow by displaying Actions or Variables in the Library pane, selecting the name of the application or category you want to use from the Library list, specifying what you want it to do with it in the Action or Variable list, and dragging it into the Workflow pane to assemble the steps you want to automate.

Automator Window

The Automator window consists of different parts, including Toolbar buttons, Library pane, Library list, Action or Variable list, Search field, Description view, and Workflow pane.

Toolbar buttons

The top part of the Automator window displays a toolbar with buttons you can use to make it easier to work with Automator. On the left side of the toolbar, Automator provides two default buttons: Hide/Show Library and Media. The Hide/Show Library button) hides or shows the Library pane, while the Media but-

ton makes it easy to add media to your workflows. On the right-side of the toolbar, Automator provides three default buttons, known as Workflow control buttons: Record, Stop, and Run. The Record button creates a workflow by recording of your mouse movements, while the Stop and Run buttons stop and play back the current workflow. These are not the only toolbar buttons available in Automator. You can use the Customize Toolbar command on the View menu to add and remove the buttons you want and change the button size and display.

Library pane

The left side of the Automator window is the Library pane, which displays the available actions and variables you can use to create Automator workflows.

Action list

When you click the Actions button at the top of the Library pane, a Library list and Action list appear. The Library list displays every program, including some OS utilities, on your Mac that you can use to create Automator workflows. When you select a program, the Action list changes to show the actions related to the program. OS X provides improved and new actions, for Preview, the Internet, RSS, and the Finder. At the bottom of the Library list, you can use Smart Groups, including Most Relevant, Most Used, and Recently Added, or create your own to make it easier to displays the actions you want to use.

Variable list

When you click the Variables button at the top of the Library pane, a Library list and Variable

list appear. The Library list displays OS utilities categories on your Mac that you can use to create Automator workflows. When you select a program, the Variable list changes to show the available variables you can use to store values and create more flexible workflows.

Search field

The Search field at the top of the Library pane is similar to the one you find in other parts of OS X. In Automator, the Search field makes it easier to find the actions or variables you want to use. Before you start a search, select a category from the Library list. As you type in the Search field, Automator displays the actions or variables that match your criteria from the selected category. If you want to search through more than one category, you can press ⌘⌘ to select the ones you want. If you want to search all the categories, click Library at the top of the Library list. The results of your search appear in the Action or Variable list in order of relevance to your search criteria. When you're done, you can click the small gray X button in the Search field to return to the complete list of actions.

Description view

The Description view at the bottom of the Library pane displays a description of the selected action or variable. The description provides information about what the action or variable does, what requirements it needs to get started, what kind of data it needs as input, what options are available, and what kind of action it performs as a result. If you need more room to display the Action or Variable list, you can click the Show Or Hide The Description View button at the bottom of the Library pane.

Workflow pane

The Workflow pane is where you place the actions and variables you want to use to create a workflow. The Workflow pane displays and tracks a flow of information from one action or variable to the next creating the results you want. In the Workflow pane, you can change the order of items, set item specific settings and options, display item descriptions, and show the results for specific ones.

Workflow log

The Show Or Hide The Workflow Log button at the bottom of the Workflow pane shows or hides the workflow log, which allows you to track what your workflow is doing.

Workflow variable list

The Show Or Hide The Workflow Variable List button at the bottom of the Workflow pane shows or hides the workflow variable list, which allows you to track the current values for the variables you use in your workflow.

More to come

Developers are always creating new actions for you to use. Check out the Apple Developer web site at *developer.apple.com* and then search *automator* for more information and details, or visit *www.automatorworld.com*. After you download them to your computer, you can use the Import Actions command on the File menu to add them to your Library list in Automator. Writing your own actions is out of the scope of this book. For details, see the Apple Developer web site or search the web for *automator*.

Getting Started with Automator

When you start Automator, a dialog box appears asking you to choose from a group of templates, also known as starting points, that help you create the first part of your workflow. You can use any of the following templates to help you get started: Workflow, Application, Service, Folder Action, Print Plugin, Calendar Alarm, and Image Capture Plugin. After you choose a template, you see an untitled workflow with an action in the Workflow pane you can fill in.

Get Started with Automator

1 Click the **Launchpad** icon in the Dock, click the **Other** folder, and then click the **Automator** icon.

Automator opens, displaying the Templates dialog.

2 Click a template icon:

 ◆ **Workflow.** Use to creates a workflow document.

 ◆ **Application.** Use to create an executable workflow application.

 ◆ **Service.** Use to create a service for use in another application or the Finder; a plug-in workflow.

 ◆ **Folder Actions.** Use to perform batch folder operations, such as opening or adding files; a plug-in workflow.

 ◆ **Print Plugin.** Use to run a workflow when you print a file. An item appears on the PDF menu in the Print dialog box; a plug-in workflow.

 ◆ **Calendar Alarm.** Use to open Calendar and create a new event; a plug-in workflow.

 ◆ **Image Capture Plugin.** Use to import photos from a camera or scanner with Image Capture; a plug-in workflow.

3 Click **Choose**. If prompted, select your content, and then click **Add**.

 ◆ Click **Close** to exit the dialog without taking any action.

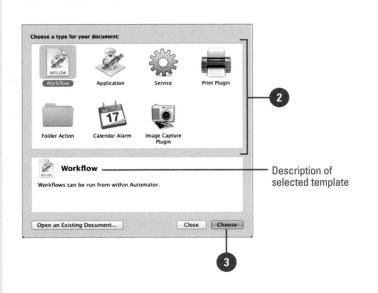

Description of selected template

For Your Information

Starting a Workflow with a Set of Files

If you wanted to create a new workflow with a specific set of files, you can use the shortcut menu in the Finder to quickly get started. In Finder, select the files you want to use in the new workflow. Control-click the selected files, point to Automator, and then click Create Workflow. Automator opens with a new workflow and the selected files are in the first action.

Opening an Existing Workflow

After you save a workflow as a Workflow (.workflow) or Application (.app) file, you can open either one at any time to modify or run it. You can open a workflow by using the standard Open dialog box in Automator. You can access the Open dialog box from the New dialog box when you start Automator from the Finder or from the Open command on the File menu in Automator.

Open an Existing Workflow

1. Use one of the following methods:

 ◆ **In Finder.** Click the **Launchpad** icon in the Dock, click the **Automator** icon, and then click **Open an Existing Workflow**.

 ◆ **In Automator.** Click the **File** menu, and then click **Open**.

 TIMESAVER *Press* ⌘+O *to open the Open dialog.*

2. Click the **Type** pop-up, and then select **All** or a workflow type.

3. Select the place from which you want to open the file.

 TIMESAVER *Click the Where pop-up to select from a list of recent places you already visited.*

4. Click the document you want to open.

5. Click **Open**.

6. To close a workflow, click the **File** menu, and then click **Close**.

Did You Know?

You can open a workflow file directly. In Finder, double-click the workflow file icon (.workflow) you want to open.

You can create a new workflow. Click the File menu, and then click New. The templates dialog box appears or a blank custom workflow appears.

Working with an Example Workflow

The best way to learn how to create a workflow is to go through an example. Automator comes with three example workflows you can open to see what a completed one looks like. The examples show you how to a workflow can display movie trailers in Safari, and process images with the Quartz composition filter. The process images workflow is a good example of batch processing images. The example processes images with the Quartz composition filter. However, you can easily change the workflow to modify the image size or convert it to another format.

Work with an Example Workflow

1. Start Automator, click the **Workflow** icon, and then click **Choose** to open Automator with a blank workflow.

2. Click the **Help** menu, and then click **Open Example Folder**.

3. Double-click the **Process Images .workflow** icon.

4. Examine the following actions in the Workflow pane:

 ◆ **Ask for Confirmation.** Displays a dialog box with information you provide for the user's benefit. You can change the button names and click the Robot icon to change it.

 ◆ **Get Specified Finder Items.** Lets you specify the files you want to process. You can use the Add or Remove buttons or drag files from the Finder.

 ◆ **Copy Finder Items.** Makes copies of the files to protect the originals.

 ◆ **Apply Quartz Composition Filter to Image Files.** Applies the filter to the selected image files.

 ◆ **Open Images in Preview.** Opens the specified image file in Preview.

5. To execute the workflow, click the **Run** button on the toolbar.

Modify an Example Workflow

① Start Automator, click the **Workflow** icon, and then click **Choose** to open Automator with a blank workflow.

② Click the **Help** menu, and then click **Open Example Folder**.

③ Double-click the **Process Images .workflow** icon.

④ Instead of working from a specified folder, let's have the Finder ask you where to get the image files.

 ◆ **Get Specified Finder Items.** Click the **Delete** button (X) on the Get Specified Finder Items title bar, click **Files & Folders** in the Library list, and then drag the **Ask for Finder Items** action to the same place as the deleted action.

⑤ Instead of applying the Quartz filter, let's change the image type.

 ◆ **Change Type of Images.** Click the **Delete** button (X) on the Apply Quartz Composition Filter to Image Files title bar, click **Photos** in the Library list, and then drag the **Change Type of Images** action to the same place as the deleted action.

⑥ Click the **File** menu, click **Save A**s, specify a new name, any tags, and then click **Save**.

⑦ To execute the workflow, click the **Run** button on the toolbar.

Ask for Finder Items action

For Your Information

Controlling Input and Output

You can control the input and output within a workflow. Some actions allow you to choose whether you want to receive results from a previous action. If so, select this check box (names vary depending on action). If available, select the Use Results from Previous Action option from the pop-up menu on the action in the Workflow pane. When you start a workflow from the shortcut menu in Finder (see "Using a Workflow as Plug-ins" on page 520), any items you select are passed into the workflow as input. If you don't want this to happen, you can set the first action to ignore input. Control-click the title bar for the first action, and then click Ignore Input.

Adding Actions to a Workflow

You can add one or more actions to create the workflow you want. Automator includes actions that can turn text into images, turn text documents into ePub books, display and retrieve web content, and enable encoding for video and audio files. Many text-based actions support RTF (Rich Text Format). When you have more than one action in a workflow, Automator frequently passes information from one action to another starting from the top. When you run a workflow, each action receives information from the previous action (input) and passes information to the following action (output). Data detector text input objects—such as URLs, addresses, and phone numbers—have the option to pass full text selection or only found text. If an action needs to receive a certain type of information, it needs to be placed in the workflow following an action that outputs that type of information. The type of input an action needs appears in the title bar. If the input and output don't match or it's not being received from the previous action, the information appears in red to indicate a problem.

Add Actions to a Workflow

1. Start Automator and use a template or open the workflow you want.

2. Click the **Actions** button in the Library pane.

3. Click the category or application from the Library list to display the actions you want.

4. Drag the action you want to the Workflow pane.

5. Enter information and specify the settings you want for the action; the information and settings vary depending on the action.

6. To show and set additional options, click the **Options** button, and then specify the ones you want to set. To hide the options, click the **Options** button again.

 ◆ To allow a user to select action settings, select the **Show Action When Run** check box.

 The availability of the Options button varies depending on the action.

Adding Variables to an Action

A variable stores a value that you can use in a workflow. For example, you can use variables to get the current time or today's date, unique text and data, or even a script. You can add variables directly to a workflow or to a compatible editable field or pop-up of an action. If you need a variable, yet you're not ready to use it, you can declare it in the Variables log for later use. In some cases, you can declare or create a a variable directly in an action.

Add Variables to an Action

1 Start Automator and use a template or open the workflow you want to add variables to an action.

2 Click the **Variables** button in the Library pane.

3 Click the category from the Library list to display the actions you want.

4 Use any of the following methods to add a variable to an action:

◆ **Add to Workflow.** Drag variable into the Workflow pane. The "Get Value of Variable" action appears.

◆ **Add to Action.** Drag variable into an editable field or pop-up menu of an action. The variable is added to the Variables log.

◆ **Declare in Log.** Drag the variable to the Variables log. You can declare it without using it immediately.

5 Enter information and specify the settings you want for the variable; the information and settings vary depending on the variable.

6 To show and set additional options, click the **Options** button, and then specify the ones you want to set. To hide the options, click the **Options** button again.

Selected variable

Drag variable into an editable pop-up

Recording an Action

If you can't find a pre-built action that meets your needs, you can record your own. Automator records your keyboard and mouse event to create a custom action, known as the "Watch Me Do" action. After you record the "Watch Me Do" action, you can adjust the playback speed and timeout settings, as well as delete any events you don't want. Before you can record an action, you need to select the "Enable Access For Assistive Devices check box in the Universal Access Preferences.

Record an Action

1. Set up your environment the way you expect it to be before you start to record.

2. Start Automator and create or open the workflow you want to add a recorded action.

 ◆ If a dialog appears, click the **Open Accessibility** button, select the **Enable access for assistive device** check box, and then click the **Close** button.

3. Click the **Record** button on the toolbar.

 The Automator Recording message appears with the Stop button.

4. Perform the steps you want to record, and then click the **Stop** button.

5. To test your recording, click the **Run** button on the toolbar.

6. Adjust the settings you want for the recorded action.

 ◆ **Delete Event.** Select the event, and then type Delete.

 ◆ **Rearrange Event.** Drag an event to change the order.

 ◆ **Adjust Timeout.** Click the Timeout up and down arrows.

 ◆ **Adjust Speed.** Drag the **Playback speed** slider.

Working with Workflows

After you add actions to your workflow, you can work with them to create the results you want. In the Workflow pane you can arrange actions in a different order; remember the input and output needs to match. If you need the same action in another place, you can copy and paste it. If you don't always need an action, you can disable it for now and then enable later. If you want to add media to a workflow, you can use the Media browser. If you can't locate a certain action, you can use the Search field to try and find it. If you still can't find it, you can import actions developed by others.

Work with Workflows

◆ **Collapse/Expand.** Click the triangle to the left of the action title.

◆ **Arrange.** Drag the action title bar in the Workflow pane to a new place.

◆ **Copy.** Select the action in the Workflow pane, click the **Edit** menu, click **Copy**, click in the workflow where you want to insert the action, click the **Edit** menu, and then click **Paste**.

◆ **Disable.** Control-click the action title bar, then click **Disable**.

◆ **Enable.** Control-click the action title bar, then click **Enable**.

◆ **Delete.** Click the **Delete** button (X) on the title bar of the action in the Workflow pane.

◆ **Browse Media.** Click the **Media** button on the toolbar. Displays the media browser where you can select and use audio, photos, and movies.

◆ **Import.** Click the **File** menu, click **Import Actions**, navigate to and select the actions you want, and then click **Import**.

◆ **Find.** Enter a word or phrase in the Search field, and then press Return. To clear the search, click the **Delete** button (X) in the Search field.

◆ **View Log.** Click the **View** menu, and then click **Show Log**. You can also use the View Results action in a workflow.

Find Collapse/Expand Enable/Disable

View log of variables or events

Browse Media

Running and Stopping a Workflow

When you finishing creating a workflow, it's important to test (run) it to make sure it works the way you want it to. When you run a workflow (all at once with the Run button or one step at a time with the Step button), Automator executes each action from top to bottom, displaying status messages at the bottom of the window. As each action completes, a green checkmark appears in the bottom left-corner of the action indicating the action worked correctly. If a problem occurred, such as the input and output not matching, a red x appears.

Run and Stop a Workflow

1 Start Automator and create or open the workflow you want to run.

2 To view the values stored in variables as a debugging tool, click the **Show or hide the workflow log** button to display the log.

3 Click the **Run** button on the toolbar to play the entire workflow or click the **Step** button to play the workflow one step at a time.

Automator executes each action from top to bottom, displaying status messages at the bottom of the window.

TIMESAVER *Click the View menu, and then click Show Log to view all the status messages.*

4 If a dialog box appears, requesting information or files, fulfill the request.

As each action completes, a green checkmark appears in the bottom left-corner of the action indicating the action worked correctly. If a problem occurred, such as the input and output not matching, a red x appears.

5 To stop the workflow, click the **Stop** button on the toolbar.

6 To show the results of a specific action, click the **Results** button at the bottom of the action. To hide the results, click the **Results** button again.

Saving a Workflow

As you work on a workflow, Automator automatically saves it with Auto Save. If the workflow is Untitled, you can give it a name. Automator periodically saves your workflow. With the Duplicate To command on the File menu, you can resave a workflow to a different template type. If you want to change a file's name or location, you can use the Rename or Move To commands on the File menu. When you use the Workflow or Application templates, you can save a workflow as a .workflow) or .app file. A Workflow file is one you open, modify, and run in Automator. An Application file is one you can double-click to start, drag it to the Dock, and assign a shortcut to make it easier to launch.

Save a Workflow

1. Start Automator and create (Workflow or Application) or open the workflow you want to save.

2. Click the **File** menu, and then click **Save...** (for new Untitled workflows) or **Save** (for existing named workflows).

3. For new Untitled, type the name you want for the workflow file, and then click in the Tags box, select or enter one or more tags (**New!**).

4. Click the **Where** pop-up, and then select a save location.

5. Click the **File Format** pop-up, and then click **Workflow** or **Application**.

6. Click **Save**.

Did You Know?

You can revert to the previously saved workflow. Click the File menu, point to Revert To, and then click Browser All Versions.

You can customize the toolbar. Click the View menu, click Customize Toolbar, drag items to the toolbar, specify options, and then click Done.

You can print a workflow. Click the File menu, click Print, select the print options you want, and then click Print.

Click to expand dialog

File options to rename, tag, move, and lock

Click Document title to display menu

Using a Workflow as Plug-ins

When you create a workflow with the template type Folder Actions, Print Plugin, Calendar Alarm, or Image Capture Plugin, Automator saves it as a plug-in type. Saving your workflows as a plug-in allows you to automate tasks in different places and situations on your Mac. For example, you can run a workflow from the Finder's shortcut menu, an event in Calendar, the import feature in Image Capture, or a print dialog box.

Use a Workflow as a Plug-in

1 Start Automator and create or open the workflow with the following type:

- ◆ **Service.** Use to create a service for use in another application or the Finder.

- ◆ **Folder Actions.** Use to perform batch folder operations, such as opening or adding files.

- ◆ **Print Plugin.** Use to run a workflow when you print a file. An item appears on the PDF menu in the Print dialog box.

- ◆ **Calendar Alarm.** Use to open Calendar and create a new event named after plug-in.

- ◆ **Image Capture Plugin.** Use to import photos from a camera or scanner with Image Capture.

2 Click the **File** menu, and then click **Save As**.

3 Type the name you want for the plug-in.

4 Click **Save**.

Did You Know?

You can create self-installing actions and services. As with Safari plug-ins, Automator actions and services can be installed from the desktop by double-clicking their icons and approving the permission dialog.

Understanding AppleScript Basics

The AppleScript language is your way of communicating with your operating system; instructing it to perform specific tasks. Who wants to do the same tasks over and over again... no one. For example, adding the .jpg extension to 150 graphic files that have to move to a system that requires extensions. There is an easier way to perform repetitive tasks, and that's with AppleScript. **AppleScript** is an English-like scripting language that is used to write script files, and those files automate actions performed by the computer (like adding an extension 150 times).

ActionScripting is more than a language that repeats recorded actions; AppleScript can make decisions based on user-interaction or by analyzing data, documents, or situations. And with OS X and the AppleScript Studio, you can create powerful OS X applications with the Aqua look-and-feel written entirely in AppleScript. AppleScript is an automation language that helps us get through the mundane tasks of working on a computer and that's more than worth the time and effort spent in learning AppleScript.

AppleScript provides shortcuts for complex tasks such as naming files, resetting preferences, or connecting to the Internet, and the AppleScript Studio comes bundled with dozens of pre-written scripts that can immediately help you with your daily computer tasks. In addition, the automated workflow gives consistency, and speed to any Macintosh project. Since more can be accomplished in the same amount of time, you become more efficient—all through the power of AppleScript. To create your own AppleScripts, open the AppleScript editor, and type the script using precise language limitations.

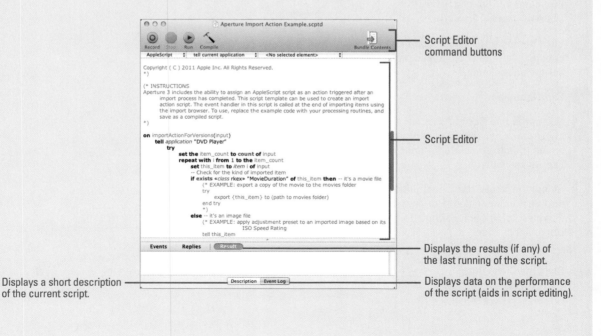

Script Editor command buttons

Script Editor

Displays the results (if any) of the last running of the script.

Displays a short description of the current script.

Displays data on the performance of the script (aids in script editing).

Using Ready-Made AppleScripts

You can use AppleScript right away, by working with AppleScripts created by the friendly folks at Apple. To gain access to the ready-made scripts, open the Applications folder, select the AppleScript folder, and then select Example Scripts, or do it the easy way by activating the built-in Script menu. When you activate (display) the Script menu, the Script icon appears on the right side of the menu bar and is available in the Finder and whenever you open an application. For example, you can click the Scripts icon, point to Printing Scripts, and then click Convert To PDF.

Display the Script menu and Enable Script Helpers

1. Click the **Launchpad** icon in the Dock, click the **Other** folder, and then click the **AppleScript Editor** icon.

2. Click the **AppleScript Editor** menu, and then click **Preferences**.

3. Click **General**.

4. Select the **Show Script menu in menu bar** check box.

5. Select or clear the **Show Computer scripts** check box to show or hide library scripts.

6. Click the **top** or **bottom** option to specify where to show application scripts on the menu.

7. Click **Editing**.

8. Select the **Use Script Assistant** check box to enable the assistant, which tries to complete portions of scripts as you type.

9. Select the **Show "tell" application pop-up menu** check box to enable it, which helps create scripts to be run in applications, such as Mail rule scripts.

10. Click the **Close** button.

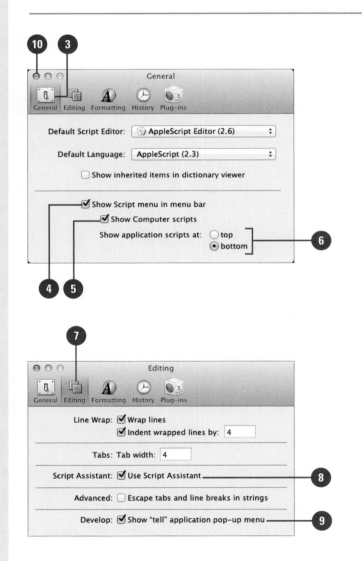

Use Ready-Made AppleScripts

1 On the right side of the menu bar, click the **Scripts** icon.

2 Point to a script category, if necessary.

3 Select a script option. Some of the useful scripts include:

◆ **Add to File Names** and **Add to Folder Names**. Add text to the beginning or end of every file or folder in the active Finder window.

◆ **Replace Text in Item Names**. Replaces text in file and folder names.

◆ **Trim File Names** and **Trim Folder Names**. Removes file extensions or text from the beginning or end of every file or folder in the active Finder window.

Open Example Scripts Folder

1 On the right side of the menu bar, click the **Scripts** icon.

2 Point to **Open Scripts Folder**, and then click one of the Scripts Folder (Finder, User, or Computer).

3 Double-click the example folder you want, if necessary.

4 Double-click the script you want to execute.

Did You Know?

You can add your scripts to the Scripts menu. Open the Example Scripts folder in the AppleScripts folder, create a folder with the name you want on the Scripts menu, and then drag your script into the folder. The script name appears on the Scripts menu.

Writing and Recording AppleScripts

Anyone can write AppleScripts. All it requires is the Script Editor application available with OS X, and knowledge of the AppleScript language. The AppleScript editor lets you type script directly into the editor window, or you can click the Record button, and then perform some Mac operation, as the editor records each step as you work. There are many places where you can go to increase your AppleScript understanding; however, point your browser to *www.apple.com*, and then search for *applescript resources* to access current resources dealing the creative techniques for AppleScript.

Write and Record AppleScripts

1 Click the **Launchpad** icon in the Dock, click the **Other** folder, and then click the **AppleScript Editor** icon.

2 Type the Script directly into the Script Editor window.

◆ **Start New.** Click the **File** menu, and then click **New**.

◆ **Start New with a Template.** Click the **File** menu, point to **New** from **Template**, point to category (Aperture, Droplets, Messages, or Mail), and then select a template.

3 To record within the active script, click the **Record** button.

4 Click the **Run** button to run the active script.

5 Click the **Stop** button to stop the running of the active script.

6 Click the **Compile** button to create a version of the active script.

7 Click the **File** menu, and then click **Save**, or **Save As** to save the script using a unique name and location.

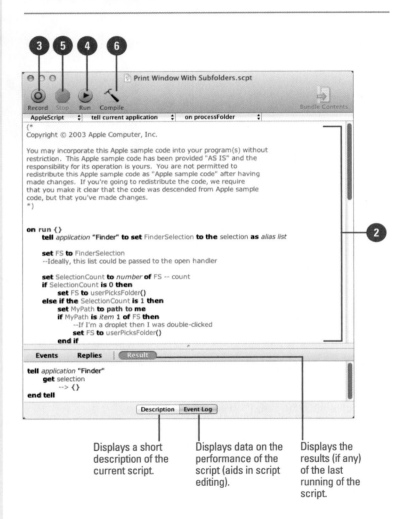

Displays a short description of the current script.

Displays data on the performance of the script (aids in script editing).

Displays the results (if any) of the last running of the script.

Open and Modify a Script from the Scripts Menu

 On the right side of the menu bar, click the **Scripts** icon.

 Point to a script category, if necessary.

❸ Option-click the script you want to open.

The Script Editor opens, displaying the selected script.

❹ Modify the script as you want.

◆ **Use the Script Assistant.** As you type, it looks for possible matches. You'll see the suggestion in gray. Press Esc to accept it. Press Option+Esc to see a list of suggestions. Enable in Editing preferences.

◆ **Use the "tell" application pop-up menu.** It create scripts to be run within specific applications, such as a Mail rule script. The menu appears in the Navigation Bar above the script, next to the language selection pop-up. Enable in Editing preferences.

❺ Click the **Run** button to run the active script.

❻ Click the **Stop** button to stop the running of the active script.

❼ Click the **Compile** button to create a version of the active script.

❽ Click the **File** menu, and then click **Save As** to save the script using a unique name and location.

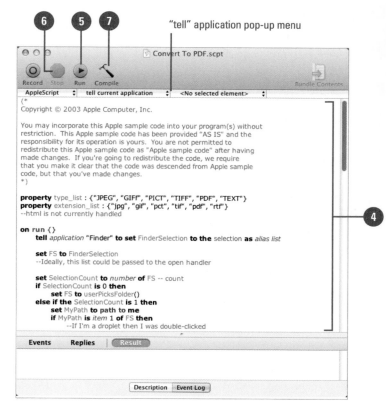

"tell" application pop-up menu

Using AppleScript with Automator

You can add an AppleScript script to a workflow. Simply, drag the Run AppleScript action into your workflow, and then enter your script into the small script editor within the action. Automator is a scriptable application. You can use AppleScript in the Script Editor to develop and execute workflows. To help you write the scripts, you can view the Automator's AppleScript dictionary. Open the Utilities folder window, open another window with the Applications window. Drag the Automator icon (located in the Applications folder) onto the Script Editor icon (located in the Utilities folder).

Use AppleScript with Automator

1. Start Automator and use a template or open the workflow you want.

2. Click the **Actions** button in the Library pane.

3. Click the **Utilities** category from the Library list.

4. Drag the **Run AppleScript** action you want to the Workflow pane.

5. Type the script you want in the action.

6. To run the script, click the **Run** button in the action below the title bar.

7. To compile the script, click the **Compile** button to create a version of the active script.

8. To run the workflow, click the **Run** button on the toolbar.

Appendix: Installing OS X Mavericks

A

Introduction

If you're upgrading to OS X Mavericks from a previous version of OS X, this appendix describes how to prepare and install OS X Mavericks. The temptation is to download the Installation app from the Mac App Store and start the installation, but you can avoid problems by making sure your computer is ready for OS X Mavericks. Before you install Mavericks, you need to check your computer hardware and software and make several setup decisions that relate to your computer. When you're ready to start the installation, the OS X Mavericks Setup Assistant walks you through the process.

What You'll Do

Prepare to Install OS X Mavericks

Determine the Current OS X Version

Get Mac Information

Get OS X from the App Store

Install OS X Mavericks

Reinstall OS X Mavericks

Preparing to Install OS X Mavericks

The Apple Installer guides you through many of the choices you need to make, but there are some decisions and actions you need to make before you start the installation. In order to run OS X, you'll need at least 2 or 3 GB (4 GB recommended) of physical RAM, and at least 8 GB of available space on your hard disk for the installation. And your Mac needs to be one of the models that can run OS X with OS X 10.6.8 or later and the Mac App Store installed. If you have OS X 10.5 Leopard or earlier, you'll need to upgrade to Snow Leopard 10.6 first, and then update it to 10.6.8.

Confirm that your hardware can run OS X Mavericks Version 10.9

OS X Mavericks Version 10.9 (**New!**) requires a Macintosh with a 64-bit Intel Core 2 Duo or better, Advanced GPU chipset, at least 2GB MB of physical RAM, and a built-in display or a display connected to an Apple-supplied video card supported by your computer.

OS X Mavericks supports the following Mac models: iMac (Mid 2007 or newer), MacBook, (Late 2008 Aluminum, or Early 2009 or newer), MacBook Pro (Mid/Late 2007 or newer), MacBook Air (late 2008 or newer), Mac mini (Early 2009 or newer), Mac Pro (Early 2008 or newer) and Xserve (Early 2009).

Verify you have enough hard drive space.

While the amount of disk space required depends on your computer and the way you are installing OS X, you are recommended to have at least 8 GB of available space on your hard drive.

Update computer firmware.

You may need to update your computer's firmware. You can check the Apple Software Updates web site at *www.apple.com/support/downloads* to see if your computer needs it.

Check out third party hardware compatibility

Third Party Hardware. OS X Version 10.9 Mavericks includes out-of-the-box functionality for many hardware devices. OS X will automatically configure itself to support most hardware. However, some devices may need additional driver support from the manufacturer. Please check with the manufacturer of your product to see if OS X Version 10.9 compatible drivers are available.

Third Party Hardware Specifics. If you have a third-party SCSI card or video card attached to your computer and the installer or OS indicates there are problems, try removing the cards or adding a terminator or disk drive to the SCSI card.

Reinstall OS X Mavericks

If you have problems with your installation and want to reinstall the OS X Mavericks software to correct it, you can do it without the installation discs. Hold down ⌘+R during a restart bootup. To erase a disk first, click Disk Utility, and then click Continue. To reinstall Mavericks, click Reinstall OS X, click Continue, and then follow the onscreen installation instructions.

Uninstall OS X Mavericks

Unfortunately, there isn't any clean way, like an uninstall application, to uninstall OS X10.9. The only real way is to backup your Home folder, Applications folder, Library folder, and anything else you want to save, and then erase the hard drive and install the operating system you want to use.

Determining the Current OS X Version

If you're not sure what version of the Mac operating system you've currently installed on your computer, you can use the About This Mac command or the Startup Disk utility to find out. The About This Mac command on the Apple menu displays the currently installed version and provides access to Software Update to upgrade it and More Info about the hardware with the System Information application. If you have multiple versions installed on different drives, you can use the Startup Disk Utility to quickly find out what is installed. You can access the Startup Disk utility from System Preferences in the Dock.

Check About This Mac for OS X Version

1. Click the **Apple** menu.

2. Click **About This Mac**.

 The OS version appears in the window.

3. Click the **Close** button.

OS X version

Check Startup Disk Utility for OS X Version

1. Click the **System Preferences** in the Dock.

2. Click the **Startup Disk** icon.

 The OS version for the connected hard drives appear in the pane.

3. Click the **Close** button.

OS X versions

Getting Mac Information

With the About This Mac Command, you can get quick and easy access to information about your Mac. The About This Mac dialog provides a centralized place to view information on your Mac's displays, storage, and memory. In addition, you can get access to support information, such Apple's Help Center, OS X Support, User Manuals, Specifications, and hardware support, and service information, such as service and repair coverage and status.

Get Mac Information

1. Click the **Apple** menu, and then click **About This Mac**.

2. Click **More Info**.

 The OS version appears in the window.

3. Click the tab with the information you want to view.

 ◆ **Overview.** Displays processor, memory, graphics, serial number and software version information.

 ◆ **Displays.** Displays display information, and access to user manual and Display preferences.

 ◆ **Storage.** Displays disc information and access to Disk Utility.

 ◆ **Memory.** Displays memory usage and upgrade instructions.

 ◆ **Support.** Provides access to Apple support and documentation.

 ◆ **Service.** Provides access to service and repair information for your Mac.

4. Click the **Close** button.

Overview tab

Memory tab

Support tab

Getting OS X from the App Store

If your Mac hardware can run OS X Mavericks—a computer with a 64-bit Intel Core 2 Duo, or better—and you have installed the latest version of Snow Leopard 10.6.8 or later, you can buy and download Mavericks from the App Store. After you download the software, you can run the installer to complete the process. You can install it on all your authorized Mac computers.

Get OS X Mavericks from the App Store

① Click the **App Store** icon in the Dock.

② Click **Sign In** in Quick Links, enter your Apple ID and password, and then click **Sign In**.

③ If needed, search for OS X Mavericks in the Search field.

④ Click the OS X Mavericks preview, icon or name, and then click **Buy App** and **Install App**.

⑤ If prompted, enter an administrator's name and password, and click **Done** to download and install.

⑥ To get download and install status, click the **Purchases** button on the toolbar, or click the **Launchpad** icon in the Dock, and then view the app's icon and progress bar.

Installing OS X Mavericks

There are several different kinds of installation: clean (new or erased disk), upgrade from OS X 10.6.8 (Snow Leopard) or later, reinstall Mac OS X 10.9, or restore Mac OS 10.9 using Time Machine. The OS X Setup Assistant guides you step-by-step through the process of installing OS X Mavericks no matter what the installation type. You start the downloaded version from the App Store, and then follow the on-screen instructions (read the instructions, select options, and then click Continue) to complete the process. As you go through the process, you can click the Back button at any time to change option in previous screens. The installation process takes about 30 to 45 minutes if all goes well, which is faster than previous versions.

Install OS X Mavericks

1 Download the OS X Mavericks installation software from the Mac Apps Store to your Mac hard drive.

See page 531, "Getting OS X from the App Store" for specific details.

2 Double-click (from Applications folder) or click (from Launchpad) the **OS X Mavericks** installer icon, and then click **Continue**.

3 If you want, read the license agreement, and then click **Agree**, and then click **Agree** again to continue.

4 In the Select Destination screen, select the disk or partition to install OS X (click **Show All Disks** as needed).

5 Click **Install**.

Please wait while OS X prepares your computer for installation, restarts your computer, and starts to install files.

6 Step through the Setup Assistant and click **Continue** as you go (click **Back** to change options):

◆ Welcome. Read the material and select a country.

◆ Keyboard. Select a language for the keyboard.

- ◆ **Wi-Fi Network.** Select a wi-fi network and enter a password.
- ◆ **Transfer Information.** Select an option.
- ◆ **Apple ID.** Enter your Apple ID and password.
- ◆ **iCloud Keychain.** Enter your Apple ID password as prompted, enter a four-digit numeric iCloud security code (**New!**) for use to restore your passwords on a new device, and then enter a phone number (**New!**) for a SMS message to verify your identity.
- ◆ **Enable Location Services.** Select the check box to enable location services.
- ◆ **Terms and Conditions.** Agree to the OS X terms and conditions.
- ◆ **Create Your Computer Account.** Enter your computer account information.
- ◆ **Select Time Zone.** Select a time zone.
- ◆ **Register.** Enter your individual information.

7 Upon completion, click **Start using your Mac**.

Did You Know?

You can use Recovery HD to help with installation problems. OS X Mavericks provides Recovery HD, which takes the place of an installation DVD by providing recovery tools such as Disk Utility. to access the Recovery HD, shutdown the computer and hold ⌘+R while booting.

You can use other languages. OS X Mavericks is available in Arabic, Czech, Turkish, and Hungarian.

For Your Information

Erasing and Partitioning a Hard Disk

During the OS X install, you can erase the hard disk you plan to install Mavericks and install a clean version with the factory settings. Click the Apple menu, click Restart, and then click Restart. During bootup, hold down ⌘+R. In OS X Utilities, click Disk Utility, click Continue, select a hard drive, and then click the Erase tab. Click the Format pop-up menu, select Mac OS Extended (Journaled), type a name for the disk, and then click Erase. In addition, you can partition your hard disk into several volumes before you install OS X. When you partition a disk into volumes, the entire disk is erased, so it's important to back up your files first. In Disk Utility, click Partition. When you partition the disk, you need to select a disk format. The typical choice in most cases is Mac OS Extended (Journaled). Upon completion, quit Disk Utility, and then follow the remaining on-screen instructions to complete the install.

Reinstalling Mac OS X Mavericks

OS X includes a built-in restore partition, allowing you to repair or reinstall OS X without the need for installation discs. OS X can be reinstalled on your Mac from Recovery HD mode. Recovery HD mode includes access to Time Machine for backup restores and the Safari web browser, so you can check your e-mail or browse the Apple Support site. In order to access Recovery HD mode, shut down the computer and hold ⌘+R while booting.

Reinstall OS X Mavericks

1 Click the **Apple** menu, click **Restart**, and then click **Restart**.

2 During bootup, hold down ⌘+R.

The built-in OS X Utilities program starts.

3 Select an option for the Start Up window:

◆ **Restore From Time Machine Backup.** Re-install OS X from a Time Machine backup. You need to previously backed up your entire computer.

◆ **Reinstall OS X.** Re-install a clean version of the OS X.

◆ **Get Help Online.** Access the web for online help. You need an Internet connection on your computer or click the Wi-Fi menu (upper right corner).

◆ **Disk Utility.** Start the Disk Utility program for erase disk options.

4 Click **Continue**.

5 Follow the on-screen instructions to re-install OS X; steps vary depending on the re-install option.

Did You Know?

You can access other utilities. In OS X Utilities, you can access the Firmware Password Utility, Network Utility, and Terminal app from the Utilities menu.

New! Features

OS X Mavericks

OS X Mavericks means superior results faster, with new features and enhancements that help you build Web sites and Internet applications. It provides a combination of visual layout tools, application development features, and code editing support, enabling developers and designers at every skill level to create visually appealing, standards-based sites and applications quickly and easily.

Only New Features

If you're already familiar with OS X Mountain Lion, you can access and download OS X Mavericks New Features to help make your transition to the new version simple and smooth. The OS X Mavericks New Features—including a more detailed list of new features—as well as other OS X Mountain Lion to OS X Mavericks transition helpers are available on the web at *www.perspection.com.*

What's New

If you're searching for what's new in OS X Mavericks, just look for the icon: **New!**. The new icon appears in the table of contents and throughout this book so you can quickly and easily identify a new or improved feature in OS X Mavericks. The following is a brief description of each new feature and its location in this book.

OS X Mavericks (version 10.9)

- **Tab Bar in Finder (p. 12, 16-17, 78, 80)** With the Tab bar in the Finder, you can work with multiple windows in a single window. The Tab bar displays a tab for each open window and an Add Tab (+) button to open a new tab. You can click a tab to make it active and work with its contents. In Finder Preferences, you can set an option to open folders in tabs instead of new windows.

- **Full Screen in Finder (p. 12, 14-16)** Finder windows come with a Full Screen button (diagonal double-arrows) in the window title bar that allows you to work using the full screen, just like full screen apps.

- **Tags (p. 18-19, 33-34, 42-43, 46-47, 52-53, 68-70, 86-87, 164, 200-201, 219, 256, 287, 502, 519)** With a tag, you can assign a color or name to an item, such as files or folders, to help you organize and find it later. When you save or edit a document, you can also assign tags to it. After you tag items, you can use a tag in the Sidebar to quickly display them. You can also use tags with the Find command to search for items with a particular tag.

- ◆ **Tags Preferences (p. 42-43, 78)** In Finder Preferences, you can manage tags—colors and names—for Finder items, which you can use as search criteria in the Find window.

- ◆ **Tags in Sidebar Preferences (p. 78, 86-87)** You can customize the Sidebar to show or hide tags that you can assign to items in the Finder.

- ◆ **Mission Control Options (p. 92-93)** You can select an option in the Mission Control pane in System Preferences to use separate Spaces in Displays.

- ◆ **Wallpapers (p. 102)** There are 9 new wallpapers in the Desktop & Screen Saver pane in System Preferences. The wallpapers include Mavericks wave, Abstract, Death Valley, Desert, Foxtail barley, Mountain range, Rolling waves, Foggy forest, and Underwater.

- ◆ **Language & Region (p. 106-107)** The improved Language & Region pane in System Preferences makes it easier to add and organize languages and specify region settings for display use with date, time, and currencies.

- ◆ **Text Substitution (p. 108-109, 181)** Text substitution options have been moved from the Language & Text pane (changed to Language & Region) in System Preferences to the Keyboard pane in System Preferences. However, you can still access the options from the Language & Region pane.

- ◆ **App Nap (p. 110, 458-459)** App Nap looks at which apps are not doing anything in the background, or which have their windows out of view, and puts them to sleep, just like when you close the lid on your MacBook. When a sleeping app is activated or needed, it immediately wakes up and is ready to go. This is done all behind the scenes.

- ◆ **Start Dictation (p. 117)** The keyboard shortcut to start dictation was changed from fn fn to ⌃⌘ ⌃⌘.

- ◆ **Captions in Accessibility (p. 120-121)** In the Accessibility pane of System Preferences, you can use captions to define and select styles for screen subtitles and captions or enable Closed Captions and SDH (subtitles for the deaf and hard of hearing).

- ◆ **Switch Control in Accessibility (p. 122-123)** In the Accessibility pane of System Preferences, you can use Switch Control for those with mobility issues to auto scan panels and UI elements—such as Keyboard, Pointer, App, Dock, Menu bar, System, Custom, and Location—to make it easy to select and use them.

- ◆ **iBooks (p. 154-157)** The iBooks app is an electronic bookshelf that allows you to purchase (from the iBooks Store), organize, read, and mark up online books. If you use iBooks on your iPad, iPhone, or iPod touch, the books in your Apple ID account are available in iBooks on your Mac via iCloud. When you take notes, highlight passages, or add a bookmark, iCloud syncs them to all your devices.

- ◆ **Maps (p. 158-159)** The Maps app allows you to view map locations and get directions. With Location Services, you can keep track of your current location. Maps makes it easy to get information on points of interest showing you phone numbers, photos, and even Yelp reviews. Once you find a place, you can get directions, real-time traffic conditions, and suggested alternate routes. If you like a place, you can bookmark it or drop a pin. When you're ready to go, you can send your map to your iPhone for voice navigation. Whenever you see an address in Mail, Contacts, and Calendar, you can display a map for its location.

- **Edit Toolbar in Preview (p. 162-163)** The buttons on the Edit Toolbar in Preview have been reorganized for easy access and to provide more room for other options. Along with normal text, you can annotate with outlined text in Preview.

- **Bookmarks in Preview (p. 162-163)** The Bookmarks menu and preferences tab have been replaced by the Bookmarks pane, which you can access from the View menu. You can select a bookmark and press Delete to remove it.

- **TextEdit (p. 199)** The Attached Files command has been moved from the File menu to the Edit menu.

- **Printers & Scanners Preferences (p. 208)** The name has been changed from Print & Scan to Printers & Scanners.

- **Internet Accounts Preferences (p. 236, 268, 270, 273, 302-303, 308)** The name has been changed from Mail, Contacts & Calendars to Internet Accounts. You can set up a Linkedin account for use with Shared Links in Safari. You can also access Internet Accounts from Messages.

- **Account option in Mail (p. 272)** If a POP or IMAP mail server requires a TLS certificate for security purposes, you can select one under Account Information in the Accounts pane in Mail Preferences.

- **Contacts in Mail (p. 275-276)** An inline Add Contact button appears in the To or Cc fields to make it easy to address an email using information from Contacts.

- **Export as a PDF (p. 292)** You can use the Export as PDF command on the File menu to export an e-mail as a PDF file.

- **Multiple Displays (p. 344, 471-473)** There's no longer a primary or secondary display. Each display has its own menu bar, and the Dock is available on whichever display you're working on. Mission Control can show you the displays in Spaces and make it easy to drag app thumbnails between them to customize your view. You can use AirPlay and Apple TV to turn your HDTV into a display. In the Display pane in System Preferences, you can arrange displays as a mirror (same displays) or as a separate extended display.

- **iCloud Keychain (p. 356-358, 413, 416-418)** iCloud Keychain stores your website user names and passwords on your Mac and updates them to your approved iCloud devices using AES 256-bit encryption. iCloud Keychain also works with credit card information. You can use AutoFill in Safari to automatically insert the information on a website.

- **App Store Preferences (p. 357)** The Software Updates pane in System Preferences has been changed to App Store. In the App Store pane of System Preferences, you can select an option to install app updates.

- **iCloud on the Web (p. 362-363)** iCloud on the web has added web-based versions of Notes, Reminders, and iWork apps: Keynote, Pages, and Numbers.

- **Calendar Views (p. 370-371, 373)** Month view includes highlights for the current week to make it easier to identify and allows you to continuously scroll through weeks and months. Week view includes Facebook events in the Calendar identified by a Facebook symbol.

- **Preferences in Calendar (p. 373)** You can select an account for alerts in the Alerts pane in Calendar Preferences.

- **Calendar Events (p. 374-375)** When you start typing an address for an event, Calendar suggests matching locations to help you out. You can include the travel time it takes to get to an event along with maps and weather forecast information to the event location.

- **Notifications (p. 390-393, 469)** When you're away from your Mac, you can see a summary of the notifications on the lock screen. When you receive an email, message or FaceTime call, you can respond to notifications without having to leave the app you're in. You can receive notifications from a website, such as breaking news, even if Safari isn't running. You can also set options for the Notification Center gesture in the Trackpad pane in System Preferences.

- **Post to Social Media (p. 394)** With the Notification Center, you can quickly send posts to social media, such as Linkedin and Facebook, as well as Messages.

- **Parental Controls (p. 401)** You can select an option to disable the built-in camera on the Other tab in the Parental Control pane in System Preferences.

- **App Update Options (p. 446-447)** In the Updates pane of the App Store, you can use the Update All button (or the Later button in a notification) arrow to set options: Install Now, Try in an Hour, Try Tonight, or Remind Me Tomorrow.

- **Timer Coalescing (p. 458-459)** Timer coalescing groups low-level operations together in the background, creating tiny periods of idle time that allow your CPU to enter a low-power state more often to save battery life on laptops. This is done all behind the scenes. You don't have to do anything.

- **Use Windows 8 on a Mac (p. 482)** In addition to Windows 7, you can use Windows 8 on a Mac using Boot Camp.

Safari (7.0)

- **Sidebar (p. 236-237, 242-243, 244)** The Sidebar displays a pane for Bookmarks, Reading List, and Share Links.

- **Favorites Bar (p. 236-237, 245, 247)** The Bookmarks bar has been changed to the Favorites bar.

- **Shared Links (p. 236-237, 244, 268)** If you have a Twitter or Linkedin account, you can view and share links from those social networking services directly in Safari. After you setup your Twitter or Linkedin account in the Internet Accounts pane in System Preferences, you can view and work with links in the Sidebar.

- **Open Safari with (p. 236-237, 260)** You can set an option in the General pane in Safari Preferences to open a new window or all windows from your last session.

- **Add (+) button (p. 242-243, 247)** The Add (+) button in the Address bar allows you to add web pages to the Reading List, Top Sites, Favorites bar, or Bookmarks.

- **Share button (p. 244)** The Share button allows you to share web pages using AirDrop.

- **Top Sites (p. 245, 260)** The improved Top Sites allows you to quickly add sites using the Add (+) button in the Address bar and directly remove sites, mark or unmark sites as permanent, and rearrange sites in Top Sites. In Safari Preferences, you can specify the number of Top Sites shown to 6, 12, or 24.

- **Bookmarks (p. 247-249)** The improved Bookmarks allow you to quickly add sites using the Add (+) button in the Address bar and work with bookmarks in the Bookmarks Sidebar or Library, where you can view, edit, rename, delete, and organize bookmarks.

- **Credit Card Information in AutoFill (p. 250-251)** You can add, edit, or remove credit card information for use in AutoFill on websites.

- **Export as a PDF (p. 255)** You can use the Export as PDF command on the File menu to export a web page as a PDF file.

- **Allow and Manage Plug-ins (p. 262-263)** You can set an option in the Security pane in Safari Preferences to allow the use of Internet plug-ins and manage the access each plug-in has to your documents and data. You can also set an option in the Advanced pane of Safari Preferences to stop plug-ins to save power.

- **Smart Search Field (p. 263)** You can set an option in the Privacy pane in Safari Preferences to not preload search Top Hits in the background.

iTunes (11.1)

- **Up Next List (p. 327, 329, 336)** The Up Next list allows you to take control of the media in the queue for playing in iTunes. You can view the Up Next list, add media to it at the beginning or end, or remove media from it. When you start a playlist, it goes into the Up Next list.

- **MiniPlayer (p. 327)** The MiniPlayer is back and better than ever. It's smaller and contains more features, like a Search field to find music, and the Up Next list.

- **iTunes Store (p. 330-331)** The iTunes Store has a redesigned home page to make it easier to navigate and find the media you want. New media items appear at the top in a scrolling cover flow list. You can use the History button to see your iTunes previews, radio station songs, and wish list media.

- **Show or Hide iCloud Media (p. 331, 336)** You can use the Show/Hide Music in the Cloud command on the View menu to show or hide music from iCloud.

- **General Preferences (p. 333)** The General pane in iTunes Preferences includes the following notification options: When songs changes, and Keep all song changes in Notification Center.

- **Playlists (p. 334)** The improved playlist allows you to quickly add media to a playlist by simply starting a drag where ever you are in iTunes. The Source pane appears where you can place the media in the playlist you want.

- **iTunes Radio (p. 336, 338)** iTunes Radio allows you to listen to music from the iTunes Store just like you would a radio station. You can select from the built-in radio stations or create your own. If you like a song, you can easily purchase it.

- **Internet Radio (p. 339)** The button to access Internet Radio has changed from Radio to Internet on the toolbar.

- **Preferences in iTunes (p. 343)** The Automatically download missing album artwork option and Check for new software updates automatically option in the General pane in iTunes Preferences have been moved to the Store pane and Advanced pane respectively.

- **Store Preferences (p. 343)** The Store pane in iTunes Preferences includes the following options: Show iTunes in the Cloud purchases, Sync playback information across devices, Sync podcast subscriptions and settings, and Limit Ad Tracking.

- **Advanced Preferences (p. 343)** The Advanced pane in iTunes Preferences includes the following notification options: Keep MiniPlayer on top of all other windows and Keep movie window on top of all other windows.

What Happen To ...

- **Text Smoothing for Font Sizes** The Turn off text smoothing for font sizes x and smaller option has been removed from the General pane in System Preferences.

- **Text to Speech option** The Announce when an application required your attention option has been removed from the Text to Speech tab in the Dictation & Speech pane in System Preferences.

- **Energy Saver option** The Allow power button to put the computer to sleep option has been removed in the Energy Saver pane in System Preferences.

- **Security & Privacy Preference Advanced option** The Automatically update safe downloads list option in the Advanced dialog box has been removed in the Security & Privacy pane in System Preferences.

- **Contacts UI** The book user interface for the Contacts app has been removed to be more consistent with other apps.

- **Enable Java in Safari** The Enable Java option on the Security tab in Safari preferences has been removed.

- **Text Encoding in Mail** The Text Encoding menu on the Message menu in the Mail app has been removed.

- **Preferences in Mail** The Show online buddy status option on the Viewing tab and the Automatically complete address option on the Composing tab in Mail Preferences have been removed.

- **Record Chat in Messages** The Record Chat command in the Messages app has been removed.

- **Preferences in iTunes** The Audio Language, Subtitle Language, and Show closed captioning when available options in the Playback pane have been removed. You can enable these options in the Accessibility pane in System Preferences. The Allow iTunes audio control from remote speakers option in the Devices pane has been removed.

- **Ping in iTunes** The connection to the Ping service in iTunes has been removed.

- **Preferences in Calendar** The Automatically retrieve CalDAV invitations from Mail in the Advanced pane in Calendar Preferences has been removed.

Index